Horsemen in
No Man's Land

Horsemen in No Man's Land

British Cavalry and Trench Warfare, 1914–1918

David Kenyon

Pen & Sword
MILITARY

First published in Great Britain in 2011 by
Pen & Sword Military
an imprint of
Pen & Sword Books Ltd
47 Church Street
Barnsley
South Yorkshire
S70 2AS

ISBN 978-1-84884-364-6

Typeset in 11/13 Ehrhardt by Concept, Huddersfield, West Yorkshire
Printed and bound in England by CPI UK

Pen & Sword Books Ltd incorporates the Imprints of Pen & Sword Aviation,
Pen & Sword Family History, Pen & Sword Maritime, Pen & Sword Military,
Pen & Sword Discovery, Wharncliffe Local History, Wharncliffe True Crime,
Wharncliffe Transport, Pen & Sword Select, Pen & Sword Military Classics,
Leo Cooper, The Praetorian Press, Remember When, Seaforth Publishing and
Frontline Publishing.

For a complete list of Pen & Sword titles please contact
PEN & SWORD BOOKS LIMITED
47 Church Street, Barnsley, South Yorkshire, S70 2AS, England
E-mail: enquiries@pen-and-sword.co.uk
Website: www.pen-and-sword.co.uk

Contents

DEDICATION

Ian Kenyon

(1939–2008)

Foreword
by Professor Richard Holmes

David Kenyon is a keen horseman, and in tackling the subject of British cavalry on the Western Front he is taking on the literary equivalent of a vast hedge with a slippery take-off and a ditch on the landing side. For although, over the past thirty years, a veritable galaxy of scholars has illuminated so many aspects of the First World War, the cavalry still stands, as Stephen Badsey observed as long ago as 1982, as a metaphor for all that is foolish and outdated about the conflict. Even the most astute historians tend to brush aside British attempts to use cavalry in the great offensive battles of 1915–17 as doomed to irredeemable failure by unsuitable terrain and hostile firepower, while for those playing to the popular gallery the spectacle of massed cavalry awaiting a breakthrough that never came is an easy way of summing up the intellectual bankruptcy of senior commanders who, as legend has it, were mostly cavalrymen themselves.

This is the first book to focus on the performance of the cavalry during the years of trench warfare. It benefits from the author's deep understanding of the structure, organisation and equipment of British and (let it never be forgotten) Indian cavalry, and of the practical issues of horse management that made it so hard to keep mounts in good condition in the inhospitable surroundings of the Western Front in wintertime. By careful analysis of its role in successive offensives, from the Somme in 1916, through Cambrai the following year and on to the last victorious Hundred Days of the war, Kenyon concludes that the cavalry did indeed have an important contribution to make.

Its mobility was by no means as badly circumscribed by the ground and German defences as might be supposed, in part because of the development of mobile trench-crossing bridges that could be quickly erected and the use of specialist route-clearance units. Its firepower, always superior, thanks to the fact that it carried the same superb Lee Enfield rifle as the infantry, to that of German cavalry, was enhanced by the use of the Vickers medium machine guns deployed by the Machine Gun Corps (Cavalry) and the Hotchkiss light machine guns that were integral to cavalry regiments. And despite the guffaws still aroused by the prospect of sword-wielding horsemen trying to get to grips with rifle-armed infantry, it is evident that there were times when mounted shock action did indeed succeed, and aggressive and determined horsemen played an important part in undermining German morale on 8 August 1918.

However, Kenyon concludes that while the cavalry could boast numerous tactical successes, it failed to make the operational contribution hoped for by some of its advocates. This had less to do with the inherent weaknesses of the arm itself than with failures at various levels in the command structure. Field Marshal Sir Douglas Haig, who remained the cavalry's greatest champion, and without whose support there would have been far fewer cavalry units in France, tended to the pre-war view that cavalry was an arm of decisive exploitation, best husbanded for use in mass once a breakthrough had been identified. In fact, as Kenyon so capably demonstrates, the development of the 'multi-layered' battle meant that there were many occasions when relatively small numbers of horsemen, held very close to the front, were more valuable than much larger quantities even a short distance further back. Lieutenant General Kavanagh of the Cavalry Corps had made his reputation as a brave and competent brigadier in 1914, but was out of his depth as a corps commander. His attempts to retain tactical command of his horsemen once battle was joined not only added an unnecessary link to the chain of command but allowed him, most notably at Cambrai, to hector his subordinates into pressing attacks when they themselves recognised that the opportunity had passed.

Kenyon's work chimes sonorously with some of the best recent research by emphasising that the main problems facing the British sprang from command, control and communications. His examination of the arrangements that were intended to enable the cavalry to exploit success shows that while communications generally worked well enough straight up and down the chain of command, they were very poor laterally, and infantry commanders, presented with a fleeting opportunity, often found themselves with no cavalry to hand and no means of summoning any. Kenyon, who is by no means a blinkered advocate for his arm of choice, recognises that there were indeed times when thrusting cavalry leaders caused avoidable casualties by insisting on mounted shock action in inappropriate circumstances, but he points to numerous examples of junior cavalry officers injecting fresh momentum into a stalled battle by dash and determination – the same qualities that were to prove so crucial a generation later when tanks had replaced horses.

The tactical circumstances of the Western Front, most notably the burgeoning role of artillery, meant that successful offensive battles would always require careful planning, preparation and co-ordination. But there usually came a moment when the situation had evolved beyond that envisaged by the planners, and comparatively junior commanders needed to generate purposeful activity in the absence of detailed orders if they were to prevent the defender from cauterising his wound before the attacker could widen it. In one sense the British army's conduct of operations on the Western Front was intimately bound up with the relationship between detailed orders and individual initiative, and it is not hard to see at least part of the reason for the cavalry's failure to achieve more dramatic results as a reflection of an overall style of command which, at least until 1918, remorselessly subordinated initiative to process. In fairness, there were good reasons (not least the army's huge wartime expansion and the extemporisation of headquarters at all levels) why this should have been the case. But as I read David Kenyon's thoughtful and scholarly study, there are times when I suspect that one of the army's real problems was not that there was too much cavalry dash – but too little.

Richard Holmes
April 2011

Professor Holmes contributed this Foreword in November 2010 after reading the final draft of this book. Sadly Richard died in April 2011 and thus did not see the project to its conclusion. His inspiration and friendship will be greatly missed by the author, and by everyone in the world of military history.

Acknowledgements

This book began life as a doctoral thesis submitted at Cranfield University in 2008. The research was carried out as a student in the Defence College of Management and Technology (DCMT) at UK Defence Academy, Shrivenham. I was supervised over nearly seven years by Professor Richard Holmes, and enormous thanks are due to him for his guidance, moral support and enthusiasm for the subject throughout that time. I was also assisted by other staff members at Shrivenham, including Gary Sheffield, Chris Bellamy and Peter Caddick-Adams, along with Steph Muir and the support staff. Visits to the department were always a highlight in the otherwise lonely task of research and writing. Additional advice and support were provided by Stephen Badsey and John Bourne. My thanks go to all of them, and to all who sat through, and commented on, my various conference lectures and public expositions of my ideas.

Research would get nowhere without the assistance of dedicated librarians and archivists. The assistance of the staff of the following libraries and institutions is also gratefully acknowledged: DCMT Shrivenham Library; JSCSC Shrivenham Library; RMA Sandhurst Library; National Archives, Kew, London; Gloucestershire County Library Service; and Bovington Tank Museum.

Thanks are also due to Peter Moore who prepared all the maps for the thesis, and then revised them all for publication here.

Lastly I would like to thank my family and friends: my parents, who supported me both morally and financially through the process, my sister, who provided a free spare bed within walking distance of Kew, and most of all my father, who was the first reader and editor of every chapter, and my sternest critic. Sadly, although present at my graduation, he did not live to see this project through to publication.

David Kenyon
Wiltshire, 2010

A Note on Terminology and Organisation

In the following text unit nomenclature follows the pattern established by the BEF itself and subsequently the *Official History;* thus, Fourth Army, XV Corps, 1st Division, 5th Brigade, etc. Where they appear, German formations are italicised.

The British cavalry divisions on the Western Front were known throughout the war as the 1st, 2nd and 3rd 'Cavalry Divisions'. By 1916 the Indian cavalry divisions were the only Indian divisions remaining in France, and were thus referred to simply as the 1st and 2nd 'Indian Divisions'. Later these were to become the 4th and 5th 'Cavalry Divisions'. British cavalry brigades were numbered, while Indian brigades were known by their home stations, e.g. 'Lucknow', 'Meerut', etc. It should also be remembered that each Indian brigade contained one British regiment, as well as British artillery and supporting elements.

Unlike the infantry, which had abandoned (at least officially) the old regimental numbers, cavalry regiments retained their numbers as well as their titles. Regiments are therefore normally referred to by number and type, e.g. the 7th Dragoon Guards, the 15th Hussars, etc. However, historic distinctions between dragoons and hussars, or 'heavy' and 'light' cavalry, survived in name only. All British cavalry used the same basic 'Universal Pattern' equipment and drills, the only variation being the issue of lances to 'Lancer' regiments.

Indian cavalry units were also listed in a numerical sequence, and were divided into 'Light Cavalry', 'Cavalry', 'Horse', and 'Lancers', thus the 4th Cavalry, the 19th Lancers, etc. Conveniently, no Indian Lancer regiments duplicated the number of a British Lancer regiment. For clarity in the text Indian regiments are usually additionally referred to by their regimental title, e.g. the 34th Poona Horse. Some regiments styled themselves in Roman numerals, such as the 'XXth Deccan Horse'; for clarity, Arabic numerals are used throughout the text.

The term 'cavalry' is used in the text to denote the arm of service, whether mounted or not. In higher formations, brigade and above, this includes the attached RHA, signallers and other supporting services. Where the term 'mounted troops' is used, this specifically implies soldiers remaining on horseback in the battle area, or dismounting to fight but with their horses kept nearby.

Measures of weight and distance quoted directly from original sources have been left unaltered, but with a metric equivalent given. All distances measured by the author are metric.

Glossary of Terms and Abbreviations

ADVS	Assistant Director Veterinary Services. Officer in charge of veterinary services, typically for a division.
BEF	British Expeditionary Force. The British army in France and Belgium, 1914–18.
BGGS	Brigadier General General Staff. Chief staff officer with the HQ of an army corps.
BGRA	Brigadier General Royal Artillery. Commander of artillery forces within an army corps, later GOCRA.
Brigadier General	Officer typically commanding a brigade.
CIGS	Chief of the Imperial General Staff.
DDVS	Deputy Director Veterinary Services. Officer in charge of veterinary services, typically for an army corps.
FGH	Fort Garry Horse. Regiment within the Canadian Cavalry Brigade.
General Officer	Typically commanding an army.
GOCRA	General Officer commanding Royal Artillery. See BGRA
KEH	King Edward's Horse. Regiment of Special Reserve, comprised of men returned from residence in overseas colonies.
LAC	Light armoured car.
LSH	Lord Strathcona's Horse. Regiment within the Canadian Cavalry Brigade.
Lieutenant General	Officer typically commanding an army corps.
Major General	Officer typically commanding a division.
MGC(C)	Machine Gun Corps (Cavalry).
RCD	Royal Canadian Dragoons. Regiment within the Canadian Cavalry Brigade.
RCHA	Royal Canadian Horse Artillery.
RHA	Royal Horse Artillery.
Sqn	Squadron: sub-unit of cavalry regiment, typically comprising approximately 100 men.

Maps

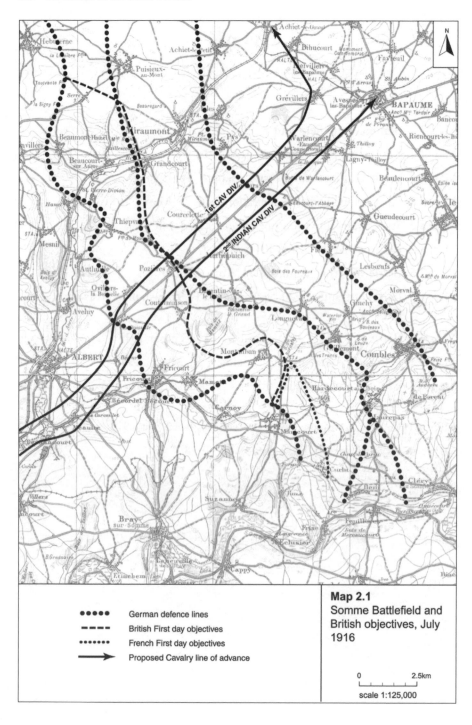

Map 2.1
Somme Battlefield and
British objectives, July
1916

German defence lines
British First day objectives
French First day objectives
Proposed Cavalry line of advance

0   2.5km

scale 1:125,000

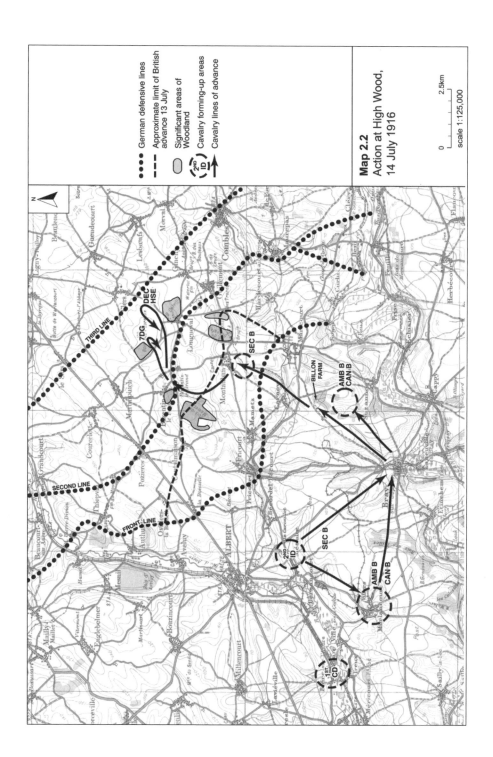

N

German defensive lines

Approximate limit of British
advance 13 July

Significant areas of
Woodland

2ND
ID

Cavalry forming-up areas

Cavalry lines of advance

Map 2.2
Action at High Wood,
14 July 1916

0   2.5km

scale 1:125,000

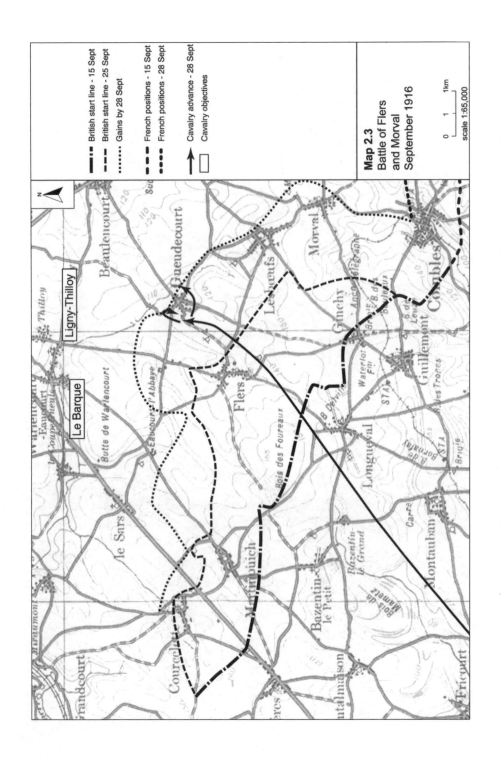

Legend

British start line - 15 Sept
British start line - 25 Sept
Gains by 28 Sept
French positions - 15 Sept
French positions - 28 Sept

Cavalry advance - 28 Sept
Cavalry objectives

Map 2.3
Battle of Flers and Morval
September 1916

0   1   1km

scale 1:65,000

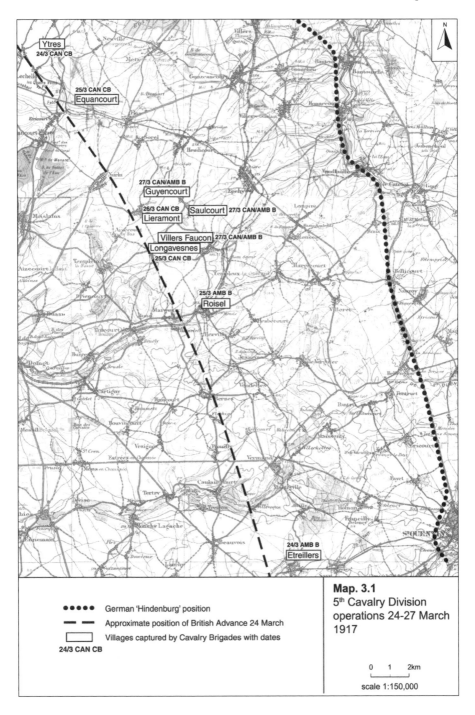

N

Ytres
24/3 CAN CB

25/3 CAN CB
Equancourt

27/3 CAN/AMB B
Guyencourt

26/3 CAN CB
Lieramont

Saulcourt 27/3 CAN/AMB B

Villers Faucon 27/3 CAN/AMB B
Longavesnes
25/3 CAN CB

25/3 AMB B
Roisel

24/3 AMB B
Etreillers

Map. 3.1

5th Cavalry Division
operations 24-27 March
1917

●●●●● German 'Hindenburg' position

– – – Approximate position of British Advance 24 March

☐ Villages captured by Cavalry Brigades with dates
24/3 CAN CB

0   1   2km

scale 1:150,000

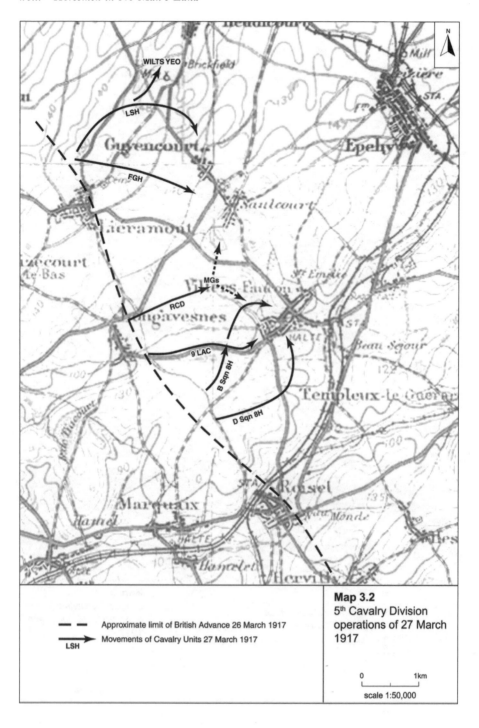

Map 3.2
5th Cavalry Division operations of 27 March 1917

– – –   Approximate limit of British Advance 26 March 1917
→   Movements of Cavalry Units 27 March 1917
LSH

0   1km

scale 1:50,000

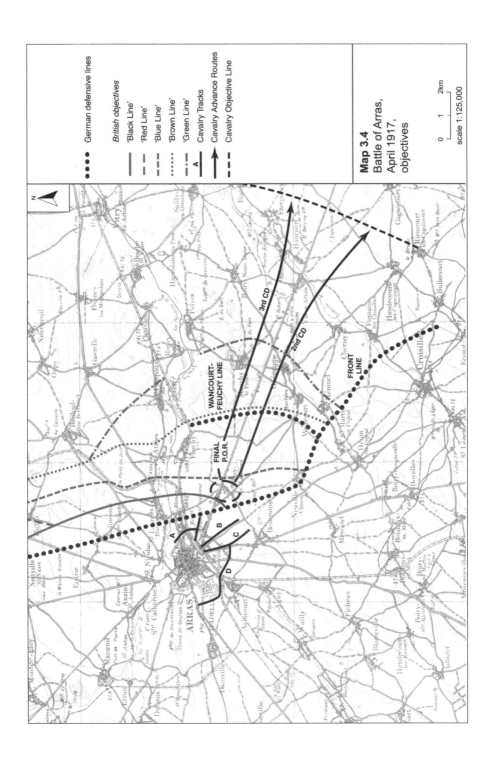

German defensive lines

British objectives
'Black Line'
'Red Line'
'Blue Line'
'Brown Line'
'Green Line'
Cavalry Tracks
Cavalry Advance Routes
Cavalry Objective Line

N

3rd CD

2nd CD

WANCOURT-
FEUCHY LINE

FINAL
P.O.R.

FRONT
LINE

A

B

C

D

ARRAS

Map 3.4
Battle of Arras,
April 1917,
objectives

0   1   2km

scale 1:125,000

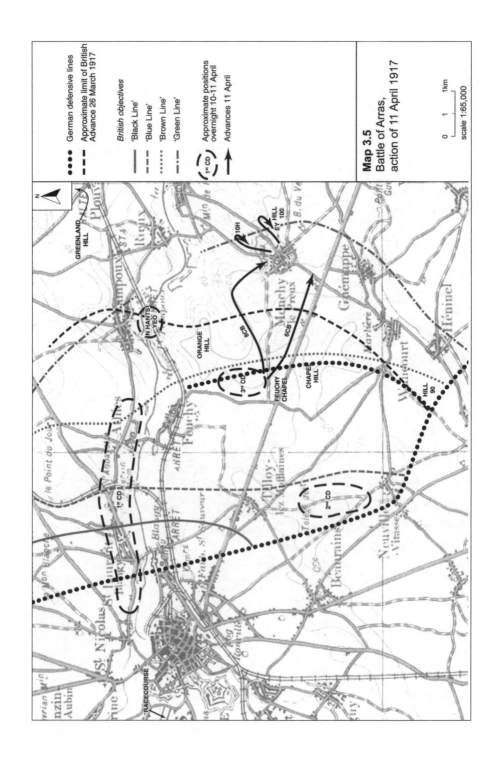

Legend:

German defensive lines

Approximate limit of British Advance 26 March 1917

British objectives

'Black Line'

'Blue Line'

'Brown Line'

'Green Line'

(1st CD) Approximate positions overnight 10-11 April

Advances 11 April

Map 3.5
Battle of Arras,
action of 11 April 1917

0   1   1km
scale 1:65,000

GREENLAND HILL

Plouvain

N HANTS VEO

ORANGE HILL

6CB

Monchy le Preux

EY HILL 100

10H

Guémappe

Héninel

Marlière

FEUCHY CHAPEL

3rd CD

CHAPEL HILL

6CB

Wancourt

HILL 90

Feuchy

1st CD

Tilloy-lez-Mofflaines

2nd CD

Neuville-Vitasse

Beaurains

St. Nicolas

RACECOURSE

ARRAS

le Point du Jour

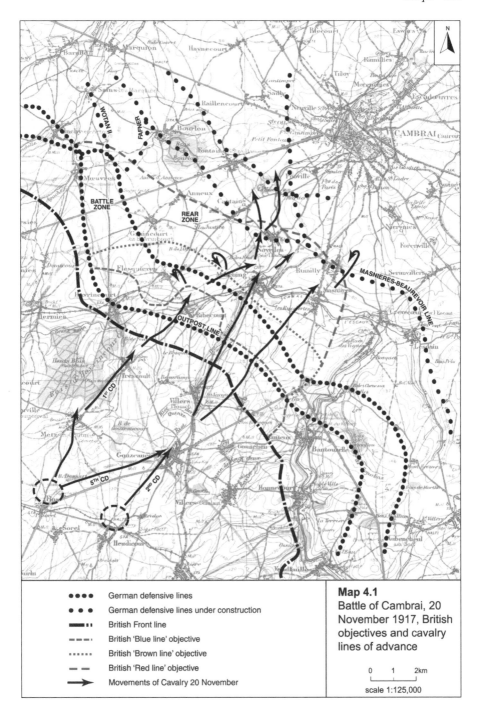

••••	German defensive lines
• • •	German defensive lines under construction
▬▬▪▪	British Front line
▬ ▬ ▪ ▬	British 'Blue line' objective
....	British 'Brown line' objective
▬ ▬ ▬	British 'Red line' objective
➜	Movements of Cavalry 20 November

Map 4.1
Battle of Cambrai, 20 November 1917, British objectives and cavalry lines of advance

0   1   2km

scale 1:125,000

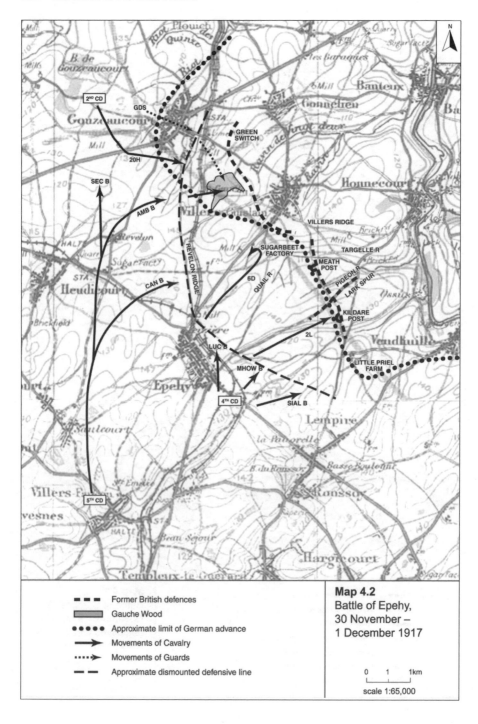

Map 4.2
Battle of Epehy,
30 November –
1 December 1917

- - - - Former British defences
�
Gauche Wood
•••••• Approximate limit of German advance
→ Movements of Cavalry
•••••➤ Movements of Guards
- - Approximate dismounted defensive line

0   1   1km
scale 1:65,000

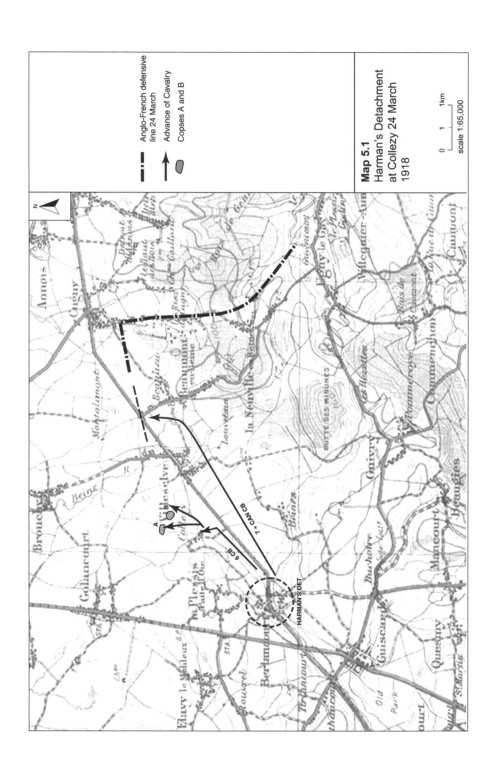

Map 5.1
Harman's Detachment
at Collezy 24 March
1918

Anglo-French defensive
line 24 March

Advance of Cavalry

Copses A and B

scale 1:65,000

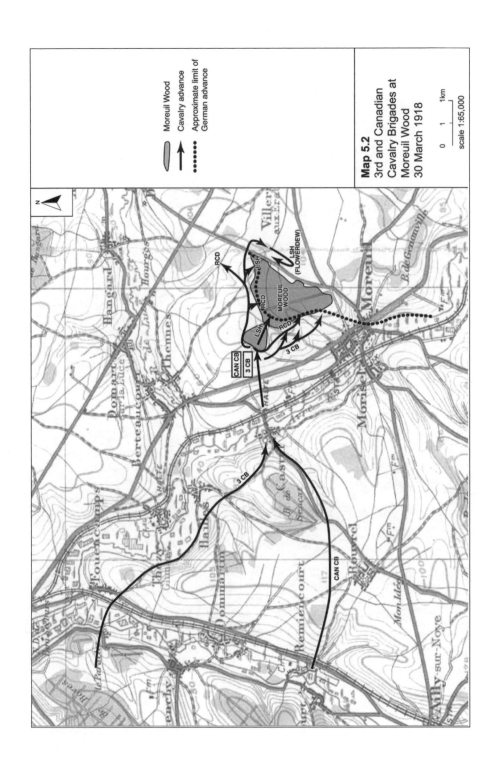

Map 5.2
3rd and Canadian
Cavalry Brigades at
Moreuil Wood
30 March 1918

Moreuil Wood

Cavalry advance

Approximate limit of
German advance

0   1   1km

scale 1:65,000

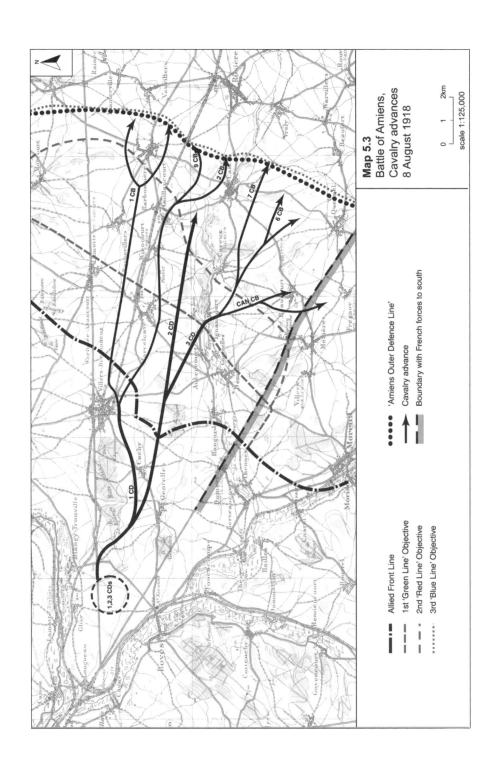

Map 5.3
Battle of Amiens,
Cavalry advances
8 August 1918

scale 1:125,000

0 1 2km

Allied Front Line
1st 'Green Line' Objective
2nd 'Red Line' Objective
3rd 'Blue Line' Objective

'Amiens Outer Defence Line'
Cavalry advance
Boundary with French forces to south

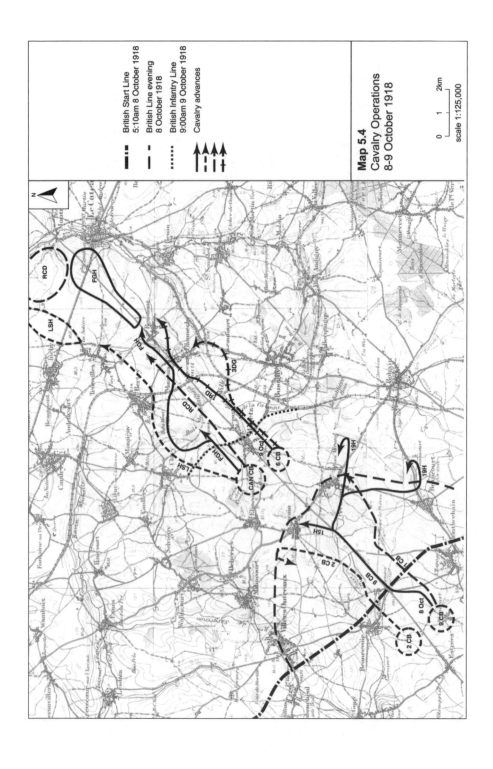

Map 5.4
Cavalry Operations
8-9 October 1918

scale 1:125,000

0   1   2km

British Start Line
5:10am 8 October 1918

British Line evening
8 October 1918

British Infantry Line
9:00am 9 October 1918

Cavalry advances

Chapter 1

Introduction:
The Opening Stages, 1914–1915

Justice has never been done to the part played by the cavalry in France and Flanders during the years 1915 to 1918.

The Marquess of Anglesey[1]

With these words Anglesey opened the final part of his magnificent eight-volume *History of the British Cavalry,* in 1997. More than a decade later his remark remains true, for while he provided a fine narrative account of the efforts of the British cavalry on the Western Front, and created a worthy literary monument to the arm, a detailed modern analytical investigation of the cavalry remains to be undertaken. Nor does it appear that any regard has been paid to his efforts in the wider community of historians of the war.

A survey of the constantly growing corpus of literature relating to the Western Front reveals (with the honorable exception of Anglesey) hardly any significant published works devoted wholly to the cavalry. Steven Badsey's chapter in Paddy Griffith's *British Fighting Methods in the Great War,*[2] published in 1996, stood virtually alone in this regard for many years, and in any case formed a small part, less than forty pages, of a larger work devoted to other arms. Badsey has recently published (in 2008) *Doctrine and Reform in the British Cavalry 1880–1918*[3] based on his 1981 PhD thesis on the '*Arme Blanche* Controversy'.[4] The Western Front did not form the main focus of this research, but Badsey concluded his thesis with the rueful observation that

> The metaphor of the charge against machine guns, or of the incompetent Victorian cavalry general attempting to control a tank battle, has spread beyond military studies into the general vocabulary of historians and readers of history, as a touchstone of all that is reactionary, foolish, and futile. It is probably too well established ever to be removed.[5]

Richard Holmes put the point rather more succinctly when he observed 'There are few subjects where prejudice has a clearer run than with the mounted arm in the First World War.'[6] As a result, what little has been written on the cavalry has, of necessity, largely limited itself to attempting to overcome this significant body of ingrained negative opinion expressed concerning the arm, and to attacking the wealth of myth and uncritically repeated half-truths which surrounds its activities. Cavalry chapters in recent works by both Holmes and Gordon Corrigan are honourable examples of this.[7] However, little or no time has yet been devoted to passing beyond assaults upon the old myths and preconceptions, and moving on to make a fresh and detailed assessment of the real history of cavalry in trench fighting. Thus there remains a significant gap in the literature of the First World War with regard to the analysis of the cavalry. It is the purpose of this book to move on to just such a detailed assessment.

It is necessary first to examine how the omission of the cavalry from First World War research has occurred, and why, in a field of study where lengthy works are devoted to a bewildering diversity of topics, more or less obscure, no major research effort has been directed specifically at the cavalry arm. The little research that has taken place has also concentrated on various rather narrow and oft-repeated questions. This omission can be discerned in the evolution of historical ideas concerning the Western Front as a whole, and in the changing orthodoxies surrounding the major issues of historical debate, such as the competence of command, the evolution of tactics and the influence of technology.

An examination of the historiography of the First World War shows that a significant change of view has taken place, in particular over the last two or three decades. This is most readily apparent in the interpretation of the rôle of the infantry and artillery, and the men who commanded them. The old myths of bungling incompetent leadership and of futile repeated sacrifice have largely been demolished. The roots of this change lie in the works over the last thirty years of John Terraine, and more recently in the efforts of scholars such as the late Paddy Griffith and Gary Sheffield in the UK, or Robin Prior and Trevor Wilson in Australia, Tim Travers in Canada, and others.[8] Indeed these writers have built up a body of opinion so large that it may be argued that their school of thought has passed out of the realms of historical revisionism and become the new orthodoxy.

This quiet revolution in First World War studies has, however, largely passed without a detailed re-examination of the cavalry. Several of the old 'incompetence' myths which have been ably refuted in relation to the infantry have been allowed to stand in relation to the cavalry, and have even been reinforced by writers who take a much more modern and revisionist view with regard to other arms. This is at least partly because the debate has been viewed in terms of the battle between 'modernism' and 'reaction' in military thought, and the cavalry arm is an easy (if erroneous) shorthand for the latter. Badsey observed 'even those academic historians who write on operational matters take the uselessness of cavalry and the *arme blanche* for granted'.[9]

An example of this is Tim Travers, who, in expounding a lengthy and at times vitriolic critique of Field Marshal Haig, set up an opposition between the 'traditional' (i.e. 'bad') and the 'professional' (i.e. 'good'). In this distinctly black and white world he firmly placed Haig, 'clinging to traditional nineteenth-century ideas about moral and cavalry',[10] at the head of the former camp. The word 'cavalry' is inserted in this context as a metaphor for all that is out-dated and unrealistic.

The roots of this 'anti-cavalry' stance can be traced to some of the earliest and most influential writers on the war. Terraine[11] and Badsey[12] have both placed the early responsibility for this on Sir James Edmonds, in Badsey's words the 'now slightly notorious'[13] Official Historian. Edmonds was an engineer officer, and clearly no great supporter of cavalry or cavalrymen. Three of the most tenacious, and erroneous, 'myths' can be directly attributed to him, at least in part, and may be summarised as follows:

- The 'cavalry generals' myth: that the high command was dominated by cavalry officers and was thus, by extension, incompetent;
- The 'last machine gun' myth: that machine guns in any quantity, and in virtually any circumstances, rendered mounted operations suicidally costly;
- The 'fodder' myth: that the support of the Cavalry Corps was a drain on vital resources, particularly of shipping, and that those resources would have been better spent in the support of other arms.

The post-war debate over mechanisation also assisted in the demonisation of the cavalry arm. Writers such as J.F.C. Fuller and Basil Liddell Hart, in their advocacy of the future of armour, were quick to use the cavalry as a counterpoint to this, and as a symbol of all that was traditional and outdated.[14] This train of thought has been adopted by more recent writers seeking to show that victory on the Western Front was achieved through the advance of technology, and through the success in particular of the tank, to the extent that a fourth myth, 'the victory of the tanks', may also be discerned.

The curious feature of all these allegations is that while a series of articles have appeared over the years individually demolishing each one, they are somehow so ingrained in the psyche of First World War writers that they do not really go away. Rather they persist, below the surface, as it were, to colour those writers' subsequent views. Although, as has already been stated, it is intended here to move beyond these old arguments, the history and pernicious influence of each is worthy of brief examination.

Broadly stated, the 'cavalry generals' myth alleges that the presence of Field Marshal Haig amongst the ranks of the cavalry supports a (rather circular) thesis within which the man is used to denigrate the arm, and *vice versa*. The argument runs that Haig was the figurehead of a wider group of out-of-touch nineteenth-century cavalry officers, who succeeded in gaining positions of high command due to their mutual influence and support, and who, to a man, proved incapable of dealing with the technological and intellectual challenges of a conflict on the scale of the Western Front. The usual suspects commonly listed among these 'cavalry generals' include, besides Haig, his predecessor Sir John French, and the army commanders Gough, Byng, Allenby and Birdwood. (A concise summary of the history and chief proponents of this viewpoint can be found in Anglesey, *A History of the British Cavalry*, vol. VIII.)[15]

John Terraine's article 'Cavalry Generals and the "G" in Gap'[16] was the first to present a full, statistically supported refutation of this argument. The piece was more widely viewed as a model of the new (at the time in 1980) revisionist thinking on the war, and the demolition of the old mythologies. Terraine was able to marshal a range of statistics to disprove the notion that the senior ranks of the BEF were disproportionately filled with cavalry officers. He was also able to show the origins of the myth in the published opinions of Edmonds (in the *Official History*) and Lloyd George, neither of whom was a particular supporter of Haig, or of the cavalry arm. It is largely Terraine's model which has been followed by later scholars tackling the same question (e.g. Neillands[17] and Anglesey).[18] Indeed, Ian Malcolm Brown was sufficiently confident of the expiry of this controversy in 1998 to state simply: '. . . the very idea that Britain, France and Germany (as well as Austria-Hungary and Russia) all managed simultaneously to produce a generation of complete incompetents at the highest levels of command is patently ludicrous.'[19]

That might well be considered to be the end of the matter. However, in spite of the destruction of the myth itself, it continued to cast a shadow over subsequent thinking. On closer scrutiny, even Terraine's own views on 'cavalry generals' are not as benign towards the cavalry as might at first appear. The chief plank of his argument seems to be that the majority of commanders were not cavalrymen, and therefore by implication were not incompetent. The inference can be drawn from this that to be a cavalry officer somehow implied a degree of incompetence. Terraine's own biography of Haig, *Douglas Haig, The Educated Soldier*, albeit written seventeen years before '*The "G" in Gap'*, also showed that he was not quite able, in spite of his later protestations, to throw off an anti-cavalry prejudice. Examination of the earlier work reveals a marked degree of ambivalence towards the idea of Haig being a cavalryman. Terraine is at pains on a number of occasions to distance Haig from his own arm of service, observing, for example, 'There was very little "Tally Ho" about Douglas Haig.'[20]

In seeking to exclude certain generals from such a group, the 'cavalry generals' debate tacitly acknowledges the existence of it. It is tempting to reverse this chain of logic, and to argue that if the leading Allied commanders were, as is suggested by Terraine, Griffith and others, actually quite good at their jobs, then their arm of service is irrelevant. Indeed further, the fact that so many of the senior commanders came from a cavalry background shows the pool of expertise and ability which existed within that arm, contrary to the opinion of those outside it, or of later historians.

The second, or 'last machine gun' myth, which holds that a mounted soldier was hopelessly vulnerable on the modern battlefield of 1914–18, is also clearly traceable to Sir James Edmonds and the *Official History*. Therein he quoted the observation by an anonymous American officer that 'you can't have a cavalry charge until you have captured the enemy's last machine-gun'.[21] Even Edmonds does not offer us any suggestion as to the qualifications of this commentator, and his opinion, for that is clearly what it is, is not borne out by the facts of a number of successful cavalry engagements, as we shall see. However, this viewpoint survives even into very recent literature on the subject.

The longevity of this myth can also, at least in part, be laid at the feet of John Terraine, albeit with the assistance of later writers who followed his line of argument. Edmonds' opinion was extracted from the *Official History* and quoted by Terraine as if it were a substantial fact both in *To Win a War* in 1978[22] and again in *White Heat* in 1982.[23] Terraine extended this argument to provide a blanket assessment of the cavalry's contribution on the Western Front: that cavalry was out-dated and vulnerable, and that its contribution to the outcome of the war was insignificant. In his discussion of the battle of Neuve Chapelle in 1915 he observed:

> To exploit a success, five divisions of cavalry were brought up behind the offensive front; this would also continue to be standard procedure. Occasion after occasion on the Western Front would show, until the changed conditions of the very last days, that cavalry were quite incapable of performing this function.[24]

Similarly, in a discussion of the Cambrai offensive in 1917: 'The complete ineffectiveness of horse soldiers on a modern battlefield was demonstrated.'[25] And finally, as late as 1918: 'For one branch, however, there was no change. The Western Front remained an impossible theatre for cavalry to the end.'[26] Terraine is probably correct in his assertion that the overall contribution made by the cavalry to the outcome of the war was not great (they certainly did not 'win the war'). It is, however, by no means equally obvious that the cavalry was an inherently useless and obsolete fighting arm. As so often in history, an assertion that is deemed to be so self-evident as to require no further elaboration is found on closer examination to rest on extremely shaky foundations.

This same dismissal of the cavalry as useless, and requiring no further comment or investigation, has also continued to permeate other more recent and otherwise highly balanced and analytical studies of the war. Robin Prior and Trevor Wilson's *Command on the Western Front* (1992) has been widely praised as an important and penetrating work, yet their attitude to 'Horse soldiers' (by which epithet the cavalry are frequently described in their book) is dismissive to a degree. Indeed their keenness to denigrate the cavalry led the authors to offer an interpretation of events which undermines the credibility of the remainder of their work. In commenting on the action at High Wood on 14 July 1916 they observed: 'Unhappily a regiment of cavalry which had reached the front in the late afternoon accompanied the attack. The cavalry were soon dealt with by German machine-gunners. The infantry by contrast initially made good progress.'[27]

This action will be examined in detail later, but it takes little reading, even of Edmonds' *Official History*,[28] to discover that on that particular occasion a *brigade* of cavalry was able to advance successfully, undertake at least one mounted charge, capture a number of prisoners and machine guns, and hold the position until relieved by supporting infantry. Such distortions reflect little credit on their authors, but are typical of the curious historical blinkers by which many historians seem constrained when dealing with cavalry matters.

Even very modern works by those who place themselves firmly within the 'new thinking' on the war suffer from this burden of received wisdom. Gary Sheffield, in his *Forgotten Victory* (2001), is able to take a much more balanced view of the detail, calling the cavalry operations at High Wood 'a considerable success'.[29] However, when it comes to generalities, he follows the old line: 'under the conditions usually pertaining to trench warfare, a combination of barbed wire and modern weapons rendered cavalry obsolete'.[30] This remark might well have been lifted from any one of Terraine's writings of twenty years earlier.

The failure of these writers to examine fully the relationship between mounted soldiers and machine guns also leads to a failure to appreciate the further point that this new technology was applied as often *by* the cavalry as *at* them. Even before the war *Cavalry Training* stated 'the characteristics of machine guns as described in the previous section render them valuable for employment with cavalry'.[31] This potential was further enhanced after the creation of the Machine Gun Corps (Cavalry) in 1916, as well as by the issue of as many as sixteen Hotchkiss guns per regiment. Thus in the later part of the war a cavalry brigade had a large and highly mobile source of potential firepower. This question will also be examined in more detail later, but the wider point, often missed, is that the machine gun was at least as much the friend of the mounted soldier as his enemy.

The third and final 'fodder' myth is perhaps the most often repeated of Edmonds' assertions, and despite a number of thorough rebuttals in print continues to recur in First World War literature. Referring to the Canadian

Cavalry Brigade's successful action at Reumont in October 1918, the official historian wrote:

> The cavalry had done nothing that the infantry, with artillery support and cyclists, could not have done for itself at less cost; and the supply of the large force of horses with water and forage had gravely interfered with the sending up of ammunition and the rations for the other arms, and with the allotment of the limited water facilities.[32]

It is possible that in this observation Edmonds was referring to the specifics of that operation, but it is equally probable that he intended a more general criticism. Either way, the remark has been taken and widened as a critique of the cavalry in the war as a whole; it is quoted at length by Terraine, both in *To Win a War*[33] and again in *White Heat*, where he refers to it as 'the final verdict' on the cavalry.[34] The Cavalry Corps, the argument runs, sat uselessly behind the line, eating its way through a vast amount of shipping resources which would have been better disposed winning the war. Statistics to support this view can be extracted from official figures. That the tonnage of fodder (5.8 million tons) shipped to France during the war exceeded even the tonnage of ammunition (5.2 million tons)[35] is a statistic so often quoted as to have become something of an old chestnut. However, the comprehensive demolition of this myth by several writers seems to have passed largely unnoticed by historians. Badsey provides convincing chapter and verse (and statistics) in his unpublished thesis of 1981,[36] and while a published version of the same arguments was presented by Anglesey in 1997[37] a tone of resignation is detectable in the latter's comments on this topic:

> There is one particularly pernicious myth that needs banishing from the minds of future historians. Even the most authoritative and reliable of those who have written about the Western Front repeat time and time again the fallacious idea that vast quantities of shipping had to be devoted to the provision of forage for the cavalry's horses. This is nonsense. If the disquisition on p. 286 will not dismiss once and for all this too often propagated falsehood, the present author presumes to believe that nothing will.[38]

Sadly, one is inclined to agree with this depressing forecast. In Ian Malcolm Brown's *British Logistics on the Western Front 1914–1919* (1998) one might expect to find a detailed account of the fodder question. This is not the case. Brown offers only one paragraph in the whole book on the question of cavalry supply[39] and even this serves only to muddy the waters as the relative statistics quoted relate only to the much smaller BEF of 1914. He is no doubt correct that in October 1914 the cavalry represented 16.7 per cent of the manpower and 34.4 per cent of the equine strength of the army in France. However, this ignores the fact that the vast growth of the army after 1915 saw a decline in the relative strength of the cavalry to as little as 1.1 per cent of overall BEF man-power[40] and 6 per cent of its horses by 1918.[41] The figures offered by Brown are therefore misleading by omission, if nothing else. Ironically, Brown's most telling comment on the question is probably the very lack of any further discussion of the cavalry in his work. The absence of cavalry supply questions from his wider analysis of the supply problems of the BEF, and their solutions, allows the inference that these were simply not an issue. It is, however, a reflection of the state of the cavalry debate that a book of this sort can be considered complete without a proper examination of supply questions relating to an entire arm of service. It is also unfortunate that such a work, which might otherwise justly be considered the 'last word' on the subject, at least for the present, shies away from a significant and controversial aspect of its principal subject.

The tenacity not only of the fodder question but of all three great (Edmonds-inspired) myths concerning the cavalry is reflected in the work of Steven Badsey, whose thesis of 1981[42] offered a comprehensive critique of all three. In his contribution to Griffith's *British Fighting Methods In The Great War* (1996)[43] he was obliged to reiterate, at least in *precis* in his opening pages, all that he had previously argued fifteen years before. His earlier observation concerning the deep roots of these prejudices, quoted at the outset of this chapter, seems painfully apt. Indeed, these debates have been rehearsed again here lest critics of what follows fall back on them as a basis for argument. What could and should have been laid to rest thirty years ago continues to be given currency, often by historians who frankly should know better.

Reference has also already been made to the use of the cavalry as a metaphor for the obsolescent, in contrast to new 'modern' methods of warfare. This practice has become particularly prevalent among writers examining the rôle of tanks in the First World War. A school of thought has developed that sees victory on the Western Front gained through technological advance; the new tanks are the instrument that breaks the trench deadlock, supported by aircraft, new artillery shells, wireless and other new-fangled devices.[44] In this brave new world there is no place for the outdated horseman or his medieval *arme blanche*. This 'technological determinism' has been subject to a thorough critique by Gervaise Phillips (2002), who observed:

> The rôle played by cavalry in the First World War has been obscured by the appearance of an (allegedly) alternative weapon system, combining mobility, firepower and the potential for undertaking shock action: the tank. Naturally the technologically minded military historian has seized upon the tank as the obvious replacement for the horse.[45]

Once again the mounted arm has provided an easy target for criticism, and more specifically, a place to lay the blame for some of the failures of the new technology. For example, much has been made of the faltering progress, or for some commentators outright failure, of cavalry–tank cooperation in the latter stages of the war. Terraine commented: 'Much had been expected of the collaboration between the Whippets and the cavalry, but this proved to be an illusion. . . . By themselves the Whippets were very successful.'[46] Prior and Wilson went further, suggesting that the concept 'made no sense at all',[47] and that when attempted it was a 'predictable fiasco . . . Cavalry soon out-distanced the tanks and proceeded on their own. Fortunately for the horse-soldiers, by this stage most German resistance had collapsed.'[48] This statement is open to challenge on a number of points, but in this context it is their placing of the blame for this failure firmly on the cavalry which is most noteworthy.

The argument continues that not only were the cavalry incapable of cooperation with tanks, but at a higher level 'cavalry generals' (in particular Haig) failed to properly exploit the potential of the new technology. Phillips observed: 'For Tim Travers the tank's impact on the conflict was only limited by the lack of imagination of cavalry generals, who were unable to grasp the potential for waging mechanised warfare.'[49] Thus the failure of tanks to play a more decisive rôle was not inherent in their technological immaturity, but imposed upon them by a 'rival' arm of service in the form of the cavalry. Paddy Griffith summarised this tendency:

> If the tank's experience on the Western Front was unfortunate and rather disappointing, that of the horsed cavalry was sadder still. They actually enjoyed little less battlefield success than tanks, but found themselves heaped with unjustified vilification in proportion as the latter were accorded unjustified accolades. This was doubly irksome since the pre-war cavalry had actually been tactically more aware and more advanced than the infantry.[50]

His last point is particularly significant as, rather than the cavalry failing to embrace the new technology, the reverse was true: large numbers of tank officers had come from the cavalry. Badsey has pointed out that this trend had been specifically encouraged at the time of the introduction of the 'Whippet' tank, with precisely such cooperation in mind.[51]

The battles of Cambrai in 1917 and Amiens in 1918 both had a significant cavalry component as well as tanks. These two offensives form the subjects of later chapters, and the relationship between horses and armour will be examined in some detail. However, in order to produce a balanced picture of the rôle of the cavalry in this context it is necessary to overcome a substantial weight of technologically driven prejudice, and to filter the large mass of armour-focused writing on these battles, to draw out the parallel, but to date largely untold, story of the cavalry.

Many of the writers who have been considered in this chapter are viewed as important progressive thinkers by those concerned with topics other than the cavalry. However, starting from a position of conscious or unconscious disregard for the relevance or usefulness of cavalry, these writers of the new 'External' school of thought on the Western Front (as it has become known)[52] are confronted with a significant difficulty. One of the major platforms of their position is that the generals of the period, and Haig in particular, were possessed of more understanding of the military realities of their situation than history had latterly given them credit. And yet it was these same generals who persisted in retaining a cavalry force and building it into their plans for attack year after year, in spite of its repeated failure to play a decisive rôle. If these commanders were to be fully exonerated, the continued presence of cavalry must be accounted for, or to put it more bluntly 'explained away'. Once again John Terraine serves as an exemplar, as it was he who set the tone for much of the following debate.

Despite his frequent repetition of the obsolescence and uselessness of cavalry, Terraine had no doubt that in the absence of a suitable alternative, cavalry was a vital part of offensive planning during the war:

> Cavalry were always held in readiness behind every large-scale attack . . . Since the attacks failed, time after time, to break through the German defences, the cavalry found little opportunity for mounted action, and their presence has been the subject of much derisive comment. The fact remains that, with all its evident weaknesses, cavalry was the *only* mobile arm available during the First World War. What comment would be appropriate for a high command, which planned and launched great assaults, without making any provision for mobile exploitation, is not difficult to see.[53]

He leaves us in no doubt what that 'comment' would be in his scathing criticism of the German high command for its failure to support the offensive of 21 March 1918 with any mounted troops (the remaining German cavalry divisions in the West having been dismounted, the reasons for which will be examined later): 'To launch an offensive intended to win the war with none at all was not just foolish: it was criminal.'[54] Similar strong language occurs elsewhere: 'A general who launches what he hopes will be a decisive offensive without an arm of exploitation (as Ludendorff did in 1918) strikes me as criminally culpable.'[55] It is curious that he should make specific reference to 'derisive comment' about the cavalry when he himself is the author of a good deal of it. He also makes no reference to the inherent contradiction contained in his view that the cavalry was both a vital component of a decisive effort, and an arm which he variously dismisses elsewhere as 'feeble', 'incapable' and ultimately 'obsolete'.

Terraine never fully resolved this dichotomy; while reluctant to dismiss the cavalry entirely, acknowledgement of its usefulness ran counter to the 'modernist' argument. One solution to this lay in the manipulation of terminology: 'In the crisis of March [1918] the cavalry proved useful by virtue of its mobility, and its dismounted brigades, though weak ... gave great help in puttying gaps and supporting counter-attacks. Thus they won great credit in the capacity that cavalry had always affected to despise – mounted infantry.'[56]

The underlying argument supporting this statement runs that 'cavalry' are an *arme blanche* shock weapon, and that as soon as they are engaged in a firepower-based rôle, they cease to be 'cavalry' proper and become merely a more mobile offshoot of the infantry. By extension, this argument continues, the rôle of 'mounted infantry' could have been filled equally satisfactorily by the infantry themselves. Badsey has thoroughly demonstrated the falseness of this hypothesis,[57] showing that the British cavalrymen were able to absorb fire-power doctrine and combine it with shock tactics to produce a highly flexible and effective tactical method, and that by contrast, simply putting infantry on horses was never a satisfactory solution. Arguably, the fact that cavalrymen were able to fulfil a firepower (or 'mounted infantry') rôle, as well as a more traditional shock (or 'cavalry') function, should be weighed in their favour when balancing their overall usefulness. Many historians, including Terraine, have, however, sought to argue for the removal of these achievements from the scales, as being somehow outside the cavalry's formal brief. This kind of sophistry would have meant little to the cavalrymen doing the fighting.

In recent years there has been some new progress in studies of the cavalry. Griffith,[58] Badsey[59] and most recently Sheffield[60] have identified the embryonic, but significant rôle of horse-mounted troops in the development of mobile warfare. It has been recognised that, in spite of the efforts of the propagandists of the 1930s to argue the contrary, the roots of 'modern' mobile warfare doctrine lay not in the tanks of the Western Front but in what could be termed in modern parlance 'softskin' transport. That the tanks of the day were not capable of the exploitation rôle that many have postulated for them is slowly becoming more widely accepted. These historians have gone further to consider the development of what Griffith calls the 'cavalry brigade battlegroup',[61] an all-arms force consisting not only of cavalry and horse artillery, but also of motor machine-guns, lorry mounted infantry, and mobile medical and other supporting services. Badsey pursued this line further still, to make the analogy between cavalry and parachute forces, in their capacity to seize by *coup de main* positions ahead of the main force.[62] These views are indeed a breath of fresh air in the cavalry debate, and it is arguable that they represent the *start* of the real debate on cavalry, rather than the old myth-based arguments.

There is a danger, however, that this sort of thinking can result in what J.P. Harris (in relation to the armour debate) terms 'reading history backwards'.[63] The application of late twentieth-century terminology and doctrine as a model for interpreting the Western Front immediately encounters the problem that Haig and Kavanagh, the Cavalry Corps commander, probably seldom used the word 'battlegroup', and could hardly have dreamed of paratroops. In order to evaluate the doctrines of the time they must be viewed from within their own contemporary framework. Haig has been subject to years of unjustified vilification because he failed to be prescient enough to discern the roots of Rommel's panzer divisions or Operation *Desert Storm* in the faltering progress of the Mark I tanks at Flers. Travers is a particular proponent of this critique, observing: 'The greatest problem was the way in which the late nineteenth-century paradigm failed to come to grips with the twentieth-century paradigm – one set of ideas simply did not engage the other emerging set of ideas.'[64]

Yet it was not Haig's concern to explore ideas that might win wars in twenty or seventy-five years' time; he had to win the war he was fighting then, and with the tools immediately available. To suggest that the shape warfare would take in the later twentieth century was apparent to observers living in its first decades is quite unreasonable, despite the hindsight-driven protestations of Fuller or Liddell Hart. In any case, even if Haig had been able to develop in theory a late twentieth-century style armoured warfare doctrine, the tanks at his disposal were simply not up to the job.

Thus, while interesting with the benefit of hindsight, the 'birth of later doctrine' argument misses the real point. The overall question, which this argument fails to address, is not whether seeds for the future were sown, but whether the retention of an (albeit by 1918 pitifully weak) force of cavalry on the Western Front was a reasonable decision by the high command at the time. Alternatively, was it, as has so often been argued, the result of a failure to understand the prevailing conditions of the fighting? The answer to this lies not in teasing out the roots of mobile warfare advances that would not fully develop until later conflicts, but in determining whether the cavalry soldiers there and then were able to fight effectively in a mounted rôle when called upon to do so.

The various issues outlined in this chapter leave a basic overall question about the cavalry yet to be answered by historians: how significant was the contribution of British and Dominion mounted troops to the fighting on the Western Front in the First World War? Answering this question is the principal purpose of this book.

Within this broader question a series of subsidiary themes and questions can be defined, and these can in turn be used as tools of measurement to assess the broader performance of the arm. The first of these is the most basic, and relates in part to the old 'last machine-gun' myth. That is, how did mounted troops fight? Not only against machine guns, but also against the whole range of opposition, including artillery and wire, and to what degree of effectiveness? That is, to what extent were they able to manoeuvre and survive within the prevailing battlefield environment, inflict casualties on the enemy and obtain battlefield objectives? Many of the answers to this question are somewhat counter–intuitive, as episodes of cavalry galloping into enemy positions with swords drawn were neither as rare nor as suicidally ineffective as it has suited some critics to assume. Nor was the ground over which many of the battles took place the wilderness of wire and shell-holes, as typified by the latter stages of Third Ypres, which fills the popular imagination. For example, large portions of the Somme front in 1916 had yet to be fought over at the outset of the offensive, and the ground over which the Cambrai offensive was launched was specifically chosen for its lack of shell damage. In spite of this, trench lines did form a significant obstacle that taxed those wishing to see a cavalry advance. This obstacle was, however, by no means insurmountable and thought was given to the means, technical and logistical, of overcoming it. While previous writers have referred in passing to 'cavalry tracks' and mobile trench bridging,[65] no detailed study of these developments has yet been made. The sheer size of even a brigade of cavalry in terms of road space (although more often confined to cross-country routes), and its requirements in terms of shelter and water behind the line must also have provided a major challenge to those developing offensives. Thus the fact that it was possible for any mounted troops to reach the scene of action at all must indicate a significant level of planning and 'behind the scenes' work not yet adequately explored by historians.

This question inevitably has its focus at the tactical level, in the activities of brigade-sized and smaller formations, and in some cases in the exploits of individual regiments, squadrons and even troops of cavalry. It is only at this level that the true texture of the fighting, and the effectiveness or otherwise of various weapons and techniques, becomes apparent. Griffith[66] and others have already demonstrated the crucial importance of tactical and technical changes at this low level of command to the outcome of infantry and artillery fighting. The attitude taken to Lewis guns at platoon level or to the exact weight and speed of a creeping barrage have been shown to make the difference between success and costly failure. A similar level of analysis remains to be undertaken for the mounted arm.

Many modern studies of the First World War, and in particular those concerned more at the tactical rather than strategic level, have also stressed the importance of 'evolution' in the development of the BEF and in its ultimate success.[67] This process is often described in terms of a 'learning curve' along which the British army moved, developing its equipment and fighting methods with each new offensive. This raises the question as to what extent the cavalry underwent a similar process. It will be shown that while a variety of changes were made in the planning of cavalry operations at the divisional and corps level, and in the planning of army level offensives as a whole, there was a remarkable consistency in lower level cavalry tactics. The fighting methods spelt out in pre-war manuals, in particular *Cavalry Training*, published in 1912 (incidentally edited and partially written by Douglas Haig), continued to be applied by junior commanders and continued to be effective. This was increasingly the case in the later stages of the war. However, this was not a result of an evolution in tactics by the cavalry themselves. Instead, as will be shown in later chapters, the character of the war had evolved around the cavalry; in particular the changes in German defensive systems, and the adoption of deep defence, made existing cavalry methods ever more appropriate on the battlefield.

If, however, cavalry were more effective tactically during the First World War than they have hitherto been given credit for, their failure to make a larger overall contribution to the fighting needs to be explained. The answer to this lies in Command, Control and Communications (or 'C3' in modern parlance), the major factor hindering greater cavalry effectiveness, and the key to so many missed opportunities on the Western Front. The attitude of army and corps commanders, and of the commander-in-chief, to cavalry operations needs to be examined. The slowness of these men to grasp the potential (and indeed the limitations) of cavalry forces in the set-piece offensives of 1915–18, was a major factor in their performance. The rôle of Haig in particular, as commander-in-chief, and his enthusiasm for the arm, but his fundamental misunderstanding of their rôle, was also a key issue.

It will also be apparent that failures of communications, and an inability to appreciate the limitations of what communication methods were available, were critical factors in hindering cavalry operations. Attempts were made to address these difficulties by practical solutions in the form of increased use of wireless, and of RFC/RAF contact patrols, for example. However, more important was the reordering of the chain of command to allow those nearer the 'sharp end' of the fighting a greater degree of control over the resources deployed on their battlefield. The degree to which this was achieved remains to be seen.

Another key factor in the effectiveness or otherwise of the cavalry in the period under consideration was the rôle of the Cavalry Corps as an institution, and of its commander 'Black Jack' Kavanagh. He was to play a significant part in the functioning (or otherwise) of the chain of command, and to exert a powerful influence over the effectiveness of the corps. Examination of this also leads to the question of what exactly the Cavalry Corps headquarters was supposed to do, and indeed whether it even needed to exist in the form it took from the end of 1916 onwards, or whether it was a hindrance to operations, and should have modelled itself after the fashion of the newly created Tank Corps.

Mention of the Tank Corps raises the question of cavalry–tank cooperation, and of new technology more generally. The significant anti-cavalry and pro-armour bias of much of the existing literature has already been discussed. The examination of this relationship is also critical. The tank forms only one part of this picture, as armour in the form of armoured cars served alongside the cavalry from the outset of the war. These vehicles were to fight alongside the cavalry in the Somme battles as well as in the operations of spring 1917. Tanks themselves cooperated with the cavalry at Cambrai in 1917, and particularly significantly at Amiens in 1918. The relative performance of the two arms, horsed and mechanical, and their degree of compatibility needs to be considered. Far from being a replacement for the cavalry, tanks had at best a complementary rôle on the battlefield, and in some cases performed an entirely different function. Thus the relationship between the two is far more complex than simply the 'new' taking over from the 'old'.

The final aspect of the contribution of the cavalry to the conflict to be considered, and one that draws together the conclusions from all the earlier themes, is operational success. Were the cavalry able to accomplish the tasks set out for them by their higher commanders? Or were they ultimately unsuccessful when measured against these goals? Typically this analysis is undertaken at the 'operational' level, that of offensives as a whole, at the command level of corps and army, as often the lower level tactical effectiveness of the arm was neutralised by poor command and control or other factors. Tactical battlefield effectiveness is relevant, and command and control systems function well only when they bring the troops concerned into contact with the enemy at the right place and time. For each of the British offensives between 1914 and 1918 it is necessary to make a judgement on the success of the cavalry operations therein.

In most cases the cavalry failed to obtain the objectives set out for them by their commanders, and by Haig, the commander-in-chief, in particular, and to that extent they were unsuccessful. However, this conclusion has to be balanced by consideration of the objectives, which in many cases were unrealistic, and provide a poor yardstick for assessment of the success of the arm. As was discussed earlier in this chapter, this has also been compounded by the keenness of many historians to use these objectives to denigrate not only the arm but also the commanders, notwithstanding the circular character of this argument.

It would have been possible to structure this study on a thematic basis, but it was felt that, unlike some other aspects of First World War studies, the history of the cavalry has been so little investigated that a statement of the basic narrative history was required in order to provide a context for the analytical parts of the study. Also in a number of cases the narratives of events offered by previous writers are simply factually incorrect, so a retelling of the course of events is required. As was discussed earlier in this chapter, many of the conclusions of these earlier scholars were also based on little or no analysis of events, or on the hearsay opinions of participants in the war whose position could hardly be considered neutral.

The narrative herein was constructed to a great extent from contemporary unit war diaries. These documents, consulted in the original in the National Archives, have the advantage of being written very close to the events described, and contain a significant amount of hard data, including texts of messages and operations orders, times, map locations and grid references, and casualty figures. Comparison of the diaries from different participating units and levels of command was also instructive. Reference was also made to the diaries of individuals and published memoirs, particularly those in positions of command, as well as other eye-witnesses. However, the difficulties of taking some of this material at face value will become apparent, particularly with regard to the Somme battles.

Secondary sources of particular importance are the *Official History* of the conflict (although this too is not without its own faults and internal biases), and the inter-war volumes of *Cavalry Journal*. The latter is a particularly important source as during the period 1919–1939 a significant body of not only personal accounts of the war but also analytical articles appeared in its pages. These pieces were also subject to peer review and discussion published in the letters pages of subsequent editions, much of which is highly illuminating. From these various sources a narrative of events has been created that forms the core of each chapter.

When Donald R. Morris set out to write *The Washing of the Spears*, his classic account of the Anglo–Zulu war of 1879, he discovered that the story, in order to make sense, had to start in 1807.[68] Likewise, the amount of mounted activity revealed by research for this book was something of a surprise. Indeed particularly with the fighting of 1914, and again of later 1918, it became impossible to deal exhaustively with every mounted cavalry action in a work of this length. However, rather than narrowing the focus, it was felt that a broader, if slightly less detailed, overview of the whole period was critical to the understanding of the subject. The nature of much of the fighting in 1914, prior to the development of trench warfare, means that the rôle of the cavalry during that period, while interesting, bears only a little on the questions raised by the later offensives. Equally, although the cavalry played a vital and costly part, largely on foot, in a defensive capacity at Ypres in 1915, they were not significantly involved in the major offensives attempted earlier that year. Thereafter the focus of attention narrows to a field which encompasses the principal attempts by the British to break the trench deadlock from 1916 onwards. It was not possible to devote space to Third Ypres in 1917. Although crucial to the understanding of the evolution of other arms, the Cavalry Corps was rapidly excluded from that battle as the true nature of the fighting became evident, and mounted forces played little significant rôle in it. The core of this work therefore concentrates on what for many was the heart of the war: the trench fighting in France from 1915 to early 1918.

*   *   *

Nonetheless one must start at the beginning, in August 1914. It is arguable that more men were mobilised on horseback in 1914 than at any other period in history. The *Field Service Pocket* Book of 1914 included a handy table of the forces of various principal foreign armies on mobilisation. From it can be listed the cavalry forces of the major belligerents: France had at her disposal ten cavalry divisions consisting of around sixty regiments or 45,000 men, Germany eleven divisions, or sixty-six regiments, totalling about 55,000 men, Austria-Hungary a further ten divisions and five independent brigades, equivalent to around fifty regiments or 45,000 men, while Russia's European army included a massive twenty-three divisions of cavalry totalling around 80,000 men.[69] This provided the Central Powers with a total of around 100,000 cavalry, while the Allies could field nearly 150,000. This can be compared with the cavalry portion of Napoleon's Grande Armée of 1812, possibly one of the largest single military forces ever previously assembled, which amounted to only 80,000 horsemen.[70]

Reference to the army of Napoleon is also relevant in as much as most of the cavalry of Europe in 1914 would have been quite recognisable to soldiers of that earlier period. French cavalry still wore the brightly coloured uniforms, brass helmets and in some cases the steel cuirasses of their predecessors from the nineteenth century. They were armed with a modern bolt-action carbine but this was a short-barrelled and rather ineffective weapon. The cavalry of imperial Germany were slightly more modern but also carried an inferior rifle, and retained a distinctly antiquated outlook. These powers had clashed previously in the Franco–Prussian War of 1870, and even though that conflict provided lessons in the effectiveness of modern firepower for those who chose to learn them, it also provided enough examples of the success of old-style *arme blanche* cavalry charges for the conservatives to win the tactical debate in many armies.[71]

The initial cavalry force sent to the continent from the UK was small in comparison to the continental armies (as indeed was the BEF itself). At the outset of the war in 1914 the BEF included five brigades of cavalry. Of these, four were under the command of the newly created Cavalry Division, while the other, the 5th Cavalry Brigade under Brigadier General Chetwode, was nominally independent.[72] This provided a force of fifteen regiments, along with a further two regiments broken up by squadrons among the six infantry divisions of the BEF as divisional cavalry. All of these units, including those forming the divisional squadrons, were regular, rather than yeomanry regiments. (One Regiment of Special Reserve, the North Irish Horse, was also attached to the BEF at Army level.) This made up a total force of some 9,269 men and 9,815 horses, along with attached artillery and ancillary units.[73]

This represented only a portion of the total cavalry force available to the British Empire. In 1914 there were thirty-one regiments of regular cavalry in the British army. These consisted of the three regiments of Household Cavalry (two of Life Guards, and the Royal Horse Guards or 'Blues'), seven regiments of Dragoon Guards, three regiments of Dragoons, and a further eighteen regiments of 'light cavalry' – Hussars and Lancers. Many of these regiments were scattered in postings around the Empire, mostly in India and South Africa, and only about half were in the UK at any one time. Most of the overseas-based regiments were recalled to serve on the Western Front in the two additional British cavalry divisions raised at the end of 1914, while others were to arrive in France as part of Indian cavalry divisions, meaning that by 1918 nearly every British regular cavalry regiment had been involved in fighting on one front or another, and in that year twenty-seven regiments were serving in France and Belgium.

Also available were a further fifty-five regiments of yeomanry. These were part-time territorial soldiers, organised under the same system as their infantry counterparts following the Haldane reforms of 1908. In theory, territorial soldiers were intended for the defence of the UK and were not required to serve overseas, but nearly all immediately volunteered for foreign service and the first yeomanry regiments arrived in France in September 1914.[74] As we shall see, these regiments were soon integrated into the cavalry divisions, and there was little to distinguish their performance from that of the regular cavalry.

The Indian army also included a further forty-three regiments of cavalry of various types. Twelve of these regiments were to serve on the Western Front between late 1914 and January 1918, while of the rest some remained in India, and others fought with distinction (alongside yeomanry regiments) in Palestine and Mesopotamia. The line-up was completed by a brigade of Canadian cavalry, which arrived in France in 1915, and of course the legendary Australian Light Horse, although only one regiment of the latter, the 13th, served on the Western Front. These overseas forces will be discussed in more detail later, but much of what follows in terms of training and efficiency was equally applicable to them as well as to their British counterparts.

The crucial difference between all of these cavalrymen, whether regular, territorial or imperial, and their continental cousins was the experience of the Boer War in South Africa from 1899 to 1902. In this campaign the battlefield had been dominated by the mounted rifleman. The Boer farmers and, as the war progressed, also the imperial forces relied heavily on the mobility of horses combined with the firepower of magazine rifles in the hands of men who could shoot. The response to this in the British cavalry was the adoption of doctrines which, while retaining the sword and lance, emphasised the power of the rifle and machine gun.[75] Gone were the elaborate nineteenth-century uniforms. The British cavalryman of 1914 wore the same dull but functional khaki tunic and cap as his colleagues in the infantry, and carried the same excellent 'Short Magazine Lee Enfield' rifle or SMLE. This had in fact been designed with use by cavalrymen specifically in mind and gave them a weapon that was comparable to the infantry weapons of their opponents, and significantly superior to the cavalry carbines of the French and Germans. The importance of individual marksmanship was also recognised and cavalrymen were taught to shoot with the same 'fifteen rounds a minute' efficiency as the infantry, receiving the same incentives for good shooting in the form of proficiency pay.

Gone also were the distinctions between 'heavy' and 'light' cavalry. Universal patterns of saddle and bridle were introduced in 1902,[76] and dragoons trained and drilled in the same way as hussars or lifeguards and carried identical equipment. The only distinction was in lancer regiments, which had campaigned successfully for the reintroduction of the lance after it was temporarily phased out, and all lancer regiments were so armed in 1914. Incidentally non-lancer regiments serving with the Indian cavalry divisions also equipped one squadron with lances, so as will be seen in 1916 the 7th Dragoon Guards were able to charge with lances on at least one memorable occasion (described later).

The other key area of improvement resulting from the South African experience was in horse-mastership. The loss rate of horses in South Africa had been virtually unsustainable, and was attributable not only to the harsh climate but also to putting horses in the hands of men who did not know how to look after them properly. Out of the 518,000 horses employed by the British army in the course of the Boer War, no fewer than 326,000 (or 66 per cent) died.[77] By 1914 this situation had changed radically and the care and management of his mount was one of the key skills of any British cavalryman. The habit of marching dismounted and leading the horses for a portion of every hour, practised by British cavalry throughout the war, but particularly in 1914, attracted the derision of their French counterparts, but its benefits were evident in the relative horse-loss rates of the two armies. Tom Bridges, who in 1914 was serving as a major in the 4th Dragoon Guards (but was later to reach the rank of lieutenant general), summed up the condition of the British cavalry in 1914:

> The Cavalry division under Allenby, consisting of four brigades with
> a total of twelve regiments and nine batteries of Horse Artillery,
> was a fine and well mounted command, and its fighting value was

probably much greater than that of any force of its size in the Allied or enemy armies. It was well trained not only to shock but to fire tactics (the results of long experience of colonial warfare) and while our horse-mastership was good, that of the Germans was inferior and that of the French (who like James Pigg never got off) was bad. The British cavalryman walked nearly as much as he rode, with the result that his horse whom he regarded as a friend and comrade kept condition remarkably well.[78]

One factor which acted against the best efforts of the cavalryman to look after his horse was simply the weight of kit and equipment he was expected to carry. The soldier was expected to be able to move and fight independently for up to 24–48 hours, and even when they were united with the wagons and limbers of the regimental transport, the latter largely carried heavier communal items and reserve stores. Thus almost everything required day to day by horse and man had to be carried by horse and man. Once again the *Field Service Pocket Book* provided an itemised (albeit perhaps slightly idealised) list. In addition to his uniform the cavalry private carried 100 rounds of .303″ ammunition for his rifle, 90 rounds of which were in a leather bandolier slung over his shoulder; he also had a haversack over his other shoulder for rations, and a felt-covered enamel water bottle. On his saddle were mounted his sword, usually on the 'near' or left side, and his rifle in a leather bucket on the 'off' side. Attached to these were his mess tin, picketing peg, water bucket and a feedbag with a ration of corn or oats for the horse. In addition, strapped on to the saddle were a pair of wallets containing his spare socks and underwear, shaving kit, horse-grooming brushes, etc., along with a waterproof groundsheet and on some occasions his greatcoat. All of this, along with the saddlery itself and blankets underneath, weighed about 100lb (50kg), or nearly as much as the rider himself. With him in the saddle the total weight was quoted as 'about 18 stone'[79] (125kg). As the war progressed, he was also issued with a second bandolier of ammunition to fit around the horse's neck, a bayonet for his rifle and in 1916 a steel helmet, not to mention Mills bombs, wire cutters and all the other impedimenta of modern warfare. This weight was clearly excessive, and every effort was made to leave out items not considered to be urgently required; greatcoats, for example, were often gone-without, but it was an unfortunate military fact that almost all of the kit was required at some stage and little could be left behind without seriously hampering efficiency. The cost in horseflesh of this heavy burden was to become apparent as the war progressed (in particular at Arras in 1917) but there was little to be done, except to dismount whenever possible and unsaddle whenever it was reasonable to do so. Much grumbling probably accompanied the constant tacking up and untacking and marching, but the necessity for it was clear.

Much of the equipment was deliberately attached to the saddle rather than to the man; for example, he no longer wore a sword belt as this weapon was slung from the saddle. The sword was intended only for use while mounted, and so was left behind when on foot, rather than dragging along and tripping up its owner. When dismounted the soldier had only his rifle, ammunition, haversack and water-bottle, the items immediately required, and was nimble as a result. The problem with this was that from late 1914 onwards the cavalry-man was often completely separated from his horse to do duty in the trenches, or in several offensives (described later) to provide reserves for his infantry counterparts. On these occasions, as he was not supplied with a backpack, all a soldier's bits and pieces had to be stuffed into the pockets of his greatcoat, or rolled up in the coat itself, and the whole strapped sausage-like *en-banderole* around his body. On foot at least this was a very unsatisfactory arrangement.

Outfitted with all this modern and well designed but inevitably heavy equipment, men and horses were grouped into regiments. The soldier's immediate circle, and the smallest organisational unit in a regiment was the section of eight men, commanded by a corporal. On parade, on the march or in battle, this group formed up in two ranks of four men, and was the basic building block of all drills mounted and dismounted. Four sections formed a troop of about thirty men, commanded by a junior officer, typically a lieutenant, assisted by an experienced troop sergeant. In turn, four troops formed a squadron, numbering around 120–130 men, led by a major or captain, and three squadrons made up a regiment.[80] This gave an overall regimental strength of around 400, significantly smaller than an equivalent infantry battalion, which had an establishment of over 800.

Each regiment also started the war with an integral machine-gun section armed with two Vickers machine guns. These were a significant addition to the firepower of the unit and somewhat made up for the lack of rifle fire-power resulting from the small size of the regiment, and the need for one in four men to be told off as horse-holders, and therefore unable to shoot. Three regiments formed a brigade, and at this level the formation also included a battery of Royal Horse Artillery, firing 13-pdr 'Quick-firing' (QF) guns (identical to those used by the King's Troop RHA on ceremonial occasions today). The cavalry brigade also had a field squadron of Royal Engineers, a signal squadron, a cavalry field ambulance unit, a veterinary section, and integral supply and ammunition columns. This meant that the brigade was a virtually self-contained formation with all the elements and troop types required to act independently and sustain itself in the field for short periods without additional support. As has been described, four such brigades formed the Cavalry Division in August 1914 along with an additional 'Independent' brigade.

Unfortunately, while the individual regiments and the soldiers within them were arguably at the peak of efficiency on mobilisation in 1914, this could not be said of the higher command of the cavalry, and indeed the problems that developed then were to persist for much of the war. The sources of some of the later command and control problems can be traced in its early structure. The particular problem was one facing the BEF as a whole at this period: its lack of pre-existing divisional and corps level command elements. The infantry was divided into two corps, but headquarters for these had to be created *ad-hoc* as no higher formation than the division had previously existed in the peacetime army. In the cavalry the situation was worse; only brigade staffs had existed before the war, and when Major General Allenby was given command of the Cavalry Division (later the 1st Cavalry Division), he had to create a staff essentially by co-opting officers he knew to be available and suitably qualified.[81] In any case a four-brigade division was too large to handle effectively, and as the summer of 1914 wore on the division was split into two groups. In part this was prompted by rivalries among the senior cavalrymen themselves. The controversy over the rôle of the cavalry in the 'Curragh Incident' of earlier in 1914 had damaged the relationships between many of these men, in particular Hubert Gough, initially commanding 3rd Cavalry Brigade, and Allenby himself.[82] These personal difficulties also extended beyond the Cavalry Division to the higher levels of command. There was little love lost between the two senior cavalrymen in France, Douglas Haig, now commanding I Corps, and Sir John French, the commander of the BEF. If nothing else, these rivalries give the lie to the idea that there was a club of 'cavalry generals' in the BEF helping one another.

By Christmas 1914 the command situation was exacerbated as more cavalry arrived in France. The existing force was split into two divisions, and a third, initially commanded by Julian Byng, was created. A Cavalry Corps was formed in October 1914, initially commanded by Allenby and then briefly by Byng, before in the course of 1915 the former was moved sideways to command an infantry corps and the latter departed for Gallipoli.[83] Two divisions of cavalry also arrived from India in November and December 1914, forming a separate Indian Cavalry Corps under Major General Frederic Rimington.[84] (These divisions included a mix of Indian and British regiments, of which more later.) Counted together, these two corps represented a force of forty-five regiments of cavalry, or around 20,000 men, but few of its leaders had commanded more than a regiment in combat prior to 1914, and none more than a brigade even under peacetime conditions.

No specific criticism of these men is implied by the observation that they lacked experience; Allenby, Byng and Gough all rose to army command and their performance in that capacity will be considered in later chapters. However, taken in conjunction with the fact that there were no pre-existing administrative or logistical structures for the cavalry at even divisional, let alone corps, level, and (in spite of years of debate on the matter)[85] no clear doctrinal model for how such large forces of horsemen should be used operationally, it is clear that those planning the rôle of cavalry in the coming battles were working essentially in the dark. The extent to which a consistent operational method could be developed by these commanders remained to be seen.

* * *

The operations of the BEF and of the cavalry in August and September 1914 have been well described in any number of different accounts.[86] As this work is mainly concerned with the more neglected activities of the cavalry in the trench warfare that characterised the Western Front from the end of the year onwards, there is not space to cover the activities of the mounted arm in that early period in great detail. However, there were several occasions of mounted combat which merit examination as exemplars of the spirit in which the cavalry began the war, and indeed in which they were to continue it through all the trials and frustrations of the next four years.

The first was the tiny but famous action at Casteau on 22 August. As the BEF arrived in France at the end of August and took up positions on the left of the French line around Mons in Belgium, the regiments forming the divisional cavalry squadrons as well as large numbers of men from the Cavalry Division itself were broken up into small patrols both to provide a screen for the activities of their own forces and to spy out the movements of the advancing Germans.[87] This was doubly necessary as the weather had turned misty and the reconnaissance efforts of the fledgling Royal Flying Corps were much hampered by the poor visibility.[88] As dawn broke on 22 August one of these screening patrols, C Squadron of the 4th Dragoon Guards, found itself in the little village of Casteau, on the main road north out of Mons to Brussels. Probing northwards in search of the enemy, the dragoons spotted a patrol of German Uhlans advancing down the road.[89] In fact these were members of the German *4th Cuirassiers*, but as at the time all German cavalry regardless of their regimental title were lance-armed, they tend to always appear in British accounts as Uhlans (i.e., 'Lancers'). The commander of C Squadron, Major Tom Bridges, whose remarks were quoted earlier, dismounted two troops to provide fire support, and kept two troops mounted for shock action. These he hid behind a farm, hoping to ambush the enemy as they came closer; however, the Germans spotted something suspicious and turned back before the trap could be sprung. Surprisingly for such a small battle, the precise sequence of events which followed differs in various accounts. Two things certainly happened: the two mounted troops commanded by Captain Hornby charged down the road and came into hand-to-hand contact with the German cavalry, winning the fight and driving them back on to their supports. Meanwhile, some of the enemy were engaged with rifle fire and Corporal Thomas was credited with being the first BEF soldier to inflict a casualty on the German army with a rifle. By his own account,

> I could see a German cavalry officer some four hundred yards away standing mounted in full view of me, gesticulating as he disposed his dismounted men and ordered them to take up their firing positions to engage us. Immediately I saw him I took aim, pulled the trigger and automatically, almost instantaneously, he fell to the ground obviously wounded, but whether he was killed or not is a matter I do not think was ever cleared up.[90]

Another 'first kill' was credited that day, Captain Hornby being the first man to use the new 1908 pattern cavalry sword in anger and 'run through' a German with it. For this rather gruesome achievement he was immediately recommended for the DSO, as the brigade commander General De Lisle had promised this reward to whoever was the first to do so.[91]

Apart from being the first time that casualties were inflicted on the Germans by the BEF, Casteau was not a particularly significant engagement, and was followed by many similar skirmishes over the coming days and weeks. Nonetheless, it set the tone for what was to follow. It is arguable that the reverse experienced by the German cavalry on the 22nd established the moral ascendancy of the British cavalry over their opponents, which was retained for the remainder of the campaign. Tom Bridges reflected on this:

> This was the first action of the British Expeditionary Force and one of the very few occasions when the *arme blanche* was used during the war. [An arguable point perhaps, as will become apparent.] The actual casualties inflicted were few, but the moral effect on both sides was great. We did not quite know what would happen when we got up against the German cavalry of which there were great masses all trained to shock action. But Hornby had solved the problem for us, and when Uhlan [*sic*] prisoners, captured Prussian horses and a stack of lances in a buggy were brought in by the Squadron Sergeant-Major past the whole cavalry division, there was no further doubt.[92]

Thus the British cavalry was in the ascendancy in what in earlier years would have been known as a 'war of outposts', involving reconnaissance, patrolling and skirmishing in small units. The bigger question was whether cavalry could contribute to the battle in larger set-piece encounters at regimental level and above. Two actions in the last week of August 1914 will serve as good examples of regimental- and brigade-level mounted action: the charge of the 2nd Cavalry Brigade at Audregnies on 24 August, and the action of the 5th Cavalry Brigade at Cerizy (or in some accounts Moy) on 28 August. The outcomes of these two engagements were very different. Anglesey covered both in his *A History of the British Cavalry*, and his reasoning for doing so bears repetition:

> The excuse for going into so much of the details of both the Audregnies and Cerisy [*sic*] actions is that they provide the best examples of early First World War chiefly mounted actions by the British regular cavalry: the former illustrating *how not*, and the latter *how to* do it.[93]

After first contacting the German advanced guards on 22 August, the BEF carried out a successful holding action along the canal line at Mons. However, by the 24th their position had become exposed by the retreat of French forces on their right, and their left was essentially in the air and vulnerable to out-flanking by the German *IV Corps*, the right wing of which was feeling its way around the western extremity of the Allied line. Much of the British force was able to disengage successfully from its attackers and begin a retreat, but the German advance around the open left flank risked cutting off the westernmost infantry units, including Sir Charles Fergusson's 5th Division.[94] Allenby's cavalry division, which had been protecting this open flank, had sent out patrols early in the morning and encountered no Germans, so had begun its own retreat southward. This potentially left the flank of 5th Division exposed. A message was sent by Fergusson to Allenby's cavalry division headquarters and the nearest cavalry unit, De Lisle's 2nd Cavalry Brigade, asking for support to enable the infantry to retire. An account of subsequent events from De Lisle's 2nd Brigade headquarters is contained in the brigade War Diary.[95] After consultation with Allenby, De Lisle moved his brigade back northward to a covering position (vacated by the brigade earlier that morning) around the village of Audregnies. From here he pushed out the 18th Hussars and L Battery RHA into defensive positions, and they were soon dismounted and unlimbered and engaging the advancing German infantry at a range of 'about 800 yards' (750m). He then went on to give a fateful order:

> I rode back to the village where I met Lieutenant Colonel Campbell commanding 9th Lancers and ordered him at all costs to check the hostile advance, adding 'It may be necessary for your regiment to charge.' I then rode to meet the 4th DGs and ordered Lieutenant Colonel Mullens to support the 9th Lancers with his regiment and to assume charge of defence NE of the river until my return.[96]

The consequences of inviting a British regular cavalry regiment, at the opening of the first continental campaign for nearly a hundred years, to charge if 'necessary', even one honed in the new doctrines of fire and movement, were inevitable. John Terraine summarised the mood:

British cavalry rarely need urging to dash at the enemy. All through the Peninsular war the Duke of Wellington complained bitterly of this habit of rushing headlong at the foe. . . . The British cavalry had learned much since then, but old habits die hard, and we seem to see a survival of this one in what followed.[97]

Colonel Campbell immediately ordered his Lancers to mount up (they had been waiting behind the village and had, quite correctly, dismounted to rest the horses), and led them at a gallop out of the village in column of squadrons, lances 'engaged' (lowered). Two squadrons of the 4th Dragoon Guards followed in column of troops, while the third diverted to the west to capture a cottage guarding the flank of the attack.[98] Major Leveson, commanding B Squadron of the 18th Hussars, was occupying a dismounted firing line in the railway cutting to the east of the line of attack. He described what he saw in a letter to the War Office Historical Branch, compilers of the *Official History*:

Suddenly there was a tremendous increase in the hostile gun and machine-gun fire on our left. I looked in that direction down the railway line (we were at the left (west) end of the cutting) and I saw our cavalry moving forward at a gallop. They appeared to be charging. They were some 1,500 yards away on my left and I could not tell if it was the 2nd Brigade or not. The first three squadrons carried lances and were in open column of squadrons. The remainder had no lances and appeared to be in column of troops as near as possible, but in both cases the formation, if ever made, was being rapidly lost. They were being exposed to terrific shell and m.g. fire. A dozen shells bursting over them at a time – I could distinctly see the men falling off their horses, others evidently wounded just clinging on.[99]

Colonel Campbell, leading the 9th Lancers, was a pre-war Grand National-winning jockey, and he set a fierce pace. There is some suggestion that the lancers attempted to deploy into line of squadrons on leaving the village but if so this made little difference to their already ragged formation. Second Lieutenant Roger Chance was following in the ranks of the Dragoon Guards: 'If there is a hail of bullets I am not aware of it, as with Sergeant Talbot glimpsed alongside, and the men thundering after us, I endeavour one-handed to control my almost runaway steed.'[100]

Gallant though this charge was, the problem facing 2nd Cavalry Brigade was simple; as Major Leveson commented, 'I could not see any objective they might have had.'[101] While there were isolated groups of German infantry in the cornfields to the north of the village, the enemy's main body was still some distance away and their artillery further still. Thus the charge petered out long before it reached any appreciable target. Some sources suggest that the ground was divided by wire fences and these caused the attack to halt, but this is disputed.[102] After galloping approximately a mile (1.6km) the cavalry reached a mineral railway, which marked the limit of their advance, and a sugar factory, or 'Sucrerie', which offered some shelter and a rallying point. By this time they were under intense artillery fire. Captain Francis Grenfell of the Lancers described how 'We simply galloped about like rabbits in front of a line of guns, men and horses falling in all directions.'[103] After that it was simply a matter of individuals and small groups trying to fall back and save themselves. Leveson of the 18th Hussars, still in the cutting, was on the receiving end of this pell-mell retreat:

> Between 5 and 10 minutes later, the remnants of this charge, a mob of men and horses, many wounded, poured into our cutting. I recognised Captain Sewell of the 4th DGs and Captain Grenfell of the 9th Lancers, and I believe Colonel David Campbell of the 9th Lancers. They galloped on down the cutting taking some of my led horses with them.[104]

The charge was a clear failure. The two regiments involved, the 9th Lancers and 4th Dragoon Guards, had suffered 169 men killed, wounded or taken prisoner and lost over 300 horses[105] without contacting a significant body of enemy forces. De Lisle, however, claimed credit for his brigade for inflicting a significant delay on the German advance:

> The charge was well led and gallantly executed by all squadrons. The actual effect was marred by a line of fence between the squadrons and the enemy, the moral effect was complete. The enemy did not advance beyond the wire fence for 4 hours and gave time for the 5th Div. to retire in good order.[106]

While the final sentence is true, it is much more likely that the German infantry attacks that followed the charge were broken up by effective artillery fire from the three RHA batteries of the cavalry division which had joined the defence line, as well as the guns of the 5th Division, which were brought into action against them. Meanwhile a cavalry brigade had been reduced to the strength of a regiment. Naturally the press at home in the UK seized on the story of cavalry heroism, and a painting was produced of Captain Grenfell riding over the German guns, despite the fact that by his own admission he never 'reached a point closer than 800 yards' from them.[107] Somehow the losses had to be justified. Grenfell was awarded a VC for his efforts in helping to recover some of the guns at a later stage of the battle, and a similar decoration was recommended for Lieutenant Colonel Campbell. His caustic reply sums up his jaundiced view of the battle: 'I want my squadrons back, not VCs or medals.'[108]

There is little that can be claimed from this action to the credit of the cavalry. The 18th Hussars and the artillery had already established a firm defence line to the east of the village, with the 5th Division infantry and more guns on their right, and it was this position which was successfully defended for much of the rest of the day. There was nothing to be achieved by charging at that moment, and even had there been, it should have been carried out with far more circumspection, in good order, and after proper objectives had been identified and the ground reconnoitred. Some sources suggest that De Lisle ordered the charge himself, telling Campbell 'I'm going to charge the enemy'.[109] If so, much of the blame for the losses rests with him, and this would explain Campbell's strong words about his squadrons, quoted above. It seems on this occasion that enthusiasm got the better of good judgement, at brigade and divisional headquarters at least.

The action at Cerizy could not be more of a contrast (and interestingly was fought largely in the absence of the brigade commander). Fought on 28 August, this was an action involving the cavalry, which, while not of great strategic significance, definitely demonstrated their high level of training, flexibility and aggression. In many ways it was a textbook encounter that might have come directly from the pages of *Cavalry Training*. It is worthy of examination here because in many ways it set the tone of what was to follow over the next four-and-a-half years. As will be shown in later chapters, similar adherence to pre-war tactics and standards of skill and training was to pay dividends far more often than has been credited by many historians. The summer of 1914 was not, as some have argued, the last chance for mounted action, but rather a precursor to years of hard campaigning.

By 28 August the two corps of the BEF had become separated. Lieutenant General Smith-Dorrien's II Corps, after its stanch defensive action at Le Cateau on the 26th, was falling back on Ham, to the west of St Quentin. Meanwhile Lieutenant General Haig's I Corps was following a line about 10 miles east, via Guise and La Fere. The inner (western) flank of Haig's force was thus exposed in the gap between the corps, but was protected by Brigadier General Chetwode's independent 5th Cavalry Brigade acting as flank- and rearguard, moving southwards broadly following the line of the river Oise. The brigade had been working steadily southwards, posting detachments on strategic points and then recalling them as the force moved past out of danger (a tactic learned on the northwest frontier of India, as well as elsewhere).[110] By late morning on the 28th the brigade headquarters, accompanied by the 20th Hussars, was established at a farm near Cerizy on the main St Quentin–La Fere road. The other two regiments of the brigade, the 2nd Dragoons (Royal Scots Greys) and the 12th Lancers, along with J Battery RHA, were about a mile and a half (2km) to the east in the village of Moy, which lay on the river Oise itself. The Scots Greys were the duty regiment for the day and had detachments and patrols posted at key points.[111] Meanwhile for the Lancers it was a rare opportunity for a break in the incessant marching and the regiment took the chance to relax. Captain Stewart, the regimental historian, records,

> There was an idyllic air about the place, miles and ages removed from the agony and press of war. 'Lunch', wrote an officer, 'off some of the finest pears, white wine, bread and cheese. Then we wandered about. . . . Rolly busied himself writing to his wife that there were no Germans near and all was quiet.' The men settled down to some sorely needed sleep and the drowsy summer afternoon settled about the chateau walls.[112]

Many men took the opportunity to bathe and shave in the chateau lakes, and the men of the machine gun section decided to strip down and sort out their equipment.[113]

Meanwhile, unknown to the Lancers, a German column led by two squadrons of the German *2nd Guard Dragoons* was advancing south down the main road from St Quentin. This force quickly drove in a Scots Greys detachment at La Folie farm, about 1,000 yards (900m) north of the brigade headquarters, but was engaged by dismounted rifle fire by the remainder of the Greys' squadron on the ridgeline to the east, a fire-fight developing at a range of about 600 yards (550m) across the intervening valley. This fight was supported by the two guns of the Greys' machine-gun section, and continued for some time.[114] The sound of firing was heard in the valley at Moy and the artillery and lancers were roused rapidly from their slumbers. Lieutenant Colonel Wormald immediately ordered the lancers to mount up, and set off himself with his adjutant and staff to find out what was happening. He was rapidly followed by C Squadron under Captain Mitchell and Lieutenant Styles's machine-gun section, who rapidly reassembled their dispersed kit and moved off.[115]

On arriving on the ridge-line C Squadron dismounted, shifted their led horses into dead ground in the rear, and accompanied by their machine-guns joined the Greys in the dismounted fight. At about this time the German cavalry made an attempt to close the range and moved mounted down the forward slope towards the British firing line, through fields of stubble and stooks of ripening grain. Why this was attempted is unclear as the result was predictable; they could make no progress, and were forced to dismount and recommence the rifle duel, this time lying among the stubble with their led horses in full view on the forward slope. To add to their discomfort a two-gun section of J Battery arrived at this point and joined in, firing at the Germans over open sights. The Germans attempted to withdraw their led horses, but under the combined rifle, artillery and machine-gun fire many stampeded and were lost to the rear. Meanwhile their dismounted men fell back gradually to the crest of the opposite ridge, where they had first been engaged.[116]

When A and B Squadrons of the lancers arrived, Wormald sent them around to the right via some dead ground to come up on to the left flank of the German squadrons and once again engage them dismounted. This was successfully accomplished, and the Germans now faced fire from two directions. It was around this time that the brigade commander, Brigadier General Chetwode, returned from a conference elsewhere to find his brigade engaged in a full-scale battle; however, he could find no fault with Wormald's management of the situation, ordering only that the so-far unengaged 20th Hussars move around the western (left) side of the enemy position and attack their other flank. The Hussars advanced until they encountered some German artillery, which was part of the larger column behind the *Guard Dragoons*; some hostile fire was taken, but the hussars dismounted and engaged the enemy guns with rifle fire, losing a number of led horses in the exchange.[117]

Seeking to put further pressure on the enemy, Wormald ordered C Squadron of the lancers to remount with a view to moving forwards to a fire position closer to the German line. The ground was reconnoitred by the adjutant, Captain Bryant, who returned with the news that the shape of the slope on the far side of the valley made it possible to get within 50 yards of the Germans while remaining out of sight, and that a bolder mounted attack might be possible. Covered by the fire of the whole of J Battery, which had by now come into action, and with the Germans distracted by the fire of A and B Squadrons from the flank, C Squadron advanced at the walk, in line of troop columns, across the valley and nearly up to the German position. At the last moment both the 'Gallop' and the 'Charge' were sounded by the trumpeters and the squadron formed line and fell on the surprised enemy, led (perhaps somewhat unnecessarily) by Wormald and the regimental HQ party. The colonel was wounded almost immediately, as was Mowlam, his trumpet major, while one of his orderlies was killed and the other unhorsed. Only the adjutant, Bryant, survived unscathed, accounting for five of the enemy with his sword. Some 20 yards behind the HQ group the lances of C Squadron wrought havoc among the dismounted Germans, many of whom attempted at the last minute to surrender; only four were captured unwounded, while another seventy or more were either killed or wounded as the squadron rallied and charged back through the position twice more. The loss to the lancers was only four killed (including the commander of C Squadron, Captain Mitchell), with the colonel and five others wounded.[118]

J Battery had meanwhile raised its fire on to woods in the rear of the German position, and largely by accident caught the supporting *jäger* battalion of the German cavalry brigade, inflicting further losses. No further resistance was offered by the German cavalry, who fell back on their main body and broke contact with the 5th Cavalry Brigade. The lancers were able to reorganise on the captured position without interference, and indeed the German column was judged to have been delayed for most of the day in its pursuit of I Corps to the south-east.[119]

One slightly bizarre feature of this action concerned the part played by the Greys. As C Squadron of the Lancers attacked, the two squadrons of Scots Greys who had not been engaged in the dismounted action charged in support of the Lancers, but by the time they arrived the battle was essentially over and no enemy remained for them to fight. This bloodless charge was seized on by the press, and the *Illustrated London News* printed a Richard Caton-Woodville painting of the event, complete with kilted infantry soldiers of the Black Watch hanging from the stirrups of the cavalry. This recalled an almost certainly apocryphal story of the Scots Greys' charge at Waterloo, where infantrymen were said to have accompanied the charge in this fashion. It almost certainly didn't happen in 1815 and it definitely didn't in 1914, as no British infantry were to be found within several miles of the battle. However, the myth stuck and a bronze figure group depicting the same fictional event remains in the collection of the National Army Museum in London.[120]

As was noted earlier, the action at Cerizy was probably not of major strategic importance, although it certainly blunted the advance of the German columns from St Quentin, and allowed Haig's I Corps to continue its retreat unmolested until it was ready to turn at bay in early September and stabilise the front. For the student of cavalry fighting, on the other hand, the action is of some significance. Here was a classic case of fire and manoeuvre, of the combination of firepower and shock action, vindicating the pre-war drills and training of the British cavalry. General Gough, who will play a large part later in this story, wrote of this action after the war, 'On my right, General Chetwode brought off what has always seemed to me a model action, illustrating the combination of fire and shock, use of ground, and surprise.'[121] Likewise, anticipating those who despised mounted action, Colonel Howard-Vyse, whose account of the battle appeared in the *Cavalry Journal* in 1921, argued:

> To those who scoff at the value of the *arme blanche* one might address four questions. First, do they consider time to be of importance in war? Secondly, how long do they suppose it would take to carry out a dismounted attack across a steep open valley three-quarters of a mile wide? Thirdly, do they think that such an attack would suffer less than forty casualties? And fourthly, given an enemy whose moral is already shaken, which kind of attack do they conceive will impress him most, three squadrons (250 men) galloping at him, or the same number of squadrons (180 men) walking towards him?[122]

It is certainly hard to disagree.

Cerizy was certainly a much more successful action than Audregnies, bearing out Anglesey's remarks about how, and how not, to conduct cavalry fighting. Nonetheless the fighting at Audregnies did include elements of the doctrine that were demonstrated so well in the later encounter. Part of the brigade, the 18th Hussars, was put in a dismounted position on one flank along with the RHA, to provide fire support to the charge, while the main body was readied for shock action. It is unfortunate that the possibility of shock action seems to have so over-excited De Lisle or his subordinates that the action developed its own momentum and two regiments were 'carried away' in the moment.

What cannot be denied is that the units concerned had no lack of aggression and were ready to take on whatever task was given to them, however risky it might appear. Their German counterparts by contrast do not seem to have acted with the same vigour. At Cerizy the Germans were also tactically unimaginative and paid a heavy price for it. Howard-Vyse also raised the question of 'moral' (morale). The consequence of Cerizy, along with a number of other actions in a similar vein, was to leave the British cavalry with a distinct confidence and moral ascendancy over their enemy. When pre-war training was put into practice, it proved effective and successful. Vyse concluded his article,

> Moreover, it is suggested that the moral value of this small success was out of all proportion to its material results. Of its effect outside the brigade mention has already been made, and those who served in the 5th Cavalry Brigade will, the writer feels sure, agree that Cerizy [Moy] created a spirit in the brigade which lasted until the end of the war.[123]

Archibald Wavell, who was with the BEF headquarters in 1914, commented in his biography of Allenby on the apparent disparity between the cavalry of the two nations:

> The record of the Cavalry Division during the great retreat from Mons may not sound brilliant. The fact remains that the British flank and rear were protected from a greatly superior force of hostile horsemen, who were roughly handled whenever they came within reach.[124]

Corporal Lawrence of the 12th Lancers put things more simply when he remarked that the regiment 'felt very "Chin-up" with ourselves'.[125]

* * *

September and October 1914 saw a significant expansion of the cavalry force of the BEF. Both regular and yeomanry regiments arrived, allowing the formation of three cavalry divisions, slightly reduced in size to three brigades, or nine regiments, each. In turn, a Cavalry Corps headquarters was established under the command of Allenby, now promoted to lieutenant general.[126] In addition to these wholly British units, in November the Indian Cavalry Corps of two divisions started to arrive via Marseilles. The Indian cavalry will play a significant part in this narrative right up until January 1918, so it is appropriate to examine their characteristics relative to their wholly British counterparts.

On the outbreak of war in August 1914 the 'Army in India' numbered some 236,000 men.[127] Of these, roughly two-thirds were Indian army troops, and one-third British army units based in India. The primary functions of this force were the protection of India's frontiers, particularly the north-west, and the maintenance of civil order within India itself. However, the provision of an expeditionary force to serve outside India had already been anticipated, and the mobilisation of this force began immediately in August 1914. The Indian Expeditionary Force A, intended for France, initially consisted of two infantry divisions and an attached cavalry brigade. (Smaller Expeditionary Forces B, C and D were also assembled for East Africa, Egypt and Mesopotamia.) At the same time the expansion of Force A to include an additional two divisions of cavalry was also taken in hand, orders being received by the relevant regiments on 31 August.[128] These two cavalry divisions reached France in November 1914, the 1st Indian Cavalry Division arriving on 7 November and the 2nd Indian Cavalry Division arriving on the 14th. The Indian Cavalry Corps was formed from the two divisions under the command of Major General Rimington, a man with a high reputation for his command of cavalry in the Boer War, but a poor choice to command Indian units owing to his low opinion of colonial troops.[129]

Each division consisted of three brigades, each of three regiments. In accordance with standard practice, each brigade had two Indian army regiments and one British army regiment. Artillery for each brigade was provided by British RHA units, and much of the logistic tail of each division was assembled on arrival in France as the units had sailed quite 'light' and had to receive significant allocations of equipment and personnel on arrival. The consequence of this was that each division, and the corps as a whole, was formed only of between a half and two-thirds of ethnic Indian personnel. Three of the nine regiments in each division were British, as were the artillery and support units, and the Indian regiments themselves were partially led by British officers (around a dozen per regiment). This ethnic balance was further altered by the addition of a Canadian brigade in 1916, as will be discussed later.

Each regiment had a combat strength of around 400 men. These were divided among four squadrons (lettered A to D), each of three troops. This organisation differed from UK-based cavalry regiments which had three squadrons each of four troops, but the four-squadron system allowed for the ethnic and religious mix within India to be more easily accommodated. For example, the two Indian regiments most closely involved in the Somme fighting in 1916 were the 20th Deccan Horse and the 34th Poona Horse. The former had one squadron of Sikhs, one of Jats and two of Deccani Muslims, while the latter had two squadrons of Rathore Rajputs, one of Kaimkhanis and one of Punjabi Muslims.[130] The potential for religious and ethnic diversity was reduced, however, by a strong recruiting bias towards the north and northwest of India. The great majority of soldiers recruited by the Raj originated from the Punjab and frontier districts, it being received wisdom among the British that these were the 'martial races' of the sub-continent, unlike their urbanised southern compatriots.[131]

The first task of the Indian Cavalry Corps after it completed its assembly in December 1914 was to support the Indian Infantry Corps on foot in the Bethune area near the Franco–Belgian border. This proved to be its lot for the remainder of 1914 and much of 1915. Units were broken down into working parties to carry out construction tasks, or were rotated through the trenches to give respite to infantry units. The only favourable aspect of this period was the impression Indian soldiers made on their hosts when billeted on French farmers, who developed a strong rapport with their guests.[132] 'Les Hindous', as the Indian soldiers were universally known, were often preferred to troops of other nations by the local populace, including in some cases their own.[133]

After Loos in September 1915 the Indian infantry component of the BEF, the Indian Army Corps, was withdrawn from France. It had taken massive losses in the fighting of the past year and was proving difficult to sustain and reinforce at so long a distance from India. The Indian units within the corps alone had suffered 21,000 casualties.[134] Shortage of shipping was acute and Lord Curzon, Chair of the Shipping Control Committee, argued for the removal of the Indian cavalry divisions as well, at least as far as Egypt. Douglas Haig, however, who had taken over from Sir John French in December 1915 as commander in chief of the BEF, argued strongly for the retention of as many cavalry as possible in France. In the event he lost only the Meerut Cavalry Brigade from the 2nd Indian Cavalry Division, which was sent back to India and subsequently to Mesopotamia; this was replaced by the Canadian Cavalry Brigade.[135] This British, Indian and Canadian division was to become one of the busiest and most successful cavalry formations within the BEF, as will be seen in later chapters.

* * *

The British and Indian Cavalry Corps were engaged in significant fighting both in the winter of 1914/15 and in the first half of the following year. They played a major part in resisting the German thrusts that became known as the First and Second Battles of Ypres. However, this fighting was almost entirely of a defensive nature and took place on foot in trenches. The cavalry were able to demonstrate that they were a match for their colleagues in the infantry in shooting and fighting, but at a heavy cost in casualties.[136] Horses were used to provide mobility for reserves which could be rushed to whichever part of the British line was threatened, but no opportunity for mounted action as such arose. This practice became known as 'fire brigade' work, and the 7th Cavalry Brigade, nicknamed 'Kavanagh's Fire Brigade', developed a particular reputation for it, under the command of Brigadier General George Kavanagh, who would rise to command the reformed Cavalry Corps in 1916.[137] Kavanagh seems to have been a popular and successful brigade commander. Unfortunately, as will be examined in more detail later, these skills did not necessarily translate to the command of the corps as a whole in the later part of the war.

The first opportunity for the cavalry to look forward to genuine mounted offensive action was in the attack around Loos planned for September 1915. Although this offensive did not lead to significant cavalry combat, except again on foot, it is worthy of brief consideration as it offers an insight into General Haig's thinking about cavalry in offensive planning at a point when he was still an army commander and had yet to step up the rôle of commander in chief. Here he was to spell out some of the ideas on the function of cavalry, and indeed some of the contradictions in his thinking, which were to remain with him for the remainder of the war.

The Loos operation was mounted at the behest of the French (in support of a larger offensive planned on two sections of the front further south), and many of the British higher commanders were sceptical of its chances of success. The resources of the BEF in terms of men and materiel were inadequate, and the chosen battlefield unsuitable, but Allied cooperative strategy made it necessary and an attack plan was produced which tried to make the best of a bad situation.[138] (Similar situations were to occur on the Somme and at Arras in later years: such was the price of coalition warfare.)

The plan for the attack called for the British First Army under General Haig to attack with two corps (a total of six divisions in the first attack) on a front of about 7km (4.5 miles) between Lens in the south and the canal at La Bassée in the north. Once the initial German defences had been pierced, the First Army, supported by a division of cavalry, would push on to the crossings of the Haute Deule Canal some 8km (5 miles) from the start line.[139] Although the attack did not reach its intended objectives, and was widely considered to have been disappointing in its results, the plan drawn up for the involvement of the cavalry is worthy of examination in detail.

What is notable about the rôle of the cavalry at Loos is that it was multi-layered. Mounted troops were intended to participate in the battle at a number of levels of command, from local divisional control to directly under GHQ. Each of the six attacking divisions already had an attached divisional cavalry squadron. This was a rôle taken by yeomanry regiments, as the squadrons of regular cavalry serving as divisional cavalry had been withdrawn into the Cavalry Corps in April 1915.[140] Normally, during an offensive, the greater part of each of these squadrons would be busy with a variety of jobs, for example serving as messengers, traffic controllers and escorts to commanders and prisoners, so few of them would be available to act as a unified fighting force. Haig ordered that one squadron of yeomanry in each of the lead divisions (1st and 9th Divisions) should be retained intact in order to provide a mobile element for each of the leading divisional commanders; these were to work in concert with an attached battery of motor machine-guns and the cyclist companies of the infantry divisions, and 'be sent forward as circumstances permit'.[141] Rawlinson, at that time a lieutenant general commanding IV Corps in Haig's First Army, requested a more senior cavalry officer to command each of these forces than would otherwise have been present, pointing out that a yeomanry squadron commander (a captain) would lack sufficient experience. Haig supported this idea, which strongly suggests both men saw this force acting substantially on its own initiative once the battle had started.[142] This devolution of cavalry forces to front-line infantry divisions is one of the more significant aspects of the planning for Loos. As will be shown in later chapters, Haig was to argue for a similar use of mounted troops on numerous subsequent occasions. Once he had advanced beyond army command to become commander in chief, however, few of his subordinates seem to have seen fit to apply the idea in practice.

Thus cavalry was available at divisional level at the head of the attack. No cavalry was controlled by Rawlinson directly at corps level, the next tier of cavalry command being First Army. Two brigades of the 3rd Cavalry Division (6th and 8th Brigades) were placed under (Haig's) First Army Headquarters, with the task of supporting and exploiting the First Army attack between Loos and La Bassée.[143] They were to form up before the attack at the Bois des Dames, west of Béthune and about 14km (9 miles) from the attack front, and were given the objective of Carvin, the same distance again beyond the front and across the Haute Deule Canal.[144] The remainder of the Cavalry Corps (two divisions) and the two divisions of the Indian Cavalry Corps were retained at the highest level of command, under GHQ control, with the rather grandiose idea that they would be used either to exploit the gains of First Army, or to work in concert with the French cavalry to exploit their allies' gains possibly as far south as Vimy. To support these sweeping cavalry moves the bus companies of First and Second Armies were concentrated under GHQ control, providing motor transport for up to a brigade of infantry.[145] This latter idea is notable as it prefigured developments that were to become more widespread in 1918. Haig was to advocate infantry in buses to support the Cavalry Corps in September of that year (discussed in a later chapter) but such ideas seem to have been neglected in the intervening years, possibly due to their lack of success on this earlier occasion.

It is possible that the then commander in chief, Sir John French, retained direct control of the bulk of the Cavalry Corps because he lacked confidence in Haig's ability to judge when best to use it. Haig seems to have thought so, remarking in his diary on 22 September, 'He seemed afraid that I might push the cavalry forward too soon.'[146] It was perhaps understandable for French as a cavalryman to wish to retain control over his own arm. If so, he was not alone in these attachments. Haig himself was to be equally guilty of keeping cavalry 'under his hand' when he became commander in chief. This tendency for commanders at corps, army and even GHQ level to hold on to the power to determine the advance of the cavalry was first seen at Loos, but it was to be a feature of nearly all subsequent offensives by the BEF right up to 1918. It was to be a significant brake on the success of the cavalry on each occasion.

Among the rank and file of the cavalry there was much optimism about the attack. Colonel Preston, who at the time was a machine-gun officer serving with the Essex Yeomanry, recorded in his diary: 'Everyone was very optimistic about the "Push"; our Brigade Major (Bethell) told us "it was all worked out from A to Z".'[147] Unfortunately, as was to be so often the case in the future, although the 3rd Cavalry Division closed up behind the attack front, no significant breach in the German defences was achieved on the first day of the attack (25 September) and the cavalry could get no further forward. The 6th and 8th Cavalry Brigades were to see a good deal of action over the following days (26–28 September) as lack of reserves in First Army forced Haig to commit them as infantry to the defence of the captured village of Loos, a job the brigades performed with some distinction,[148] although it was not a particularly appropriate use for specialist cavalry soldiers. This too set a pattern that was to be repeated in later offensives, particularly at Cambrai in 1917, when the 1st Cavalry Division was to suffer significant losses on foot in Bourlon Wood.

Inevitably the two Cavalry Corps under GHQ control made no contribution to the battle; they were too far away, and at the wrong end of too long a chain of command to serve any useful purpose. Loos set the tone for much of what was to follow. An over-optimistic vision of what the infantry battle would achieve led to the conception of a rôle for the cavalry which it could never fulfill. Secondly, control of the cavalry's movements was placed in the hands of GHQ and Army headquarters, which were inadequately informed about the progress on the ongoing battle and thus were unable to respond to events. Finally the cavalry were thrown into battle as an emergency stop-gap in a dismounted, defensive rôle, which they were quite capable of carrying out efficiently, but which was a waste of their wider specialist talents. As will be shown in the following chapters, each of these mistakes was to be repeated, in varying combinations, throughout 1916 and 1917.

After what can be argued was a quite successful year in 1914, both mounted and dismounted, 1915 must have been a disappointing time for the cavalry.

Forces were assembled in anticipation of a breakthrough of German defences during the offensives at Neuve Chapelle in April and Loos in September, but no call was made on their services. In short, as Anglesey put it,

> During the whole of 1915 the cavalry was virtually never employed in action other than as infantry or pioneers ... In the course of the year's three large-scale allied offensives of Neuve Chapelle, Festubert and Loos, it had to look on impotently for nothing approaching an exploitable breakthrough was ever achieved.[149]

Traditionally the history of British cavalry on the Western Front has terminated at this point. It is widely thought that the cavalry spent the rest of the war as inactive as they had been in 1915. As we shall see, this is very far from the truth, as 1916 was to bring both technical and organisational change, and a surprising amount of combat. Techniques and attitudes developed in those early days of 1914 were to continue to be successfully applied in the years that followed.

Chapter 2

The Somme Battles,
July–September 1916

It's like staying somewhere for Ascot and not going to the races.

Lieutenant Lascelles, Bedfordshire Yeomanry,
4 July 1916[1]

Mounted troops played little or no part in much of the Somme fighting, and none in the famous first day. However, examination of the plans made for them and the part in the fighting envisaged for them by Haig and by the army commanders, in particular Rawlinson at Fourth Army, reveals a good deal about the command and control problems which were to blight, and largely negate, any chance of operational success by the cavalry in the campaign.

By contrast, the two occasions when mounted troops were able to enter battle in 1916 show a force which was not only well prepared for the battle it was to fight, but also surprisingly capable, able to move around the battlefield with a degree of flexibility, without taking catastrophic casualties, and able to inflict both physical losses and psychological damage on the enemy. Cavalry units also took on the German machine guns with their own firepower, and won the duel for fire superiority. In spite of this, the 14 July battle in particular has been used by many historians as a shorthand for the vulnerability and ineffectiveness of the cavalry. This argument is frequently supported in the literature by accounts of events that characterise them as late into battle and quickly killed. It will become apparent in the course of this chapter that this was not the case.

* * *

On 3 March 1916, following – and possibly reflecting – the lack of mounted action by the cavalry at Loos, both the British and the Indian Cavalry Corps were broken up and the divisions attached to the headquarters of the individual armies.[2] Stephen Badsey has interpreted this as a change in Haig's conception of the rôle of the cavalry, moving towards more devolved forces exploiting local advantages rather than a decisive, multi-division cavalry breakthrough.[3] It should also be seen, however, in the context of the political pressure Haig was under to reduce his cavalry force in France, and it may have been a way of making cosmetic changes without losing actual fighting power. Notable in the orders for the abolition of the two corps is the retention of a skeleton corps headquarters staff, available to allow the rapid recreation of a new corps if required (as indeed happened in September 1916).[4]

On 1 April 1916 Haig also appointed General Gough as Temporary Inspector General of Training of Cavalry Divisions.[5] Haig urged Gough to be vigorous in instilling his combined-arms ideas through the ranks of the cavalry, recording in his diary, 'Above all he is to spread the "doctrine", and get cavalry officers to believe in the power of their arm when acting in co-operation with guns and infantry.'[6] Any officers deemed insufficiently flexible were removed.[7] The question arises as to what exactly Haig meant by this 'co-operation' with other arms. There is no doubt that he believed in the tactical combination of dismounted firepower from rifles and machine guns, and support from artillery in the cavalry battle. Chapter 10 of *Cavalry Training*, 'General Principles of Cavalry Tactics', makes this point explicitly.[8] This manual was drafted at least in part by Haig himself. However, it is implicit in *Cavalry Training* that these dismounted elements are subordinate parts of what is essentially a separate *cavalry* battle. There is little in the pre-war manual to suggest that Haig and the cavalry considered the possibility of fighting as subordinate players in an *infantry* battle. Thus the combined-arms ideas of the commander in chief should always be viewed in the context of his conception of a mounted breakthrough, which was the keynote of his thinking throughout the war. As Loos had demonstrated, however, this thinking was always combined with (or possibly clouded by) an idea of integrating the cavalry into the battle at an early stage. Haig would never satisfactorily address this dichotomy.

An interesting by-product of this proposal was that in placing all the cavalry divisions back under a single (cavalry) commander, a corps was formed almost by default, and this would have implications for Rawlinson's plan for the coming offensive. Gough himself referred to 'the whole Cavalry Corps'[9] when describing his rôle during this period. Clearly, while advocating localised, combined-arms fighting, Haig had still not entirely lost his vision of large-scale cavalry operations, as the subsequent creation of the 'Reserve Army' under Gough was to indicate.

Meanwhile, undismayed by the disappointments of Loos, preparations were made at lower levels within the cavalry divisions through the spring and summer of 1916, in the form of reorganisation, new equipment and training, for a renewed offensive that was expected in the course of the year. Many of the new techniques prepared for the 1 July 1916 attack were successfully applied on a small scale on 14 July and later in September. These battles served to vindicate in practice many of the ideas developed during this training period, and show that contrary to popular belief the cavalry arm was, at a regimental level at least, far from unprepared for the conditions of warfare it was to meet on the Western Front, and able to fight effectively. A variety of organisational changes had already taken place by March 1916, and others were to follow during the period leading up to the Somme offensive. This reorganisation took place within all five cavalry divisions (mirroring in some cases similar changes in the infantry), but will be examined with reference to one division in particular, the 2nd Indian Division, as this formation was later to play a key rôle in the fighting on 14 July.

Preparations in the division began in the spring of 1916, taking the form of a variety of equipment and organisational changes. The first of these changes took place in February. This was the withdrawal of the regimental machine-gun sections and the establishment of centralised brigade machine-gun squadrons. These squadrons were formed into the separate Machine Gun Corps (Cavalry) or MGC(C). This mirrored an equivalent process taking place in the infantry brigades to form the MGC companies. Initially these squadrons consisted simply of the guns, horses and men detached from the regiments, but over time their establishments were made up by drafts, and horses as well as other equipment could be returned to the parent regiments.[10] These squadrons had a final establishment of six sections, each consisting of two Vickers machine guns, carried on packhorses, and commanded by a lieutenant. In addition Hotchkiss machine guns were issued to the regiments themselves along the same lines as the issue of Lewis guns in the infantry. This was a gradual process but by the time of the 1 July attack the 2nd Indian Division had been brought up to strength with sixteen Hotchkiss guns per regiment.[11] The machine guns in the brigade MG squadrons, combined with the Hotchkiss guns integral to the regiments, represented a marked increase in the firepower available to the cavalry, both defensively and offensively, since the guns were all pack-mounted, and were as mobile as the regiments themselves. The guns also served to counter the lack of firepower available to cavalry regiments due to the relatively small number of men available to form a dismounted firing line. One MGC(C) section was to play a notable rôle in the battle on 14 July, and the integral Hotchkiss machine guns of the 19th Lancers were to prove valuable in September.

The second important change took place towards the end of June when the 9th Light Armoured Car Battery was attached to the 2nd Indian Division with its six Rolls-Royce armoured cars.[12] Again this represented a boost to the firepower available to the division, and this asset was devolved down to brigade level as the cars were divided in pairs between the individual brigades. Unfortunately the armoured cars struggled to deal with the mud, and even on roads were unable to live up to their full potential. In spite of this, however, the addition of the 'Lambs' (as they became known) to the cavalry can be seen as representative of the forward-thinking, combined-arms culture evolving within the cavalry arm, which Haig was at pains to develop. Much has been made of the supposed mis-match between cavalry and armour by supporters of the latter. This will be examined in more detail later, particularly in connection with tanks, but it should not be forgotten that cavalry–armour cooperation had its roots in working with armoured cars long before the first tank made its appearance. Further, when these changes are considered alongside the other existing assets within each cavalry brigade, including a battery of horse artillery and integral mounted signal and engineer troops, it can be seen that these formations were becoming increasingly mobile and potent units.

In addition to the organisational changes, Gough instituted a vigorous training programme, which was implemented both in divisional level manoeuvres and at regimental level. The various war diaries of the 2nd Indian Division record this process: on 9 May a divisional 'Scheme' was undertaken including 'Practice in passing through Trench system and concentrating beyond'. On subsequent days exercises included the optimistic 'Action against a beaten enemy', as well as 'Tactical exercise against an enemy in position', and 'Practice in crossing trenches by blowing up with explosive and by filling in with picks and shovels'.[13] The Secunderabad Brigade diary for May also records 'Training in mounted and dismounted work, bomb throwing, trench warfare, Hotchkiss gun, bayonet fighting and physical training continued throughout the month'.[14] One feature of this training that shows the new seriousness with which it was undertaken was that for the first time troops on exercise were allowed to ride through standing crops.[15] It is perhaps more surprising that such constraints on training had earlier been enforced, even after nearly two years of war.

At divisional level, exercises in 'liaison with RFC' were also carried out on 2 and 3 June.[16] The rôle that aircraft could fulfil in keeping forward troops in contact with headquarters and in the directing of supporting artillery was quickly recognised, and training with lamps and wireless was undertaken. Officers from the cavalry were detached to the RFC and *vice versa*.[17] The usefulness of this training (as well as some of its limitations) would be demonstrated in the course of the 14 July battle.

A further change to the organisation and training of the 2nd Indian Cavalry Division was the addition of the Canadians. The Canadian Cavalry Brigade was briefly attached to the division in March, then reverted to direct command from GHQ before being permanently allocated to the 2nd Indian Division in June (after the removal from the division of the Meerut Brigade).[18] The Canadian cavalry had been formed into a mounted brigade in the UK in 1915, but were initially sent to France on foot to reinforce the depleted Canadian infantry after losses suffered during the German attack at Ypres in April of that year.[19] Only in January 1916 was the brigade reconstituted as a mounted unit.[20] Prior to their permanent attachment to the division, the Canadian Brigade had been a part of Gough's training regime and they took to one aspect of their training with particular vigour. This was the question of trench crossing. On 27 May 'Experiments were made in the various methods of crossing trenches with cavalry and guns, by bridging and filling in.'[21] This led on 31 May to the testing of two specially designed portable bridges, an 'RCHA Bridge' weighing 550lbs (250kg), designed for use by guns or wagons, and a 'Fort Garry Bridge', weighing 202lbs (90kg), devised for horses in single file. Tests were carried out and times recorded; the artillery bridge could be assembled and in position in just under three-and-a-half minutes, while the Fort Garry Bridge could be thrown across a trench in less than 45 seconds. Both bridges were formally demonstrated before Haig at Helfaut on 3 June.[22] His response is not recorded but it is likely to have been favourable as the Fort Garry Horse was subsequently adapted as a specialist bridging unit and its squadrons dispersed among the individual brigades of the 2nd Indian Division.

Besides training, specific preparations for the upcoming offensive were also carried out. It was necessary for the cavalry to have a properly reconnoitred and prepared line of advance in the event of an attack. To this end the 2nd Indian Cavalry Division spent the latter part of June preparing and marking two tracks from their assembly areas around Meaulte, north-eastwards around either side of Bécourt Château woods, and on up to the British front line in Sausage Valley.[23] This task was not made any easier by the fact that they were specifically proscribed from using any roads usable by wheeled traffic, but had to cut a new track across country. On the day of the offensive these tracks were to be extended across the British and German trenches to just beyond Pozières. The Secunderabad Brigade, forming the advanced guard of the division, was to be specifically responsible for establishing and manning four trench crossing-points suitable for both cavalry and guns in Sausage Valley. In this they were to be assisted by detachments of Canadians equipped with their mobile bridges, to 'make and indicate' trench crossings and to handle any prisoners.[24]

It is clear from this wealth of training and logistical preparations that the cavalry divisions were far from idle in the period leading up to the Somme battles. Inevitably the limitations of their preparations became apparent when battle was joined, but many of these faults were only readily apparent in hindsight. At a regimental level the cavalry should be seen as at least as well prepared for the Somme battles as its infantry counterparts, and in some respects more sanguine and realistic about forthcoming events. Unlike many of the New Army divisions, for which the Somme would be their first taste of offensive fighting, many of the cavalry had been 'out since '14' and had significant combat experience. It should be remembered that many cavalrymen were not only training behind the lines but also spent periods dismounted in the front line, and such service would have provided a good understanding of the realities of the war. Corporal of Horse Lloyd of the Life Guards summed up the prevailing attitude:

Every man of us had taken some part in trench warfare as infantry, and in many sectors no–man's–land was as familiar to us as our own billets. We considered ourselves more than a match for Fritz, and had proved it in the past. But we realized he was a fine soldier, brave and tenacious, especially in defence, who would not give way without 'having a go'.... Thus we smiled at the optimistic blitherings of our superiors and moved up to the undertaking without any particular feelings of either elation or misgiving.[25]

*   *   *

As things turned out, cavalry played no part in the fighting on the first day of the Somme offensive. Writers on the battle have not generally examined the rôle of these mounted forces, or their lack of one, in any more detail than this. The cavalry tend only to appear in narratives of the Somme battles waiting hopefully behind the lines, their presence serving as a metaphor for the wider failures and 'loss of innocence' which the offensive has come to represent. For example, John Keegan observed 'Haig had three cavalry divisions brought up to the Somme front, but they were neither expected to, nor did they, play any part on July 1st or any other day in 1916.'[26] This simplistic view, however, ignores the fact that cavalry forces did become involved in the fighting as the campaign progressed, and that, although they did not play a major part in the final outcome, they were not entirely idle.

Where more detailed accounts of the campaign do refer to the activities of the cavalry, this coverage has also tended to be highly critical of the arm, and of those who defined its rôle. As has been discussed earlier, these criticisms start at the top, with the implication that the senior commanders' inclusion of cavalry in their plans was characteristic of their wider lack of understanding of the nature of the battle being fought. At a lower level, the part in the fighting played by mounted troops is offered as evidence both of their inherent obsolescence and unsuitability for the war being fought and, perhaps more surprisingly, of their own lack of appreciation of this.

The rôle of the cavalry in the Somme fighting, as envisaged by Haig, the commander in chief, and by General Rawlinson, as commander of Fourth Army, is illustrated on the four principal occasions on which they were incorporated in the plans of attack: the initial 1 July offensive, the fighting at High Wood on 14 July, and the battles of Flers-Courcelette on 15 September and Morval on 25–26 September. In only two of these four battles did cavalry become involved in the fighting, in brigade strength at High Wood on 14 July, and in squadron strength at Gueudecourt on 26 September. Neither action was decisive in the outcome of the offensive, and the Gueudecourt action formed only a minute fraction of the fighting on that day.

By looking at these two episodes it is possible to evaluate the effectiveness of mounted troops in action, and to compare this with the aspirations of their commanders, and the criticism which has been made of the arm, both by contemporaries and by later historians. The overall strategic plan for each attack, as well as the detailed planning within the cavalry formations, reveals the faltering progress of the senior commanders in understanding how to use mounted troops in the prevailing conditions. The differences in attitude between Haig and Rawlinson towards the function of cavalry also become apparent. Haig was remarkably consistent in his views of what the cavalry should do, clinging on, right up until November 1918, to a vision of a large-scale breakthrough and pursuit. Rawlinson, by contrast, was initially sceptical of the value of cavalry, but learned later to incorporate them into his operations. In 1916, however, his views had yet to soften towards the mounted arm, and his plans for them reflected that early scepticism.

* * *

The planning for the 1 July offensive on the Somme has been characterised as a conflict between the conservative 'Bite and Hold' tactics of Rawlinson as Fourth Army commander, and the more ambitious 'Breakthrough' objectives of Haig as commander in chief.[27] The difference between the two commanders' thinking with regard to mounted forces illustrates this, with Rawlinson, an infantryman, making no provision in his plan for cavalry, and Haig, the cavalryman, eagerly awaiting 'the "G" in Gap'.[28] With the benefit of hindsight, some historians have tended to favour Rawlinson's less ambitious plan, seeing in it a more realistic appraisal of the likely outcome of events, as opposed to Haig's over-optimism. Liddell Hart commented 'The very belief in such far-reaching possibilities suggests a failure to diagnose the actual conditions.'[29] Others by contrast have castigated Rawlinson for his timidity and for opportunities missed, especially on the southern flank of the attack, where a rapid follow-up of the successes of Congreve's XIII Corps might have reaped significant rewards.[30]

In fact the difference between the two views is more subtle. Rawlinson was prepared to permit the cavalry exploitation that Haig urged, but saw it essentially as a second, separate, phase of battle from the breaking into and through the German main positions, which was primarily a matter for infantry and artillery. Only when a clear hole had been made in the enemy line would the cavalry advance (and Rawlinson frankly did not expect such a gap to be easily or quickly produced). This view was, paradoxically, in line with much pre-war thinking within the cavalry, in which the arm had seen itself, assisted by integral machine guns and accompanied by horse artillery, as an increasingly mobile force, independent of the support of other arms.[31]

Haig, even before the war, had advocated this independent rôle for the cavalry, exploiting the success of a separate infantry battle. At the same time he was keen to see mounted forces involved in each offensive at an early stage. This had been reflected the year before in the plan for the Loos offensive. His own thinking was thus irreconcilably split, and his proposals for the Somme offensive were shot through with recommendations that the cavalry be brought into the fighting at as early a stage as possible. Unfortunately his thinking about this combined-arms doctrine was obscured by his optimism about the outcome of the offensive as a whole. His advocacy of the early commitment of cavalry to the battle was increasingly overtaken by visions of a substantial breakthrough of the German position and exploitation beyond the trench lines into open country. It was difficult for Rawlinson to devise a strategy that reconciled both of these ideas, and in the end he opted for a plan that relegated the cavalry to the more traditional independent exploitation rôle, at the expense of combined-arms fighting.

This difference of view can be followed through the sequence of plans for the attack produced by Rawlinson and Fourth Army, and Haig's comments on those plans. Rawlinson took command of the newly formed Fourth Army in March 1916. On 26 March he was formally requested by Robertson (as Chief of the General Staff) to produce a plan of attack on his army frontage for a force of approximately fifteen divisions, supported by one cavalry division.[32] This was no great surprise as discussions of such an offensive had been in train since the New Year, and Fourth Army had been formed with this attack in mind.

Rawlinson and Major General Montgomery, his chief of staff, produced their first formal plan for the Somme attack for Haig's consideration on 3 April 1916.[33] This envisaged an attack on a front of some 20,000 yards (18km) with a penetration of the German line to a depth of between 2,000 and 5,000 yards (1.8–4.5km). This was quite a conservative plan but reflected concerns about the range up to which infantry could be supported by artillery, and the man-power and guns available.

Haig was disappointed by what he saw as the lack of ambition in this plan. He recorded in his diary of 5 April:

> I studied Sir H. Rawlinson's proposals for attack. His intention is merely to take the Enemy's first and second system of trenches and 'kill Germans'. He looks upon the gaining of 3 or 4 kilometres more or less of ground [as] immaterial. I think we can do better than this by aiming at getting as large a combined force of French and British across the Somme and fighting the enemy in the open![34]

In particular, to Haig's disappointment, the 5,000-yard maximum advance proposed by Rawlinson took in the whole of the German first line of defence, but only about two-thirds of the second, and offered no prospect of outright penetration of the enemy position. Indeed Rawlinson's plan explicitly stated that 'I do not therefore propose to include the Second Line south of Pozières in the objectives allotted to corps'.[35] Haig criticised Rawlinson's strictly limited objectives, commenting: 'It is therefore usually wiser to act boldly in order to secure, at the outset, points of tactical value it may be possible to reach, rather than to determine beforehand to stop short of what may prove to be possible, in order to avoid risks.'[36]

Nor had any rôle been defined for cavalry, beyond a general position in reserve behind the attack. At this stage, however, Rawlinson had at his disposal only the single division of cavalry allocated to Fourth Army when the Cavalry Corps was dissolved at the beginning of March.[37] No additional cavalry had been specially earmarked for the attack, although reserve divisions were available under the command of Haig at GHQ. Rawlinson might therefore be forgiven for failing to consider a single cavalry division (with a rifle strength equivalent only to an infantry brigade), among a force of fifteen infantry divisions, as the decisive force at his disposal.

In spite of this, Haig demanded a larger rôle for mounted troops in the plan: 'Opportunities to use cavalry, supported by guns, machine guns etc, and infantry, should be sought for, both during the early stages of the attack and subsequently.'[38] Two parts of this remark are significant. The first is that the cavalry were not expected to act alone, but in concert with all arms, and the second that their involvement should not await the eventual hoped-for breakthrough, but should take place 'during the early stages'. This reflected the combined-arms part of Haig's view of the rôle of the cavalry. In his eyes the cavalry was not only to serve in exploiting the breakthrough but also in making it, and the subsequent mission he provided for them beyond the German lines was also intended to be carried out in conjunction with supporting arms.

Rawlinson in contrast still envisioned an infantry and artillery battle, followed, if successful, by a cavalry phase. He responded to Haig's remarks on 19 April with revisions to his plan of attack:

> As regards the employment of cavalry, it appears to me that the best use we can make of them is immediately after the attack on the line Grandcourt–Pozières has been successful, and that they may be of the greatest assistance in enabling us to reach the further objectives, if we succeed in inflicting upon the enemy a serious state of demoralisation.[39]

The final part of this remark is revealing. In Rawlinson's mind the cavalry were only to be used to pursue a beaten and fleeing enemy. He continued to see the cavalry battle as a separate phase following on from a successful infantry and artillery attack, and furthermore was sceptical of such an opportune moment arising. A manuscript note alongside this paragraph in Haig's own hand argues for an earlier and more integrated involvement of the horse: 'This seems to indicate the use of "the Cavalry" as <u>one</u> unit, this is not my view of its involvement <u>during</u> the fight. Certain corps commanders ought to have some cav. regts at their disposal.'[40] Here Haig can be seen advocating a multi-layered cavalry battle similar to that proposed at Loos the year before, with some units operating locally in concert with the infantry to create the break, and others subsequently exploiting it.

The two men met again on 6 May.[41] Haig once again pressed his case for a deeper attack into at least the German second line, and for the first time outlined specific geographical objectives for the cavalry, proposing a thrust as far as Bapaume, followed by a turning movement to the north towards Arras. At the same time, however, Haig still expected these ambitious objectives to be reached by a single division of cavalry: 'One division of cavalry (the 2nd Indian Cavalry Division) will be at your disposal during the operations.'[42]

Significantly, much of the debate over the nature of the offensive was conducted at this stage in rather abstract terms. Haig in particular may be criticised for advocating the use of cavalry without ever defining what exactly they should do, or indeed whether they should fight at an early stage or be retained for exploitation (reflecting his own divided thinking). This problem had its roots in the wider flaw within the whole offensive, which was the lack of any serious strategic objective behind the relevant portion of the front. The attack was to be made north of the Somme in order to oblige the French to the south, but otherwise had no particular goal in sight.

Rawlinson does not seem to have been unduly troubled by this as his objectives had always been limited to the destruction of the German positions immediately in front of him, rather than a more sweeping strategic mission. In his formal *Fourth Army Operation Order* of 14 June the objectives were defined simply as 'breaking up the enemy's defensive system' and 'defeating his forces within reach'.[43] The detailed plans that followed outlined a relatively modest 'Bite and Hold' mission. Indeed Rawlinson stressed the need to consolidate on early objectives and not get carried away by ideas of deep penetration:

> the success of the operations as a whole largely depends on the consolidation of the definite objectives which have been allotted to each corps. Beyond these objectives no serious advance is to be made until preparations have been completed for entering on the next phase of the operations.[44]

Haig's response to these plans seems to reflect a view of the battle that was sharply different from that of Rawlinson, but at the same time did not acknowledge this difference. On 16 June he suggested that 'The enemy's resistance may break down, in which case our advance will be pressed eastwards far enough to enable our cavalry to push through into the open country beyond the enemy's prepared lines of defence.'[45] In addition, in a note of 21 June he went on to propose not only 'pushing the cavalry through to seize Bapaume and establish itself in good positions in that neighbourhood'[46] but subsequently 'When the cavalry has reached Bapaume it should be relieved there by the supporting troops so that it may be set free for co-operation in a further move northward.'[47]

To Haig's credit, he no longer expected a breakout on this scale to be achieved by a single division of cavalry; in addition to the 2nd Indian Division, the 1st and 3rd (British) Cavalry Divisions were placed at the disposal of Fourth Army under the command of General Gough.[48] Significantly, the troops allotted to Gough, ultimately to become the 'Reserve Army', also included three divisions of infantry from II Corps, which Haig no doubt intended would fulfil a combined-arms rôle in support of the cavalry breakout. (In an interesting aside, Stephen Badsey notes that it was at this time that one of these infantry divisions, the 25th, adopted the horseshoe as its divisional sign.[49] The dissolution of the two Cavalry Corps headquarters (British and Indian) earlier in the year has already been discussed. In the creation of a separate layer of command for the three cavalry divisions used in the opening Somme attack (in this case in the form of Reserve Army Headquarters), the reconstitution of the Cavalry Corps was prefigured. It may be argued from this that the specific exploitation rôle allocated to Gough's force would colour the conception of the rôle of the later Cavalry Corps, both by those within it and by those under whose command it was placed. This will be examined in more detail in a later chapter.

Rawlinson never supported this addition to the chain of command, and he later succeeded in detaching II Corps from Gough's control.[50] Even without the loss of the infantry, Gough was set a stiff task with the resources available to him. He later observed: 'When the very comprehensive task which was set me in these orders is considered, in conjunction with the fact that I had only three cavalry and two infantry divisions with which to carry it out, I certainly think that I should have required early reinforcements!'[51]

Nonetheless it is difficult to see how even with three divisions of cavalry available these strategic opportunities would arise out of Rawlinson's limited offensive plans. Also, in spite of setting these grandiose goals for the cavalry, as late as 16 June Haig was continuing to define the objectives of the offensive as a whole in only the loosest terms. He described the objective simply as 'relieving the pressure on the French at Verdun and inflicting loss on the enemy'.[52]

Rawlinson was extremely sceptical of the ever-more ambitious cavalry objectives. At a command conference on 22 June he observed:

> An opportunity may occur to push the cavalry through ... and in this connection I will read you the orders I have received on the subject from the Commander-in-Chief this morning. But before I read them I had better make it quite clear that it may not be possible to break the enemy's line and push the cavalry through at the first rush ... A situation may supervene later ... for pushing the cavalry through, but until we can see what is the course of the battle, it is impossible to predict at what moment we shall be able to undertake this, and the decision will rest in my hands to say when it can be carried out.[53]

Rawlinson acknowledged the possibility of Haig's wider vision coming to fruition in a memorandum entitled 'With regard to action to be taken if the Enemy's resistance breaks down' issued on 28 June.[54] In this, however, he reiterated the point that any immediate exploitation of gaps in the German resistance was to be the job of the infantry. Indeed the cavalry were obliged to 'Remain in their places of assembly until these [infantry] divisions have moved forward and cleared their line of advance.'[55] Thus the rôle of the cavalry in Rawlinson's eyes remained confined to a secondary phase of the battle, after the initial infantry combat had been fought and won.

The other major question debated by Rawlinson and Haig was the precise line of advance along which any cavalry operation would proceed. This was not a matter that could be decided once the offensive had begun. Not only would it be necessary to bridge the enemy trenches once the attack was under way, but also routes had to be prepared and marked on the British side of the line to allow the cavalry to move up through the mass of men and materiel behind the attack. Any moves would also have to take place over ground already disturbed by German shelling. These factors significantly constrained the location and direction of any proposed cavalry breakthrough.

Haig had initially envisioned an attack northwards from the right (south) end of the Fourth Army front through Montauban, taking advantage of the eastward turn of the German line north of the Somme to roll up their position from south to north.[56] Unfortunately two factors mitigated against this. The first was the presence of French troops north of the river, with the boundary between the national armies passing through Maricourt. This made the area south of Mametz and Montauban very crowded and the insertion of cavalry forces from their forming-up areas in the west into this area across the line of advance of the reserves already there would have been extremely difficult. Secondly, the German second line position in this southern sector of the front was set back from the first line, and did not fall within Rawlinson's immediate objectives for the infantry attack. The axis of any cavalry exploitation had therefore to be at a point that could be reached sufficiently easily by the cavalry without interfering with other troops, and where the infantry attack was expected to penetrate sufficiently far into the German position for a breakthrough to be possible.

The potentially rather unimaginative answer to this was to define the cavalry axis of advance straight through the middle of the offensive front, along the Albert to Bapaume road. The 2nd Indian Division was given the initial objective of Bapaume, with a line of advance south of the road, while the 1st Cavalry Division was given the objective of Achiet-le-Grand, 5km (3 miles) north-west of Bapaume, with a line of advance north of the road. The 3rd Cavalry Division was to remain in reserve east of Albert.[57] It was also made clear, not only in the Fourth Army operation orders[58] but also in divisional orders that the assault was to be primarily an infantry affair right up as far as Courcelette and Martinpuich. Only when a substantial hole had been punched in the German lines and the infantry reserves of III and X Corps had been pushed through would the cavalry advance begin.[59]

What becomes apparent from this is that the cavalry divisions, although described as a 'reserve' force, were committed to battle before the offensive started. While Rawlinson retained the decision over *when* they were to move off, their objectives and line of advance were pre-determined, and to attempt to change these 'on the hoof' during the course of the battle would have been a recipe for chaos. Unlike commanders of previous eras, who were able to retain a large force of reserve cavalry and, as Napoleon demonstrated at Eylau in 1807,[60] launch it both at a time and on a part of the battlefield of their choosing, Rawlinson had to decide in advance where he thought this critical point would be. One flaw in his plan was that having reached this conclusion over the axis of potential cavalry breakthrough, he did not focus the strength of his initial infantry attack in this area in order to facilitate it. Instead he retained an even, broad-front attack all along the line. This made a critical collapse of part of the German defences not only less likely, but also less predictable in terms of where the line might break. This lack of offensive focus is another sign that Rawlinson did not really believe that such a collapse of enemy resistance would actually occur, and that his plan anticipated only limited 'Bite and Hold' gains over a wide front. Rawlinson's conservative attitude to the likely outcome of the attack was probably born of his experiences as a corps commander in 1915. He had seen the limited gains achieved in the attacks of that year, and indeed as early as March 1915 had himself coined the term 'Bite and Hold' in response to the results of the battle of Neuve Chapelle.[61]

It is arguable that Rawlinson could have partially overcome this problem by dividing his cavalry force. As he was distributing guns and infantry along the 20 miles of his attacking front, he could have been distributing cavalry, either as complete divisions or in brigade strength, to his infantry commanders at corps level. This would have had the effect of multiplying his chances for success, albeit in each case on a smaller scale. It would also have fulfilled the 'small print' of Haig's ideas for the use of cavalry 'supported by guns, machine guns etc., and infantry ... during the early stages of the attack',[62] even if it was at the cost of the great turning movement through Bapaume which was the commander in chief's wider objective.

In the event, under Rawlinson's 'Bite and Hold' plan other assets such as infantry and artillery were distributed more or less evenly along the front, and given relatively modest operational objectives. Meanwhile his plan for the cavalry was a response to Haig's vision of a strategic breakthrough, albeit filtered through his own traditional ideas of the rôle of cavalry. He collected all the cavalry together as an old-style 'Mass of Decision' at a single point behind the front. Haig's appointment of Gough and the assembling of the Reserve Army allowed the three cavalry divisions on the Somme front to coalesce informally into a corps-like cavalry formation. Rawlinson's plan, placing all three divisions together on one axis of attack, did nothing to prevent or dilute this effect. As a result the offensive for which the cavalry was prepared was quite different in character from the offensive which the infantry and guns actually carried out.

*   *   *

The consequences of Rawlinson's plan for 1 July 1916 are well known, but the specific part played (or rather not played) by the cavalry is nonetheless worthy of consideration in some detail. On the morning of 1 July the three cavalry divisions left their billets at 3.30am and were in place in their positions of assembly behind the III and X Corps front by 5.30am. Rawlinson had originally intended to keep the cavalry very much 'under his hand', holding them in a position near his own Fourth Army headquarters at Querrieu. This would have left them more than 20km (12 miles) from the infantry start line at Zero hour. This was altered after Haig's intervention on 21 June and the 1st Cavalry and 2nd Indian Divisions were advanced during the night of the 30/31 to positions around Bresle and Buire-sur-Ancre.[63] This left them some 9km (5 miles) behind the start line. As soon as the offensive began, at 7.30am, patrols were sent to Bécourt and to Sausage Valley to monitor the progress of the infantry attack.[64] Sadly this progress was negligible, and by 8.30am it was clear that this part of the offensive had failed. Orders were received from General Gough (at Fourth Army HQ) at 11.30am that no move would be made before 2.30pm. Meanwhile Rawlinson, the Fourth Army commander, had decided by midday that there was no chance for the cavalry, recording in his diary at 12.15pm, 'There is of course no hope of getting the cavalry through today.'[65] At 3.00pm the cavalry were stood down, and by 6.00pm had withdrawn to billets further to the west. In short, when the particular portion of the offensive which was intended to open the door to a cavalry advance failed, all three cavalry divisions were left with no other option but to return, frustrated, to their billets.

Meanwhile, opportunities for mounted exploitation on other parts of the front withered for lack of cavalry support. A collapse of enemy resistance did occur opposite XIII Corps in the south (ironically where Haig had initially proposed), but since this was not anticipated in the plan, nothing could be done to exploit it. Martin Middlebrook suggests that 'Two or three cavalry regiments boldly handled could have achieved results out of all proportion to their numbers'[66] if they had been available to exploit XIII Corps' success. While theoretically this was true, it neglects the fact that once the cavalry had been committed to another part of the battle, little could be done to divert them. It has been suggested that 'reserves included 2nd Indian Cavalry Division, saddled-up three miles behind XIII Corps jumping-off point'.[67] In fact the bulk of the cavalry remained around Buire and Bresle, some 14km (or 9 miles) from Montauban as the crow flies, but this suggestion also ignores the fact that this distance was measured diagonally across the British front line in the midst of a major attack. Whether 3 miles or 20, such a move was not practical for the cavalry except along previously prepared and reconnoitred lines of advance, and those lines of advance had been prepared towards another part of the battle. Corporal of Horse Lloyd again summed up the mood of expectation (albeit not shared by all ranks) and disappointment in the cavalry in the course of 1 July:

> Our worthy Troop Officer called our Troop together on the evening of 30 June 1916, and proceeded to deliver to us an inspiring speech. He began: 'Boys, it's the eve of Waterloo!' Jock Morrison exploded and covered his mouth with his hand like a schoolboy. I'm afraid we were an unappreciative audience.
>
> The bombardment of 1 July saw us saddled up and standing to at dawn. There followed several hours on our toes. In the evening we were still waiting for something to turn up when our Troop officer came along, called us together and proceeded to form a bombing section from the troop. . . . This threw some light on the prospects of the 'Gap' and served to show how matters really stood.[68]

Once again, as at Loos ten months before, the initial infantry and artillery assault had failed to create a breach in the German defences for the cavalry to exploit, or at least not on a part of the line where cavalry were available. This failure was so complete that any critique of the cavalry's plans and preparations is rendered somewhat irrelevant. No alterations in the command arrangements or planning within the cavalry could have changed the outcome of the infantry battle, and without that, the mounted arm was powerless. However, the cavalry did not have long to wait before a successful infantry attack would present a potential opportunity for them to show their worth.

* * *

Despite the disappointments of 1 July the cavalry remained hopeful of a rôle in the fighting. The 2nd Indian Division remained at 4 hours' notice to move until 7 July.[69] However, no advance was ordered. It was not until Rawlinson mounted his next large-scale set-piece attack that a rôle for mounted troops would once again be proposed. On this next occasion the cavalry would come to grips with the enemy at High Wood during what has become known as the 'Battle of Bazentin Ridge' on 14 July. The small part played by the cavalry in this battle was probably no more significant in terms of the overall outcome of the Somme campaign than their part in the 1 July attack, but this action sheds light on the usefulness or otherwise of the arm, and on the appropriateness of their preparations. In particular the movements of the cavalry forces involved demonstrates their battlefield mobility, which was a key part of their overall effectiveness, and over which they have suffered significant and undeserved vilification.

The course of events on that day is salutary in demonstrating how the actions of the cavalry have been misrepresented in many subsequent accounts of the battle. As early as 1938 the Official History painted an erroneous picture of the cavalry stuck in the mud, unable to arrive at the scene of the action until the evening.[70] This image has been accepted uncritically by most of those subsequently dealing with the battle.[71]

On the basis of this supposed immobility, many historians have gone on to criticise the senior commanders for having unrealistic expectations of what the cavalry could achieve. Others have gone even further and suggested that Rawlinson's inclusion of any cavalry in his plans was a grave error. Prior and Wilson argue that:

> These orders [for the cavalry] do no credit to Rawlinson's command. . . . The result could only be a slaughter of the mounted force. Rawlinson's orders therefore only make any sense if he was expecting the enemy to flee. And if that was his expectation then the boundaries of cloud cuckoo-land should be moved down a stage from their usual location around GHQ.[72]

Harsh words indeed, but as will be shown, this was not an observation borne out by the facts of the battle.

In the aftermath of 1 July Haig and Rawlinson seem to have continued to hold divergent views on the nature of the battle. The infantry attacks along the proposed cavalry line of advance, those of X and III Corps, had failed completely. Rawlinson was keen to renew these failed attacks from the British centre and left, possibly in order to try to wipe away the embarrassment of complete failure on this part of the front. Haig, on the other hand, was keen to exploit the success on the right, in particular Congreve's XIII Corps gains around Montauban. In due course Rawlinson accepted this latter line of attack (although Haig was to have a much harder job selling the idea to the French, on whose immediate flank the attack would take place).[73]

Curiously a form of rôle reversal seems to have followed Rawlinson's acceptance of a renewed attack on the British right. His plan for this offensive was both tactically inventive and incorporated his chief's vision of a significant cavalry rôle in the early stages.[74] It also made provision for a complete break-through of the German position. Indeed, as Rawlinson wrote in his diary, 'if we are wholly successful, it will have far reaching results – especially if I can get the cavalry through and catch the guns and break up their commands'.[75] This was a far cry from his pessimistic forecasts of the prospects for mounted troops before 1 July. Possibly Rawlinson was starting to succumb to the constant pressure for a larger rôle for the cavalry placed upon him over the past months by the commander in chief. Equally, he may have recognised that in an attack on the German second and third lines of defence, even a shallow 'bite' might fully penetrate the formal defensive system. Haig meanwhile seems to have become increasingly conservative. In particular he was sceptical of the ability of his relatively untrained troops to carry out the complex form-up by night in no man's land envisaged in Rawlinson's new scheme of attack, and saw altogether too much risk in the plan as a whole.[76] He was also worried that the cavalry might be committed too early, before the time was quite right, arguing, some-what uncharacteristically, that 'The divisions were not to go forward until we had got through the enemy's fortifications, except a few squadrons to take High Wood.'[77] (His earlier remarks about Sir John French before Loos come to mind in this context.) True to form, however, Haig did eventually let his subordinate have his way and the attack proposed by Rawlinson and his corps commanders went ahead. Interestingly, Liddell Hart suggested that 'For once, Horne, who was usually as apt to agree with Haig's views as he was dependable in other ways, agreed instead with his immediate superior [Rawlinson], and this fact may have helped tilt the scales.'[78] (The influence of Lieutenant General Horne, commander of XV Corps, not only on the planning but also on the outcome of the battle will be examined in more detail later.)

In brief, the overall plan for the attack on 14 July comprised an attack northwards from Montauban (captured on 1 July) into and through the German second line position on the Ginchy–Pozières ridge.[79] The main attacking front was to be approximately 3,500 yards (3.2km) wide, with its flanks defined by Mametz Wood to the east and Trones and Delville Woods to the west. The initial objective was the German second line itself, followed by the villages of

Bazentin-le-Petit to the west, Bazentin-le-Grand in the centre and Longueval in the east. These three villages lay immediately behind the German line. If the attack was successful up to this point, cavalry would be pushed through with the immediate objective of High Wood, in order to make a lodgement in the as yet only partially constructed German third (or 'Switch') line. Potential further exploitation by additional divisions of cavalry was also postulated.

The initial infantry attack would be conducted by four divisions, from right to left, the 9th and 3rd Divisions of XIII Corps, and the 7th and 21st Divisions of XV Corps. An additional supporting attack would be made by III Corps on the left beyond Mametz Wood. The initial assault would be made at first light of dawn, 3.25am, from forming-up positions out in no man's land, as close to the German positions as possible. To reinforce the element of surprise this would be preceded by only five minutes of 'hurricane' bombardment (although a less intensive wire-cutting bombardment had already been taking place for several days).[80]

The cavalry force to take part in the attack was the same as for 1 July: the 2nd Indian Division and the 1st and 3rd Cavalry Divisions. The 2nd Indian Division was to start immediately to the south of Albert, in the vicinity of Meaulte, 9km (5 miles) from Montauban, but by Zero hour (i.e. 3.25am on the 14th) would have one brigade immediately behind the infantry attack to the south of Montauban. One regiment of this brigade was to support each of XIII and XV Corps in their attacks on their second objectives, the villages behind the line, and the third regiment was to be ready to seize High Wood by *coup de main* as soon as an opportunity arose. The other two divisions were assembled further away, the 1st Division at Buire, 14km (9 miles) from Montauban, and the 3rd Division at La Neuville, 22km (13 miles) from Montauban.[81]

Further clarification of the cavalry orders was issued by Fourth Army on 12 July: 'In the event of our attack on the enemy's second line being successful',[82] the three cavalry divisions would advance sequentially through the German second line, the 2nd Indian leading and the 1st and 3rd following. The 1st Division would form a flank guard towards Leuze Wood to the south-east, and the 3rd Division would play a similar role towards Martinpuich to the north-west, while the 2nd Indian Division pushed on towards Flers and Le Sars. Significantly these advances would take place under the control of XIII and XV Corps rather than Fourth Army, and thus not only would cavalry units be immediately available behind the infantry attack, but the local corps commanders would have control of them. This devolution of control of the cavalry from army to corps level was a vital first step in improving their effectiveness but, as will be shown, it still did not provide the flexibility required to allow local commanders to fully exploit their tactical potential.

Subsequently it appears that Rawlinson became uncomfortable with the placing of his entire cavalry force beyond his own immediate control, and a further memorandum was issued on 13 July. In this he reclaimed the 1st and 3rd Divisions under his own hand:

> The Army Commander does not consider that the entire responsi-bility for launching the 1st and 3rd Cavalry Divisions should rest on the Commanders of the XIII and XV Corps. He has decided therefore that although the actual orders for the advance of these two divisions will be issued by the XIII and XV Corps, the final decision as to whether the suitable time has come for launching them will rest in his hands.[83]

Events would prove that the immediate effect of this change was to write the two British cavalry divisions out of the battle entirely, as a 'suitable time' never presented itself to Fourth Army. In the case of the 2nd Indian Division, however, Rawlinson used the memorandum to reiterate their vital rôle:

> He [Rawlinson] places the greatest importance on the seizure of High Wood and the enemy's new line to the east and west of it, as a stepping stone to a further advance.
>
> The GOC XIII Corps will therefore issue orders for the 2nd Indian Cavalry Division to advance, on his own responsibility, when he considers the situation permits of it.[84]

Thus Congreve, commanding XIII Corps, would not only have at least one regiment of cavalry under his hand from the outset of the battle, he would in due course also acquire control over the whole Indian cavalry division. The possibility of a true combined-arms attack thus presented itself. The plan has been criticised because the cavalry division was under XIII Corps control while their objective, High Wood, was in the XV Corps area,[85] but this objection neglects the fact that the cavalry line of advance to reach High Wood crossed the portion of the German second line attacked by XIII Corps. Thus only XIII Corps would be able to judge when such an advance was practical. This confusion of command and objectives was, however, to become a significant factor in the failure of the attack.

Such were the broad outlines of the attack ordered by Fourth Army. How this was to be carried out by the troops involved is revealed in the orders issued lower down the chain of command at corps, division and brigade level. As always on the Western Front, the primary difficulty was communications. Rawlinson and Fourth Army HQ were 25km (15 miles) behind the front at Querrieu. General Congreve, in command of XIII Corps, was based at Chipilly, some 14km (9 miles) from Montauban, while XV Corps HQ was at Heilly, roughly between the two. In turn the headquarters of the three cavalry divisions would start the battle in their points of concentration, but the commanders would soon be on the move with their divisions. In order to overcome this problem the headquarters of the 3rd (Infantry) Division was nominated as an advanced reporting centre. This division, under Major General Haldane, formed the left of XIII Corps' line, and was thus roughly in the centre of the attack. Haldane's main headquarters was initially located about 1km (1,100 yards) north-east of Bray-sur-Somme.[86] Subsequently, an advanced headquarters was established at Billon Farm 1km south of Carnoy.[87] This placed it only about 4km (5,000 yards) behind the start line of the attack. As the attack began, the commander of the cavalry advanced guard, Brigadier General Gregory, and subsequently the commander of 2nd Indian Division, Major General MacAndrew, were both to establish themselves at these headquarters. Cavalry liaison officers were also sent to all the other attacking infantry divisions (with motor cyclists and mounted despatch riders) with orders to report to MacAndrew at 3rd Division headquarters. It was at the advanced headquarters that much of the immediate business of fighting the battle was conducted through *ad-hoc* conferences among the commanders at divisional and brigade level.

The second difficulty faced by the cavalry divisions was their line of advance. As on 1 July, the route to be taken up to the start line of the attack was prepared in advance by the construction of cavalry tracks. These were formally defined in the 2nd Indian Division's operation orders of 12 July:

> Four new routes across country have been marked by flags from the new bivouack towards Carnoy and thence towards Montauban.... It is extremely important that all units should be thoroughly familiar with these tracks. They will be referred to in future orders as A, B, C and D from south to north.[88]

This must have been a substantial undertaking as each track ran for between 10 and 15km across country. Much of the route in the rear areas would have required relatively little repair, but the portions between Carnoy and Montauban would have crossed the former British and German front lines of 1 July, and the devastated area resulting from the British bombardment. The Secunderabad Brigade, at least, must have been 'thoroughly familiar' with the tracks as working parties detailed for their construction are recorded in the brigade War Diary on 7, 9, 10 and 11 July.[89]

Once the start line of the attack had been crossed, similar provision was to be made for the cavalry to advance over the German second-line trenches, and it was the responsibility of the attacking infantry to provide this. The attack orders for Haldane's 3rd Division include:

> The 8th Inf. Brigade will arrange to cut ramps 12 feet wide down to the captured German trenches in two places for the passage of cavalry in such a way as not to block the passageway in the trenches. The wire

opposite these ramps will be cleared away by the infantry and the gaps clearly marked by flags.[90]

In addition, the leading cavalry brigade would once again be accompanied by the Canadians with their portable bridges. Thus comprehensive preparations had been made to get the cavalry into position for their rôle in the attack; all that remained was for the infantry corps commanders to launch them forward into battle.

*   *   *

The battle of Bazentin Ridge began with an infantry attack, on schedule at 3.25am on 14 July. The part played by mounted troops in the battle can be reconstructed from reports contained within the war diaries of the formations concerned. Although at times vague and contradictory, these accounts, taken as a whole, provide a fairly comprehensive narrative of the events of the day. This narrative is somewhat at variance with that typically appearing in published accounts of the battle. During the battle itself there was a good deal of confusion among the other arms concerning the progress of the cavalry. Bodies of horsemen were reported in various locations when in fact these were only patrols, or in some cases no cavalry were present at all. This confusion has been perpetuated in accounts of the action which refer loosely and interchangeably to the 7th Dragoon Guards, the Secunderabad Brigade, the 2nd Indian Division, or even simply 'the cavalry' as if these terms represented a single body of troops. This was not the case. Operational orders split the division into a series of separated bodies,[91] each moving on a different timetable and by different routes; only when the path of each is followed does the situation become clear.

On 13 July two of the three cavalry divisions allocated to the attack were in reserve to the west of Albert, the closer of the two being the 1st Cavalry Division around Buire-sur-Ancre, some 14km (9 miles) from the front line at Montauban. These two divisions were held directly under Rawlinson's hand, under Fourth Army command. As discussed above, Rawlinson never issued orders for these forces to move from their points of concentration. It is sufficient to say therefore that these divisions took no part in the battle and no further reference need be made to them here.

The 2nd Indian Division, by contrast, was to have an exceptionally busy day. At midnight on the night of 13/14 July they were in billets around Meaulte, to the south of Albert and perhaps 5km (3 miles) closer to the front than the other two wholly British divisions. The infantry attack was scheduled to begin at 3.25am, but deployment by the lead infantry brigades into no man's land began several hours before. In keeping with this, the first elements of the 2nd Indian Division were also on the move soon after midnight, so as to be as close to the front line as possible at the moment when they might be needed. It is something

of a misrepresentation to refer to the location of large forces in precise terms –
the *Xth* Division was at map reference *000* – as these formations took up large
amounts of ground. For example, a cavalry division moving in road column
(half sections) is estimated to have formed a column up to 12 miles (19km)
long.[92] It is possible, however, to break down the 2nd Indian Division into
some of its component parts and follow these parts individually, recording the
locations of the head of each column at various times. The division was divided
up as follows:[93]

- The 2nd Indian Division headquarters party, including Major
  General MacAndrew (GOC 2nd Ind. Div.)

- Secunderabad Brigade headquarters party, including Brigadier
  General Gregory (GOC Sec. Brig.)

- The 'Vanguard' formed from elements of Secunderabad Brigade,
  consisting of:

  7th Dragoon Guards
  1 squadron Fort Garry Horse (with trench bridges)
  2 sections brigade machine gun squadron (with four Vickers guns)

- The 'Advanced Guard', formed of the remainder of Secunderabad
  Brigade, consisting of

  20th Deccan Horse
  34th Poona Horse
  four sections brigade machine gun squadron (with eight Vickers
    guns)
  N Battery RHA (with six 13pdr guns)
  1 Field Troop RE
  2 Rolls-Royce armoured cars from 9th LAC Battery
  1 Squadron Fort Garry Horse (with portable trench bridges)

- The remainder of the 2nd Indian Cavalry Division, consisting of
  Ambala Cavalry Brigade
  Canadian Cavalry Brigade (less two squadrons)
  Remainder 9th LAC Battery (four cars)

At the risk of providing a tedious amount of detail, it is important to follow each
of these bodies of troops individually, since only then is the real truth about
their mobility revealed. At some time shortly after midnight the Ambala Brigade
and the Canadian Cavalry Brigade moved from billets to their divisional point
of concentration at Morlancourt. This was 4km (2.5 miles) south of Meaulte, and
actually marginally further from the front line. This assembly was complete by
3.30am. Here they were to stay until around 8.00am.[94]

Also at around midnight the two HQ parties set out from Meaulte. MacAndrew arrived at the main HQ 3rd Division, just outside Bray, at 3.30am;[95] Gregory went ahead, arriving at advanced HQ 3rd Division at Billon Farm by about the same time.[96] At about 1.30am the two portions of the Secunderabad Brigade completed their assembly at Meaulte and moved off, the vanguard leading, towards Bray. The advanced guard halted just to the north-west of Bray, near the main HQ 3rd Division, arriving at about 3.45am.[97] The vanguard pushed on, crossing the Albert–Peronne road just south of Carnoy at 5.05am and moving on to a position in a valley immediately to the south of Montauban. Once across the old front lines the 7th Dragoon Guards (part of the vanguard) closed up into column of squadrons, B Squadron leading, and advanced through moderate shelling, four horses being wounded.[98] It is not clear at what time the vanguard reached Montauban, but it is not likely to have been later than about 7.00am. In due course, after resting and watering the horses at Bray, the advanced guard moved off at 6.15am and had arrived at 3rd Division advanced HQ at Billon Farm by 7.15am.[99]

Thus by 7.00am the cavalry advance was proceeding on schedule, with the various portions of the 2nd Indian Division advancing by stages along its prepared routes. The vanguard of the division had crossed the old 1 July front lines without difficulty and was in a position of support behind the infantry attack at Montauban, the remainder of the advanced guard was 4km (2.5 miles) to the rear at Billon Farm, and the balance of the division still at Morlancourt. At this stage the infantry attack was proceeding well on many parts of the front, and for the first time that day a report reached Rawlinson (at around 7.00am) that Longueval, the key objective on the right hand side of the attack, had been captured.[100]

Eager to begin the next phase of the battle, Rawlinson (via XIII Corps) ordered the remainder of the 2nd Indian Division to close up to the front and for the advanced guard to proceed with its attack towards High Wood. These orders were received at 7.40am and the advanced guard moved up from Billon Farm across the old front lines to the position south of Montauban occupied by the vanguard, mostly arriving probably around 8.30am. Meanwhile the other brigades of the division, at Morlancourt, received orders at around 7.45 and were on the move by 8.20, advancing through Bray to positions in the vicinity of Billon Farm.[101] It was at this stage that the division encountered its first difficulties. The two armoured cars attached to the advanced guard, commanded by Second Lieutenants Williams and Pocock, set off from Billon at about 9.00am. Unfortunately the road across the old front lines was bad (a situation no doubt made worse by the recent bad weather and the passage a few minutes before of the hooves of a brigade of cavalry), and the two armoured cars became hopelessly bogged in the mud. It was to be midday before the two cars had been dug free and returned to Billon.[102] Some wheeled transport was, however, able to make the passage as N Battery RHA was able to join the brigade concentrated behind Montauban by 9.30am.[103] At about this time MacAndrew and the 2nd Indian Division HQ group also moved up from Bray to the 3rd Division advanced HQ at Billon Farm, joining Gregory and the Secunderabad Brigade HQ.[104]

The advance of the Indian cavalry was vividly described by one of its members, Shah Mirza of the Deccan Horse, in a letter home written a few days later:

> That morning at 3.30 a very heavy bombardment was made on the enemy's trenches. Every kind of cannon was used and the bombardment lasted for an hour. The terrible noise of that hurricane of shot and shell was such that I am not able to describe it. When the enemy's trenches were sufficiently demolished, the infantry attacked and took them. We were ready waiting close by.
>
> When we learnt that there were not many enemy trenches in the rear, we were ordered to advance. The trenches that were taken had to be filled in places or bridged to enable us to cross. At certain places we were unable to cross at all. After a while another way was found for us to cross but we crossed with difficulty. What I saw in the course of the advance I shall never forget. We had to pass amongst the dead bodies of the men who had fallen during the morning's attack, and the trenches were full of German dead. The ground was torn and rent to pieces by the shell fire and there were holes five and six feet deep.[105]

Sadly, the reports reaching Fourth Army of progress in Longueval did not reflect the real situation, as a see-saw battle was taking place for the possession of the village; the struggle would last all day, with reports of capture or loss coming in every few hours, but usually hopelessly out of date by the time they were read. Also from about 8.00am onwards there occurred one of the fatal breakdowns of communications and confidence that characterised British attacks on the Western Front. At about 8.15am, as the fighting for Longueval continued, the 7th Dragoon Guards sent out two patrols under Lieutenants Malone and Hastings to reconnoitre their route towards High Wood.[106] Unfortunately, the route proposed for the advance was via the trench crossings prepared immediately to the west of Longueval, and on approaching the village the patrols came under machine-gun fire from it, and from machine guns surviving in the German second-line trenches to the west. These patrols returned to the brigade and reported the route impassable, and when this information reached Congreve at XIII Corps, 'it was decided by the Corps Commander not to push on to the allotted objectives until the situation became more favourable'.[107] At this point the XIII Corps attack was effectively halted, halting the cavalry with it, waiting for the complete capture of Longueval.

On the left flank of the attack, on XV Corps' front, however, the situation was rather different. By 9.00am all of the first and second phase objectives had been secured and the ground between Bazentin-le-Grand and High Wood was mostly clear of Germans. Indeed at about 10.00am Brigadier General Potter of 9th Brigade was able to make his famous walk, unmolested, up the hill to High Wood.[108] In the course of the morning several of the infantry divisional commanders proposed attacks into this gap; both Watts, commanding 7th Division (XV Corps), and Haldane, commanding 3rd Division (XIII Corps), offered their reserve brigades, but were told by their respective corps and by Fourth Army that these brigades were required as a reserve in case of counter-attack, and to 'wait for the cavalry'.[109] Ironically, the cavalry were also waiting, behind Montauban, for renewed orders from XIII Corps to advance.

Further cavalry patrols were sent out in the course of the morning to the west around Bazentin-le-Grand and into Bazentin-le-Petit. These patrols, under Lieutenants Adair and Struben (7th Dragoon Guards), witnessed a German counter-attack on the north end of Bazentin-le-Petit at around 11.45am,[110] but must also have been able to determine the viability of an attack along the more westerly line; still no orders were given. Indeed, the presence of mounted men advancing and then withdrawing in the vicinity of the Bazentins was reported to XV Corps as the failure of the cavalry advanced guard attack.[111] Meanwhile the Secunderabad Brigade itself, with elements of the 7th Dragoon Guards out patrolling, occupied its Indian regiments by sending work parties to repair the cavalry tracks across the old front lines.[112]

By noon it seems to have become apparent to Rawlinson at Fourth Army that no cavalry advance had taken place on High Wood. Indeed, no advance of any sort had taken place beyond that of the lone brigadier at around 10.00am. He therefore authorised the infantry attack on High Wood by the 7th Division (XV Corps), originally proposed by its commander Major General Watts earlier that morning. It was now the turn of Lieutenant General Horne, commanding XV Corps, to develop the same concern over Longueval that had constrained Congreve at XIII Corps from ordering the cavalry forward in the morning. Horne delayed the 7th Division's attack on XV Corps' front until such time as Longueval had fallen to XIII Corps.[113] It is difficult to see the justification for this decision. Horne may have felt that with German troops still in positions immediately to the north and west of Bazentin-le-Petit, as well as in Longueval, an attack on High Wood would be exposed to fire from both flanks. On the other hand, the capture of High Wood could equally be seen as a method of outflanking and rendering untenable the position of the German forces in Longueval itself. Either way, Horne's decision once again stalled the attack as a whole, while the 9th Division on the right continued to struggle for Longueval.

At 3.10pm reports reached XV Corps of the capture of Longueval by XIII Corps. Once again these reports were out of date, as the struggle for the village continued.[114] Nonetheless Horne authorised the attack on High Wood by the 7th Division for 5.15pm. Word of this attack reached Gregory, who was with the Secunderabad Brigade behind Montauban, at 4.35pm, via a telephone line laid by the brigade signal squadron from 3rd Division advanced HQ at Billon Farm to the brigade position at Montauban.[115] He returned to Billon Farm, and was briefed by MacAndrew on the attack orders passed down by XIII Corps. The Secunderabad Brigade was to provide flank protection to the 7th Division's attack, with the objective of the German third-line trenches east of High Wood, while the infantry attacked into the wood itself. (The cavalry was not tasked with attacking into the wood, and the significance of this point will become apparent later.) During the briefing orders were received postponing the attack until 6.15pm. Gregory had returned to the brigade by 5.40pm, at which time he received a final version of his orders. Under these, he was to take two regiments, the 7th Dragoon Guards and the 20th Deccan Horse (plus the machine guns and the Canadian bridging squadron), north-west to Sabot Copse, where they would be placed under the command of XV Corps. From that point they would move on their objectives to the east of High Wood. The third regiment, the 34th Poona Horse, would stay at Montauban.[116]

The two regiments left Montauban at 6.00pm, crossing the British front line of that morning in 'Montauban alley' via ramps prepared during the day by the brigade field squadron of the Royal Engineers. The regiments had arrived at Sabot Copse, some 3km (2 miles) away in a straight line, by 6.25pm. Here Gregory attended further briefings with Brigadier General Minshull-Ford, the commander of 91st Brigade, 7th Division, and the whole force moved off at around 7.00pm.[117] The advance was conducted with 91st Brigade on the left, advancing on High Wood. On their right came the 7th Dragoon Guards, in column of squadrons, B Squadron leading. (Column of squadrons was such a common attacking formation in the operations covered by this study that it is described in detail in Appendix 1.) On the right of the dragoons were the Deccan Horse in similar order (with A Squadron leading).[118] N Battery RHA deployed in support on a reverse slope to the south of the German second-line position, with a forward observer in the German reserve trench. However, although the first round was fired by the battery at 8.10pm, failing light restricted observation and only twenty-one rounds were fired in total in support of the cavalry.[119]

As the cavalry advanced across the broad valley behind the German second line they were visible to observers on the ridge behind, and to the Germans in Longueval and Delville Wood, as well as to scattered parties of the enemy in the fields between. The regiments came under machine-gun and rifle fire, but sustained relatively few casualties. The lead squadron of the 7th Dragoon

Guards came abreast of the eastern side of High Wood at about 8.00pm. Here they encountered a larger concentration of Germans sheltering in shell holes within a crop of standing corn. The lead squadron under Lieutenant Pope charged these troops, who immediately fled. Sixteen Germans were ridden down and 'speared' (the leading squadron of all Indian-based regiments being lance armed), while another thirty-two were made prisoner.[120] In order to retain contact with the infantry attack the dragoons then halted and established a defensive line, taking advantage of a bank along the side of the road from the southern corner of High Wood to Longueval. This position came under machine-gun fire from Longueval at about 9.00pm, and the brigade machine guns were pushed out to the right flank to deal with this. The German guns were silenced, but not before one gun horse had been hit. Second Lieutenant Hartley, commanding one of the sections, made an attempt to retrieve the gun but was killed in the process, while the gun itself was found to be damaged beyond repair. Second Lieutenant Anson, who took over command of the party, was also wounded while withdrawing the remainder of the machine-gun squadron.[121]

The Deccan Horse advanced on the right of the dragoons. Meanwhile the true situation in Longueval had become clear as the High Wood attack was being prepared, and new orders were issued to the Deccan Horse at 7.30pm.[122] According to these, the regiment was to maintain contact with the dragoon guards on the left, but their new objective was to support a renewed attack by the 9th Division into Longueval village and Delville Wood. The Deccan Horse were to advance right around the north end of Delville Wood as far as the German third line towards Flers. This manoeuvre was carried out successfully, and ten soldiers of the *16th Bavarian Regt.* were captured. This advance, and its moral effect on the enemy, was described by a participant, Lieutenant Colonel Tennant:

> As each squadron cleared the defile it formed line and advanced at a gallop in the direction taken by the advanced guard, which lay through a broad belt of standing corn, in which small parties of the enemy lay concealed. Individual Germans now commenced popping up on all sides, throwing up their arms and shouting 'Kamerad' and not a few, evidently under the impression that no quarter would be given, flung their arms around the horses' necks and begged for mercy – all of which impeded the advance.[123]

A notable feature of this account is the exaggerated fear that a few mounted men could inspire in the enemy. This was an additional factor in the tactical effectiveness of cavalry which should not be underestimated, and which was to be significant in the fighting of 1918, discussed later.

Enemy fire from Flers and from Delville Wood meant the regiment could not advance further than about 500m short of the German third-line trenches; no sign of the 9th Division's progress into Delville Wood was evident, and to attack it unsupported would have been futile. In due course, as darkness fell at around 9.30pm, the Deccan Horse withdrew and took up a defensive position extending the line already established by the 7th Dragoon Guards along the High Wood–Longueval road.[124]

Earlier in the evening, the 7th Dragoon Guards had come under fire from German troops and machine guns in a sunken road extending from the eastern corner of High Wood. An RFC contact aircraft spotted these troops and indicated their position to the cavalry by firing on them with tracer. The observer was also able to make a sketch of the situation and drop it onto N Battery. The Secunderabad Brigade narrative records that: 'An endeavour was made to communicate with the plane by lamp, to find its identity, but without success.'[125] Further light is shed on this incident by the brigade signal squadron war diary, which includes the complaint that the drills and codes for liaison with RFC contact aircraft had only been taught to the signallers attached to the divisional headquarters, back at Billon Farm. The brigade signallers at Gregory's advanced headquarters in the fields behind the 7th Dragoon Guards thus had no means of communicating intelligently with the aircraft.[126] This episode demonstrates once again the problem of lack of devolution to lower levels of command not only the authority to take command decisions, but also the means of communication in order to do so. The purpose of contact aircraft was surely to provide up-to-date, or even real time, reconnaissance information, but if this information had to travel along a long and unreliable chain of command before it could be acted upon, much of its value would be negated.

In the course of the night the Secunderabad Brigade was relieved, and the position taken over by infantry. The 7th Dragoon Guards and the Deccan Horse began a gradual withdrawal at 3.30am on the 15th, and were able to depart without further loss.[127] Meanwhile the remainder of the division had also been withdrawn. The Ambala Brigade was ordered up to Sabot Copse in the early hours of the 15th to be available to support the renewed infantry attack on High Wood, but as the day wore on the impracticality of any further cavalry action became apparent and the 2nd Indian Division was stood down at 6.15pm on 15 July.[128]

*   *   *

It is instructive to compare the course of events contained in this narrative with the way the battle has been described in published accounts. It rapidly becomes clear that preconceptions about the capabilities and vulnerabilities of cavalry have clouded these accounts from the outset, and the tactical effectiveness of the cavalry has been ignored. Some of these preconceptions have been touched on earlier, but two in particular stand out. The first of these is the lack of mobility of cavalry in the face of trenches and shell-damaged ground. The *Official History* stated that:

> At 7.40am the XIII Corps had ordered forward the 2nd Indian Cavalry Division from its place of assembly around Morlancourt (4 miles south of Albert). The division moved at 8.20am, but its progress across slippery ground cut up by trenches and pitted with shell holes proved very slow: it was well past noon when its advanced guard, the Secunderabad Cavalry Brigade (Brigadier-General C.L. Gregory) with attached troops, arrived in the valley south of Montauban.[129]

It is true that the weather had deteriorated since 1 July, a factor which was to halt the advance of the armoured cars, but there is no evidence that it interfered with the planned timetable of cavalry movement. The above account conflates the movement of the 2nd Indian Cavalry Division main body, which left Morlancourt at 8.20am but only to march as far as Billon Farm, where it was formed up and halted as ordered by about 9.30am, and the Secunderabad Brigade, which had its vanguard (the 7th Dragoon Guards) 'south of Montauban' by 7.00am and was closed up in that location as a complete brigade including supporting artillery, by 9.30am. The *Official History* also observes that 'the brigade did not begin to cross the old British front line until the evening'.[130] Assuming this remark refers to the front line of 14 July, not 1 July, this is strictly true, but it fails to point out that this was after the whole day had been spent waiting behind Montauban. Taken in the context of the previous quoted statement it is easy to infer that this late advance was due to difficulties experienced in the cavalry getting forward. It was not.

Sadly, once errors of this sort reach print, they tend to be replicated. Anglesey falls into this trap, suggesting:

> It was now that the daunting nature of progress by mounted troops across soft and slippery terrain cut up by the elaborate trench system and pitted with innumerable shell-holes made itself painfully clear. It was a long time past midday before the leading squadrons began to show near Montauban.[131]

Similarly, Liddle suggests that 'it took the Deccan Horse four hours to move the six–seven miles [from Bray] to Montauban'.[132] In fact this move was done in two stages: 3.5km (2 miles) from Bray to Billon Farm, achieved in under an hour (6.15am–7.15am), and 4.5km (3 miles) from Billon Farm to Montauban, carried out in 50 minutes (7.40am–8.30am). Unfortunately, this erroneous picture of the cavalry stuck in the mud continues to recur, appearing most recently in Peter Hart's work on the Somme, published in 2005.[133]

It should not be inferred from these movement schedules that the cavalry were free to roam over the battlefield unhindered. All of the above writers were correct to state that shell holes, trenches and particularly wire were serious obstacles to cavalry. What is incorrect is to suggest that somehow the cavalry commanders were surprised by this, and were seriously delayed by it. Liddle also suggests that 'During the morning infantry commanders were waiting for the cavalry to arrive, although nothing had been done to speed up their movement, for example by clearing the road.'[134] On the contrary, the cavalry had spent most of the previous fortnight clearing a road, and on the day of the attack infantry battalions were specifically tasked with continuing this work through the German line. After its arrival at Montauban, the Secunderabad Brigade also spent much of the day dispersed in working parties. The result of this detailed preparation was a relatively smooth and timely advance. The success of this work on trench crossings carried out by the cavalry itself and by the infantry is indicated by the fact that the squadron of the Fort Garry Horse attached to the Secunderabad Brigade specifically to provide trench bridging returned to its billets on 15 July with its portable bridges unused.[135]

Such an advance, however, could only take place along lines predicted and prepared before the battle. The significant difference between the 14 July attack and the failures on 1 July lay in the relative narrowness of the offensive front, which made it easy for the cavalry commanders to predict where the cavalry might be needed, and to construct an access route to that point. On 1 July the construction of a cavalry track to cover every contingency would have been logistically impossible and, as has been shown, the point of breakthrough selected and prepared for by Rawlinson proved to be the wrong one.

The second aspect of the battle which has been frequently misrepresented is the extent to which the cavalry were vulnerable to enemy machine-gun fire, and the casualties they suffered in their advance across the open ground towards High Wood. The casualties suffered by the Secunderabad Brigade were not high. A breakdown of these is included in the brigade war diary.[136] In the 7th Dragoon Guards, Lieutenant Anson was wounded in rescuing the machine-gunners, and two other ranks were killed and twenty wounded. Sixteen horses were killed or missing with a further twenty-three wounded. The 20th Deccan Horse suffered higher losses, mostly probably when bumping up against the German third-line trenches: two Indian officers were wounded, and three other ranks killed and fifty wounded. Eighteen horses were killed or missing and fifty-two wounded. The machine gun squadron lost Lieutenant Hartley killed, ten other ranks wounded and twelve horses killed. N Battery was shelled briefly at around 11.00pm; three shells fell on the wagon lines, killing two men and wounding twelve, and killing twelve horses.[137] Two other men in the brigade were wounded.

Compared with an initial brigade strength of probably in excess of 1,500 men, eight killed and slightly fewer than a hundred wounded might be considered a trifling loss by Western Front standards. The loss in horses was slightly greater, with roughly fifty killed and a hundred wounded. It must be considered, however, that in the absence of horse ambulances, a 'wounded' horse was one that was sufficiently lightly injured to keep up with the regiment on its own feet. Many of these are therefore likely to have recovered and returned to service. Horses wounded more seriously would have been destroyed in the field by regimental farriers, and thus come under the 'killed' totals. This situation is a long way from the outcome for cavalry in the open on the Western Front both as predicted at the time and assumed by subsequent historians. Prior and Wilson's remark that 'the cavalry were soon dealt with by the German machine-gunners'[138] is clearly wide of the mark, to say the least. Indeed, on the basis of the successful suppression of German fire from Longueval by the cavalry machine gun sections, it is tempting to suggest that the reverse was true.

It might be argued that the brigade was not very seriously engaged, and the enemy soldiers charged by the 7th Dragoon Guards seem to have been mostly occupied in surrendering and running away. The two regiments were, however, deployed under fire and in sight of the enemy for at least 2 hours, from around 7.00pm until it got dark at around 9.30. They also occupied a position that was not entrenched, at least initially, and had to rely for cover on folds in the rolling ground and the height of the standing crops.

Yet the idea that cavalry were somehow doomed to fail seems to have become rooted in popular imagination. One eye-witness, Lieutenant Beadle, an artillery observer with the 33rd Division (XV Corps reserve) allegedly observed the cavalry attack on High Wood:

> It was an incredible sight, an unbelievable sight. They galloped up with their lances and with pennants [*sic*] flying, up the slope to High Wood and straight into it. Of course they were falling all the way ... I've never seen anything like it! They simply galloped on through all that and horses and men dropping on the ground, with no hope against machine guns, because the Germans up on the ridge were firing down into the valley where the soldiers were. It was an absolute rout, a magnificent sight. Tragic.[139]

This account appeared originally in Lyn Macdonald's *Somme*, and was subsequently quoted in a number of published sources where it was accorded the weight due to eye-witness testimony.[140] It should be noted, however, that Lieutenant Beadle was listed by Macdonald as a 'Direct contributor' to her work, i.e. an interviewee recalling events around sixty years later, and the 'Valley of death' tone of his account is notable, especially when the number of casualties in the overall operation is considered. With all due respect to a veteran of the battle, it would appear that Lieutenant Beadle was letting his preconceptions and his poetic imagination get in the way of his powers of recollection. A clue to this is the fact that he saw 'pennants flying', when lance pennons had been discontinued for active service since before 1914,[141] and that the horsemen are described as riding *into* the woods, a feat which was not attempted, nor did it form part of their orders or objectives. To be charitable, the squadrons may have been carrying trench crossing marker and signal flags, but the impression is of a recollection coloured by romantic expectations of what a cavalry charge on the Western Front *ought* to have been like, rather than the reality. Other historians have found the romantic idea of senseless cavalry sacrifice equally hard to resist; A.J.P. Taylor, for example, described 'a sight unique on the Western Front: cavalry riding into action through the waving corn with bugles blowing and lances glittering. The glorious vision crumbled into slaughter as the German machine guns opened fire.'[142] Certainly it is a powerful image – but it is not borne out by the facts.

Perhaps the most spectacular of the descriptions of the fighting that day comes from another supposed eye-witness, Lieutenant Colonel G. Seton Hutchison, whose memoirs described the advance of the Deccan Horse:

> I descried a squadron of Indian cavalry, dark faces under glistening helmets, galloping across the valley towards the slope. No troops could have presented a more inspiring sight than these natives of India with lance and sword, tearing in mad cavalcade onto the skyline. A few disappeared over it: they never came back. The remainder became the target of every gun and rifle. Turning the horses heads with shrill cries these masters of horsemanship galloped through a hell of fire, lifting their mounts lightly over yawning shell holes; turning and twisting through the barrage of great shells: the ranks thinned, not a man escaped. Months later the wail of the dying was re-echoed among the Himalayan foothills ... 'weeping for her children and would not be comforted'.[143]

The assertion that 'not a man escaped' is a poor description of an engagement where the regiment in question suffered only three fatal casualties. It also contrasts sharply with the more mundane description of the fight given by one of the participants, Mirza Ahmed Baig, in a letter home: 'Well, our lot went into the attack, and returned from it safely.'[144]

Other contemporary observers were influenced by their own experience of the fighting, and without seeing the cavalry actually in action, were cynical about their prospects. Lance Corporal Crask of the 8th Battalion, Suffolk Regiment, was passed by the cavalry on its way to the front: 'Unfortunately they are of no use and suffer very heavy casualties without getting near the Bosche from the fact that their horses cannot pass over the debris and the barbed wire that is lying about.'[145] It is not difficult to appreciate in what terms infantry soldiers would come to view a force that, in their eyes, had spent most of the war thus far in 'comfort' behind the lines, waiting for a moment which the infantry no longer believed would arrive. It is, however, potentially misleading to place too much emphasis on the clearly rather jaundiced viewpoint of such a primary source. Caught between cynicism within other arms of the BEF itself and the popular demand for tragic heroism, it is easy to see how an exaggerated idea of cavalry casualties could develop and become embedded in subsequent interpretations of their rôle.

This erroneous view of the vulnerability of men on horseback appears to have been quite widely held by those on foot, including infantry officers who might otherwise have chosen to ride. At least one cavalryman, however, considered that this was a misapprehension. The Ambala Brigade, although never committed to action, spent a large part of 14–15 July in the forward area in support of the Secunderabad Brigade, and the 18th Lancers in particular remained in readiness about Sabot Copse throughout 15 July until the division as a whole was stood down that evening. An (anonymous) officer of the 18th Lancers considered that:

> Infantry officers should have made more use of their horses; the experience of the regiment in these days goes to prove that a man on a horse stands a better chance of getting through a hostile barrage than a man on foot. At the same time one feels extraordinarily naked and vulnerable when mounted and heavy shelling is going on, but that is only when standing still![146]

Clearly when shells began to fall the advantages of being able to move rapidly somewhere else were not lost on at least one participant in the battle.

* * *

Nonetheless the question remains whether 14 July represents an opportunity missed by the cavalry. It has been demonstrated that at least part of the cavalry force was available behind Montauban early in the battle on 14 July, and also that when this force was finally released it was able to operate effectively in the battle zone without catastrophic loss. In spite of this there is little doubt that a tactical opportunity for cavalry exploitation was missed that morning, and the arm was operationally unsuccessful. Whether this opportunity had wider implications for the offensive as a whole is more difficult to prove one way or the other, although the early capture of High Wood would undoubtedly have lowered the price paid in casualties for this objective over the weeks that followed. With these points in view it must be asked why the moment was missed, and why the early opportunities were not seized upon.

As so often on the Western Front the answer lies in command and communications, in all arms including the cavalry, and at all levels. At the highest level Rawlinson must bear some responsibility. His decision to retain direct control over two of the three available cavalry divisions excluded them from the battle from the start. The 2nd Indian Division was able to participate in the battle from a relatively early stage, but only because these troops were on the move towards pre-determined objectives several hours before the infantry attack even started. The idea that cavalry could be moved up from rear areas after the battle had begun, in response to front-line events, was clearly unrealistic. As later chapters will show, this continued to be a problem throughout the war. Only cavalry already on the move towards pre-determined objectives prior to 'Zero hour' would ever play a part in the fighting.

At the next level down the corps commanders are also culpable. The decision to place the Indians under the command of XIII Corps was an admirable start, as was the decision to deploy them forward at an early stage. XIII Corps, however, was in no better position to understand the unfolding events on the battlefield than was Fourth Army. There was also a significant breakdown in communications between XIII Corps and XV Corps in the course of the morning. The result was that when the cavalry was held up on the XIII Corps front opposite Longueval, neither they nor Congreve at XIII Corps was aware of the 'Gap' developing on XV Corps' front around the Bazentins. The divisions on XV Corps' front meanwhile dug in awaiting the imminent arrival of the cavalry from XIII Corps. By the time this had been resolved and the cavalry made available to XV Corps at around noon (although the two regiments of the Secunderabad Brigade were not formally assigned to XV Corps until around 6.00pm), the commander of XV Corps, Horne, had become so obsessed with the battle for Longueval, *on XIII Corps' front*, that he did not sanction an attack towards High Wood until nearly 4.00pm, despite Rawlinson's eagerness for the attack to be pressed on from midday onwards. By the time the assault began in the evening not only had the German third line been significantly deepened and reinforced, but the attacking forces simply ran out of daylight.

At divisional and brigade level command seems to have been more effective. The infantry commanders were near enough to the battle to know what was actually going on, and seem to have been prepared to improvise and develop any opportunities that arose. There are also a number of examples of these commanders getting together for *ad-hoc* conferences to develop combined operations between their units. The meetings at Haldane's 3rd Division advanced headquarters and between Gregory and Minshull-Ford at Sabot Copse are examples of this. Unfortunately this initiative seems to have been hamstrung by the necessity to clear all plans through corps and army commanders, whose understanding of the battle was out of date, and whose offensive attitude was deeply cautious. 'Bite and Hold' with the emphasis on 'Hold' seems to have been the watchword at corps and above.

Ironically, two commanders at divisional level stand out from their more flexible peers: Gregory and MacAndrew. Contrary to Haig's demands that cavalry commanders think ever more flexibly, on 14 July these two seem to have become quite narrow-minded and unimaginative, unable literally to think outside the tracks built for them across the battlefield and the terms of their formal operation orders. The move up to Montauban was well executed. At that point orders prescribed a move across the German second line immediately to the west of Longueval. When patrols found these crossings to be impracticable, at around 7.00am, there seems to have been little urgency in exploring an alternative, despite the possibilities available further west near Bazentin-le-Grand Wood. Rather, the Secunderabad Brigade seems to have been content to wait for the infantry to finish its battle, and then call upon them in accordance with the plan. Patrols did not report back from the western side of the field until mid-morning, by which time the German defences, especially around Bazentin-le-Petit, had hardened significantly. Thus the force that was potentially best placed to take advantage of any fleeting chances to regain the momentum of the offensive was the least well led. It has been argued that two years of inactivity had resulted in a tactical stagnation of the cavalry officer corps, and the loss of its best talents to other arms.[147] If so, then 14 July stands as an example of that phenomenon.

In defence of these commanders, the difficulties presented by the available means of communication must be taken into account. Although miles of telephone cable were laid before the attack, this was vulnerable to shelling, and laborious to extend beyond the forward positions as units advanced. Curiously, it was also vulnerable to damage from friendly troops. Almost all cavalry movement orders for the battle include a post-script enjoining troops to watch out for and avoid telephone cables, and where they crossed the line of advance, these had to be specially buried by the parties building cavalry tracks.[148] The telephone system also tended to follow the command hierarchy, with the result that adjacent brigades in the front line might have to pass messages through several higher formations in the rear in order to communicate laterally along the front, not least because corps headquarters wished to retain tactical command over events on the battlefield. The consequences of this in terms of confusion and delay have already been discussed.

As far as the cavalry were concerned, these problems were spelled out by an anonymous, but clearly disgruntled, signals officer of the Secunderabad Brigade signal squadron in their war diary.[149] During the time the various parts of the brigade were on the move in the morning, communication was maintained up and down the various columns, and with Gregory at Billon Farm, by motor-cycle and horse-mounted despatch riders. When the brigade assembled behind

Montauban it was found that, although this location had been determined in advance and lay behind the British front line, no telephone link had been provided for communication by the cavalry between the Secunderabad Brigade itself and its commander, still at Billon Farm. Telephone lines existed between 3rd Division headquarters at Billon and Montauban and beyond, but these all belonged to infantry and artillery formations which were busy with their own signal traffic. The cavalry brigade signallers laid a telephone line to link these two positions, but in so doing used up their entire stock of cable. The consequence of this was that when the brigade moved off to Sabot Copse, and subsequently out towards High Wood, runners and lamps had to be used to communicate with the end of the telephone line at Montauban. This was to become a significant problem when the 7th Dragoon Guards and the Deccan Horse established their positions to the east of High Wood and night fell. Communications after that time rapidly deteriorated as runners and despatch riders got lost in the dark.

Fourth Army also issued orders for the use of wireless communications between XIII and XV Corps headquarters and the cavalry divisions,[150] but there is no evidence that significant use was made of this. The headquarters of the 1st and 3rd Divisions never advanced, and MacAndrew and the 2nd Indian Division headquarters remained with the 3rd (Infantry) Division headquarters, which was in direct touch with XIII Corps by land line. It is arguable that wireless would have been more useful further down the chain of command at brigade level, but the bulk and complexity of the available equipment, and its unreliability, may have made this difficult.

Only one wireless message concerning the movements of the cavalry was broadcast on 14 July, when at around 10.30am an aircraft was used to broadcast the message that 'Enemy second line of defence has been captured on a front of 6,000 yards. British cavalry is now passing through in pursuit of the demoralised enemy.' Sadly this did not reflect the real situation on the ground but was rather a (possibly slightly naïve) attempt at signals deception, intended to confuse and alarm German wireless listening stations.[151] Whether any Germans were actually deceived by it is not recorded.

* * *

After the missed opportunities of 14 July, the Somme fighting degenerated once again into a period of smaller scale attacks, and small areas of ground won at great cost. By mid-August, however, Haig started to feel that this 'wearing-out battle' was reaching a critical stage, in which a final decisive blow might be possible to end the campaign. In his view a renewed offensive in mid-September offered the possibility of finally breaking entirely through the German prepared defences and into open country beyond. It was this offensive initiative that was to form the basis for the battle of Flers-Courcelette on

15 September, and its follow-up the battle of Morval ten days later. These battles, like those of 1 and 14 July, show limited (but promising) tactical effectiveness on the part of the cavalry, negated once again by a failure of higher command and control.

Haig's vision was spelled out in a GHQ memorandum of 19 August, calling for plans of attack to be prepared by Fourth and Reserve Armies, 'with the object of securing the enemy's last line of prepared defences between Morval and Le Sars, with a view to opening the way for the cavalry'.[152] The main thrust of this attack was to be the responsibility of Fourth Army, with Gough's Reserve Army in a supporting rôle on the northern flank. Rawlinson responded with a characteristically conservative plan, involving a series of sequential, limited, 'Bite and Hold' attacks, conducted by night. Haig did not feel that these were decisive enough and spelled out his own more expansive scheme in a further memorandum of 31 August. Once again the attack was to be 'planned as a decisive operation'.[153] In particular, once the main defensive lines had been broken, 'as strong as possible a force of cavalry, supported by other arms, will be passed through'[154] with the aim of making a grand strategic sweep through Bapaume and rolling up the German lines to the north, in the fashion first proposed back in June.

To this end the Cavalry Corps, dissolved back in March, was to be reformed under Lieutenant General Kavanagh, and all five divisions of cavalry available in France were to be included within it. This was intended as a temporary measure, but in fact the corps was to continue in being (albeit at reduced strength after 1917) until the end of the war. This was a larger force of cavalry than was assembled for the 1 July attack, and shows Haig's determination to exploit fully any opportunity that might be created. But while other arms were urged to support the cavalry advance, Haig did not specifically allocate any infantry to the Cavalry Corps as had been attempted in June, when he had initially conceived the Reserve Army. He may have felt that in the light of 14 July his 'combined-arms' vision was starting to be absorbed anyway and did not need to be specifically reiterated; if so, he was to be disappointed.

Rawlinson issued detailed orders for this attack on 11 September.[155] In these he specified that once the infantry had reached the last line of German defences, an advance in four timed bounds over a total of around 4,000m (2.5 miles), cavalry would be pushed through to secure objectives on the high ground beyond the Bapaume–Peronne road. However, he once again entirely separated the cavalry from the initial infantry battle. None of the cavalry divisions was to move until the infantry were firmly established on their final objectives:

> The Cavalry Divisions will not move forward to where they will mask the guns or interfere with the advance of the infantry supports and reserves, until the infantry have secured a sufficiently strong hold of

the villages of Morval, Lesboeufs and Flers to admit of the Cavalry Divisions advancing to their objectives.[156]

Indeed, on 13 September Rawlinson went even further to restrict the freedom of movement of the cavalry. His 'Instruction on the event of a general advance'[157] reiterated the necessity of avoiding clogging the rear areas and masking the guns with advancing cavalry. It insisted not only that the cavalry should wait until the infantry were established on the 'Red Line' final objectives, but also that they should wait until the artillery had been leap-frogged forward into supporting positions behind the new infantry line. Only after that were the rôles reversed and the infantry tasked to support the further advance of the cavalry, 'the rapidity of whose advance at this period of the battle is all important'.[158] It is hard to see how any 'rapidity of advance' would be achieved by forces queuing up behind the advancing artillery. Indeed, it is hard to read in Rawlinson's orders for the cavalry any sense that he saw them as anything other than a bulky inconvenience and even a liability; this tone becomes very clear in the last paragraph of the 'Instructions':

> The Cavalry Corps must ensure that the forward areas now in our hands are not blocked with cavalry prematurely ... The cavalry advance must be continuous, but it must also be very methodical, any attempt to push too much cavalry through at one time will only lead to confusion and consequent delay.[159]

Despite the reservations of the Fourth Army commander, the newly reformed Cavalry Corps began life in buoyant mood. On 1 September Archibald Home, newly appointed as Kavanagh's chief of staff, wrote, 'I wonder if the old Cavalry will come into its own at last. To be with it if it does will be stupendous.'[160] Nonetheless he cannot have been alone in feeling that the corps was under scrutiny by many of its opponents, both in France and in the government at home, and success was potentially vital to their future. As the battle progressed on 15 September his tone was less optimistic: 'It would appear that if the cavalry does not get a chance this time it will be the end of them.'[161] On 10 September Kavanagh himself issued an upbeat assessment of the prospects for the corps. Besides setting out the divisional objectives for the coming attack he urged his subordinates to make the most of the opportunity to show their worth:

> Everything points to the probability of the Cavalry having its long wished for chance of proving its value in the near future, but in order to do so it must be used with the greatest boldness, and all risks must be taken and heavy losses occasionally expected, which will be amply repaid by the great results that will almost certainly be obtained.[162]

He was, however restrained by the strictures of the Fourth Army commander concerning his movements, and a memorandum was attached to the formal operation order issued by Cavalry Corps headquarters on 13 September. This highlighted Kavanagh's concern not to upset other arms: 'The Corps Commander wishes Divisions to be very careful as regards questions of traffic and water. They must remember that they are only guests in the different Corps areas, and a great deal of tact is required to avoid friction.'[163]

The appearance of words like 'guests' and 'tact' are curious in the context of a military operational order. The Cavalry Corps thus began the September battles on the horns of a dilemma. On the one hand they had been given the opportunity finally to participate in the battle in strength and potentially show their true fighting value, but on the other they were not to be permitted even to advance until Rawlinson's infantry and artillery battle had been fought and won. Indeed, their mere appearance in the rear areas prior to the appointed moment would be seriously frowned upon by Fourth Army. It is difficult to see how any meaningful exploitation of successes by infantry could be obtained under these circumstances.

* * *

Zero hour on 15 September, for what was to become known as the battle of Flers, was set for 6.20am.[164] The four phases of infantry attack and the associated artillery barrages were timed to place the infantry on their final objectives by approximately 11.00am (Zero plus 4.30). The lead cavalry divisions were therefore in position ready to advance by 10.00am,[165] although it was not intended that all five divisions should come into action immediately. The 1st Cavalry Division and the 2nd Indian Division were in place between Mametz and Carnoy, some 6km (3.5 miles) behind the infantry start line and around 10km (6 miles) from the 'Red Line' objectives at Gueudecourt. On receiving the order to advance, these divisions were to move on parallel tracks either side of Delville Wood to objectives beyond the Bapaume–Peronne road, to the south-east of Bapaume and around 5km (3 miles) in advance of the infantry objectives. A Cavalry Corps forward reporting centre was located a little to their rear at Billon Farm (familiar to the Indians from 14 July). The remaining divisions were strung out in the rear and would only advance sequentially as each of their predecessors cleared the narrow line of advance. The 2nd Cavalry Division had two brigades at Bray, 5km (3 miles) behind the lead divisions, with orders to move off at around noon; the remainder of this division and the 1st Indian Division were concentrated at Dernancourt to the south-west of Albert. Finally the 3rd Cavalry Division was assembled at Bonnay, 12km (7.5 miles) from Albert and nearly 30km (19 miles) from the infantry objectives at Gueudecourt. It is difficult to see how any decisive exploitation of the infantry's gains could be developed by means of this stately progress of the cavalry from deep behind their own lines, even without taking into account the priority given by Rawlinson to artillery movements ahead of the cavalry advance.

When the infantry attack went in, these difficulties became academic. In spite of the maiden use of 'tanks' and the associated public rejoicing at their modest successes, in the laconic words of the Cavalry Corps war diary, 'the attack did not develop sufficiently for the cavalry to advance'.[166] Flers, Courcelette and Martinpuich all fell, but the strongpoint villages behind the German third line, Morval, Lesboeufs and Gueudecourt, all remained in enemy hands, and 'until these three localities could be occupied there could be no question of a breakthrough'.[167] The weather also deteriorated on the evening of the 15th and hopes for any cavalry advance faded. On 16 September the 1st Cavalry, 3rd Cavalry and 2nd Indian Divisions were stood down and withdrawn from the battle area.[168] Later in the month, although still nominally under Cavalry Corps command, two of these divisions would be posted out of the Fourth Army area, the 1st Cavalry going to Third Army, and the 3rd Cavalry to GHQ reserve.[169] Kavanagh could not have known, but the action on 15 September 1916 was to be the only operation in the whole war where all five cavalry divisions operated within the corps under his direct command. Although they remained within the Cavalry Corps, divisions were to be detached to other armies or fight under direct infantry corps command in later battles, such that he never again had direct control of more than three. Home was therefore probably correct to consider the day something of a high-water mark in the aspirations of the arm.

The diminished Cavalry Corps continued to await its chance. Corps advanced headquarters remained at Billon Farm, and the 2nd Cavalry and 1st Indian Divisions remained in readiness at Dernancourt, in support of XIV and XV Corps respectively. During this period of waiting one significant step was taken, when from 18 September onwards each division was ordered to provide a daily duty squadron in support of its respective infantry corps. These squadrons were held in the vicinity of Carnoy and were directly on call from XIV and XV Corps, although any orders would be repeated to the Cavalry Corps for information.[170] A single squadron was not a large force, but this marked a return to the principle of cavalry formations directly controlled by the attacking infantry commanders, as had been the case on 14 July (or as far back as Loos), and circumvented the lengthy chain of command resulting from the recreation of the Cavalry Corps. It was one of these squadrons that would see action on 26 September.

Rawlinson renewed the offensive on 25 September. By this time, however, the tone was quite different. The infantry objectives remained only those parts of the 15 September objectives not yet obtained, Morval, Lesboeufs and Gueudecourt, an advance of around 1,500 metres (1 mile). 'Bite and Hold' was once again the guiding principle. The influence of this on the Cavalry Corps is apparent from the corps orders issued on 20 September.[171] Of the three divisions available to Kavanagh, only one, the 1st Indian, was given formal orders to participate in the attack. The 2nd Cavalry and 2nd Indian Divisions would remain in their billets at Dernancourt at 2 hours' notice to move. Only two brigades of the 1st Indian Division were moved up behind the attack, the Mhow and Sialkot Brigades taking up positions around Mametz and as far forward as Montauban, around 5km (3 miles) from the infantry start line. Their objectives were stated as Ligny-Thilloy and La Barque, a modest 3km (2 miles) beyond the infantry final objectives. Also, whereas on 15 September corps orders had urged the cavalry on to attack German headquarters and rail termini as far away as Marcoing, 25km (16 miles) beyond the enemy front,[172] the new orders contained the following pessimistic prediction:

> In the event of the Cavalry advance contemplated above being possible, two situations may arise:-
>
> (a) The advanced cavalry troops may successfully seize part or all of the above villages.
> (b) These villages may be strongly held and the Cavalry forced to retire.[173]

Clearly the new-found optimism of early September had been short-lived. There was also an additional factor constraining the ambitions of the cavalry. In order to conform with an attack by the French to the south-east at Combles, Zero hour was set for 12.35pm.[174] This meant that in contrast to the dawn start on 15 September, the infantry were unlikely to be on their final objectives before 3.00pm at the earliest, leaving little of the autumn daylight for the cavalry. Corps orders acknowledged this, stating that if the lead brigades could not pass the final 'Blue line' by 6.30pm at the latest, no large-scale move should be attempted.[175]

The battle of Morval, as it became known, followed a now-familiar pattern. Initial reports were good and the Mhow Brigade, lead brigade of the 1st Indian Division, sent squadrons of the 6th Dragoons (Inniskillings) and 2nd Lancers (Gardner's Horse) as far as the 110th Infantry Brigade headquarters at Flers.[176] However, a situation now developed which was to bear striking similarities to the delays and failures of 14 July. The right of the British attack was a complete success. The 5th, 6th and Guards Divisions of XIV Corps captured the villages of Morval and Lesboeufs on schedule. Word of this success reached the corps commander Lord Cavan in the course of the afternoon, but due to uncertainty concerning the progress of both XV Corps on his left and the French on his right, he chose to take no further action to exploit it, choosing instead simply to consolidate the positions gained.[177] In fairness to Cavan, no cavalry had been allocated to this portion of the attack (apart from the daily corps duty squadron, and his integral corps cavalry regiment). The line of advance prescribed for the 1st Indian Division was through Gueudecourt in XV Corps' area, and this part of the attack was held up. Thus no mounted exploitation of the successes of XIV Corps took place.

Meanwhile XV Corps had made good initial progress into the German third line position in front of Gueudecourt, but parties of Germans remained in the 'Gird' trench line and no advance to the village itself was possible. At 4.00pm the 1st Indian Division 'received definite orders not to advance until the whole village was in our hands'.[178] And by 7.00pm:

> Owing to the fact that the whole of Gueudecourt was not captured, and that a party of Germans still held out in Gird Trench, which was in the direct route of the proposed cavalry advance, it was not possible to get the cavalry through ... and the 1st Indian cavalry division was ordered back to billets near Dernancourt.[179]

This was easier said than done in the dark, on the congested routes behind the attack front, and it was not until past midnight that the division reached Dernancourt.[180] Once again a battle plan that restricted all the cavalry to a single line of advance had prevented flexible exploitation of the day's successes on XIV Corps' front, while the cavalry waited behind the day's failures on that of XV Corps.

The attack was renewed on 26 September, but only with the aim of capturing the final objectives of the previous day, and no large-scale cavalry involvement was proposed.[181] Starting at about 6.30am, the 110th Brigade, assisted by a single tank, began clearing the final pockets of German resistance out of Gird trench in front of Gueudecourt. This was completed by around 11.00am. At this point the situation became uncertain. Gueudecourt village lay about 500m (550 yards) beyond Gird and Gird Support trenches and no enemy could be seen, but it was not known whether the Germans continued to hold the village. Lieutenant General Horne, commanding XV Corps, now took an unusually imaginative step and called up all the cavalry available to him to advance into the gap and explore the situation, with the aim of securing the village and taking up defensive positions on the ridge to the north-east.[182] Unfortunately, the only cavalry units remaining in the battle area were the daily duty squadron allocated to his corps from the 1st Indian Division (D Squadron, 19th Lancers (Fane's Horse), under Captain Fitzgerald), and a single troop of the corps cavalry regiment, the South Irish Horse, a force amounting to no more than about a hundred men.

Fitzgerald's personal account of subsequent events is contained in his official report to the Cavalry Corps.[183] Leaving Mametz at 11.55am, the squadron advanced east of Flers and across the open ground towards Gueudecourt. They crossed the two Gird trenches 'without any difficulty' and moved on at a trot 'in line of troop columns in half sections' (i.e., four parallel columns each two men abreast), reaching the sunken road at the south-western corner of the village by 2.15pm. The squadron was 'heavily shelled' and fired on by at least one machine gun during this advance but suffered only a single casualty. Basing himself in the cover of the sunken road at the entrance to the village, Fitzgerald then sent mounted patrols of his own squadron around the north side of the village, and of the South Irish Horse around the southern side. The latter made little progress due to machine-gun fire from the east, and returned. The northern patrol got as far as a sunken road running east to west into the northern corner of the village. This was occupied by battalions of the King's Liverpool Regiment of the neighbouring 165th Brigade, who had advanced to this point on the previous day. Heavy shelling prevented any further advance, and the patrol returned to the south-west of the village. Fitzgerald then dismounted the remainder of the force and advanced into the village on foot, taking up a line in extension of that of the 165th Brigade, through the centre of the village and facing roughly north-east. Using the squadron's four Hotchkiss machine guns and rifle fire he was able to repel a series of probes by German forces from the north-east, aiming at retaking the village, and held on until around 6.00pm when infantry of 110th Brigade took over his positions.

The encounter was also summarised in a letter home written the following week by Risaldar Kushal Khan of the 19th Lancers:

> We got the orders to go on patrol duty beyond a village which the infantry had taken, and to occupy an eminence there. But when we got into the village itself, we found heaps of the enemy, and bombs and machine guns were very active. In fact our infantry had not taken the village but were all round it. Our squadron dashed into the village with great bravery and surrounded a number of Germans, but they managed to break away and get into a trench in the corner of the village. We dismounted, and holding our horses, took up a position in the middle of the village. There were few casualties owing to God's mercy. We held that village for five hours, and then the infantry came up and relieved us.[184]

D Squadron suffered total human casualties of three killed and seven wounded, a surprisingly modest loss. Unfortunately the German artillery located the horse lines in the sunken road to the south-west of the village, and shelling killed thirty-five horses and wounded a further twenty-four, equivalent to more than half the equine strength of the force. Fitzgerald felt in hindsight that the horses might have been safer dispersed in the open, rather than concentrated out of sight but vulnerable to shelling.[185]

Although a small-scale affair overall, Kavanagh expressed himself 'thoroughly satisfied' with this operation. Fitzgerald was called to report to the corps commander in person and subsequently received the Military Cross.[186] In many respects Kavanagh was entitled to be satisfied. Once again mounted forces had demonstrated the characteristics first apparent at High Wood. Cavalry had been able to move relatively speedily up to the front line (Fitzgerald managed the 12km (7.5 miles) from Mametz to Gueudecourt in a little over 2 hours), cross the front-line trenches without difficulty, and advance in the face of shelling and machine-gun fire without sustaining significant casualties. Furthermore the force had been able to improvise a defensive position on its objective, and using integral machine guns repelled enemy counter-attacks until relieved by supporting infantry. Unfortunately, while the horses provided the key to reducing losses by speed of movement, as soon as the force halted they became a vulnerable impediment and suffered accordingly.

The Gueudecourt action can be viewed as an exemplar of a key role cavalry could have adopted on the Western Front, and towards which it moved gradually, particularly in 1918: small forces, at the disposal of front-line commanders, used to seize advanced positions and exploit small tactical advantages. This point was evident to some as early as 14 July, the anonymous officer of the 18th Lancers quoted earlier also wrote: 'It is an interesting speculation whether it would not have been sounder at this stage of the war to have split up say, one, of the five cavalry Divisions in being, and to have increased the numbers of Corps and Divisional cavalry.'[187]

It is unlikely, however, that Kavanagh would have seen it that way. He would more probably have taken the success of 26 September as vindication of the larger *strategic* rôle of cavalry as a force of wider exploitation, a concept which the offensives of 1916 had so far shown to be beyond reach.

* * *

The involvement of the cavalry in the Somme campaign can be judged against the three key themes set out at the opening of this study:

- First, a close examination of the two occasions when cavalry became involved in fighting during the Somme battles has served largely to vindicate them at a tactical level. Their combination of mobility and firepower made them tactically effective. Much of the criticism levelled at the arm, both at the time and since, is seen to be unfounded.

- Secondly, however, at a higher operational and strategic level, it is difficult to detect any clear understanding by their commanders of their capabilities, or indeed their shortcomings. This led to a failure to achieve the wider operational objectives allocated to the arm.

- Thirdly, at this stage of the war no particular process of evolution or development was apparent in the thinking of the senior commanders, although as will be demonstrated in later chapters, it is arguable that this did develop later in the war.

When the four offensive operations considered in this chapter are viewed together, a series of observations may be made. Haig appears remarkably single-minded in his thinking. He laid out his objectives for the campaign in June, and in his GHQ Instructions as late as September he was able simply to refer his subordinates to these earlier orders.[188] The same villages recur as cavalry objectives; Ligny-Thilloy, Achiet le Grand and Bapaume itself, the main strategic prize of the offensive (although its value was largely psychological rather than strategic). The main change was that as the Fourth Army painfully advanced, these objectives became closer to the attacking front. The holding positions in which the cavalry divisions awaited the orders to advance also become familiar – especially the villages in the valley of the Ancre to the south-west of Albert, Dernancourt, Morlancourt, Buire and Bonnay. Haig seems throughout to have been wedded to the concept of a breakthrough and cavalry exploitation. He was constantly anticipating a decisive collapse of the German defences. This was a keynote of his attitude throughout the remainder of the war, despite the fact that even up to November 1918 arguably it never took place.

A distinction may be drawn, however, between the two occasions when the commander in chief was able to insist on his vision of a decisive stroke, 1 July and 15 September, and the two more limited attacks of 14 July and 25 September. On 1 July the contrast between Haig's strategic breakthrough vision and Rawlinson's own plans for a 'Bite and Hold' attack have already been discussed. In addition, it has been shown that Rawlinson expected to win each battle with infantry and artillery before allowing the cavalry to participate. Thus where he was asked by Haig to plan a deep thrust into the enemy position he did so by setting ever deeper objectives for the infantry, and thereby delaying ever further the involvement of the cavalry, rather than following Haig's vision of early cavalry action. An example of this can be seen in Rawlinson's plans for III and X Corps on 1 July. In the event that they achieved their initial objective of Pozières, an advance of around 4km (2.5 miles), this would be followed not by cavalry exploitation, but by a further infantry push as far as Courcelette and Martinpuich, another 4km (2.5 miles). Equally, in the plans for 15 September, when the 'Red Line' was reached the cavalry had to wait until the artillery had advanced and the infantry attack began again before they were allowed to move.

By contrast, where Rawlinson set more limited objectives and the whole scale of the battle was smaller, such as at Bazentin Ridge or Morval, an opportunity arose not only for the cavalry to begin the battle closer to the infantry start line, but also to perhaps become involved in the battle at an earlier stage. It is not clear at this stage of the war whether this was a deliberate policy on Rawlinson's part, as he still planned these offensives as essentially two-stage (infantry, then cavalry) affairs. It will be shown in later chapters that as his conception of the 'Bite and Hold' battle developed, particularly in 1918, the integration of cavalry into the early stages became more pronounced, but there was only shadowy evidence of this in 1916.

A second recurring feature of these attacks was the narrowness and rigidity of the cavalry line of advance. Again this has been examined in relation to 1 July, but the same difficulty arose on the 14th, where it has been shown that the 2nd Indian Division became stalled behind the failing attack on Longueval on the British right while opportunities for exploitation withered on the left of the attack. The same phenomenon is discernible on 25 September; the cavalry waited for Gueudecourt and Gird Trench to be captured on the left, while Cavan's XIV Corps on the right was content to consolidate on captured trenches although the ground ahead was essentially clear of Germans. Clearly large-scale strategic diversions of the cavalry as some have advocated in relation to 1 July were not viable, but the case for more flexibility on a smaller scale at Bazentin Ridge or Morval/Gueudecourt is harder to refute.

The difficulties of cavalry movement behind the lines, and the need for cleared tracks, has been examined, but it has also been shown that the cavalry were not nearly as constrained in their movements as has often been suggested. Their lack of flexibility has thus to be accounted for elsewhere, and it would seem likely that these constraints must have been mental rather than physical. These may have been imposed from above by Rawlinson's repeated strictures concerning the risk of clogging the rear areas, which seem to have severely curbed any aggressive spirit that Kavanagh and the Cavalry Corps might other- wise have possessed. They may also have been self-imposed by a lack of tactical imagination on the part of more junior cavalry commanders. Most critically, however, any tactical imagination which might have been shown at lower levels was stifled by a system of command that required decisions to be referred up a slow and unreliable chain of command before they could be acted upon. Thus any possibility of rapid or spontaneous action was denied to local commanders.

Finally, it must be asked whether any commanders (apart from Haig himself, who was inevitably too divorced from the direct control of battles to greatly influence their progress) fully grasped their commander in chief's ideas of combined-arms doctrine, that is the insertion of smaller mounted forces into the infantry/artillery battle at a stage prior to a complete 'breakthrough', and sought to apply them on the field of battle. Only one commander shows any evidence of such an understanding: Lieutenant General Horne, commander of XV Corps. It is surely more than coincidence that the only two occasions when mounted troops were committed to battle during the Somme campaign were on his corps front. Significantly, in neither case were the cavalry committed to battle in precisely the manner predicted in their orders. The evening attack on High Wood by the 7th Division and the Secunderabad Brigade was broadly in line with earlier stated objectives, but was at least in part developed *ad-hoc* in the course of the fighting. Equally, on 26 September, after the capture of Gird trench, an opportunity opened up for mounted troops not perhaps to ride for a gap in the traditional sense, but certainly to explore and possibly exploit a fluid and uncertain situation. Again, despite the fact that this was not specifically provided for in the battle plan, Horne was to be seen reaching out for cavalry. Unfortunately on this occasion the cavalry divisions available a day earlier had been stood down and he had to settle for a scratch force of a little over a squadron.

Horne went on to command First Army in 1917. He was also well acquainted with Haig, having been his Commander Royal Artillery (CRA) when Haig commanded I Corps at the beginning of the war.[189] He was not a 'cavalry general' (a term whose validity has already been challenged), having served his earlier career in the Royal Horse Artillery.[190] However, were his branch of service to be considered relevant to his grasp of combined-arms fighting, it would perhaps be more significant to note that, unlike his commander at Fourth Army headquarters, he was *not* an infantryman.

* * *

Detailed historical analysis of the Somme campaign may well serve to vindicate the cavalry as an arm to some degree, but perhaps the last word on the experience of cavalrymen in 1916 should be left to one of the participants, Corporal of Horse Lloyd:

> The bones of many cavalrymen lie in the chalk of the Somme battle-fields. But our men were not killed in the excitement of the attack, nor in putting up a desperate resistance to counter-attacks. For the most part they perished under shell-fire in lousy bivouacs just behind the line, or out in no-man's-land at night while manipulating picks, shovels or rolls of barbed wire. And all detested the whole daft business.[191]

Chapter 3

The Hindenburg Line and Arras, November 1916–April 1917

It seems rather a pity to lose all these chaps who were perfect cavalrymen for the sake of a village which is a complete shell-trap for the British side.

Julian Byng, May 1917[1]

The usefulness of cavalry in the spring of 1917 has typically been characterised in much the same vein as their efforts the year before. John Terraine, for example, commented of Arras, 'The astonishing spectacle was seen of cavalry trying to charge in crater fields; the result, as one might suppose, was high mounds of dead horses, much wasted gallantry, and no progress worth mentioning.'[2] Nor is this a recent phenomenon. The propagation of this view can be detected as early as 1920, when J.F.C. Fuller (never a friend to cavalry) observed 'in 1917 Cavalry, though used in the battles of Arras and Cambrai, accomplished practically nothing save on foot'.[3] Even Richard Holmes, who generally offers a more positive view of the mounted arm, describes how at Arras 'cavalry loyally trotted off to calamity in the crater fields around Monchy-le-Preux: some sang the Eton Boating Song as they disappeared into a blizzard'.[4] The latter part of this remark, although true, tends to create the familiar image of cavalry as socially elite but out of touch with reality, gallantly riding to their inevitable doom. (It also neglects the fact that the regiment referred to was the Royal Horse Guards (Blues), which might be expected to include more Old Etonians than most, and ignores the ironic humour of the BEF, which would inevitably prompt soldiers to sing of 'jolly boating weather' in the middle of a snowstorm.) As will be shown, none of these comments does justice to the part played by the cavalry in these battles.

A more specific charge levelled at the cavalry is that the static warfare of the preceding years had dulled their senses and led to a tactical staleness which left them unable to exploit fully the opportunities created in 1917, in particular the German retreat to the Hindenburg Line. Terraine observed

> cavalry and infantry alike, after years of trench warfare, had lost the habit and art of movement. Broad horizons and empty country

bewildered and frightened them; long dependence on massive artillery support created another inhibition, and further delays occurred as the guns struggled forward along the mined and miry roads.[5]

This was a significant misrepresentation of the success of the cavalry in these operations.

*   *   *

First, however, it is necessary to take a look at how the cavalry fared in the aftermath of the Somme battle, and during the winter of 1916/17. Lack of supplies and reinforcements combined with one of the worst winters of the century to leave the arm weak in manpower and sickly in horsepower. As Anglesey put it, 'the BEF's mounted arm entered the year of *L'Affaire Nivelle*, and the battles of Arras and Cambrai noticeably weak'.[6] As the autumn of 1916 progressed the weather became increasingly worse, and it became evident that no opportunity for mounted work by the cavalry would arise until the following year.[7] In mid-November the five divisions of the reformed Cavalry Corps were withdrawn to winter billets on the Channel coast. These billets stretched from Boulogne in the north 80km (50 miles) south as far as Le Treport at the mouth of the River Bresle. The 1st, 3rd and 2nd Cavalry Divisions respectively were allocated areas from Boulogne as far south as the mouth of the River Somme, north-west of Abbeville, while the two Indian divisions were billeted south of the Somme.[8] The wide dispersal of the corps was intended both to provide space for training and to reduce the load on the various billeting areas. Positions near the coast were also intended to ease the logistical difficulties of forage supply,[9] although problems with this were to arise nonetheless.

Brigadier General Home, Brigadier General, General Staff (BGGS) of the Cavalry Corps, was concerned at the end of the Somme battles that the cavalry had lost their edge: 'Our cavalry has got slow, it wants speeding up. They want ginger and to forget that such things as trenches exist.'[10] While his own preference was for front-line action, even in the infantry, he recognised that training was vital over the winter if the cavalry were to make an impression when the weather improved:

> It is very dull back here with the Cavalry. We have got all our Divisions back now and they are busy settling into their winter quarters – then we shall be able to commence some training. A great deal will be required from the Cavalry next Spring and I hope that they all realise it.[11]

The nature of what would be required of the corps, at least in the minds of its commanders and of GHQ, had been spelled out as early as September 1916 in a document signed by Home entitled 'Winter Training'.[12] This stated that a 'clear task for the cavalry' had been laid down by the commander in chief (Haig), and that unlike the previous winter, where much training was devoted to the conversion of mounted troops to trench fighting on foot (described in the previous chapter), the reverse was now true. The 'mission statement' (in modern parlance) embodied in this document merits quotation at length:

> Up to the present the Cavalry in France has played a dual rôle – trained as Cavalry but at the same time [it] has had the shadow of trench warfare continually hanging over its head. The result has been that attempts were made to have the Cavalry equally good for both these rôles, and trench warfare being the nearest, a great deal of time and labour was devoted to fitting Cavalry to take its place in the trenches, and fighting equally well as infantry.
>
> There is no doubt that this training has left its mark on the Cavalry. The horizon has been narrowed, movement and suitable ground for training have been non-existent, men have been away from their horses for long periods, and the characteristics of Cavalry, laid down in Cavalry Training 1916, namely 'the power to move with rapidity, to fight when moving, to seize fleeting opportunities, and to cover long distances in a short time' have been sometimes forgotten.
>
> The task laid down by the Commander-in-Chief for the Cavalry embodies all the characteristics quoted above, and all training must work towards this end.[13]

In short, mobile warfare remained the vision towards which training should be focused. In Haig's mind the breakthrough remained a dominant motif, despite the disappointments of 1916. The document acknowledged that service in the trenches was likely, but discouraged undue time spent on preparation for this, the implication being that time in the line was inherently a suitable education. It was in this spirit that the cavalry divisions began their winter training programmes.

In spite of the dogged ambitions of their overall commander, however, a subtle but significant change had taken place in the emphasis of this training, and the type of operations for which the corps was preparing. This was described by Major Darling, serving with the 20th Hussars, 5th Cavalry Brigade:

> It was known that a great Allied offensive was to take place in the spring, so we had once more to prepare to go through the 'gap'. Officially the expression 'gap' had long since been dropped as it had become almost a term of derision. We had been told to speak of 'operations beyond the trench system', or some such phrase. However, 'gap' was shorter and the term continued to be used to describe the cavalry's share in the offensive.[14]

Training was carried out in cooperation with infantry, the cavalry practising the capture of relatively nearby objectives, which were then consolidated and handed over to supporting troops. Darling continued:

> We were not to pursue blindly whooping and yelling through the night, as the Prussian cavalry are said to have done after Waterloo. Nor were we to make raids on distant aerodromes, railway junctions and headquarters, as we were to have done on the Somme in 1916. Every detail was cut and dried, but I do not remember that anyone was told off to bring back the Kaiser's head on a charger. On the whole, it was a modest programme compared to former ones.[15]

It is possible to discern in these remarks a transition in cavalry thinking away from an optimistic but ultimately unrealistic ambition of a distant breakthrough rôle, as had been postulated in 1916, towards more limited local tactical objectives. It is important to note the appearance and development in embryonic form in the winter of 1916/17 of concepts which were to become key in 1918. At this stage, however, while it is important to acknowledge that this change in thinking was taking place, it was not yet fully understood or reflected in the organisation, command and tactical handling of the cavalry. Nor were combined-arms operations in cooperation with infantry, and in particular artillery, well enough developed. The situation was further complicated by the changes in the defensive battle the Germans were to fight in 1917. The Arras offensive, as will be explored later in this chapter, demonstrated the gap between the development of these new tactical ideas on paper and in training, and their practical application on the battlefield.

'Winter Training' also contained more detailed training objectives, and several of these are noteworthy. The first of these was communications: 'The question of communications requires a great deal of attention. Trench warfare has wedded us to the telephone, and when moving the telephone will hardly be used.'[16] Training of despatch riders, both horse and motorcycle mounted, was urged. Secondly, cooperation with armoured cars was to be practised: 'The Corps Commander is of the opinion that these cars should be used with troops both in reconnaissance and attack and that they seldom – if ever – be employed on distant expeditions by themselves.'[17] The latter part of this instruction may reflect Home's own scepticism. In January 1917 he recorded: '[I] Went down to inspect the 5th Cav. Div. armoured cars today. They want some brushing-up, I think.'[18] The failure of combined cavalry/armour operations on the Somme has already been examined, but such operations were also to be a feature of the fighting in the spring of 1917, with varying degrees of success.

Several organisational changes were also carried out over the winter. The first of these was simply of nomenclature, the 1st and 2nd Indian Divisions becoming respectively the 4th and 5th Cavalry Divisions.[19] This acknowledged their presence within a unified Cavalry Corps, but also reflected the fact that in the 5th Division in particular Indians were in a minority; the division contained four Indian regiments, two British and three (a brigade) Canadian. Secondly, in the spring sufficient specially trained reinforcements were received to start posting men directly to the cavalry machine-gun squadrons, allowing some cavalrymen to return to their parent units. The Indian brigades' squadrons in particular were entirely remanned with British troops sent as formed units from the MGC(C) training centre at Maresfield in Sussex, both British and Indian officers and Indian other ranks being returned to their regiments.[20]

These reinforcements, however, should be considered the exception rather than the rule. More generally an on-going manpower crisis was developing in the BEF.[21] Trained British reinforcements were at a premium and Robertson, Chief of the Imperial General Staff (CIGS), started to send trained men from the cavalry reserve to the infantry and engineers in France, blocking reinforcement of the cavalry.[22] This left many regiments below strength. The reinforcement of the MGC(C) may be seen in this light as a ploy to circumvent this block and free more cavalrymen to return to the ranks of the cavalry regiments.

This general shortage of men was not the only obstacle to Home and Kavanagh's vision of winter training. From October 1916 each cavalry brigade was required to furnish a pioneer battalion for dismounted service.[23] Theoretically only two of these battalions would be formed within each division at any one time, leaving one brigade free for mounted training, and they were to be disbanded at the end of January. In fact most of the pioneer battalions continued work until March, at which point, although nominally disbanded, working parties were still supplied to start on the construction of cavalry tracks for the Arras battle.[24] Given that the remaining men in each brigade were obliged to tend the horses of their dismounted colleagues, it is clear that the impact on training as formed units must have been significant. In addition, virtually all of the machine-gun squadrons were required to spend periods in the front line,[25] and the corps RHA batteries were all removed over the winter and sent to support infantry formations, not returning until mid-March.[26] Thus despite the pious hopes of 'Winter Training', the 'shadow of trench warfare' continued to loom darkly over any preparations for a mobile battle that the cavalry might attempt.

Already short of men, and burdened by this range of extra responsibilities, the cavalry was further hindered by a lack of forage. Towards the end of the Somme fighting, concerns began to be expressed about the condition of the horses. This can be followed in the war diary of Colonel Harris, Deputy Director Veterinary Services (DDVS) of the Cavalry Corps. Early in October he inspected the 18th Hussars and 9th Lancers (2nd Cavalry Brigade), commenting 'There were a large number of thin horses in both these units.'[27] A few weeks later he saw the Hampshire (Carbineers) Yeomanry: 'There was a large percentage of thin horses. I recommended grazing and ordered some special tonic balls.'[28] By November shipping problems had exacerbated the problem and hard feed, particularly oats, started to become scarce. Harris visited the 5th Army Artillery School at the end of November, and commented that the horses were getting only 6lb of oats rather than the official ration of 12lb, and as a result were 'looking very poor'.[29] Similarly, hay was running short. The 1st Cavalry Division halved the ration to 6lb in November, and the 15th Hussars reported difficulty in finding even this much, feeding only 5lb per day.[30] It was not until 13 April, two days after the Monchy battle, that the full ration of 12lb of oats and 12lb of hay was restored. Harris commented rather ruefully, 'It is a pity this was not done when they were in the back area during the spell of very cold weather. There would have been fewer debilitated animals and, as we have seen by experience, fewer casualties.'[31] Once again we can turn to the experiences of Corporal of Horse Lloyd to see how these measures affected men and horses in the ranks:

> The daily ration for each horse was, say, nine pounds of corn. . . . and never a grain more nor less whatever the difference in size of the animals. Now my horse, Herbert, was the biggest and hungriest horse for miles around. Others in the troop were half his size and had half his appetite. These little devils were as fat as butter, while poor Herbert was slim and touchy on short rations.

Lloyd reverted to the age-old soldier's solution of stealing him extra corn and hay, until Herbert was 'happy and plump and shining'[32], but this is not a solution that would have succeeded had it been more commonplace.

The other great problem suffered by the cavalry, and indeed by all combatants in France, was the very cold winter of 1916/17. Frost and snow continued from November through until April. The combination of cold weather and short rations had a severe impact on the condition of the horses, and was to be a significant factor in losses during the Arras battle in April. A measure of the severity of the conditions is shown by the need to use of petrol to wash cuts and wounds to horses' legs, as water would simply freeze over the wound.[33] Opinion was divided in the cavalry over the best response to the cold. Some units worked their horses hard in an effort to acclimatise them, suffering in the process a higher casualty rate, while other units kept their mounts as far as possible under shelter. The latter policy produced fatter horses for brigade inspections but proved to be the downfall of several regiments as these animals were unprepared for the shock of work and weather when the attacks began in the spring. Either way, as Major Darling observed, 'I can only repeat that when we finally left for the battle, we were far from satisfied with the condition of the horses.'[34]

On top of all this, sarcoptic mange, widespread among the French civilian horse population, broke out within the Cavalry Corps in January 1917.[35] While not necessarily fatal, this disease created the need to constantly re-billet troops out of villages where the cases occurred, and the temporary quarantining of large numbers of horses. This led to congestion in the veterinary hospitals, already coping with the large volume of 'debilitated' horses resulting from the forage shortage.[36] A number of equine casualties were also caused by the necessity to clip the winter coats of mange cases, which subsequently left them vulnerable to the extreme wintry weather.[37]

In the light of all these difficulties it is hard to see how very much useful preparation for the up-coming campaign could have been achieved over the winter within the Cavalry Corps. Hunger, the weather and the constant demand for labour to support the troops in the front line would all have taken their toll, and it is unlikely that overall the corps was in any better shape to fight in the spring of 1917 than it had been at the close of the Somme battles. No doubt the cavalry remained keen to take their long-awaited opportunity to prove themselves, and some have interpreted this as reflecting the preparedness of the corps as a whole for the fight ahead. Preston, describing Arras and Monchy in the *Cavalry Journal*, asserted that, 'The cavalry regiments had had no serious casualties since the Second Battle of Ypres; [in 1915] their standard of training had reached a high level; if the day of the "Gap" was indeed at hand, all ranks were ready for it.'[38] However, will-power alone would not be sufficient. As will be seen, although the cavalry showed themselves keen and courageous in the battles of March and April, the cost among tired, overloaded horses in atrocious weather was tragically high.

* * *

Meanwhile, as early as September 1916, while the Somme battle was still in progress, the Germans had begun preparations for a new defensive position in the rear behind the battlefield. A network of reserve positions was mapped out stretching along the whole of the German line from the Belgian coast to the Moselle. Construction of the first of these, 'Siegfried', running from Arras to south of Laon, was begun on 27 September. This and its northern neighbour, the 'Wotan' position, were to become more commonly known both by the British and Germans as the Hindenburg Line. While originally intended as a position of last resort, a decision was taken by the German high command in February 1917, in the light of the territorial and manpower losses of the Somme battles, to make an organised and voluntary withdrawal to the Siegfried position.

The full details of this new defensive system, and the thinking behind it, were examined by G.C. Wynne in his 1940 work *If Germany Attacks*.[39] Key to understanding this new defensive method was the idea that ground may, temporarily at least, be traded for tactical advantage. Rather than seeking to halt an Allied attack against a heavily defended front line, the German plan allowed attacking troops to be absorbed within a much deeper defensive network. Once inside, the attackers would be caught in previously devised killing zones, between individual strong-points, before ultimately the *status quo* was restored by specially trained counter-attack units. This had the incidental effect of creating a battlefield that was much deeper than previously – up to 10km (6 miles) rather than 2km (1.5 miles) – but at the same time less densely defended. Also the effects of artillery would inevitably be dispersed across a wider area. Thus while the British cavalry were narrowing their horizons to look for a more limited and integrated tactical rôle on the battlefield, the Germans were simultaneously creating a defensive system that would allow the horsemen greater local offensive opportunities.

Operation 'Alberich', a staged withdrawal by the Germans to the new position via a series of intermediate defensive positions, began on 14 March 1917. This was combined with a 'scorched earth' policy in the areas abandoned, including the mining of roads, demolition of villages and destruction of anything perceived to be of use to the advancing Allies. Brigadier General 'Jack' Seely witnessed this destruction at first hand while advancing with the Canadian Cavalry Brigade: 'Every house was levelled within one metre of the ground, every tree was cut down, big or small, including the fruit trees and the gardens. Most extraordinary of all even the little rose trees on the walls had been cut through just above the ground.'[40] This was combined with mines and booby-traps. The military value of such a policy is at best debatable, but one effect it did have was to provoke significant anger in the advancing British and French forces.

The withdrawal may be compared to the swinging of a door, with its hinge at Arras in the north and its southernmost point, as far as the British were concerned, 50km (30 miles) to the south beyond Peronne, the depth of the withdrawal at this southern end being around 20km (12 miles) eastwards towards St Quentin. Opposite the northern end of this movement was General Gough's Fifth Army, faced with only a short distance to follow up, but under pressure to close up with the Germans in time to support an attack at Arras at the beginning of April. To the south was Fourth Army under General Rawlinson. His force was under less pressure of time but was both more thinly spread along its frontage and had further to go to reach the new German position.[41]

Within a few years of the war's end criticism was developing of the failure of the Fourth and Fifth Armies to make more of the German retreat to the Hindenburg position in March 1917. The adverse comment of J.F.C. Fuller, for example, was alluded to earlier in this chapter. This criticism was refuted by Cyril Falls in the Official History, in which he was at pains to explain that the organised nature of the German withdrawal, the devastation left in their wake and the strength of the defensive position to which they were known to be falling back all 'acted as a brake' upon the advance of the British forces. Further 'it was plainly useless to attack that position until the bulk of the artillery was within range and well supplied with ammunition.'[42] Nonetheless some writers have continued to propose the somewhat circular argument that on the one hand the British high command launched an all-out 'pursuit' of the Germans, but that at the same time such an operation was doomed to failure. John Terraine argued: ' "Pursuit" by the Allied armies, no matter how vehemently ordered by their higher commanders, was hardly more than a pious hope.' He went on to add, 'The Cavalry, the only weapon of exploitation that they possessed, was seen to be almost completely ineffective in these circumstances' and 'the arm was not well handled.'[43]

A closer examination of events shows that on the contrary, rather than a reckless but ineffective pursuit, Fourth and Fifth Armies conducted a methodical and largely successful follow-up of the German withdrawal. This managed to balance the twin requirements of closing up to the Hindenburg position in time for the planned Easter offensives, by the British at Arras and by the French to the south, and of minimising unnecessary losses. These twin objectives were laid out by Haig on 16 March in a GHQ letter to army commanders and to Kavanagh at the Cavalry Corps:

> 2. The general intention of the Field-Marshal Commanding-in-Chief is:-
>
> > (a) To maintain pressure on the enemy and harass his rearguards with the minimum number of troops required for that purpose.
> > (b) To strike the enemy on the Arras–Vimy front in the greatest possible strength with a view to penetrating his defences, outflanking the Hindenburg Line from the north and operating in the direction of Cambrai.
>
> Advantage should be taken of local opportunities to cause the enemy loss in his retirement, especially by means of artillery fire; but attacks in force which will be met by rearguards fully prepared, are unlikely under the conditions to give an adequate return for the losses likely to be incurred.[44]

(Incidentally this letter was an early example of Haig's tendency to include Kavanagh, a corps commander, in meetings and correspondence otherwise only addressed to the commanders of armies.) Taken in the light of these criteria, the cavalry operations of March 1917 were far from 'ineffective'. The Germans were indeed 'harassed' and 'caused loss', at the cost of a minimum of casualties to the cavalry. The operations also provided a valuable opportunity for the cavalry to put into effect some of the training undertaken over the winter, and for the tactical evolution of the arm to continue. Indeed, minor operations such as the Villers Faucon attack of 27 March (discussed below) might be considered textbook examples of the successful application of mounted units to attacks on limited objectives.

When the German withdrawal began (on 14 March opposite Fourth Army, and on 17 March opposite Fifth Army), only the corps cavalry regiments attached to the infantry corps were available to follow it up. It rapidly became apparent that these limited cavalry forces would not be sufficient and on 19 March a division from the Cavalry Corps was ordered up to support each army. The two Indian divisions, now renamed the 4th and 5th Cavalry Divisions, were selected, the 4th Division going to Fifth Army in the north, and the 5th Division going to Fourth Army in the south.[45]

However, although these additional troops represented nearly 40 per cent of the cavalry available to GHQ, they were sufficient only to replace the existing corps regiments and slightly increase the numbers of cavalry on each corps front. The 4th Cavalry Division, attached to Fifth Army (comprising I (Anzac), II and V Corps), deployed forward only the Lucknow Cavalry Brigade, providing three regiments for the three corps on the army front. Meanwhile to the south, the Canadian Cavalry Brigade (from the 5th Cavalry Division) took over the front of the two northerly corps of Fourth Army (XIV and XV), while the Ambala Brigade covered the two southerly Corps (III and IV). As the latter two brigades adopted the standard pattern of putting two regiments in the line and keeping one in reserve, this also represented a front-line reinforcement of each infantry corps equivalent to only a single regiment of cavalry. As this was intended to replace rather than augment the already exhausted corps cavalry regiments, it reflects little more than maintenance of the *status quo* in numbers of mounted troops rather than a significant increase. This simple lack of manpower should be taken into account when the impact of the cavalry on these operations is judged. This was clearly not a force large enough to deliver a decisive blow upon the retreating Germans, 'well handled' or not.

Nor was that the intention of the cavalry commanders. The modest ambitions of the cavalry divisions can be read in the orders issued by the 5th Cavalry Division HQ on its attachment to Fourth Army:

> The tasks of the Division are:-
>
> (a) To ascertain the dispositions of the advanced hostile detachments.
> (b) To ascertain the enemy's defences and strength.
> (c) To picket the enemy so as to prevent his advancing and so as to give instant information of his withdrawal.
> (d) To be ready to follow up the enemy if he withdraws.[46]

These orders clearly reflect the tone of Haig's GHQ letter of 16 March; contact was to be maintained, but no rash and costly moves made. As the following narrative will show, however, far from being overly timid in the execution of these instructions, the lead brigades of the cavalry fought extremely aggressively, not only following up the German withdrawal but forcing the pace of it. In short, within the bounds set by their orders, the operations of the cavalry during this period were a complete success.

*   *   *

The most significant cavalry operations during this advance took place during the period 23–28 March. As has been described, the task of Fifth Army in the north required a more urgent push against the retreating Germans. Their way was blocked, however, by a well-developed system of German intermediate defences, including the R1, R2 and R3 reserve lines. Although only the third of these was defended with any vigour, Gough was forced to advance by a series of methodical set-piece attacks, which left little rôle for the cavalry beyond reconnaissance patrols and flank guards.[47] Thus little significant mounted action took place on this front. On the Fourth Army front, however, covered by the 5th Cavalry Division, the greater distance to be covered and the lack of formal intermediate defensive positions left more scope for cavalry operations.

When the 5th Cavalry Division took over from the regiments of corps cavalry on 24 March, the Fourth Army front lay approximately 8km (5 miles) east of the Bapaume–Peronne road, running north-west to south-east parallel to, but some 10km (6 miles) short of, the Hindenburg position. Divisional Headquarters was established in Peronne. The Canadian Cavalry Brigade took over the northern half of the line from Bus to Longavesnes, the Royal Canadian Dragoons covering XIV Corps on the left (north) and the Fort Garry Horse covering XV Corps on the right, with Lord Strathcona's Horse in reserve. To the south the Ambala Brigade took over the front of III and IV Corps with the 8th Hussars and 18th Lancers initially in the line.[48] Brigadier Seely was quick to inspect personally his (Canadian) brigade frontage,

> My headquarters were at a place near Moland, and I received orders
> to spread my cavalry along a twelve-mile front in support of the
> infantry. Next morning, with Geoffrey Brooke, I rode all along this
> Front from end to end. We soon saw that the Germans, though well
> placed, with plenty of machine guns in position, were nevertheless in
> small numbers. They had few trenches and hardly any wire.[49]

His decision was to begin offensive operations immediately, and both the Canadians and the Indians to the south were soon in action. Having made contact with the Australians to the north and the French to the south, both brigades started to patrol forwards. The Canadians attacked the village of Ytres at the northern end of the line and 'after a sharp fight'[50] established posts there. Meanwhile the 9th Hodson's Horse, the third regiment of the Ambala Brigade, occupied Etreillers in the south, although their posts were raided during the night of 24/25 March and several men were lost.[51]

The next day, 25 March, was spent in a similar fashion, described by the divisional war diary as 'Outpost, reconnaissance and patrol fighting along whole front of Fourth Army.'[52] On 26 March the Canadians pushed forward, capturing the villages of Equancourt and Longavesnes, driving out small parties of the enemy and handing the villages over to the infantry.[53] The aggression and commitment with which these operations were undertaken can be seen from an incident described by Seely, when he went forward to inspect the ground gained:

> Major Critchley [of Lord Strathcona's Horse], who commanded the squadron which had encircled Equancourt, went round with me in the fading light. He seemed curiously sad and tired in contrast to all his men, who were elated by victory. I asked him to sit down and rest while his officers took me round. But he insisted on coming as far as the most important point. He explained the position to me lucidly but slowly and then sat down. I turned to the Sergeant Major, who said: 'He has been shot through the chest, Sir, but he made me promise not to tell until he had finished his work.'[54]

Sadly, Critchley's wound was to prove fatal and he died a few days later.

Meanwhile to the south the Ambala Brigade combined with elements of III Corps in an attack on Roisel. Earlier, on 21 March, Major General Fanshawe, commander of the 48th Division but in temporary command of III Corps, had formed an advanced guard consisting of his 'Corps Mounted Troops' (cavalry and cyclists), the 1/4th Battalion of the Oxford Light Infantry, two batteries of field artillery and two sections of engineers. This became Ward's Force, named after the corps CRA Brigadier General Ward, who was given temporary command of it.[55]

On 26 March this force, with its mounted component now formed by two squadrons of the 18th Lancers and supported by three armoured cars from the 9th LAC Battery, attacked Roisel. The cars and the infantry attacked the village frontally from the east while the lancer squadrons outflanked it north and south. The armoured car attack was very successful, driving in a post of about forty Germans on the western side of the village,[56] but the outflanking effort proved more difficult: 'B Squadron [18th Lancers] were unable to co-operate effectively as the ground south of Roisel was too marshy and intersected', while D Squadron 'co-operated on the northern flank' but machine-gun fire from the village prevented a significant advance.[57] As a result the remaining German garrison was able to make its escape and only one prisoner was captured.[58] This battle was not particularly significant in the overall campaign, but it is noteworthy because Ward's Force represented a combined-arms concept that is more often associated only with the Hundred Days in 1918. In fact, however, it is one strand of a thread which can be traced from the combined bicycle, machine gun and cavalry formations proposed at Loos in 1915, through the cavalry and armoured car operations of 1916, and eventually into the cavalry and tank operations of 1917 and 1918 described in later chapters. As will be demonstrated, far from being a revolution in 1918, the developments of that year should be seen as the culmination of a long evolutionary process.

During the night of 26/27 March the Canadians pushed a small enemy detachment out of Lieramont, before once again handing the village over to the infantry.[59] With this village taken, the front lay along a line from Lieramont through Longavesnes and Roisel. From there the next bound would include the village of Villers Faucon 3km (2 miles) to the east, and to the north the twin settlements of Guyencourt and Saulcourt. For this operation the Canadian Cavalry Brigade was reinforced by the addition of the 8th Hussars from the Ambala Brigade and the Royal Wiltshire Yeomanry (XV Corps Cavalry), as well as the armoured cars of the 9th LAC Battery and three batteries of artillery from the 48th Division, in addition to the RHA batteries of all three brigades of the 5th Cavalry Division.

The attack was to be one of envelopment from north and south, the Canadians moving into Guyencourt from the north and the 8th Hussars attacking Villers Faucon from the south. As a preliminary, at about 1.00pm one squadron of the Royal Canadian Dragoons advanced east from Longavesnes for about 1km (1,000 yards) and charged a German outpost, killing three men with the sword and capturing nine prisoners.[60] This would later allow machine guns to be pushed forward in this area to cover the attack on the villages.

A preliminary bombardment of 40 minutes' duration was begun at 4.30pm and at 5.10 the attack began. After a short delay caused by a snowstorm, the Canadian brigade advanced from the north-west in bounds, moving in open order at the gallop. The Wiltshire Yeomanry were pushed out to the north and north-east to cover the flank and rear of the attack while Lord Strathcona's Horse swung around to approach Guyencourt from the north. Meanwhile the Fort Garry Horse advanced on their right, approaching Saulcourt from the north-west. Artillery and machine-gun support from the west continued 'to the last minute',[61] halting as the Canadians dismounted to fight on foot through the ruins of the villages, which were securely in Canadian hands by 6.00pm. The defenders fled in the direction of Epehy; enemy machine guns in that village rendered a close mounted pursuit impossible, but the Hotchkiss teams of the

Fort Garry Horse rapidly deployed east of Saulcourt and were able to inflict casualties on the retreating Germans.[62]

During the course of the Guyencourt attack, Lieutenant Harvey of Lord Strathcona's Horse came upon an enemy trench protected by several strands of barbed wire. Knowing that this was an obstacle insurmountable to his horse, he dismounted, jumped the wire on foot and entered the position with his revolver, capturing a machine gun. For this he was subsequently awarded the Victoria Cross.[63]

Meanwhile a similar assault was made on Villers Faucon from the south. B and D Squadrons of the 8th Hussars moved off at 5.00pm while the bombardment was still in progress. B Squadron advanced rapidly to the cover of several copses to the west of the village and there dismounted to provide fire support, while D Squadron swung wide to the right and approached the village from the south. Again, after a short dismounted fight the village was in British hands by 6.00pm. Hussar casualties were very light: two killed and fifteen wounded, with fifteen horse casualties.[64]

Unfortunately the armoured cars fared less well. After the success of the cars at Roisel in drawing enemy fire, two were sent along the Marquaix–Villers Faucon road with the specific intention of distracting the enemy from the cavalry. Sadly, the Germans had responded to the previous battle by rushing up armour-piercing ammunition for their machine guns and both cars were quickly knocked out, their entire crews, with the exception of one officer, either killed or wounded.[65] The impact on the 9th LAC Battery of this loss is poignantly summarised in the laconic entry in the battery war diary: '27/3/17, 2 armoured cars in action. OC seriously wounded.'[66]

In general, however, all parties were well pleased with the operation. Brigadier Home visited the headquarters of the 5th Cavalry Division on 29 March and recorded in his diary that 'They were very cheerful and pleased as their men had had quite a pretty little fight and were all the better for it.'[67] MacAndrew, the divisional commander, also sent a wire to his troops offering 'Heartiest congratulations ... for the dashing attack'.[68] On the same day the division was withdrawn from the front line; it would take no further part in the advance.

* * *

It may seem odd in the light of the successes of the end of March that the 4th and 5th Cavalry Divisions were withdrawn from the battle area after only five or six operational days. However, those who have castigated the cavalry for not 'doing more' neglect the high intensity of these operations. The cavalry were in action almost every day on reconnaissance or in attack, and the intervals would have been spent digging in, awaiting infantry relief and then moving on to the next objective. Rest and shelter were almost non-existent, and the weather continued to be very cold. The Wiltshire Yeomanry (XV Corps Cavalry) recorded that 'During the operations between March 19th and 30th the Regiment was in action 9 days besides sending out troops on reconnaissance on two other days ... The horses were in the open from March 18th onwards and owing to very severe weather, hard work, and long hours saddled–up, suffered very severely in condition.'[69] Nor, as has already been discussed, did the divisions come into the line as fresh as they would have liked due to the weather and the ration situation over the winter.

It is a long–standing military truth that mobile operations are highly fatiguing and difficult to sustain for more than a short period. The highly mechanised forces involved in the invasion of Iraq in 2003 were able to sustain their momentum only for a few days before an 'operational pause' was forced upon them by their own logistical situation. On the Western Front the duties involved in garrisoning a static front–line trench were considered sufficiently fatiguing that troops relatively rarely spent more than seven or eight days in the line before relief, and four days was considered the reasonable norm.[70] The infantry system of support at all levels from company to division allowed for a rotation of troops with only a minority in the line at any one time. For the cavalry, however, there was no such reserve depth. When the German with–drawal began each infantry corps had just a single cavalry regiment available to follow up. After five or six days (19–24 March) these troops were worn out. As has been explained, over the front of Fourth and Fifth Armies a reinforcement of two divisions of cavalry provided only slightly better than one or two further regiments per corps. Five days later, on 29 March, these too were exhausted, and with the 1st, 2nd and 3rd Cavalry Divisions being held back for the Arras offensive there was simply no more cavalry available to provide a third 'rotation'. Far from having 'lost the habit and art of movement', the cavalry had worn itself out by its very mobility. The remainder of the advance to the Hindenburg Line thus took place with only very limited cavalry support.

Reference has already been made to the 'textbook' character of cavalry operations during this period. Both brigades of the 5th Cavalry Division showed themselves capable of attacking using a well coordinated combination of artillery and machine–gun support, dismounted fire–power and the astute use of mounted shock. Nearly all attacks were characterised by the use of outflanking manoeuvres and the rapid consolidation of ground gained by the advance of both integral Hotchkiss teams and supporting machine–gun squadrons.

The Canadian capture of Equancourt on 26 March is a good example. The village was first engaged by machine–gun and artillery fire from the north–west by the Canadian MG squadron and RCHA battery. Subsequently, under the cover of this fire, the Fort Garry Horse established dismounted fire positions to the west and north, A Squadron on the north side 'menacing' the village particularly vigorously.[71] With the enemy suitably distracted, two squadrons

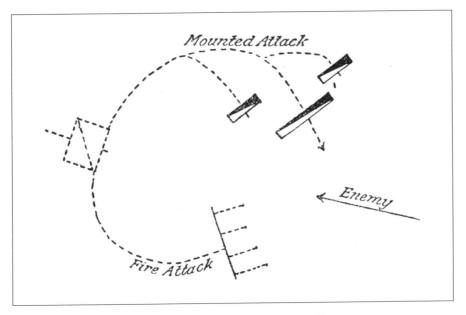

Fig. 3.3 Diagram of cavalry tactics from *Cavalry Training*, Fig. 20

of Lord Strathcona's Horse were able to gallop into the village from the south virtually unmolested. Casualties for the whole operation were five men wounded.[72] A sketch of this operation, with attack by fire on one flank masking a mounted advance on the other, would bear a striking resemblance to the model for such an attack laid out in Fig. 20 of *Cavalry Training*[73] (reproduced above). In spite of Home and Kavanagh's reservations, examined earlier, the cavalry had not forgotten the key elements of mobile warfare. These were also pre-war tactics, classical 'fire and movement' concepts that had been applicable in 1900 and remain so in the twenty-first century. Much has been made of how the citizen infantry of the BEF relearned these techniques in 1917, assisted by such documents as SS143 *Instructions for the Training of Platoons for Offensive Action 1917*, published in February of that year.[74] It is arguable that the cavalry, still leavened by a significant number of pre-war regular officers and men, had never forgotten them.

The attack on Guyencourt–Saulcourt–Villers Faucon on 28 March took essentially the same form but on a larger scale. It was also remarkable for its coordination between the several brigades and their supporting arms. Simultaneous, widely separated attacks from north and south were successfully launched, with troops advancing at high speed but moving tactically in bounds using the available cover. Crucially, the artillery and machine guns were able to suppress the defenders with fire until the cavalry were virtually among them. A German officer captured on the day considered the speed and coordination of the attack to have been key: 'The speed with which the squadrons effected their entrance from the south and north completely upset his plans, which he had no time to alter.'[75] In the light of these actions the accusation of tactical staleness among the cavalry after months of static warfare is hard to sustain.

On 10 April 1917, while the 2nd and 3rd Cavalry Divisions huddled in snow-filled shell-holes east of Arras, GHQ issued one of the few doctrinal pamphlets of the war addressed specifically at cavalry fighting. This pamphlet, entitled 'A Note on the Recent Cavalry Fighting up to 7th April 1917', is highly significant in that it gives an insight into the contemporary view of what had taken place in the advance to the Hindenburg Line in March, and of any lessons learned from it. The pamphlet is reproduced in full as Appendix 2, as the points it raises offer a valuable tool for a reassessment of the spring fighting and have relevance to the analysis of the Arras battles.

Several of the observations in the pamphlet are relatively mundane, for example, 'time spent on reconnaissance' (Paragraph (a)) is something of a military cliché, but others are more significant. Paragraph (b) highlights the problem encountered at Gueudecourt in September 1916 (which was later to be the keynote of the fighting at Monchy), that cavalry halted and dismounted on a captured objective, particularly a village, are hopelessly vulnerable to horse casualties if the enemy can bring observed artillery to bear. This was to become even more of a problem as the Germans became more adept from 1917 onwards in the creation of observed artillery 'killing zones' within their new flexible defensive systems.[76] The advice is therefore to push on beyond such 'localities', and to tell off pursuing detachments. However, it is hard to find examples of this working in practice; even the most successful of the cavalry's spring operations, the Guyencourt–Saulcourt–Villers Faucon attack, was unable to advance beyond its immediate objectives due to enemy machine-gun fire.

The main body of the pamphlet, paragraphs (c) to (g), outlines the ingredients of a classical mobile attack, combining speed and flanking assaults masked by a frontal attack, using carefully timed suppressive artillery, armoured cars and machine-gun fire on the target. Again the Guyencourt attack serves as an example, but in this case of the successful application of all these principles. It can be argued that this is not a particularly radical set of tactical principles, and indeed it has been noted earlier that a similar battle plan was presented in pre-war cavalry manuals. The contemporary value of the pamphlet, however, lies in its implicit assertion that these methods have now been tested 'for real' on the battlefield and have been shown to retain their validity, and, moreover, that although much of the character of the war may seem new and different, commanders neglect these 'old-fashioned' principles at their peril. This consistency, and the continued application of pre-war doctrine on a battlefield that evolved to make it ever more appropriate, is one of the keys to understanding the story of the British cavalry in the war.

Overall the contribution of the cavalry to the advance to the Hindenburg Line was probably not decisive. However, it was not a phase of the campaign which offered any promise of decisive results, and this fact was quickly recognised by Haig and the commanders of Fourth and Fifth Armies. An infantry advance unsupported by mounted troops would probably have been slower and potentially more costly, but would ultimately have achieved the same results. What then of the decision to commit two divisions of cavalry to the battle? This should not be seen, as some have interpreted it, as a misguided vision of a great rout of the retreating Germans, which the cavalry failed to achieve. Rather it may be viewed as a routine reinforcement of the exhausted corps cavalry of the Fourth and Fifth Armies.

It is arguable, and it was a recurrent theme of Haig's thinking, that the Cavalry Corps needed to be carefully husbanded until the 'big day'. As Home put it: 'If you think you may want Cavalry, it must be kept in a glass cage until the day arrives, no half measures are of any use.'[77] In the light of this it may seem profligate to commit a large part of the cavalry to an operation that it was already known would not be strategically decisive. However, it must be remembered that Haig was under pressure from a timetable not of his own making. The Easter deadline for the BEF to be ready for a combined offensive with the French in the south must have been a factor in his thinking. If cavalry could speed up the advance of the two southern armies into position to support this attack, then the commitment of these sparse resources would be justified. The removal over the winter of the Cavalry Corps' artillery and machine guns for service in the front line and the formation of pioneer battalions also showed that GHQ was not afraid to dip into the resources of the corps when it was convenient to do so. Equally, while the cavalry could ill afford the additional horse losses incurred during the campaign, there is no doubt that the opportunity for mounted action provided a boost to the morale not only of the divisions involved but to the whole arm. A similar although limited effect may have been produced in the ranks of the rest of the army, the appearance of horsemen still being viewed as a sign of forward progress.

As was alluded to earlier in this chapter, the March fighting is also significant in that it was one of the few occasions when Haig (whatever his motivations) provided the cavalry with a realistic and achievable set of operational objectives, which the cavalry were able to fulfill entirely. Thus judged against their operational goals as laid out by their commander they were entirely successful. Arguably this was not to happen again until Amiens in August 1918, and even there Haig widened his horizons at the last minute before the attack and inserted unrealistic additional objectives into the plan. While admittedly quite modest, this success has been almost entirely ignored by subsequent historians. There is one honourable exception, Cyril Falls, the Official Historian. His remarks on the contribution of mounted troops to the Hindenburg advance may be left as a final comment on the cavalry during this period:

> Practically all the work fell upon the infantry divisions because the corps cavalry regiments were not strong enough for much more than reconnaissance. It was perhaps unfortunate that the cavalry divisions were so carefully husbanded for the coming offensive during this phase; for the work done by the 5th Cavalry Division during the few days it was at the disposal of Fourth Army was brilliant.[78]

*   *   *

Meanwhile, as the cavalry cantered through the snow harassing the retreating Germans, plans were afoot for a renewed offensive. In the spring of 1917, as with the Somme offensive the year before, Haig as commander in chief of the BEF did not have a free hand to attack where he chose on the Western Front. He remained convinced that the decisive sector of the front was in the north, in Flanders, where an attack could clear the Germans from the Channel coast,[79] but this plan was not to be realised until the autumn. Meanwhile he was obliged to fight on in the south in cooperation with the French. The replacement of General Joffre at the head of the French armies, the appointment of General Nivelle and the politics which followed have been thoroughly examined elsewhere,[80] but the outcome of these discussions and the strategy for the coming months were laid out by GHQ in January 1917.[81] Essentially the BEF was to play a supporting rôle to the French in the south, and attacks would be launched in the Ancre Valley by Fifth Army, at Arras by Third Army (under General Allenby) and at Vimy Ridge by First Army. These would be limited affairs, intended only 'To pin the enemy to his ground, draw in his reserves, and thereby facilitate the task of the main French attack.'[82] General Nivelle had also successfully argued for the British to take over a substantial additional sector of the line south of the Somme battlefield in order to free up French divisions for the upcoming offensive. This extension of the line was to be the responsibility of Fourth Army (as was examined earlier in this chapter).

The task laid before Third Army at Arras was 'Firstly to seize the high ground about Monchy le Preux. Secondly, to turn the German defences south of Arras by a rapid advance in a south–easterly direction towards Croisilles and Bullecourt.'[83] This was to be the main thrust of the attack, and would be supported to the north by the capture of Vimy Ridge by First Army, and by the operations of Fifth Army in the south. Haig, as was his habit, called for proposals from his army commanders for the details of how these attacks should be undertaken.

Edmund Allenby, commander of Third Army, was an almost exact contemporary of Haig; both were 56 years old in 1917. His career had taken a path similar to Haig's, with Allenby following him into the post of Inspector General of Cavalry in 1910. He had gained significant combat experience in South Africa, both as a regimental officer and as a column commander, and in 1914 was appointed to lead all the British cavalry in France, as commander of the cavalry division of the original BEF. As the number of cavalry in France increased he rose to command of the Cavalry Corps (then of three divisions, with a separate Indian Cavalry Corps) in October 1914.[84] Perhaps unusually for the expanding BEF, all of these rôles were accommodated within his substantive pre-war rank of major general, which he had held since 1909. He led the corps through the costly defensive fighting of First Ypres over the winter of 1914/15, before moving on to command V Corps in May 1915, again leading that formation through the defensive fighting of Second Ypres.[85] Allenby took over command of Third Army in October 1915 when its former commander, Monro, was sent to the Dardanelles.[86] T.A. Heathcote described Allenby as 'the British Army's last and greatest captain of horse',[87] and it is probably true that he was the most experienced cavalry leader in the BEF. He was also to go on to famous success with mounted forces in Palestine. However, in the spring of 1917 Third Army, with the exception of its unsuccessful diversionary attack on 1 July 1916, had not done much fighting. Apart from his limited rôle on the Somme, Arras would be Allenby's first army-level set-piece battle, and his first major all-arms offensive action.

Opinions vary concerning the relationship between Haig and Allenby. Wavell claimed that 'He [Allenby] and Haig had never been congenial to each other',[88] while Lawrence James more recently described their relations as 'outwardly tranquil'.[89] Possibly, the similarity between the two men in their relative inarticulateness led to a degree of awkwardness in their meetings.[90] General Charteris was a witness to this, observing 'Allenby shares one peculiarity with Douglas Haig, he cannot explain verbally, with any lucidity at all, what his plans are. In a conference between the two of them it is rather amusing.'[91] He did, however, go on to point out that 'they understand one-another perfectly'.[92] In spite of their communication difficulties, James asserts that Haig found in Allenby 'a trustworthy general, in tune with his own thinking and second to none in his adherence to the principles of the aggressive spirit and wearing down the enemy'.[93] Indeed, Allenby had gained a reputation for perhaps being unnecessarily aggressive, or profligate with the lives of his men. Haldane, commander of the 3rd Division under Allenby at Ypres in 1915, remarked 'Everyone hates being in Vth Corps',[94] and Allenby himself was widely unpopular. Wavell naturally sought to excuse this, arguing that Allenby 'merely carried out the orders of superior authority', but tellingly went on: 'But Allenby's gospel of absolute loyalty to the orders of those above him made him wholehearted in his persistence to push in [sic] while any possible chance of success remained.'[95]

This 'aggressive spirit' is apparent in the 'Appreciation' produced by Third Army in February, outlining the Arras attack.[96] Allenby believed a degree of tactical surprise was possible, even in an operation on a large scale, and measures were included to hide preparations for the assault. A short but intense artillery bombardment of only 48 hours was also proposed. This combination of shock and surprise, Allenby believed, would soon carry the attacking troops through the German defences and into open country, and he advocated a change in thinking among his subordinates:

> At this period, the beginning of open warfare, it must be realised that the maintenance of the forward movement depends on the determination and power of direction of the commanders of sections, platoons, companies and battalions. The habit of digging a trench and getting into it, or of waiting for scientifically arranged artillery barrage before advancing, must be discarded.
>
> A slow advance will give time for German reinforcements to arrive. If the advance is continued with reasonable rapidity it is probable that the resistance will quickly lessen and that we shall reach places in which there are no German troops other than those running away in front of us.
>
> Artillery as well as infantry must shake off the habits of trench warfare. Battery commanders must be prepared to use their initiative and be able to make rapid reconnaissance followed by rapid movement ... direct fire will become common.[97]

Allenby's thinking about the fluid nature of the likely fighting is also in evidence in his remark that 'Staffs will move with the troops, and staff and other officers will require horses.'[98] The contrast between this optimistic all-out attack and the measured 'Bite and Hold' approach of Rawlinson a year before is obvious. It is tempting to suggest that this reflected Allenby's cavalry background as opposed to Rawlinson's infantry career, but this is probably less relevant than the contrast between Rawlinson's bitter knowledge of the Somme battles and Allenby's inexperience of this type of fighting, combined with his thrusting personality. This was the first offensive of this magnitude of which he had charge, and no doubt he wanted to make an impression.

In some respects he had good grounds for optimism. In particular, Third and First Armies were well supplied with artillery: over their 20km (12 mile) attack front they had twice the number of guns used on the 30km (18 mile) front of 1 July 1916.[99] Expertise, particularly in the use of creeping barrages, had also increased. Haig, however, was characteristically sceptical of the more innovative parts of the plan (as had been the case when he considered the proposed night attack on 14 July 1916). The 48-hour bombardment in particular was vetoed in favour of a more conventional four-day artillery preparation.[100]

As this planning progressed, the German withdrawal to the Hindenburg Line began to unfold. In some respects this ought to have rendered Haig and Nivelle's offensive plan obsolete, as the 'Bapaume salient' in the German line, which formed the original objective, no longer existed. Nivelle, however, remained adamant that the attacks at Arras by the British and on the Aisne by the French should be carried out as planned, with minor amendments, and with the (somewhat coincidental) objective of taking the Hindenburg Line position in flank at both ends. Curiously, Haig's principal concern became that further withdrawals by the Germans might take place before the offensive could be launched, preventing a sufficiently massive blow from being delivered against their forces.[101]

The Third Army infantry attack in the north, at Arras, would be supported by artillery and was divided into four main phases, corresponding with four objective lines:

- The 'Black Line', to be captured in the first few minutes, consisted of the German front-line trenches, and represented an advance of around 500–1,000 yards (450–900m);
- The 'Blue Line', to be attacked 2 hours after 'Zero Hour' included the German second line, a further 1,000 yards (900m) forward. At this point the advance would pause to allow artillery to move forward.
- The 'Brown Line' was to be attacked at 'Z plus 6 hours 40 minutes' and included the so-called 'Wancourt-Feuchy Line', an additional German defensive line some 2,200 yards (2km) beyond the 'Blue Line'.
- Finally, an advance would be made at 'Z plus 8 hours', before dusk, to a position on the 'Green Line'. This line did not reflect a specific German defensive position but was an arbitrary line drawn along the high ground beyond the village of Monchy-le-Preux, 7,000 yards (6.4km) beyond the infantry start line.

The ambitious nature of these infantry objectives is clear. They represent a significant penetration of the German position.

The rôle of the cavalry in the offensive was laid out in 'Instructions issued to the Cavalry Corps for offensive operations to be carried out by the Third Army', issued on 5 April 1917.[102] The corps was placed under Third Army command. Kavanagh, as corps commander, however, did not have unified control of all five divisions. The 1st Cavalry Division was allocated to support the Vimy Ridge attack under First Army command (later amended to GHQ Reserve), while the two Indian divisions were separated from the corps. The 4th Cavalry Division was attached to Gough's Fifth Army in support of the Bullecourt attack to the south (which was to follow the Arras and Vimy Ridge offensives), and the 5th Cavalry Division was held in GHQ Reserve. Third Army was therefore immediately supported by the remaining two divisions of the Cavalry Corps, the 2nd and 3rd, along with an attached infantry division (the 17th). The Cavalry Corps objectives lay beyond those of the infantry, and were defined as a line astride the Arras–Cambrai road stretching from Riencourt in the south to Etaing in the north, a front some 8km (5 miles) wide and some 16km (10 miles) beyond the initial British front line. This advance was to be attempted in the last hours of Z-Day, after the infantry had reached the Green Line and formed defensive flanks on either side to the north and south.

When compared with the cavalry objectives for 1 July 1916 the plans for the cavalry at Arras are superficially similar. Both required an advance by two divisions astride the main axial road through the battle front, to a depth of around 16km (10 miles). However, as noted earlier, there was less discussion at Arras of onward exploitation deep into the enemy's rear areas. The contrast with the later operations of 1916 is also discernible in the movement timetable for the cavalry. The 2nd and 3rd Cavalry Divisions were expected to be in their 'final positions of readiness' astride the Cambrai road at Tilloy les Moufflaines 'by the time the infantry attacks are expected to reach the Brown Line', i.e. around Z plus 6 hours. Indeed, the whole movement was intended to be more or less simultaneous. Instructions to the Cavalry Corps stated:

> It is the intention to issue this order ['Cavalry advance'] in such time as will enable the leading brigades of the cavalry divisions to pass through the Green Line as soon as, or very shortly after, the infantry reach that line.[103]

Further, unlike the previous year, when the cavalry had waited even in its most advanced positions of readiness behind the infantry start line, the final position of readiness was defined actually beyond the German front-line (Black Line) position. This was certainly an innovative step, but the wisdom of pushing so many cavalry so far forward before the outcome of the infantry attack was certain is not beyond criticism, as subsequent events were to prove. Allenby and Kavanagh were forced to strike a balance between placing mounted troops close enough to the battle to be of use, and potentially stranding them, out of supply, in the chaotic forward area of an on-going attack. A recognition of this potential supply problem can be seen in the orders to all arms to carry iron rations for three days, and the subsequently rather notorious order for the infantry to save weight by leaving their greatcoats behind.[104] The cavalry were issued three days' oats for the horses (around 8kg (20lb)), as well as 190 rounds of rifle ammunition.[105] In the event, the impact of this extra weight on already undernourished horses was severe.

The plan also suffered from the same command and control problems as had occurred the previous year. The final position of readiness of the two cavalry divisions was of less importance to their ability to advance than their authority to do so. Once again, instead of this being automatically timetabled, the order 'Cavalry advance' would come from Third Army via Cavalry Corps Head-quarters. The likelihood of this order being issued in a timely fashion and quickly communicated to the troops concerned was very low.

Two final features of the cavalry orders for the offensive are worthy of note. The first of these is a page of 'Variations' appended to the 'Instructions issued to the Cavalry Corps'; this envisioned possible outcomes of the attack other than that initially outlined and offered compensating changes to the plan. Of particular interest was the 'Second variation'. This gave instructions for routes to be reconnoitred so that in the event of the failure of VI Corps' attack south of the river Scarpe, but a corresponding success by XVII Corps to the north, the 2nd and 3rd Cavalry Divisions could be re-routed to exploit north of the river. The practicality of this manoeuvre in the middle of an attack is questionable, but the appearance of such flexible, contingency-based planning is significant. Such a change of plan would also be hamstrung by the length of the chain of command between the troops concerned, and those at Third Army deciding to make the change. This factor was to become apparent during the course of the battle.

Secondly, in operation orders of 8 April[106] details are given of army-level heavy artillery cooperation with the Cavalry Corps, both from Third and Fifth Armies, using long-range guns to 'shoot' the cavalry on to its distant objectives, the villages of Boiry, Vis and Fontaine les Croiselles. This was a good idea in principle, but was to prove unsuccessful, the lack of controllable artillery support for the cavalry divisions becoming a significant factor in their sub-sequent performance.

*   *   *

The Cavalry Corps began April 1917 in winter billets near the Channel coast. Two days before the start of the attack, scheduled for 9 April, the three cavalry divisions committed to the Arras battle began their movements (the 1st Cavalry Division supporting First Army, and the 2nd and 3rd Cavalry Divisions supporting Third Army). These moves were originally scheduled for 6 April, but were delayed until the 7th in the light of a 24-hour postponement of the whole operation requested by the French.[107] Initially the divisions closed up and moved to positions to the west of Arras. From north to south these were:

- 1st Cavalry Division: the valley of the Ternoise, north-west of St Pol (HQ at Croix);

- 3rd Cavalry Division: the valley of the Canche, from Frevent west as far as Conchy (HQ at Monchel); and
- 2nd Cavalry Division: the Authie valley from Doulens west to Auxi-le-Château (HQ at Wavans).[108]

In the case of the 2nd and 3rd Divisions these moves simply followed the river valleys which had formed the units' billeting areas, the Canche and the Authie. Each river valley offered water, and lay on a direct road towards Arras, the heads of the divisions lying an average of 30km (18 miles) from the city.

On 8 April ('Z–1') the three divisions closed up further and advanced to holding positions closer to Arras. The 1st Division moved to Frevin-Capelle, 10km (6 miles) to the north-west of Arras, the 3rd Division to Gouy-en-Artois, 14km (9 miles) to the west, and the 2nd Division to Pas-en-Artois, 25km (16 miles) to the south-west.[109]

The infantry attack began at 5.30am on 9 April. Significant gains were made by all three attacking corps on the Third Army front, XVII Corps to the north of the Scarpe, and VI and VII Corps to the south of it. Indeed, Falls observed in the *Official History* that 'the first day's operations of the battles of Arras were among the heaviest blows struck by British arms in the Western theatre of war'.[110] The greatest advance, some 5km (3½ miles), took place on the XVII Corps front immediately north of the Scarpe where the 9th and 4th Divisions advanced to within a few hundred yards of the final Green Line objective beyond Fampoux (the furthest advance yet in a single day in the trench war).[111] In the centre VI Corps completely overwhelmed the German first-line defences and captured a number of guns in 'Battery Valley' to the rear of this position. Unfortunately, delays in the attack meant that the artillery barrage outran the infantry advance and the attack mostly halted short of the last major German defensive position, the Wancourt-Feuchy or Brown Line. Only the 15th Division on the left (north) of the VI Corps attack was able to penetrate the Wancourt-Feuchy defences and occupy a long north–south ridge, which became known as Orange Hill, but this was only achieved late in the day and little could be done to exploit this success.[112]

In accordance with the plan,[113] the two cavalry divisions under Third Army command moved off on the morning of the 9th to positions of readiness. The 2nd Cavalry Division advanced to the suburb of Ronville, immediately behind the British line to the south-east of Arras, arriving by 9.30am, and the 3rd Cavalry Division halted on the racecourse to the north-west of Arras by 10.00am.[114] In the light of the infantry successes, the order 'Cavalry advance' was issued by Third Army. This was received at Cavalry Corps HQ by telephone at 2.40pm and wired to the divisions shortly after.[115] In response the 3rd Cavalry Division moved around the north of Arras and on to cavalry track A, the northernmost of the cavalry tracks prepared through the British front line. The 2nd Cavalry Division advanced from Ronville via tracks C and D further to the south. Each division crossed the original front-line trenches via extensions to the tracks completed by dismounted parties earlier in the afternoon.[116] Both were in position in their 'Final positions of readiness' at Tilloy, astride the Arras–Cambrai road and beyond the German first-line positions by 4.00pm, ready to advance towards their objectives beyond the Green Line.[117] Unfortunately, with the Brown Line defences still largely unbreached, such an advance was impossible and at 8.20pm the divisions were ordered to fall back to the west and south of Arras. The 2nd Cavalry Division moved back to the Crinchon valley to the south-west of the town while the 3rd Cavalry Division circled back around to the north to billets between the St Pol road and the river Scarpe[118] and on the racecourse.[119]

No cavalry support had been assigned to XVII Corps north of the Scarpe in the original plan, except as one of the 'variations' included as an appendix. At a meeting during the afternoon Allenby, ignoring the planned 'variation', asked Haig, in view of the successful advance on this front, for the use of a brigade from the 1st Cavalry Division to support XVII Corps.[120] Up to this time this division had been held in GHQ reserve at Frevin-Capelle, 10km (6 miles) north-west of Arras. (In fact the cavalry of this division had already been detached to support the Canadian Corps of First Army to the north but was not brought into action.)[121] Haig agreed, but at this point the rather tortuous nature of the command structure became apparent. Although the 1st Cavalry Division was in GHQ reserve, it was still nominally under the command of the Cavalry Corps (the remainder of which was under Third Army command). Thus orders from GHQ to the 1st Cavalry Division to detach a brigade to Third Army went through Cavalry Corps Headquarters, which was telephoned by GHQ at 4.15pm, and in turn rang the 1st Division with a warning order. Corps received a confirmatory GHQ wire at 4.55pm,[122] but this was not passed on; instead the 1st Division sought direct confirmation from GHQ, but this was not received by the division until 6.15pm,[123] by which time it was too late for anything significant to be done. The cavalry was moved up as far as Athies, but got no further.[124] The loss of this opportunity for exploitation was felt keenly by the infantry commanders of the 4th and 9th Divisions.[125] Brigadier General Carton de Wiart, himself a cavalry officer although at the time in command of the 12th Infantry Brigade (part of the 4th Division), recalled: 'We could have taken many more prisoners and much valuable ground if only cavalry had been available, but as it was we could see the guns being driven away into the distance, to be used against us another day.'[126]

Once again the length of the chain of command had prevented local commanders from exploiting situations where a rapid deployment of mounted troops might have made a significant difference.

Only one cavalry success – small-scale, but significant – is recorded from 9 April. The Northamptonshire Yeomanry were serving as the corps cavalry regiment of VI Corps, and accompanied by the corps' 6th Cyclist Battalion formed the Corps Mounted Troops. Their orders were to advance behind the 15th Division attack, and then pass through the infantry and seize the river crossings over the Scarpe at Fampoux. These crossings would be vital in retaining contact between VI Corps south of the river and XVII Corps to the north, as the two corps advanced on their respective Green Line objectives.

When Feuchy village (the northern end of the Brown Line on the VI Corps front) was captured by the 15th Division, at around 5.00pm, the yeomanry under Lieutenant Colonel Seymour, accompanied by A Company of the cyclists, advanced through the infantry. Continuing along the river bank for a further 1km (½ mile) the yeomanry reached the crossroads south of Fampoux village. B Squadron under Major Benyon turned left towards Fampoux and, despite coming under sniper fire from the houses north of the river, drove off the snipers, captured two field guns and 'made good the road bridge'. Patrols were also sent across the river to link up with the forward elements of the 4th Division north of the river. Meanwhile C Squadron under Major Nickalls advanced further east to secure the railway bridge over the river, capturing four further guns and a number of prisoners. The two squadrons then bivouacked overnight, the horses remaining saddled, in the marshes beside the river.[127] The cyclist company had been held up somewhat by the bad going along the river bank but arrived in time to throw out outposts to the south-east on the Monchy road, and to help secure the position overnight.[128]

*   *   *

Although by nightfall on 9 April no units of Third Army had reached the Green Line, their final first-day objectives, Allenby was content that the battle was going well, and was keen to push on and exploit the success of the first day. Orders were given for a renewed attack at 8.00am on the 10th in which all three corps were to secure the remainder of the Brown Line positions.[129] Orders were received from Third Army at the Cavalry Corps HQ at 11.30pm to be ready to move to support this attack at 7.00am.[130] However, VII Corps on the right (south) of the line was held up by continuing fighting in the Hindenburg Line trenches opposite its attack, and asked for a delay. A new start time was therefore agreed of 12 noon; this was telephoned to Cavalry Corps HQ at 4.10am on the 10th and duly passed on to the cavalry divisions.[131] While allowing more time for the infantry to reorganise and for artillery to be brought up, the late start reduced the opportunities for cavalry exploitation. As Falls put it, 'The prospects for the cavalry going through before dark were thus diminished.'[132] The attack on 10 April was successful in as much as the remainder of the Brown Line position, and Orange and Chapel Hills beyond were captured.[133] Further advance, however, proved difficult. The ground before Monchy-le-Preux was swept by fire not only from the village itself but also from positions to the north of the Scarpe around Mount Pleasant and Roeux. As a result the infantry attack was halted by nightfall on the forward slopes of Orange Hill and as far east as Les Fosses Farm.[134]

To the north of the Scarpe General Fergusson, commanding XVII Corps, somewhat belatedly considered that there might be a 'favourable' opportunity for cavalry along the north bank of the river from Fampoux towards Greenland Hill, supported by the 4th Infantry Division attacking on their right towards Mount Pleasant and Roeux.[135] Accordingly at 11.15am command of the whole of the 1st Cavalry Division was restored to the Cavalry Corps and Third Army from GHQ (excepting of course the 9th Brigade, still supporting the Canadians to the north). Formal orders for the operation were issued as part of Cavalry Corps Operation Order No. 4 at 11.45am.[136] Major General Mullens' 1st Cavalry Division set off from its overnight position at Fermont-Capelle 10km (6 miles) north-west of Arras at around 1.45pm,[137] closing up to the cavalry which had moved forward the previous day, and with the 5th Dragoon Guards (of 1st Brigade) as advanced guard. Progress was slow. The 1st Cavalry Brigade recorded that 'the road along the north bank of the Scarpe was not only very bad, but the congestion of traffic going both ways caused numerous blocks'.[138] When Brigadier General Makins, in command of the 1st Brigade, reached Fampoux at 4.30pm it was clear after consultation with the infantry commanders of the 4th Division that their supporting attack had made no headway against fire from Roeux chemical works and the railway embankment. Thus the cavalry attack stood no chance of success.

There was no doubt that the cavalry could not advance – dismounted action would have had no more possible result than the infantry attack, and a mounted action was evidently not feasible. There was no scope: the troops were in a 'regular neck of a bottle, with no chance of outflanking movement'.[139]

The attack was called off and the division bivouacked where it stood, strung out between St Nicholas (north of Arras) and Fampoux. The attack was intended to be renewed at noon on the following day, 11 April, but the continuing opposition from Roeux made significant advances impossible and the operation was cancelled again at 6.00pm.[140]

For the two cavalry divisions supporting the Third Army advance south of the Scarpe the delay in the infantry attack from 8.00am until noon gave a welcome respite. Retirement on the night of the 9th had been very slow against the flow of traffic moving up in support of the attack, and most units had not reached their bivouac positions until the early hours of the morning of the 10th. The 5th Cavalry Brigade recorded that their last unit in, E Battery RHA, did not arrive until 5.30am.[141] The weather had also deteriorated. Monday had been cold but fine, but overnight the wind rose, bringing heavy showers of sleet and snow.[142] The 4th Cavalry Brigade, moving in support of the 3rd and 5th Brigades of the 2nd Cavalry Division, recorded on 9 April that, 'Owing to the darkness and the state of the Cavalry track' some units did not reach bivouac positions until 3.00am, 'weather conditions miserable'.[143] Likewise on 10 April, 'Weather conditions were abominable and could not have been worse.'[144]

As daylight came on 10 April the cavalry divisions turned laboriously around and set out again on the tracks north and south of Arras. The 3rd Cavalry Division was to advance north of the Cambrai road with Monchy as its immediate objective. The 2nd Cavalry Division was to advance south of the road towards Hill 90, behind the southern end of the Wancourt-Feuchy position. Orders were issued by telephone from Cavalry Corps HQ in the early hours of the morning, and formalised in Cavalry Corps Operation Order No. 4, issued at 11.45am on the 10th.[145]

North of the Cambrai road the 3rd Cavalry Division was telephoned by the Cavalry Corps HQ at around 11.00am. It was reported that infantry of the 37th Division had been seen in Monchy-le-Preux, and that consequently the leading brigades of the 3rd Cavalry Division should advance.[146] Accordingly, Major General Vaughan, commanding the 3rd Cavalry Division, ordered an advance by the 8th Brigade north of Monchy towards Boiry-Notre-Dame, and by the 6th Brigade south of Monchy towards Vis-en-Artois. The 7th Brigade would remain in support. These movements began around 2.30pm.[147] Throughout the afternoon the 3rd Cavalry Division received reports of the faltering progress of the 37th Division towards Monchy, coupled with optimistic urgings from Kavanagh at Cavalry Corps HQ to push on and become involved in the battle at the earliest opportunity. At 3.40pm the Divisional diary records 'Patrols in touch with Infantry reported that 37th Division held up at western exits to Monchy le Preux, ... [village] believed to be held by only two battalions which 37th Division hoped soon to dislodge.' Meanwhile at 3.50pm 'Corps commander gave verbal orders on telephone that troops on south were pushing on well and that he wished division to push on rapidly and take risks.'[148] These telephone interventions were to become a common feature of Kavanagh's command style, not only at Arras but also in later battles. Unfortunately, he was rarely in command of the full facts at corps HQ and his interventions were often unhelpful.

By 5.00pm it was apparent to those at the front that the infantry attack had stalled short of Monchy. The 3rd Cavalry Division reported to Cavalry Corps at 5.20pm: 'Our infantry have not got Monchy.'[149] To get the attack moving again, the 37th Division suggested that the cavalry 'gallop' the ridge to the north of the village around Pelves Mill, as machine-gun fire from this area had the infantry pinned down.[150] (To gallop a position was to attack mounted towards a geographical feature, not knowing whether or not it contained enemy troops; it was as fast as, but less formal than, a 'Charge', which had a specific body of enemy as its target.) By this time the lead elements of the 8th Cavalry Brigade had advanced as far as the forward slopes of Orange Hill and were coming under fire from Monchy and from across the river to the north-east. At around 6.00pm an attempt to advance was made by a squadron each of the 10th Hussars (under Captain Gordon-Canning) and the Essex Yeomanry (under Major Buxton). The two squadrons galloped as far as Pelves Mill,[151] but were driven back by artillery and machine-gun fire. Fortunately their retreat was covered by a brief snowstorm. Casualties were also reduced by the Germans' use of high explosive shells, which largely buried themselves in the ground, instead of airburst shrapnel.[152] Meanwhile to the south of the 8th Brigade, the 6th Cavalry Brigade was supporting the infantry attack immediately to the west of Monchy, but this too was held up due to fire from the village and the brigade could make no progress.[153]

The armoured cars of the 7th LAC Battery (attached to the 3rd Cavalry Division) also made an attempt to advance, pushing down the Cambrai road. This proved extremely difficult as the road surface was shell damaged and blocked by fallen trees. The weather also left the going very muddy and falling snow blocked the drivers' vision slits. The battery diary records 'with the exception of the drivers the personnel of the cars was constantly outside guiding and making up the road surface'. Some Germans were engaged around La Bergère crossroads, but with nightfall the attempt was abandoned, one car having to be left at Les Fosses Farm, stuck in a shell-hole.[154]

Meanwhile, south of the Cambrai Road Major General Greenly's 2nd Cavalry Division was at its position of readiness at Tilloy by 12.30pm. The division advanced with the 5th Brigade on the left towards the south end of the Wancourt-Feuchy line, and with the 3rd Brigade on the right towards Hill 90, at around 3.00pm. The 4th Brigade remained in support. However, as Hill 90 remained in German hands little progress was made.[155]

At 6.00pm the 37th Division reported that the 'situation west of Monchy was not rosy',[156] but this fact, although clear to those at the front, seems not to have been appreciated by the higher commanders. At 6.35pm a meeting took place between Allenby and Kavanagh at which it was agreed that the cavalry should try to take Monchy that night, in cooperation with the 37th Division. Kavanagh once again telephoned Vaughan at the 3rd Cavalry Division:

> Corps Commander stated on telephone 6.35pm that both he and the Army Commander agreed that the Cavalry should make a determined effort to get Monchy tonight, as great importance was attached to the capture of Monchy. He considered that it was an opportunity for Cavalry to achieve important results by working wide round the flank in co-operation with infantry.[157]

This was clearly an overly optimistic appreciation of the situation, although it should be noted that reports were very slow in reaching Cavalry Corps HQ. Formal word of the failure of the 8th Cavalry Brigade's push on Pelves Mill, attempted at 6.00pm, did not reach corps until 8.45pm.[158] In the event there was no opportunity for an infantry advance due to continuing shelling and machine-gun fire, and indeed some battalions of the 37th Division did not receive the attack orders until after the preparatory artillery barrage had already lifted.[159] Thus no attack materialised.

The 3rd Cavalry Division retired at nightfall and bivouacked north of the Cambrai road and west of the Wancourt-Feuchy Line trenches and Orange Hill. No hot food was available and the ground was too soft to picket, so the men sheltered in shell holes holding the horses. It snowed through most of the night. Corporal of Horse Lloyd spent an uncomfortable night with the 7th Cavalry Brigade: 'We tied our horses in bunches and sat down anywhere just waiting for orders. Night fell, and some of us scrambled into holes and corners trying to sleep. The cold was severe.'[160] The 8th Cavalry Brigade was subject to overnight shelling, the 10th Hussars in particular suffered nine men and fifty-one horses killed.[161] South of the Cambrai road General Greenly, commanding the 2nd Cavalry Division, gave his brigadiers the choice of staying put overnight, or retiring, on the understanding that they would return ready to resume the attack at 5.00am on the 11th. The three brigades chose to stay put, and bedded down in shell-holes where they were, spread out between Tilloy and Neuville Vitasse.[162] They were resupplied overnight by packhorse with 6lb (3kg) of oats per horse.[163] The 5th Brigade in particular came under significant shell-fire during the night; unable to redeploy due to the darkness and the amount of wire lying around their position, they suffered over a hundred human casualties as well as losing a number of horses.[164] Overall it was a cold and miserable end to a second frustrating day for the cavalry.

*   *   *

As day dawned on 11 April, the third day of the offensive, Allenby still believed that an opportunity remained for a decisive blow. Indeed, his orders for the day suggest that he thought a collapse of enemy resistance was imminent. A telegram to corps commanders ran: 'The AC wishes all troops to understand that the Third Army is now pursuing a defeated enemy and that risks must be freely taken.'[165] How closely this represented the real situation is a moot point. The offensive was to be resumed by all three attacking corps at 5.00am. Orders for the Cavalry Corps were issued at 11.45pm on the 10th.[166] One cavalry division was to support each corps attack, the 1st Division supporting XVII Corps north of the Scarpe, the 3rd Division supporting VI Corps between the river and the Cambrai road, and the 2nd Division supporting VII Corps south of the road. The cavalry advance was to begin at 6.00am: 'Each [infantry] division will have one [cavalry] brigade close up behind, and in close touch with, the attacking infantry.'[167] Ambitious objectives were set, not only to capture the Green Line of 9 April, but to push on as far as the final German position, the so-called 'Drocourt-Queant Line' (nearly 10km (6 miles) east of Monchy), and link up with Fifth Army, attacking that morning from the south at Bullecourt.[168]

The inability of the 1st Cavalry Division to advance north of the Scarpe has already been described. The activities of the 2nd Cavalry Division on the south side of the Cambrai road are equally quickly dealt with. VII Corps to the south was tasked with the capture of Hill 90, and when this attack failed no opportunities remained for the division to advance. The 2nd Cavalry Division remained in its overnight positions and came under renewed shellfire on the 11th, suffering significant casualties among the horses, before the whole division was withdrawn to its forming up positions in the Crinchon Valley at 4.50pm.[169]

Between the Cambrai road and the Scarpe the attack was resumed by VI Corps at 5.00am, supported by the 3rd Cavalry Division. The 15th Division attacked between Monchy and the Scarpe, while the 37th Division attacked Monchy village itself. During the fighting of the previous day, 10 April, the German line to the north of Monchy had been held by the *Reserve Battalion* of the *162nd Regiment* of the *17th Reserve Division* holding a line along the Monchy–Roeux road. This was a relatively fresh battalion. The line to the south through Monchy itself and along the Wancourt road was held by remnants of the other battalions of the *162nd* and *163rd Regiments*, both of which had suffered heavily in the defence of Neuville Vitasse on 9 April, and subsequently in holding the southern part of the Wancourt-Feuchy line. They had thus already been driven out of two previous defensive positions and their divisional artillery had been almost entirely captured or destroyed.

However, by the morning of 11 April the German position in Monchy had been reinforced overnight by the *3rd Bavarian Division*. In particular the *Ist Battalion, 17th Bavarian Regiment* took over positions in the village. Unfortunately for them, as these positions were taken over at night the Bavarians had little chance to arrange a proper defence. As a result the Bavarian battalion was virtually destroyed in the 37th Division attack at dawn. By 7.30am elements of both the 15th and 37th Divisions were holding positions in, and to the north of, Monchy village; the 13th Battalion, Kings Royal Rifle Corps and 13th Battalion, Rifle Brigade of 111th Brigade (37th Division) occupied the village, while the 10th and 11th Battalions of the Highland Light Infantry (15th Division) held positions to the north.[170] Significantly, however, unlike the guns of the garrison of the village the previous day, the artillery of the *3rd Bavarian Division* survived intact, and was deployed in a great arc behind Monchy ready to pour fire on to the village.[171]

Vaughan's 3rd Cavalry Division took up a position behind the infantry attack ready to exploit around the flanks of Monchy. Their objectives were Pelves Mill on the left, and Bois Du Vert and Hill 100 in the centre, approximately 1,000m (1,100yds) beyond the village. At 7.10am the 8th Cavalry Brigade learnt that the 112th Brigade had a foothold in the western part of Monchy and reported this to the 3rd Cavalry Division.[172] Later, at 7.55am, the 6th Cavalry Brigade to the south passed on a similar report: '112 Brigade report Monchy has fallen, also considers it safe to say that La Bergère has also fallen.' Further patrol reports from the 3rd Dragoon Guards of 6th Brigade suggested that the village was not wholly in British hands but that it was at least partly captured.[173] In response to this news Brigadier General Bulkeley-Johnson, commanding the 8th Cavalry Brigade, ordered his brigade to advance on their objectives to the north of and beyond the village. He issued verbal orders to the brigade:

> Seize the ridge Bois des Aubepines to Pelves Mill; Essex Yeomanry on the right, Tenth Hussars on the left. When this is achieved, proceed to first objective, namely Bois du Sart – east end of Pelves, including Hatchet and Jigsaw woods . . . to each leading regiment two subsections machine guns. Rest of Brigade to follow in this order, G battery RHA, Blues, remainder of Machine Gun Squadron.[174]

He also reported the advance to the 3rd Cavalry Division: 'In consequence of information that Monchy is now taken I am sending off Tenth and Essex to try to get their objectives. They are both going south of Orange Hill as MG fire from the river is as bad as ever and holding up the infantry.'[175]

In the light of this advance, Brigadier General Harman of the 6th Cavalry Brigade to the south ordered forward his own lead regiment, the 3rd Dragoon Guards, to conform with the 8th Cavalry Brigade's move and to cover their southern flank.

These three regiments moved forward over prepared trench crossings in the Wancourt-Feuchy line at around 8.30am. The 10th Hussars and Essex Yeomanry of the 8th Brigade were on the left (north), intending to circle around between Monchy and the Scarpe, while the 3rd Dragoon Guards of the 6th Brigade headed south of the village. Emerging south of Orange Hill they advanced at the gallop, in line of troop columns, with one troop advanced as scouts.[176] An advance in brigade strength like this was a rare enough sight to make a significant impression on the watching infantry. Captain Cuddeford of the Highland Light Infantry witnessed this advance:

> During a lull in the snowstorm an excited shout was raised that our cavalry were coming up! Sure enough, away behind us, moving quickly in extended order down the slope of Orange Hill was line

upon line of mounted men covering the whole extent of the hillside as far as we could see. It was a thrilling moment for us infantrymen, who had never dreamt that we should see a real cavalry charge, which was evidently what was intended.[177]

It was at this moment that a decisive point was reached in the battle. The objectives of the cavalry advance lay beyond Monchy, and the squadrons had intended to skirt around the village, but after their experience the day before Bulkeley-Johnson had ordered that if fire was encountered from north of the river, the 8th Brigade should swing right and head directly for Monchy. The subsequent death of the brigadier later that morning has denied history his own account of this decision, but it was recalled by Captain Gordon-Canning of the 10th Hussars, who had led the unsuccessful reconnaissance north of Monchy the day before:

> On the morning of 11th I definitely said that it would be impossible to advance via the low ground on Pelves Mill; the advance must be made via Monchy and then directed NE, along high ground in order to outflank Pelves and Pelves Mill. This was agreed to by B.J.[178]

The advancing regiments were indeed brought under a heavy fire coming from Mount Pleasant Wood across the river and both regiments veered right into the village.[179] After a brief conference in the village square between Lieutenant Colonel Whitmore of the Essex Yeomanry and Lieutenant Colonel Hardwick of the 10th Hussars, one squadron of Essex Yeomanry advanced north-east along the Pelves road, while the lead 10th Hussars squadron moved north along the road to Pelves Mill. The remaining Germans in the village fled, but it was found to be impossible to advance beyond the village due to fire from German positions to the east and north. Lieutenant Colonel Hardwick, commanding the 10th Hussars, took a squadron around the north side of the village but he was driven back into the cover of the village via the château park on the northern side. Hardwick was severely wounded in the course of this manoeuvre and Lieutenant Colonel Whitmore of the Essex Yeomanry took command of all forces in the village.[180] These forces were quite substantial as in spite of the heavy fire received by the leading squadrons, and their inability to advance beyond the village, the remaining squadrons of both regiments had followed on closely, and rather than rallying back to Orange Hill had followed on into the village. Thus probably almost a thousand men and horses were packed into the village. Private Garnett of the Essex Yeomanry, who was at the time serving with the 8th Brigade Machine-Gun Squadron, provided a vivid account of the advance on and occupation of Monchy,

> I was riding a little horse called Nimrod and leading another with a pack saddle on his back loaded with boxes of machine-gun

ammunition. We had not gone far when a huge shell burst to my right. Someone yelled 'Garnett's pack-horse has broken its leg!' Our Corporal, Harold Mugford, shouted at me to keep going but the pack-horse fell, and as I was holding on to him so tightly, he pulled me out of the saddle. I let go and managed to stay on Nimrod, regaining my balance, but then my saddle slipped under his stomach. I rode on, hanging on for dear life, on his bare back. All the rest of the column had left me and, seeing a huge hawthorn tree, I got behind it and adjusted the saddle. I remounted and rode on alone to where the others had gone and quickly entered the village where I saw a dead pack-horse with ammunition on his back, so I dismounted and took a box. Galloping along the street I soon reached the building marked 'chateau' on my map, where I was stopped by our officer who demanded my box of ammunition and told me to follow him. By now there were a few of us and the shelling had become very heavy, so the officer ordered us to lie down under the shelter of a wall. As I was lying in a gap between two cottages, I immediately got up, still holding my horse, and lay down under the wall of the cottage opposite. I had not been there long when a light shell came through the gap in the cottages and cut down the officer and most of the others. Nimrod was terrified and reared up violently, dragging me along the street for some yards until I was forced to let go. I never saw him again after that.[181]

The infantry of the 37th Division in Monchy were found to have suffered heavily. Virtually all the officers had been killed, and a party of only about seventy exhausted men was found in the western part of the village; many were sheltering in cellars rather than making an active defence.[182] The infantrymen were set to collecting wounded, digging, and salvaging tools and ammunition while the cavalry took over the defence of the village. The Vickers guns of the machine gun squadron and the regimental Hotchkiss were deployed on the north-eastern, eastern and south-eastern exits to the village, two strong-points being constructed at the north-eastern apex of the château park and on the eastern side of the Pelves road.[183] Unfortunately a number of the tool-pack horses had been lost in the advance, so fortifying the position proved difficult; in addition, as described in the earlier account, both the machine gun squadron and the regiments had lost a number of machine-gun ammunition packs, so rounds were in short supply.[184] The Essex Yeomanry made up for this loss by salvaging two infantry Lewis guns and bringing them into action.[185]

By around 9.30am the village had been placed in a reasonable state of defence, but around this time German shelling of the village also started to intensify. While out in the open the effect of German shelling had been greatly nullified by the softness of the ground, but this was not the case among the streets and buildings and the cavalry started to suffer heavily as a result. Large numbers of led horses filled the streets of Monchy, and sought cover on the western side of the village. These streets were soon blocked with dead and injured horses.[186]

Meanwhile on the right of the 8th Cavalry Brigade the 6th Cavalry Brigade advanced as far as the Monchy–Wancourt road south of Monchy, with the 3rd Dragoon Guards leading. The regiment advanced with B Squadron in front (led by Captain Holroyd-Smith), with one troop of the squadron in line and the remaining three troops in line of troop columns behind, followed by C Squadron (Major Cliff). On reaching the road, the dragoons came upon a party of Germans attempting to dig in, in front of four guns. These troops fled, leaving the guns.[187] Very few friendly infantry were to be seen and the brigade came under fire from Guemappe, 1,000m (1,100 yards) to the south-east, so they took up dismounted positions along the road, deploying their Hotchkiss guns, and supported by the Vickers of the attached machine gun section.[188]

Towards 9.00am, in an attempt to assess the situation, Brigadier Bulkeley-Johnson, commanding the 8th Cavalry Brigade, advanced with his staff as far as the Monchy–Fampoux road, but here he was killed. As a result, command of the brigade fell to Lord Tweedmouth, commanding officer of the Blues, although in fact with the 10th Hussars and the yeomanry in Monchy, Tweedmouth's command was limited for practical purposes to his own regiment, the brigade RHA battery and the remainder of the brigade MG squadron.[189]

At around 10.30am the 63rd Brigade (the reserve brigade of the 37th Division) was ordered up to reinforce the village. These troops were able to advance only as far as an area of German practice trenches north-west of Monchy, where the bulk of the brigade took cover, feeding small parties into Monchy as opportunities arose during breaks in the firing.[190] Also at around this time the three batteries of horse artillery belonging to the 3rd Cavalry Division – C, G and K Batteries of the IV Brigade RHA – came into action in support of the 6th and 8th Brigades. Deploying in the valley between the south end of Orange Hill and Monchy itself, they fired protective barrages beyond the village,[191] no fewer than 450 rounds per battery being fired in the course of the day.[192]

As the morning wore on, the situation in the village became grim, especially for the exposed horses. Indeed Lieutenant Swire of the Essex Yeomanry had to be specially detailed for the task of shooting wounded horses in the crowded streets.[193] Colonel Whitmore reported at 11.10am:

> Have sent several messages conveying all information of EY and XRH. What remains of those regiments are holding on to the north-east, east and southern exits of the village. Require both MGs and ammunition. Am afraid we have had many casualties. Counter-attack

expected. Colonel Hardwick and several officers wounded. Reinforcements required as reserve. Majority horses casualties.[194]

An attempt was made at around 11.20am by the Royal Horse Guards (Blues),
with the remaining four guns of the 8th Machine Gun Squadron, to try to
reinforce the village but they were forced back by the weight of fire falling
around the village. Two gun-pack horses were hit and the guns lost in the
snow.[195] At this point Vaughan, in command of the 3rd Cavalry Division,
realised that no further progress was likely and a decision was made for the
division to 'strengthen any position they now hold' using machine guns and
to try to withdraw the remaining horses.[196] Those of the 6th Cavalry Brigade
(3rd Dragoon Guards) to the south of the village escaped without great loss,
but the horses of the 8th Cavalry Brigade were heavily shelled and many more
were killed during attempts to withdraw them.

A further despatch from Whitmore in Monchy at 11.45am read, 'We are
badly in need of reinforcements and machine-guns.'[197] In response to this a
second attempt was made at around 2.00pm by A Squadron of the Royal Horse
Guards and the remaining subsection of machine guns to reinforce the village.
No. 1 MG Section did make it into the village, although the accompanying
squadron of the Blues was forced back, perhaps fortuitously as their additional
presence in the village would probably have served only to provide further
targets for the German guns.

Similar concerns were expressed by the 3rd Dragoon Guards on the right
(6th Cavalry Brigade) front. Fearing being outflanked to the south, where
the line was held only by a party of about thirty infantrymen, survivors of the
morning attack, they sent a message at around 2.30pm asking for reinforcements. One squadron of the North Somerset Yeomanry (6th Cavalry Brigade)
was despatched, accompanied by four machine-guns and by regimental tool-
pack horses.[198] An initial attempt to advance mounted was met with heavy
machine-gun fire, but a second attempt on foot leading pack animals only was
successful, reinforcing the 3rd Dragoon Guards on the Wancourt road.[199]

By mid-afternoon it was appreciated at all levels of command that the
attack around Monchy had stalled. At 5.00pm Kavanagh at Cavalry Corps HQ
ordered the withdrawal of the unengaged parts of the corps (the 2nd Cavalry
Division, and the 7th Brigade of the 3rd Cavalry Division) to their former
positions to the west of Arras. The remaining brigades in Monchy were to withdraw 'when the situation permits'.[200] Indeed, despite the fact that the Hussars
and Yeomanry in Monchy and the Dragoon Guards to the south fought on into
the evening, Advanced Cavalry Corps Headquarters in Arras ignored them,
closing at 6.00pm and withdrawing to Duisans, west of the city.

In the late afternoon infantry of the 12th Division were sent into the village
under cover of snow to relieve the cavalry. These were later reinforced by the

17th Division, formerly the division attached to the Cavalry Corps as part of the Third Army reserve.[201] As night fell a line was consolidated from Fampoux through Monchy and along the Monchy–Wancourt road. The majority of the cavalry were withdrawn, handing over the defence of the village to the 37th Infantry Brigade at midnight. Due to a lack of machine guns the cavalry Hotchkiss teams as well as the Vickers guns of the 8th Brigade Machine Gun Squadron were retained in Monchy until the following day. A party of fifty men, mostly 10th Hussars, stayed on under the command of Captain Palmes.[202]

With the departure of this stay-behind party on 12 April the part played by the cavalry in the Arras offensive came to an end. On the night of the 11th Allenby had ordered all the cavalry back to its billets of 8 April, to the west of Arras. After resting there they were further withdrawn on 16 April. On 18 April Haig ordered Kavanagh to keep two brigades in readiness within 36 hours of the front line, but these were never called for and cavalry took no further part in the battle.[203]

* * *

An analysis of the overall 'success' or otherwise of the cavalry in the operations during the advance to the Hindenburg Line has already been offered. It has been argued that while strategically of limited significance, these operations were tactically well conducted and reflect credit on the mounted troops involved. The production of the GHQ pamphlet also reflects an acknowledgement of this at the time, even if it was to be forgotten by post-war commentators.

The part played by the Cavalry Corps in the Arras battles, however, is less easily defined. A simple verdict on the Arras offensive is offered by the fate of its commander. Allenby was removed from command of Third Army and sent off to Egypt.[204] Despite his later successes this move can only be viewed at the time as a demotion, and the inference from that is that the offensive was a failure. Rawlinson had learned in 1916 that such set-piece offensives have a natural internal momentum, and to push on after that has run out is to court great human loss for little territorial gain, hence 'Bite and Hold'. The latter stages of the Arras campaign follow this pattern: the battle was pushed on into the second half of April, when the Third Army was exhausted and the Germans had reorganised their defences, and became increasingly bogged-down and bloody. The early stages of the attack, however, are rightly viewed as a notable success. The Third Army advanced further, faster and with fewer losses than had been achieved hitherto in trench fighting. Unfortunately the cavalry attack at Monchy-le-Preux fell at the 'high-water mark' of the offensive. No further significant advances were made after 11 April, and the failure of the 8th Cavalry Brigade has developed into a metaphor for the failure of the offensive as a whole, and for Allenby's lack of understanding of the battle.

At first glance the cavalry fighting of 9–11 April supports this conclusion. Clearly the advance of the 3rd Cavalry Division on 11 April was, from the point of view of its operational objectives, a failure. No units reached even their first objectives of Pelves Mill and Hill 100, and exploitation beyond towards the wider operational goal of the Drocourt–Quèant Line 10km (6 miles) to the east was never a possibility. Also, as Kavanagh wrote to Allenby in a letter of 13 April, 'Altogether I am afraid it has been rather an expensive business.'[205] Just how expensive is detailed in Appendix 3. The 3rd Cavalry Division as a whole took 598 casualties over the three days, and the regiments that held the line around Monchy suffered the greater part of these losses, at over 400. Colonel Whitmore estimated that by 11.00am on 11 April the garrison of the village (formed of the 10th Hussars, Essex Yeomanry, 8th MG Squadron and some infantry) had been reduced to 'considerably less than half its strength'.[206]

This human loss, however, was overshadowed in the eyes of contemporary observers relatively accustomed to such losses (Preston described the casualties as 'Regrettable [but] proportionately no higher than in many infantry attacks'[207]) by the more unusual sight of the equally massive loss of horses. Lieutenant Alan Thomas, an infantry officer who visited Monchy on the evening of 12 April as part of the 37th Division, described the scene:

> Heaped on top of one another and blocking up the roadway for as far as one could see lay the mutilated bodies of our men and their horses. These bodies torn and gaping had stiffened into fantastic attitudes. All the hollows of the road were filled with blood. This was the cavalry.[208]

This passage has been picked up by nearly every subsequent published account of the battle,[209] and serves as a graphic image of the scale of equine loss. Exact figures for horse casualties are hard to determine, but may be estimated at somewhere between 500 and 1,000. A 10th Hussar survivor of the battle offered the higher figure, claiming that his regiment left the village after dark with only thirty horses still in hand.[210] Whatever the exact figure, the loss was enormous and the gains very limited.

It is tempting to look no further at the involvement of the cavalry at Monchy than this, and to take Thomas's final words 'This was the cavalry' as an overall verdict on their usefulness in the offensive.[211] However, while it is easy to characterise the offensive as a whole and Monchy in particular as expensive failures, when these events are viewed in more detail, from the point of view of mounted troops, some facts emerge to the credit of the cavalry and their commanders.

The precise events of the early morning of 11 April remain somewhat controversial. The 'capture' of Monchy is claimed by the 37th Division, and a fine memorial to this achievement stands in the village. However, units of the 15th Division to the north, the cavalry and even C Battalion of the Tank Corps all claimed a share of these laurels.[212] What is less in doubt is that credit for the retention of the village in British hands for the remainder of the day falls to Colonel Whitmore and the 6th and 8th Cavalry Brigades. As at Gueudecourt the previous autumn, a point had been reached where an important tactical objective fell briefly between the two armies. The German defences of the village had been more or less destroyed, but in making the effort to do so the 111th and 112th Brigades had so exhausted themselves that they were in no position to defend the ground gained against a counter-attack. The albeit somewhat accidental arrival of the cavalry secured the village for the British. Kavanagh claimed that 'if they had not gone in and occupied Monchy the Germans could have reoccupied it when they pleased'.[213] There is no evidence that the Germans made any serious attempt to recapture the village once the cavalry had arrived; concentrations of enemy infantry were noted on several occasions, but these were dispersed by artillery and machine-guns.[214] However, this should not be viewed as evidence that they would not have taken it back if they thought it practicable, rather that the presence of the cavalry rendered such a counter-attack foolhardy.

The accidental nature of the cavalry presence in the village should also be stressed (and has been examined earlier). Monchy did not form the objective of their attack; a commander who deliberately placed nearly an entire brigade of cavalry in such a position, and left it there at the mercy of enemy artillery for the remainder of the day would be open to serious censure. However, in the confused situation of the morning of 11 April, the ability of the cavalry to consolidate (albeit at great cost) the work of the infantry earlier in the day, until proper infantry relief could be coordinated, probably turned the attack of the 37th Division from a costly failure into a success.

It is possible to speculate why the Germans made no serious attempt to recapture Monchy. One answer, and possibly one of the key tactical lessons of the battle, is the effectiveness of cavalry machine-guns. Ivor Maxse is famous for observing later in the war that 'A platoon without a Lewis Gun is not a platoon at all!'[215] and the same may be said for the Hotchkiss guns in the cavalry. Since 1916 these had been issued at the level of sixteen per regiment, or at least one per troop. This overcame the earlier problem created by the numerical weakness of cavalry units, namely that their dismounted rifle strength (and thus unit firepower) was very low. The presence of pack-mounted Hotchkiss guns within the troops themselves, as well as the addition of the twelve Vickers guns in each brigade machine-gun squadron, provided cavalry units with substantial mobile firepower. This was recognised before the Arras offensive began. The Third Army appreciation of 7 February stated that:

> With the cavalry, as with the infantry, the essence of success lies in moving forward rapidly before German reinforcements arrive on the scene. Once the ground is gained it will not be difficult to hold it against counter attacks, having in view the great increase in firepower now made available by machine guns.[216]

Colonel Whitmore put this into practice at Monchy, basing his defence of the village around machine-gun strongpoints. Unfortunately many of the guns (and as importantly ammunition pack-horses) had been lost in the advance and Whitmore never had as many machine guns as he would have liked. This is reflected in the stress he placed on 'MGs and ammunition' in his messages to brigade HQ, and the necessity of salvaging two infantry Lewis guns found in the village. The remainder of the day resolved itself into a duel between the dwindling number of cavalry machine-guns firing from the village, many of which were put out of action,[217] and German machine guns and artillery seeking to silence them. In the event the cavalry were able to hang on, and the tenacity with which their guns were manned is reflected in the Victoria Cross awarded to Lance Corporal Mugford, formerly of the Essex Yeomanry, then serving in the 8th MG Squadron, who continued to man his Vickers despite suffering two broken legs, refusing to be taken to the aid post.[218]

A similar situation developed to the south of the village where the 3rd Dragoon Guards based their defence of the Wancourt road around their machine guns, receiving reinforcement of further guns from the 6th Brigade MG Squadron and from the North Somerset Yeomanry in the course of the afternoon. The 6th Brigade war diary drew attention to this, stating: 'OC 3rd D. Gds reported very favourably on Hotchkiss rifles, stating that the line held by 3rd D. Gds was defended entirely with Hotchkiss rifles which were able to break up assembly of Germans prior to counter-attack.'[219]

The ability of relatively small numbers of machine-gun armed cavalry to defend tactically important positions leads to another important question concerning their use not only in the Monchy battle but in the offensive as a whole; were there simply too many cavalry? There is little doubt that Monchy could have been defended by a significantly smaller force. To pack the whole of two regiments into the village simply resulted in the heavy casualties suffered by these units in the crowded streets, without greatly enhancing the potential defence. Kavanagh himself raised this point: 'Each Commanding Officer brought the other two squadrons of his regiment rather too close on the leading squadrons and in turn were forced to close into the village.'[220] Further reinforcements from the Royal Horse Guards and 8th MG Squadron also made several attempts to reach the village in the course of the day. But while the machine guns were desperately needed, and had been requested by Whitmore, it is hard to see what help the Blues would have been, other than to provide additional targets for the German artillery.

At a higher level, the same problem arose with the 2nd and 3rd Cavalry Divisions as a whole. Allenby deserves credit for his keenness to deploy these troops forward, and Final Positions of Readiness beyond the Black Line (German front line) reflect a useful tactical change from 1916 when such formations were typically held hopelessly far behind the line. However, it is clear that Allenby misread the battle in one critical respect. After the infantry's dramatic progress on 9 April, he seems to have concluded that the battle was very nearly won, and that the successes of the first day would continue on subsequent days. As he put it in his telegram to corps commanders on 10 April: 'The A.C. wishes all troops to understand that Third Army is now pursuing a defeated enemy and that risks must be freely taken.'[221] He expressed slightly more reservation in a letter to his wife the same day, but the tone is similar: 'The battle is not over, as we are still on the tail of the enemy, pressing and capturing their rearguards.'[222] Viewed alongside the deep objectives set out for the cavalry advance on 11 April, it is clear that he did not anticipate much organised resistance.

In drawing this conclusion Allenby was simply wrong. It has been pointed out by both Falls[223] and Wynne[224] that at Arras the new German techniques of defence in depth were not fully developed. Counter-attack divisions were held too far in reserve (to protect them from Allied artillery), and were thus not available to support the front-line divisions, which were in many cases virtually wiped out. Nonetheless, the German position was, if incomplete, still significantly deeper than those of the previous year. A typical German regimental defensive position (of three battalions) now extended to a depth of up to 10km (6 miles)[225] as opposed to the deployment over as little as 1,000m (1,100 yards) used previously on the Somme. It was therefore unrealistic to expect that after an infantry advance of only around 5km (3 miles), which had not completely overcome the enemy's existing fixed defences (much of the Brown Line was still in German hands on the night of 9 April), the cavalry would be able to advance in strength unimpeded. Instead the 2nd and 3rd Divisions were trapped, out of reach of water and supplies, in the muddy space between Arras at their backs and the remaining German defences in front of them to the east.

It is arguable that the greater progress achieved by XVII Corps north of the Scarpe offered the possibility of cavalry exploitation. Unfortunately on this side of the river the available cavalry of the 1st Division had been held so far back in reserve (in a manner reminiscent of the Somme battles the year before) that it was not able to reach the battlefield in time. E.L. Spears summed up the frustration felt by those who were witness to these events:

> As a cavalry officer I cannot but feel the deepest regret that my old arm was so mishandled. There seems to be absolutely no doubt from the evidence of infantry officers, both of the 9th and 4th Divisions, that cavalry could have got through on their fronts on the afternoon of the 9th. It is deplorable that instead of this being attempted the division north of the river was held so far back as to be useless, while south of it great masses of horsemen clogged the advance of both infantry and guns.[226]

Elsewhere Spears went on to add 'in one respect the unfortunate cavalry . . . was lucky in that the Germans had neither guns to fire nor planes to see with; for this great assembly of horses only four thousand yards from the front presented an unheard-of target'.[227] In the light of what happened at Monchy this is an important point. Fortunately, apart from those engaged at Monchy, only one brigade was exposed to significant shelling. The 5th Cavalry Brigade came under fire between 5.00pm on 10 April and 7.00am on the 11th as it occupied a position at the southern end of the cavalry line opposite Wancourt and Hill 100. Here losses were substantial, amounting to over 100 human and nearly 350 equine casualties suffered in one night.[228]

Losses from enemy artillery were not the only casualties suffered by the Cavalry Corps over the three days spent in and out of the forward area. The extreme weather also played a significant part. The generally poor condition of the horses as a result of a long cold winter on short rations has already been discussed. Added to this were the heavy weight carried (including extra ammunition and horse feed) and the dreadful going on roads and cavalry tracks, which rapidly deteriorated into deep mud and slush. Major Parks, Assistant Director Veterinary Services (ADVS) of the 2nd Cavalry Division, summed up the conditions: 'The cavalry track was deep with mud almost impassable to riding horses, quite impassable to wheels; horses suffering from exposure got down and were unable to rise.'[229] Even in the billeting areas to the west of Arras the weather made conditions terrible. Trooper Bailey of the 1st Life Guards (7th Cavalry Brigade) gave a vivid and widely quoted description of the morning of 10 April on Arras racecourse:

> The horses had pulled up their heel pegs and were huddled together. Some were dead through exposure, others had chewed their saddle blankets to pieces. It was impossible to release the head chains as they were completely frozen, and so were our fingers. . . . After a while came the order to saddle up and mount. What with the freezing night

which had weakened the horses and our combined weight, many of them just collapsed and died.[230]

Major Jolliffe, ADVS of the 3rd Cavalry Division, complained after the battle that 'There appears to be a great deal of difficulty in obtaining accurate figures for horse casualties – . . . in a large proportion of cases it was quite impossible to find out what had become of the horses that were missing.'[231] This remains the case. Accurate overall figures for horse losses are difficult to determine, not least because there was little standardisation in listing. Horses were recorded as 'killed in action', 'died', 'destroyed', 'evacuated', 'wounded' and a host of other sub-categories. A table of fatal horse casualties for the Cavalry Corps was produced by the Deputy Director Veterinary Services (DDVS) and this is reproduced as Appendix 4, but it is clear from other sources that the total of 1,208 fatalities for the corps suggested by the DDVS is an underestimate of the losses. For the 2nd Division the figure of 464 excludes a further 308 horses wounded or evacuated,[232] giving a divisional total of 772. Similarly, a further 382 horses evacuated[233] should be added to the figure of 603 for the 3rd Division, giving a total of 985. On this basis the figure of 141 for the 1st Division should perhaps be increased by around 50 per cent to 200. This gives an overall corps loss of approximately 2,000 equine casualties from all causes.

Clearly the majority of losses in the 3rd Cavalry Division were from enemy fire (in the 6th and 8th Cavalry Brigades in particular). However, for units less heavily engaged the losses from cold and exhaustion were proportionally higher. The 5th Cavalry Brigade lost 347 killed, wounded and missing from shellfire, but a further 130 died of exhaustion.[234] The 4th Cavalry Brigade, which as divisional reserve suffered very little at the hands of the Germans, lost fifteen horses killed and wounded, but a further sixty-five either died of exhaustion or had to be destroyed. In addition twenty-nine were evacuated sick.[235] In the light of these figures the 'mishandling' of the Cavalry Corps complained of by Spears becomes all the more evident as their advance not only exposed them to enemy attack to no purpose but also the very act of advancing in such atrocious conditions inflicted significant casualties on already weakened horses.

In view of all these difficulties and losses, and of Allenby's over-optimism, the question arises whether *any* useful rôle existed for cavalry in the offensive. The deepening of the German defensive system had made a 'breakthrough', in the sense of a complete strategic penetration of their organised defences, as Haig had envisioned the year before, ever less likely. It is not axiomatic, however, that this diminished the possible usefulness of mounted troops in the offensive. It has been shown earlier in the remarks of Major Darling that during the winter cavalry had been training for a redefined offensive rôle, involving relatively close 'definite objectives' and interacting with supporting infantry. It is arguable that the deepening of the German defensive zone, rather than offering fewer opportunities for mounted troops, in fact had an opposite effect. As the battle area deepened, fighting inevitably became more fluid, with a lower density of troops and artillery within it. In this more open fighting the potential for small mounted units to exploit 'gaps' at a tactical rather than operational and strategic level, and to take advantage of fleeting opportunities, was ever greater. Cavalry could also potentially extend the gains of the infantry (typically limited, as at Arras, to around 5km (3 miles)) and push on to the full depth of the enemy defences.

As we shall see, the full significance of this change was not appreciated or reflected in cavalry fighting until the following year. The seeds of it were evident at Arras, and again at Cambrai in November 1917, but it did not fully develop until Amiens in 1918. However, on both those later occasions this cavalry effort followed closely on the heels of the infantry attack on the first day, or even in the first few hours, of the battle. A significant dislocation of the German defences could be expected from the shock of the opening of an offensive, and therein lay the opportunity for the cavalry. To expect that this effect would persist until the following day or, as Allenby did, to the third day of the battle was simply unrealistic. German reinforcements could be expected if not within hours then at least within a day, and after that any forward momentum would be lost.

The operations around Monchy reflect a move towards this new style of fighting. Initial objectives were quite modest and infantry support was expected to take over the positions gained. Unfortunately the command structure and communications available to the 37th Division and to the cavalry were not flexible enough to cope with this new style of fighting. Artillery coordination in particular failed completely. Confusion reigned over the attempt to deploy guns forward to support the renewed attacks. The commander of the 111th Brigade reported of his attack on Monchy on the morning of 11 April: 'At 5.00am when the attack started my brigade had no artillery support, and I did not know what batteries had been allotted to me, or who was commanding them.'[236] Indeed, it has been suggested that the bombardment which did arrive in support of this attack actually fell on the attackers, hitting two of the four available tanks.[237] If this was the situation in a prepared infantry attack, how much more difficult it would be to support more spontaneous mobile cavalry operations can only be imagined. Allenby's remark about the need for troops to discard the habit of waiting for a 'scientifically arranged barrage' has been quoted earlier, but while the flexibility he was urging was admirable, proper artillery support remained fundamental to the success of any attack. As was mentioned above, this general deterioration in the organisation of the attackers was also exacerbated by a corresponding, inverse level of reorganisation by the Germans. By the third day of the battle the defences around Monchy had hardened out of all pro-portion to their condition on 9 April.

The fate of the 8th Cavalry Brigade at Monchy has been blamed on a neglect of these tactical basics. Captain R. Gordon-Canning, who commanded B Squadron, 10th Hussars in the battle, wrote to the *Cavalry Journal* in the 1930s making this point:

> I consider that arrangements should have been made for a machine-gun and artillery barrage on to Pelves Mill and Mt Pleasant Wood. The German garrisons were left untouched to do what they liked with us ... The invariable error of a localised attack was again brought out. No sooner were the two advanced regiments in Monchy than all further movement stopped. This permitted every German gun to concentrate on Monchy within two minutes of our arrival. If a holding attack had been carried out by the infantry on Pelves Mill and Roeux at the identical moment of our advance, I believe the cavalry could have obtained Keeling Copse and Bois des Aubepines within half-an-hour of leaving Orange Hill.[238]

In short, in the absence of diversionary attacks and suitable artillery and machine-gun support, the cavalry inevitably became trapped in the village, an easy target for enemy artillery. Of the army level artillery support proposed for the cavalry in the orders of 8 April (referred to earlier), no sign can be found on 11 April. Even the 3rd Cavalry Division's own integral RHA batteries only came into action in support of the attack at around 10.30am, by which point the lead regiments were already bogged down in Monchy and the initiative had been lost. Had proper artillery support been available to the cavalry from the outset of their attack (as had been the case in the Hindenburg Line battles in March), the result may have been very different.

A second aspect of this new style of fighting is scale. Two divisions of cavalry advanced on the VI Corps front, yet it has been suggested that Monchy was somewhat over-garrisoned by two regiments, and during the offensive as a whole only three or four regiments were seriously engaged (out of eighteen). It is arguable that very similar results could have been obtained with a far smaller force of cavalry, and indeed that a smaller force would have been more manoeuvrable and would have led to a less cumbersome command structure and more flexibility. Falls recognised this, observing 'In place of the ambitious scheme of using cavalry in masses, by divisions, as was projected south of the Scarpe, the best opportunity seems to have been for squadrons acting independently.'[239] For this to work, however, a change in command structure and philosophy would also be necessary, with far more delegation to front-line leaders. Falls again: 'responsibility and freedom of action should be delegated to subordinate commanders who are well forward. The German system which made the battalion commander the real controller of the battle proved its value again and again.'[240] Sadly there was little evidence of this on the British side at

Arras. The situation north of the Scarpe on 9 April serves as an example, where local commanders saw the potential for mounted exploitation but had no cavalry to hand and no authority to obtain them.

Much of this may seem somewhat theoretical and based upon hindsight, but the Arras fighting does offer one practical demonstration of these principles. The capture of the bridges at Fampoux by the VI Corps Mounted Troops (the Northamptonshire Yeomanry and corps cyclists) on 9 April is a brilliant example of the potential for small units to exploit the more fluid situation, advance past the leading infantry, and seize points of tactical importance. Not only did this small force successfully reach the bridges that were their objective, but they captured a number of German guns in the process, and were still holding on 36 hours later in a position to support the attack on Monchy on the morning of 11 April. Stephen Badsey's comparison of cavalry with paratroops has been referred to earlier, but in this case it is perhaps particularly apt. The seizure of bridges ahead of the main force by lightly equipped mobile forces immediately conjures up images of later airborne operations, the difference being that at Arras it was entirely successful.

Unfortunately the very success of the Northampton's advance (the regiment took only four casualties)[241] and the small scale of the operation have led to it being widely overlooked when the rôle of the cavalry in the offensive is considered. Monchy is not only a larger action but possesses the components of mass casualties and 'pointless sacrifice' that fulfil popular expectations of a First World War cavalry battle. It was at Fampoux rather than Monchy, however, that the real potential of mounted troops on the evolving trench battlefield of 1917 was demonstrated.

Chapter 4

Cambrai, November–December 1917

Then a most ludicrous thing happened; there was a great deal of clattering, galloping and shouting and a lot of our medieval horse soldiers came charging down the street; I yelled to them that the bridge was gone but they took no notice of me and went right up to it, one MG would have wiped out the lot, and then they turned about and with a very piano air trotted back the way they had come.

Major Philip Hammond, F Battalion, Tank Corps[1]

After their withdrawal from the Arras battles in April 1917 the cavalry had to wait until the autumn of that year before they were in mounted action again. The offensive near Cambrai in November 1917 was initially an enormous success, with a substantial 'break in' achieved in the German defences. Thus in theory an ideal opportunity for the cavalry to show its mettle was created. Unfortunately, the cavalry entirely failed to take advantage of this, and the arm has been vilified as a result ever since. Unlike Arras earlier in the year, which ranks as one of the 'forgotten' offensives of the First World War, the attack at Cambrai in November 1917 has received a significant amount of scholarly attention. Unfortunately from a cavalry perspective, the focus of most of these books is evident in the titles, such as *The First Tank Battle, Cambrai 1917,*[2] or *The Ironclads of Cambrai,*[3] or more recently *Cambrai: the First Great Tank Battle, 1917.*[4] The primary interest of all these writers is the tank, and Cambrai as the first manifestation of large-scale armoured warfare. This is an entirely legitimate theme, but it is all too easy when seeking to emphasise the importance of the (actually rather faltering) first steps of the tank to offer as a counterpoint the manifest uselessness of the cavalry arm. Almost all published accounts of Cambrai are guilty of this to a greater or lesser extent, characterised by the fact that the opinion on the 'medieval' cavalry expressed by Major Hammond above occurs repeatedly in them.

The use of the cavalry as a convenient scapegoat for the failures of the Cambrai offensive as a whole began almost as soon as the fighting was over. When the battle was debated in the House of Commons in December 1917 the use of cavalry was described as 'obviously absurd'.[5] This criticism continued after the war and led to the complaint by T.T. Pitman in the *Cavalry Journal* that,

> Of all the cavalry operations on the Western Front, none met with more criticism than their 'action' or as some say, 'inaction' at the Battle of Cambrai. Their failure to achieve success gave anti-cavalry critics the opportunity they had been seeking since 1915, and the result was censure by many, who neither knew their subject, nor the orders that were issued to the cavalry whom they condemned.[6]

The Cambrai volume of the *Official History*[7] was one of the last of the series to be published, appearing as late as 1948. While the compiler Wilfrid Miles gave a reasonably balanced account of the cavalry's performance, this was not so with the Preface, written by Sir James Edmonds, who took the opportunity to repeat once again the words of his anonymous American concerning 'the last machine-gun' and to observe 'It is by no means certain ... that there was any place for bodies of horse on the battlefields of 1917.'[8]

The tone was thus initially set by Edmonds, but the degree of vilification heaped on the cavalry seems if anything to have grown with the passing of the years. Robert Woollcombe, writing in 1967, devoted a chapter to 'The failure of the cavalry'.[9] A.J. Smithers in 1992 did not devote space to such an analysis, restricting himself to sweeping judgements. He quotes Colonel Baker-Carr of the Tank Corps:

> Nothing much has been said about the cavalry, for there is nothing to say ... The cavalry, after blocking all the roads for miles, sat down behind a hill, and remained there all day and then returned home-wards, again blocking up the roads which were desperately needed to bring up every sort of supplies for tanks and infantry.

He went on once again to invoke the views of Major Hammond of the Tank Corps: 'those poor horse soldiers were a pitiful sight in a modern war'.[10] The balance has been somewhat redressed in recent years with the 1997 publication of Anglesey's volume on the Western Front,[11] nonetheless it remains the case that, as Anglesey observed, Cambrai was a battle 'in which the cavalry took a controversial part which has never been adequately studied'.[12]

*   *   *

Almost from the moment of his appointment to the command of the BEF, Field Marshal Haig took the view that a decisive blow was best delivered against the Germans at the northern end of the Western Front, in Flanders.[13] This ambition was thwarted by the need for inter-Allied cooperation over both the Somme and Arras operations, as has been described earlier. With the collapse of Nivelle's offensive in the south, the disturbances in the French army that

late 1. A fully equipped cavalryman of 1917–1918. (*Taylor Library*)

Plates 2 and 3. June 1916: the Royal Canadian Horse Artillery practise assembling a trench bridge ..
(*Archives of Canada*)

... and a 13lb field gun crosses the finished bridge. (*Archives of Canada*)

Plate 4. The Fort Garry Horse demonstrate the use of a temporary trench bridge, June 1916. (*Archives of Canada*)

Plate 5. A Canadian cavalry tool-pack horse, June 1916. (*Archives of Canada*)

Plate 6. Horse lines of the Fort Garry Horse, June 1916. (*Archives of Canada*)

Plate 7. Makeshift horse lines behind the front line, winter 1916/17. (*Taylor Library*)

Plate 8. A complete cavalry regiment (the Fort Garry Horse) paraded by squadrons in June 1916. (Archives of Canada)

Plate 9. The 20th Deccan Horse in Carnoy valley prior to going into action at High Wood, July 1916. (Taylor Library)

Plate 10. Members of the 9th Hodson's Horse pause to consult a map, near Vraignes, April 1917. (*Taylor Library*)

Plate 11. Members of the 29th Lancers (Deccan Horse) near Pys, March 1917. (*Taylor Library*)

Plate 12. British cavalry crossing muddy ground near Mory in the spring of 1917. (*Taylor Library*)

Plate 13. British cavalry waiting to advance alongside the Arras–Cambrai road, April 1917. (*Taylor Library*)

Plate 14. British cavalry advancing along a cavalry track in 1917. (*Taylor Library*)

Plate 15. Scots Greys mount up beside a road, May 1918. (*Taylor Library*)

followed, and the replacement of that general by Petain as commander-in-chief of the French army in May 1917,[14] Haig finally got an opportunity to put his plan into effect. The product of this was the series of battles from August to October 1917 officially known as 'Third Ypres', but more commonly and iconically referred to as 'Passchendaele'. There was very little involvement of mounted troops in these battles, but the Cambrai battle should be considered against this backdrop. The long struggle that was Third Ypres was brought to an end after the capture of Passchendaele village by Canadian forces in mid-November 1917.[15] In the light of the effort and the cost of the fighting in Flanders, it is difficult to see why Haig launched another offensive towards Cambrai less than a fortnight later. A variety of factors influenced the decision to make another attack so late in the year. Individually none of them was a compelling reason for an offensive, but taken together they were sufficient to generate the impetus for another battle. Unfortunately, this conjunction did not lead to a coherent plan, nor were the various participants clear how their various individual motivations interacted with one another. The result of this was an under-resourced offensive that lacked clear operational objectives and turned short-term success into longer-term failure.

As early as the end of April 1917 Haig had discussed with Nivelle an attack in the Cambrai area, to draw off German reinforcements from the already faltering French attack in the south. Fourth and Fifth Army staffs were tasked to examine the question, and on 19 June III Corps, then part of Fourth Army, produced a plan for a small-scale operation. By then, however, with the ending of the spring battles at Arras and in the south, the justification for such an operation had passed. Also in June General Byng took over Third Army from Allenby, who departed for Egypt, and on 5 July Third Army took over the Fourth Army area, including III Corps. Thus the III Corps plan arrived on Byng's desk at Third Army.[16]

Simultaneously in July 1917 the Tank Corps (formerly Heavy Branch, Machine-Gun Corps) came into existence.[17] The commander of the new corps, Brigadier General Elles, and his chief of general staff, Lieutenant Colonel Fuller, were keen to develop an operation that would show off the potential of their tanks, newly upgraded in the form of the Mark IV. These had been available since June, and were now in service in substantial numbers. On 4 August Elles and Fuller submitted a plan to GHQ for a tank-based raid in the Cambrai area. This was frostily received as staff were busy with Ypres. The same plan, however, was passed the following day to Byng at Third Army. Byng was only too happy to include the tanks as part of an offensive plan already under consideration.[18]

Thirdly, on the staff of IV Corps in the line opposite Cambrai was Brigadier General Tudor, commanding the artillery of the 9th Division. He too came up with a plan, advocating a surprise attack based upon unregistered artillery bombardment. This too was passed via Lieutenant General Woollcombe, commanding IV Corps, to Third Army on 23 August.[19] Byng took a plan combining all these elements to Haig at the end of August. The situation in Flanders meant that Haig was not in a position to approve the attack or to make any firm promises of resources, but Byng was encouraged to continue planning on paper against a day when the plan might be put into effect. That day came on 13 October, when Haig formally approved the start of preparations for the attack. Following that decision a formal conference of subordinate commanders was held at Third Army on 26 October.[20]

Several reasons have been offered for Haig's approval of the Third Army plan. Both his supporters and his detractors argue that he was desperate for a spectacular success to counter the long-drawn-out failures of Ypres; the difference between them is whether this is viewed as shrewd out-manoeuvring of his opponents in Westminster, or desperate vanity. Either way, as Moore put it:

> Haig's position was not unlike that of a stage impresario whose backers begin to mutter about seeing a return on their investment. The long running Ypres show was drawing to a close without showing much profit and it was no good blaming everything on the weather.... It wasn't excuses Haig needed but a new star turn.[21]

The result of this was an offensive which was supported by Haig for political reasons, had been born in Third Army for reasons that were now obsolete, and was planned by tank-men and gunners whose objectives were technical demonstration rather than strategic success. The result of the latter in particular was that, as John Terraine observed, 'Third Army had allowed itself to be so preoccupied with the first stage of the fight that it never properly considered what would come next.'[22]

The operation was also compromised by a lack of troops. After the Italian disaster at Caporetto in October, Haig was forced to provide divisions from France to reinforce the Italian front.[23] This left barely enough to cover the Cambrai operation with virtually nothing in reserve. Charteris, Haig's intelligence chief, expressed this concern: 'We should get surprise, but we are really taking on a big job with 5 divisions less than we expected to have.' He went on: 'Our own big attack is heavily prejudiced by the withdrawal of the divisions to Italy. We shall have no reserves. We shall be alright at first, afterwards it is in the lap of the God of battle.'[24] This lack of reserves was reflected in the fact that for the first time since 1915, the cavalry divisions were dismounted in the latter stages of the Cambrai attack, and committed to battle as infantry. This was all too reminiscent of Loos in 1915, where a similar lack of manpower for reserves led to the use of cavalry in this rôle.

Fundamental to the planning for the battle of Cambrai was the ground over which it was to be fought. The British line, running broadly north-west to south-east, passed approximately 7½ miles (12km) to the south-west of the town of Cambrai itself. Facing it were the German 'Hindenburg' and 'Hindenburg support' trench systems. However, crossing the front lines from north to south were the roughly parallel Canal du Nord (to the west) and Canal de l'Escaut, also known as the Canal de St Quentin (to the east). Between these two canals was an area roughly 7 miles (11km) wide and 12 miles (19km) deep, defined to the north by the Sensée River, running east-west. This 'quadrilateral', as it was termed, was key to the plan.[25] As first devised, the plan called for the use of surprise artillery bombardment and tanks to smash through the Hindenburg defences, then an advance northwards along the corridor between the canals. This advance would be continued over Bourlon ridge and the Sensée crossings, and further along the German position to the north-east, rolling it up from the flank. However, at a series of meetings between Haig and Byng the plan was refined.[26] As a result the focus was shifted from a rolling attack north-east up the German line to a more ambitious encircling operation passing to the east of Cambrai and as far as the Sensée. Third Army expressed the objectives thus:

1. The object of the operation is to break the enemy's defensive system by a *coup de main*; with the assistance of tanks to pass the Cavalry Corps through the break thus made; to seize Cambrai, Bourlon Wood, and the passages over the Sensée river and to cut off the troops holding the German front line between Havrincourt and that river.[27]

Critically, the plan called for the capture by the infantry of the crossings over the Canal de l'Escaut on the eastern side of the attack at an early stage to allow the Cavalry Corps to cross and swing around the rear of Cambrai. Wilfrid Miles observed rather ruefully in the *Official History*:

It will be noticed how important it was to pass the cavalry divisions, without delay, across the St Quentin canal [Canal de l'Escault], which constituted a truly formidable obstacle for mounted troops. Once the way was cleared by the other arms, all would depend on the boldness and enterprise with which the cavalry was handled.[28]

Third Army had at its disposal nineteen infantry divisions. The main attack was to be made by seven of these: four divisions of Lieutenant General Woollcombe's IV Corps on the left, astride the partially built and still dry Canal du Nord, and three divisions of Lieutenant General Pulteney's III Corps on the right, with its right resting on the Canal de l'Escault. A fourth division of III Corps and three divisions of V Corps were in reserve. In addition a total of 476 tanks were to spearhead this attack.[29] The use of unregistered artillery and the lack of a preliminary bombardment would not only provide surprise, but also avoid churning up the ground, allowing these tanks to advance more easily.

The detailed rôle of the cavalry was laid out in 'Instructions for Operations GY' issued on 10 November.[30] All five divisions of the corps were to be involved, but only three were to be committed on the first day ('Z Day'). The advanced headquarters of the Cavalry Corps was to be established at Fins, approximately 5 miles (8km) behind the British front line. This was also to serve as the advanced concentration area for the 1st and 5th Cavalry Divisions, while the 2nd Cavalry Division was to concentrate at Villers Faucon, a few miles to the south-east of Fins. All divisions were to be ready to advance from these positions 2½ hours after the start of the infantry and tank attack (referred to as Zero + 2½). Three routes of advance were specified. The 1st Cavalry Division would advance from Fins via Metz, Trescault and Ribecourt to the Canal de l'Escaut at Marcoing. From there it would swing north and advance up both banks of the canal with the dual objective of isolating Cambrai from the west, and cooperating in what Haig had urged should be an 'all arms attack' on Bourlon Wood and Bourlon village to the north.

To the east of the 1st Division, the 5th Cavalry Division was to advance astride two routes: from Fins via Gouzeaucourt, beside the line of the railway through Villers Plouich to Marcoing, and from Gouzeaucourt via La Vacquerie to Masnières. This division would then cross the canal at Marcoing and Masnières, pass through the last line of German defences on the far bank, the so-called 'Masnières–Beaurevoir Line' to the north-east of the canal, and embark on a great sweep around the east side of Cambrai to the Sensée crossings in the north. The 2nd Cavalry Division would follow the routes taken by the 5th Cavalry Division and swing eastwards on the far side of the canal to guard the flank. To further disrupt the German rear areas, one brigade of the 4th Cavalry Division, the Lucknow Brigade, was to advance with the 2nd Division and raid south-east towards Walincourt. The 3rd Cavalry Division and the remainder of the 4th Division would move up to the concentration areas vacated by the first three divisions, and would be committed to follow up the advancing divisions at a time to be determined by Cavalry Corps headquarters.

This plan was, to say the least, ambitious. The divisions were concentrated on the night of 19 November (Z day −1) in villages an average of 12 miles (20km) to the west of Fins.[31] On the night prior to the attack they would have to march from there to the forward concentration areas, and in turn on to the canal and their objectives. For the 5th Cavalry Division in particular this added up to a total of some 30–35 miles (50km). Routes across the Hindenburg defences would have to be constructed, and crucially the canal bridges would have to be secured intact by the advancing infantry. The cavalry was to be criticised, as will be examined later, for its lack of 'attack', but as can be seen both distance and the physical obstacles faced by the cavalry divisions in the shape of the German defences and critically the Canal de l'Escaut weighed heavily against their success. Although written in hindsight, the remarks of 'Jack' Seely, commander of the Canadian Cavalry Brigade, summed up the heart of the problem:

> Now comes the mystery. The distance to be travelled by the tanks in order to arrive in open country was about four miles. Will it be believed that at the point selected for attack there was the one obstacle on the whole of the Western Front which formed an insurmountable barrier to the cavalry – the Canal de l'Escault. Horses can cross almost anything; they can even swim broad rivers, as they have very often done in war. But the one thing they cannot get over, unless they can bridge it, is a canal with perpendicular banks. They can get in, but they cannot get out.[32]

Communications were also likely to be vital. Although a proposed time of departure (Zero +2½) was stated, this would not be executed automatically; instead the actual time of advance of the cavalry divisions was to be determined by the Cavalry Corps headquarters, on the basis of reports from cavalry patrols and from the advancing infantry. However, in the spirit of combined-arms operations, the 1st Cavalry Division was removed from the direct control of the Cavalry Corps headquarters and placed under the command of Woollcombe's IV Corps. (Similarly but less significantly, the Lucknow Brigade was placed under the command of III Corps.) This would have been a useful step had it not been that all communication between IV Corps and the cavalry still had to pass through the advanced HQ of the Cavalry Corps at Fins. The lack of a direct link between the infantry corps (and divisions) and the cavalry, and the potential for delay and interference by the Cavalry Corps commander Kavanagh at his headquarters were to be significant problems. As during the Somme and Arras battles, this insistence by higher commanders on choosing for themselves the moment of advance was to be fatal to the cavalry's chances of seizing any fleeting opportunities, and once again was largely to exclude them from the battle.

A variety of efforts to improve communications were attempted, but in the event were not enormously helpful. A cable connection was to be laid from the Cavalry Corps HQ to an advanced report centre at Marcoing, and a contact aircraft of 35 Squadron RFC was allocated to each advancing cavalry division for liaison with the Cavalry Corps HQ. Pack-mounted wireless sets were also to accompany the divisions, to be set up on the line of the canal. Instructions also stated that tank-mounted radios would be available to take messages as they would also be in operation on the canal line. Somewhat bizarrely, however, it was determined that cavalry radios should not broadcast within 1 mile (1.6km) radius of a tank radio as this would cause interference.[33] How cavalry radios were to function given this restriction is not clear. Arguably the necessity for all of these complex technical solutions, none of which worked effectively anyway, could have been avoided simply by devolution of command of the cavalry to the divisional commanders themselves, and the establishment of a fixed time-table for advance.

* * *

Zero Hour for the offensive arrived at 6.20am on 20 November 1917. In the absence of a preliminary bombardment the Germans were caught by surprise and the successes of the tanks and infantry in capturing their initial objectives were rapid and substantial.[34] An opportunity for cavalry action thus presented itself, but how successful this would be remained to be seen. It had been calculated that the initial march of the cavalry divisions from their positions of concentration to the advanced positions at Fins would take 5 hours. Thus in order to allow the horses and men some rest on arrival the divisions set off shortly after midnight with a view to arriving at Zero Hour. The 1st Cavalry Division completed this march without mishap and arrived north of Fins at 6.15am.[35] On arrival, command of the division formally passed from the Cavalry Corps to IV Corps,[36] but as no direct link existed between IV Corps and the division, messages continued to be relayed by Cavalry Corps advanced HQ. Within the 1st Cavalry Division the 2nd Cavalry Brigade was detailed as advanced guard, with the objective of moving up the west bank of the St Quentin Canal on Cantaing and Fontaine. The 5th Dragoon Guards of the 1st Cavalry Brigade were also attached to the 2nd Cavalry Brigade, with orders to cross the canal at Marcoing and support up the eastern side.[37]

At 8.20am (equivalent to Zero +2, thus actually half an hour ahead of schedule) the division was ordered by IV Corps to advance from the forward position of concentration at Fins as far as Metz. The division duly moved forward, the lead elements reaching Metz by 9.55am.[38] Encouraging reports continued from IV Corps. At 10.08am Cavalry Corps HQ was told 'Havrincourt being mopped up. Ribecourt taken. 1st Cav. Div. to feel forward as soon as road is clear.'[39] This message was passed on to the 1st Cavalry Division and they continued their advance through Trescault. It was at this point that one of the most controversial episodes of the battle of Cambrai occurred. The village of Flesquières lay on a reverse slope roughly in the centre of the British attacking front. It lay behind the German defences and formed part of the 'rearward battle zone' known to the British as the Hindenburg Support Line. Not only was the position very heavily garrisoned and expertly defended, but for reasons which have occupied many pages of scholarship and debate since,[40] the infantry of Major General Harper's 51st Highland Division became separated from their tanks, and when the latter were mostly destroyed by German artillery fire, the infantry attack stalled short of the village.

This reverse should not have influenced the 1st Cavalry Division as their line of advance took them south of Flesquières via Ribecourt, Marcoing and east of the Bois des Neuf (described in some sources as 'Nine Wood'). However, at about 11.00am, apparently unaware that the village was still in German hands, General Harper commanding 51st Division rang General Woollcombe at IV Corps to report that 'Flesquières was in our possession and that the road from Trescault to that place was fit for cavalry.'[41] How he reached this conclusion has never been established, but he did. As a result IV Corps HQ passed on a message to the 1st Cavalry Division timed at 11.15am:

> HP14 Road from TRESCAULT through K29 Central to FLESQUIERES reported fit for cavalry AAA FLESQUIERES now taken AAA Push forward through BROWN LINE AAA No report so far about RIBECOURT road AAA[42]

[Author's note: The exact text of this and following orders is given as their content was to become highly controversial.]

This message was to become a major bone of contention in the aftermath of the battle between Lieutenant General Woollcombe of IV Corps and Major General Mullens, commanding the 1st Cavalry Division. Woollcombe would later assert that no part of HP14 changed the specific orders or route of advance of the cavalry, and that it contained only 'information'.[43] In this he is strictly correct, but the clear inference to be drawn from the message is that an advance via Flesquières might be more successful than one via Ribecourt. Mullens had also visited the reserve brigade headquarters of the 51st Division in person at 11.15am and had been advised that the capture of Flesquières was imminent. As a result of this he concluded that an advance via Flesquières 'might not only be better, but might be the only available or quicker line of advance on Cantaing, to pass to the west of the Bois des Neufs [*sic*].'[44]

In spite of Mullens' ability to talk in person to the 51st Division, his chain of command still passed from IV Corps HQ via the Cavalry Corps HQ to his own division, and it was from the Cavalry Corps commander that the final crucial interference came. At 11.50am Mullens received a message also timed at 11.15am:

> G.210 IV Corps report 11.10am the road from TRESCAULT through K29 and through FLESQUIERES is open AAA It is not yet known if RIBECOURT road is open yet [*sic*] AAA The 1st Cav. Div. will advance through FLESQUIERES AAA[45]

The final sentence of this message may be considered a direct change to Mullens' orders, albeit from a corps under whose direct command his division no longer fell. The interfering hand of Kavanagh at Cavalry Corps HQ can be sensed in this order (G.210), 'interpreting' the orders from IV Corps. It may be that this order truly reflected the wishes of Woollcombe at IV Corps at the time (although he was to deny this later), but it certainly removed any remaining discretion from Mullens as to the line of advance of his division. In the light of this, at 11.20am Mullens ordered his advanced brigade (the 2nd Cavalry Brigade) to advance on Flesquières. Unfortunately, despite Harper's claims to the contrary, Flesquières was still resisting the 51st Division. With no progress possible in this direction the advance of the 1st Cavalry Division ground to a halt.

It was not until 1.00pm that the 2nd Cavalry Brigade was able to make further forward progress. It should be noted at this point that, in circumstances reminiscent of High Wood sixteen months before, while the 1st Cavalry Division was under the command of IV Corps, its original route of advance from Ribecourt via Marcoing and Noyelles lay entirely in the III Corps area. On returning from a visit to the forward elements of his brigade in front of Flesquières, Brigadier General Beale-Brown (commanding the 2nd Cavalry Brigade) met his liaison officer with the 86th (Infantry) Brigade of 29th Division, the division tasked with the capture of Bois des Neuf for III Corps. This officer was able to tell him that the attack on Bois des Neuf was going well and that a passage through Ribecourt was possible, although he had been heavily sniped at.[46]

As a result of this new information, starting at about 1.00pm a move was made to revert to the original line of advance. At about 2.00pm, more than 1½ hours after the brigade had been unsuccessfully diverted towards Flesquières, Ribecourt was assaulted by two dismounted squadrons from the 2nd Cavalry Brigade[47] while the remainder of the brigade 'turned' the village from the south, and resumed the advance towards Bois des Neuf. Unfortunately this route lay along the forward slope south of Ribecourt and exposed the advancing troops to heavy machine-gun fire from German positions around Flesquières, so the lead regiment of the 2nd Cavalry Brigade, the 4th Dragoon Guards, did not reach the Bois until around 3.00pm. On arrival it was discovered that reports of the situation there were also incorrect, and that the Bois des Neuf was still not captured, so the 2nd Cavalry Brigade halted in the valley immediately east of Marcoing.[48]

At this point yet another change of plan for the cavalry was ordered by IV Corps. The 51st Division was to make a further attempt to carry Flesquières and several messages were sent from 2.45pm onwards to the effect that the 1st Cavalry Division, and in particular the 2nd Cavalry Brigade, should support this by doubling back in a move north-westwards over Premy Chapel Ridge towards Orival Wood to outflank Flesquières from the east. This move was attempted but on crossing the ridge patrols of the 2nd Cavalry Brigade came under such heavy fire from the north-west that the move was not considered practical.[49] Meanwhile, more orders continued to arrive from IV Corps including at 3.40pm:

> HP.19 51 Div. are attacking FLESQUIERES from west and south AAA
> 1st Cav. Div. will try to work round the north east of
> FLESQUIERES from PREMY CHAPEL RIDGE.

Mullens was later to criticise this change of orders, as he had HP.14 issued earlier in the day, pointing out that it served only to further delay the advance of the division and distract from its overall objective.[50] Woollcombe argued, with some sophistry, that as Flesquières was holding up the whole advance, to 'hasten its fall' might be considered within the 1st Cavalry Division's overall objectives, and in any case the move was only to be made by two regiments. 'This left him [Mullens] 2 cavalry brigades to carry out his original orders.'[51] The weakness of this argument is self-evident: the capture of Flesquières was never an objective of the 1st Cavalry Division, and indeed was not even on their original line of advance. In an effort to press home his case, Woollcombe spoke directly to Byng at Third Army by telephone.[52] The nature of the conversation is not recorded but Woollcombe must have lost the argument as at 4.00pm IV Corps HQ was obliged to pass on to the 1st Cavalry Division:

> HP.20 Third Army orders that you are to push on with full strength
> through MARCOING and carry out original plan.[53]

Woollcombe had been overruled, and once again Mullens was to revert to the plan to advance up the canal bank, this time on direct orders from Byng at Third Army. In the event, however, so much time had been lost that he was only in a position to order the advance of the 2nd Cavalry Brigade (supported by the 5th Dragoon Guards of the 1st Brigade) from their position south of Bois des Neuf, the remainder of the division being stuck hopelessly far back in the rear. The 1st Cavalry Brigade was still in the vicinity of Trescault, the wrong side of the Flesquières–Ribecourt bottleneck, and the 9th Cavalry Brigade remained even further back at Metz. The confusion of contradictory orders passed to the 1st Cavalry Division is recorded in the war diary of the Cavalry Corps HQ, acting as relay for the messages:

> 5.30pm 1st Cavalry Division report by telephone that after orders
> had been given to 2nd Cavalry Brigade to go to Orival Wood
> [i.e. back to Flesquières], orders were received from IV Corps
> to say that one regiment was to move on Cantaing in accord-
> ance with original scheme. GOC 2nd Cavalry Brigade had
> already ordered 4th DGs on Cantaing. GOC 1st Cavalry

Division then ordered whole brigade to move on Cantaing
with one Regt, 1st Cav. Bde. [5th Dragoon Guards] to move
to Marcoing in support.[54]

As the daylight rapidly faded and misty rain started to fall, it was left to
Brigadier General Beale-Browne's 2nd Cavalry Brigade, and in particular to his
lead regiment, the 4th Dragoon Guards, to make up this lost time and press on
towards the division's objectives. The lead troops of the 4th Dragoon Guards
were soon able to ascertain that not only was the Bois des Neuf finally free
of the enemy, but the village of Noyelles beyond it next to the canal had also
been captured (in a mounted attack at 3.00pm by elements of the 5th Cavalry
Division, discussed below). To the north of Noyelles the village of Cantaing
was 'faintly visible in the mist'[55] from the north-east corner of the Bois des
Neuf, but apparently was still occupied by the enemy. Accordingly, Lieutenant
Colonel Sewell of the 4th Dragoon Guards sent his lead squadron (A Squadron
under Captain Warter) towards Les Vallée Wood, on the canal bank to the
north of Cantaing, while B Squadron (Captain Darley) was sent to form a
defensive flank towards Cantaing to protect A Squadron's advance. Unfortunately
B Squadron were 'checked by wire and heavy machine-gun fire from Cantaing
and were unable to do more than draw the enemy's fire from that village'.[56]
This was, however, sufficient to allow A Squadron to advance. Two troops
were dropped off on the left to extend the flank of B Squadron northwards,
while Warter and the remaining two troops galloped on. In the centre of Les
Vallée Wood was La Folie Château; as they approached this, they encountered
four German ammunition wagons; the horses and crews were shot as the
cavalry rode on, charging with swords a further party of twenty enemy on foot,
killing or capturing all of them. The château itself was then approached and
further prisoners taken.

Simultaneously with the advance of the 4th Dragoon Guards, the 5th Dragoon
Guards had been sent to continue towards their objective of moving up the
eastern bank of the canal. Unfortunately this was impossible as although the
infantry had got across the canal in Marcoing, no advance could be made
beyond the bridge due to fire from Flot Farm 1,200 yards (1,000 metres) north
of the crossing. As a result the 4th Dragoon Guards were now dangerously
deep within the German positions, and receiving fire not only from Cantaing
to the west but also from across the canal to the east. Thus they were forced to
retire to the Bois des Neuf, B Squadron covering the withdrawal of A Squadron
to a position east of the Bois.[57]

The 4th Dragoon Guards were happy with their efforts: a large number of
casualties had been inflicted, with Hotchkiss, rifle and sword, between fifty and
sixty prisoners had been taken (the exact number was not recorded as they were
handed over immediately to the infantry of the 86th Brigade) and two machine

guns had been captured. Total losses in the regiment were three killed (one of whom was Captain Warter, killed during the retirement), four wounded and eight missing, with thirty horses lost. While only a small part of the overall canvas of Cambrai, the 4th Dragoon Guards had shown that they could both survive and manoeuvre in this part of the battlefield without suffering excessive casualties. The tactical effectiveness of the cavalry was once again not in doubt. One wonders what could have been done if the rest of the brigade or indeed the division had been available. The brigade then withdrew for the night to a position west of Cantaing. Lieutenant Colonel Sewell was disappointed not to have taken Cantaing: 'In my opinion had it not been for the enemy on the east of the Escault canal it would have been possible to push our advance and turn the village from the east.'[58] However, the enemy remained east of the canal and no more could be done.

* * *

While the 1st Cavalry Division spent the short daylight hours of 20 November struggling, against contradictory orders and unhelpful advice, to get forward to their objectives, the two other cavalry divisions on their right in the III Corps area underwent a similar experience. The 5th Cavalry Division, supported by the 2nd Cavalry Division, was tasked with the grand sweep around to the east of Cambrai, crossing the Canal de l'Escault at Marcoing and Masnières. This advance was to be made along two cleared cavalry tracks, the western route passing from Gouzeaucourt through Villers Plouch to Marcoing, and the eastern or 'Kavanagh' track from Gouzeaucourt via La Vacquerie to Les Rues Vertes and thence across the canal at Masnières. However, unlike the 1st Cavalry Division, which made its advance strung out in one long column along a single route of advance, both the 5th Cavalry Division in the lead and the 2nd Cavalry Division in support were split across both tracks. Their order of march may be shown schematically as follows:[59]

	Marcoing Route	Masnières ('Kavanagh') Route
5th Cav. Div.:	Secunderabad Bde 5th Cav. Div. HQ (MacAndrew) Ambala Bde	Canadian Cav. Bde
2nd Cav. Div.:	4th Cav. Bde	5th Cav. Bde 2nd Cav. Div. HQ (Greenly) 3rd Cav. Bde
4th Cav. Div.:		Lucknow Bde (Under III Corps)

The idea behind this split was presumably that it delivered a complete division (the 5th) across the canal as rapidly as possible, allowing it to advance rapidly as a coherent whole towards its objectives beyond Cambrai. However, the difficulty presented by such an arrangement was that although communications along each line of march were reasonably good, laterally they were virtually non-existent. As each division was split across the two lines of advance, the Canadian Cavalry Brigade under Brigadier General Seely would be almost entirely out of touch with 5th Division HQ, while the 4th Brigade would be similarly separated from the 2nd Division. To counter this, Major General MacAndrew commanding the 5th Cavalry Division and Major General Greenly of the 2nd Cavalry Division had agreed that should the left column be able to push on while the right was held up, command of the Canadians would pass to Greenly.[60] In any case the advance of both divisions was to be controlled from the Cavalry Corps HQ in the rear. In the light of the experiences of the 1st Cavalry Division, the consequences of these arrangements can easily be guessed at.

Unlike the experience of IV Corps where Flesquières remained a problem, the early stages of the infantry and tank battle on the III Corps front were extremely successful. The 'Outpost' and 'Battle' zones of the Hindenburg defences, forming the first and second objectives, were secured by 11.30am. The attacking divisions on the right of the III Corps front (the 12th and 20th Divisions) then swung further to the right to form a defensive flank along Bonavis Ridge, overlooking the canal, in order to allow the supporting 29th Division to push on towards the canal crossings at Marcoing and Masnières.[61]

Aside from the activities of the cavalry divisions, another feature of this advance is of interest. As had been the case at Ypres in August, as well as in earlier battles, troops of the corps cavalry regiments were attached to the attacking infantry divisions to patrol forward and exploit any opportunities during the latter stages of the advance. Two troops of the Northumberland Hussars, the III Corps' attached cavalry regiment, were advancing with the 59th Brigade in the 20th Division. Their orders were, once the 'Brown Line' (the second objective, the Hindenburg support system) had been captured, to push on quickly to the crest of the Bonavis Ridge to prevent German observation from the ridge onto the lines of advance of the 29th Division and the cavalry.

The two troops set off just before 9.00am and advanced successfully to the 'Brown Line', where they halted and dismounted. Their journey was uneventful, 'the wire being safely crossed and the trenches remaining unfilled, [having been] jumped.'[62] From there they were able to see that the advance of the 12th Division (along the spine of the ridge to the east of their position) was being held up by rifle and machine-gun fire from a position north of le Quennet farm. Taking a rather liberal interpretation of their orders, the two troops attacked this position. Lieutenant Sanders' troop dismounted and advanced frontally by short rushes, supported by the Hotchkiss guns of both troops (two guns). Meanwhile Lieutenant Ramsay's troop circled around the rear of the position, deliberately exposing themselves periodically in order to draw fire away from the frontal attack. Two tanks were also flagged down and persuaded to join the attack. These were able to contribute fire support, knocking out a machine-gun position before being themselves hit by field gun fire. Ramsay then galloped the position from the rear, resulting in its surrender and the capture of two field guns. Leaving Sanders to remount and reorganise, Ramsay then pushed on at a gallop towards Bonavis Ridge, securing positions on the crest which both troops then occupied until relieved the following morning.[63]

Once again the skill and enterprise of junior cavalry leaders was displayed, as was to be seen later in the day with the 4th Dragoon Guards at la Folie (described earlier). The two lieutenants showed that they not only grasped the wider tactical situation, but were able to use their initiative to mount successful local attacks, using a mixture of dismounted firepower and mounted shock just as their training manuals proposed. These troops were in a forward position able to assist the infantry, and even successfully to cooperate *ad-hoc* with nearby tanks. Unfortunately there was to be little opportunity for such action by the members of the cavalry divisions within the Cavalry Corps itself.

Meanwhile, the 2nd Cavalry Division had arrived at its forward point of concentration at Villers Faucon, 10km (6 miles) behind the British front line, at Zero Hour, 6.20am, having marched through the night. The 5th Cavalry Division was delayed for an hour by railway crossings, and did not arrive at Fins until 7.30am, but this delay was not significant as they were not time-tabled to move until 'Z + 2½' or 8.50am.[64] In the event they were kept waiting somewhat longer. A report timed at 9.15am (received at 10.25am) was sent by the Secunderabad Brigade, lead brigade on the western (Marcoing) route, that their contact patrols with the infantry were onto the second objective, but no orders for an advance by the 5th Cavalry Division (which had of course to come from Corps HQ) were issued. Progress to the east was slower still. As has been described above, the 12th Division had encountered some opposition on Bonavis Ridge and as a result the right flank of the advance was not considered secure. At 10.05am III Corps HQ advised the Cavalry Corps HQ that the 29th Division was being released to advance 'with caution' towards Marcoing and Masnières.[65] That division began its advance at 10.15am.[66] It was not until 10.52am, 2 hours after their scheduled start time, that Kavanagh ordered an advance by the lead brigade of the 2nd Cavalry Division (5th Cavalry Brigade). Even this was only as far as the road south-west of Gouzeaucourt.[67] Here they were to wait. It should be noted, however, that the 5th Brigade was not the lead unit time-tabled to use this route, as the order of march had them following the Canadians of the 5th Cavalry Division. The 5th Division had still not been ordered forward, and in acknowledgement of this the 2nd Division were ordered to keep south of the road and leave it clear. It is difficult to see what Kavanagh was hoping to achieve by this move, reversing the order of march of the two divisions.

Cavalry working parties had meanwhile been sent forward to consolidate the gaps in the wire and complete the construction of the two tracks. The Cavalry Corps HQ was advised that this work would be complete by about noon.[68] At 11.40am the 5th Cavalry Division finally received the order to advance by telephone from Cavalry Corps HQ. This was confirmed in writing at noon (3 hours after their planned start time); the division was to 'move forward as ordered pushing patrols in touch with advancing infantry so as to advance across the canal should the situation be favourable'. The 2nd Cavalry Division was to close up on its lead brigade to the south of the Gouzeaucourt road, so as to be 'ready to follow 5th Cav. Div. should the situation develop favourably'.[69]

On the western track the leading elements of the Secunderabad Brigade of the 5th Cavalry Division reached the southern outskirts of Marcoing by around 1.45pm, having covered the 16km (10 miles) from Fins in around 1½ hours.[70] The majority of the village had by that time been in the hands of the 87th Infantry Brigade for over an hour, but although they had been able to make good the river and canal crossings, they could make no progress beyond the railway station, which remained stubbornly defended. The advanced guard of the Secunderabad Brigade, a squadron of the 7th Dragoon Guards, crossed the canal bridge at about 2.00pm, but immediately came under machine-gun fire and opted to dismount and extend the line of the 87th Brigade infantry attacking the railway.[71] Major General MacAndrew, commanding the 5th Cavalry Division, is reported to have been somewhat displeased at his men reinforcing the infantry, as he was still hoping to make a substantial mounted advance.[72] However, the move might just as easily be seen as another example of the flexibility displayed by the cavalry at a local level on 20 November, where attacking on foot where appropriate was as common as staying mounted.

Still keen to get across the canal, a second squadron of the 7th Dragoon Guards was ordered north to try to secure the bridge at Noyelles. A report on this action was made by the squadron commander Captain Lane:

> At about 2.15pm on the 20th November I was ordered to take my squadron and make good the village of Noyelles sur l'Escault. Lieutenant Dawkins and one troop was detailed as advanced guard. They advanced rapidly to point L.11.d [immediately south of Noyelles] where they came under rifle and MG fire. I decided to gallop the village with troops at 40 yards distance. The MG fire was high and did no damage. The advance was successful and the village was captured at 3.00pm. Total captures 35 prisoners, of whom 10 were found hiding in the village.[73]

Captain Lane had good reason to be pleased, as the squadron suffered no casualties in this attack, but although infantry were able to move up and consolidate the hold on the village it was not possible to cross the canal bridge owing to hostile fire from the far bank. Several of the river bridges leading to the canal had also been destroyed.

Shortly afterwards the lead brigade of the 1st Cavalry Division arrived at Marcoing, and the 4th Dragoon Guards were able to continue probing northwards along the west bank of the canal beyond Noyelles as far as La Folie (described earlier). They were also unable to cross the canal, and the 5th Dragoon Guards' advance on Flot Farm was no more successful than that of the 7th Dragoon Guards at 2.00pm. Thus both the 1st Cavalry Division and the western portion of the 5th Cavalry Division were halted east of the canal, and made no more progress that day. This left only the Canadian Cavalry Brigade of the 5th Cavalry Division and the 3rd and 5th Cavalry Brigades of the 2nd Cavalry Division on the easternmost 'Kavanagh' track with any possibility of crossing the canal, via the bridges at Masnières.

The Canadian Cavalry Brigade, as advance guard of the column using the eastern 'Kavanagh' track, set off from Fins at around 11.40am, simultaneously with the advance of the Secunderabad Brigade on their left (on the western track). They made similar time, arriving on the southern outskirts of Les Rues Vertes, the village on the south side of the canal (Masnières was on the north side), at around 1.40pm. Here they met elements of the 88th Brigade and were subject to 'a certain amount of hostile artillery and MG fire'.[74] Les Rues Vertes had been in the hands of the 88th Infantry Brigade since some time after noon, but an event had occurred which was to be critical in the failure of the Cavalry Corps' advance, and as a result has become rather controversial.

F Battalion of the Tank Corps was tasked with the capture of Les Rues Vertes and Masnières ahead of the 88th Brigade. Major Philip Hammond, the commander of F Battalion, left a well known memoir of the capture of the villages.[75] According to his account, he was able to enter Les Rues Vertes on foot accompanied only by one other soldier and they ran for the canal bridge only to see it disappear in 'a cloud of dirty white dust' as the German defenders blew their demolition charges. The extent of the damage to the bridge is unclear, but it was still passable. When the tanks of F Battalion arrived they were accompanied by Captain Martel of the Tank Corps staff, and he, believing that the bridge might still take the weight of cavalry, prevented the tanks from attempting to cross.[76] Unfortunately, as no cavalry had arrived and as the Germans were consolidating their defence of the far bank of the canal, it was decided at 12.40pm to send a tank across. What followed has become one of the legends of the Cambrai battle: the F Battalion tank 'Flying Fox II' drove on to the bridge, carrying what Moore has termed 'the world's first "panzer grenadiers"',[77] bombers from the 11th Battalion, The Rifle Brigade. This was too much for the bridge, which collapsed, dumping the tank in the canal. The bombers and tank crew fled unharmed, concealed by the steam created by the flooding of the hot exhausts, but the bridge was gone. Incidentally, a rather bizarre aspect of this episode was recorded by one of the other tank crews present:

> The last to leave the tank was Lieutenant Edmundson. He was quite bald and always wore a wig – a most expensive one. As he climbed the girders, this wig fell into the water and floated slowly away. He was quite a strange sight without his wig and the effect was increased by the fact that the crew were wearing chain masks. The enemy did not fire at all while this was going on. It is impossible to say whether this was due to the screening effect of the steam, or to stupefaction at the strangeness of the whole spectacle.[78]

Edmundson subsequently obtained compensation from the War Office for his hairpiece, but the damage done to the cavalry's chances of crossing the canal was not so easily repaired. It was not until around an hour later (at 1.40pm) that Seely, commanding the Canadian Cavalry Brigade, arrived at the south end of Les Rues Vertes. Here he conferred with Brigadier General Nelson commanding the 88th Brigade, who was under the erroneous impression that the tanks had crossed the canal bridge and that it remained intact.[79] Accordingly Seely ordered forward his advanced guard regiment, the Fort Garry Horse. They reached the bridge at about 2.15pm, to be greeted by a broken and impassable bridge.[80] It was this appearance by the cavalry which prompted Major Hammond's often repeated remark about 'medieval horse soldiers' and 'a ludicrous thing' quoted at the head of this chapter, but it says more about the prejudices of a tank officer than about the performance of the cavalry. Indeed he places the arrival of the Fort Garry Horse in his narrative ahead of the collapse of the bridge by 'Flying Fox', implying that it was already impassable due to German fire, and thus avoiding any blame on the Tank Corps for its destruction.[81] Others have gone further. A.J. Smithers sought to argue that the destruction of the bridge somehow saved the cavalry from a worse fate on the far bank, as their advance was self-evidently doomed: 'But for the mishap of Lieutenant Edmundson's tank on Masnières bridge they [the German machine-gunners] would have collected vastly more scalps. Fortunately for themselves the British cavalry did nothing,'[82] an observation which owes more to prejudice than to fact.

Far from doing nothing, the Fort Garry Horse looked for an alternative crossing point over the canal. Subsequent events were described in a report by their commander Lieutenant Colonel Paterson.[83] Arriving at the downed canal bridge at around 2.15pm, Paterson was advised that the canal was passable by the lock gates and footbridge 1,000 yards (900m) to the east of the village. This was 'stated by civilians to be suitable for horses in single file, and over which I could see the infantry crossing'. Major Sharpe was sent to examine the crossing but did not return. At around 3.00pm Major 'Tiny' Walker of the MG Squadron reported that his unit had prepared a crossing over the lock using baulks of timber found nearby. B Squadron of the Fort Garry Horse (under Captain Campbell) was ordered across, and the remainder of the regiment prepared to follow.

Meanwhile, as the 5th Cavalry Division had been exploring the canal crossings at Marcoing and Masnières, the 2nd Cavalry Division had been waiting south of the Gouzeaucourt road with no orders. Tiring of this delay, at 1.20pm Major General Greenly sent a motorcycle to Cavalry Corps HQ to find out what was going on. A staff officer returned at 2.08pm with orders for the division to follow closely on the advance of the 5th Cavalry Division.[84] The 2nd Cavalry Division duly advanced; Greenly himself arrived in Les Rues Vertes some time after 3.00pm and found the Canadians were out of contact with the rest of their division. He rode on to the 5th Cavalry Division report centre to consult with MacAndrew, the divisional commander, but he was nowhere to be found. In accordance with the command contingency arrangements described earlier, he took command of the Canadian Brigade and called a conference with Seely, the commander of the Canadians, and Brigadier General Nelson, commander of the 88th Infantry Brigade.[85]

The outcome of this meeting was crucial as Greenly was persuaded that the single lock crossing was too precarious to push a whole brigade over, let alone most of the 2nd Cavalry Division. The approaches were marshy, the crossing was under increasing enemy fire, the weather was deteriorating, and there were perhaps only 1½ hours of daylight remaining. Orders were duly sent to the Fort Garry Horse that no more troops should cross the canal and any on the far bank should be withdrawn. The Canadian Brigade was to assist the 88th Brigade in consolidating a line along the canal, and the remainder of the 2nd Cavalry Division column, approaching in the rear of the Canadians, was to halt with its head 2 miles (3.2km) south of Les Rues Vertes.[86] As these orders were sent out, the possibility of getting significant numbers of cavalry anywhere across the canal on 20 November disappeared.

On receiving the recall orders, Lieutenant Colonel Paterson, commanding the Fort Garry Horse, set off himself in pursuit of Captain Campbell's B Squadron. Unfortunately he was not able to catch them up and they disappeared into the gloom beyond the canal.[87] The subsequent activities of B Squadron, Fort Garry Horse have become another of the legends of Cambrai. Captain Campbell was killed early in the advance, and the squadron was led by Lieutenant Strachan, who was subsequently awarded the Victoria Cross for his leadership. Strachan provided a detailed narrative of their adventures in an article for the *Cavalry Journal* in 1927.[88] According to his account, the squadron was tasked with a special mission separate from the rest of the Canadian Cavalry Brigade, that of capturing an enemy corps headquarters in the village of Escadoeuvres north-east of Cambrai, and they set off with this in mind. The squadron passed through the wire of the German Masnières–Beaurevoir line north of the canal and, cutting their way through a camouflage screen on the Crevecoeur–Masnières road, charged a battery of German guns. Many gunners were killed and the squadron rode on, past a group of around a hundred Germans with four machine-guns who tried to surrender, but who, in the light of B Squadron's special mission, were left for supporting troops to round up. After an advance of about 3 miles (5km) the squadron rallied in a sunken road and took stock of their position. It was apparent that they had taken over fifty per cent casualties, and that no support was forthcoming; in addition the Germans had identified their position and increasing fire was directed upon them. At this point Strachan decided that the mission was now impossible and, abandoning the remaining horses, the survivors of the squadron withdrew to the canal under cover of darkness.

A somewhat more sanguine account of the expedition was provided in a letter printed in the *Cavalry Journal* of 1928 in response to Strachan's article. This was produced by Lieutenant (later Captain) Cowen, who had been sent with the squadron as a German-speaking interpreter. In particular he was highly critical of Strachan's choice to ignore the German machine-gunners:

> The Germans had their hands upraised in token of surrender. I told Lieutenant Strachan that I was going to take a section and send it back with those prisoners. Instead of this he seized my reins as I started to give the order, directing me to keep going – a serious mistake which cost many lives, for the moment we had gone by, the Germans picked up their rifles and machine-guns and started firing from our rear.[89]

It is also apparent from Lieutenant Cowen's account that it was largely due to his ability to bluff enemy sentries in German that the foot party was able to return to the canal without further loss. As it was the squadron had lost Captain Campbell, 86 out of 129 other ranks, and all 140 horses,[90] as well as their Hotchkiss guns and packs. Eighteen prisoners were brought in.

On this basis B Squadron's foray across the canal can hardly be considered a great success. However, in the reports of both Strachan and Cowen the evidence of an even greater failure can be discerned. As Strachan observed, 'it will easily be seen that the whole success of the cavalry action depended upon crossing the river and the canal. It is ancient history now that a tank crossing the Masnières bridge crashed through and as this prevented the cavalry from crossing the "show" was practically called off.'[91] However, he continued, 'Judging from what one single squadron did, what could five cavalry divisions not have done?'[92] His description of the advance through the Masnières–Beaurevoir line, the last formal German defence line on the north side of the canal, shows that this was met with comparatively little resistance: 'Up to this point [the German gun battery] no opposition had been encountered from German infantry. The trenches marked on the map were merely "spit-locked" (dummy) and there was practically no wire, but there were a few concrete "pill boxes" completed and machine-guns were firing from them.'[93] He concluded: 'It appears that there would have been a remarkable opportunity for a great cavalry success, had the operation in its original form been carried out.'[94] Cowen supported this view, recalling the spit-locked trenches and absence of wire. He bemoaned the lack of air reconnaissance: 'The visibility that day had been very low, due to fog, causing many of our low flying planes to crash into the hills. Had they been able to see clearly and get reports back promptly our infantry could have advanced to the Rumilly–Crevecoeur line with little resistance.'[95] This perception by the front-line commanders that a gap in the German defences existed can be contrasted with the view from Cavalry Corps HQ:

> At 3pm the situation was that Masnières and the Masnières–Beaurevoir line was still held by the enemy, that the main bridges over the canal were broken, that the crossings that existed were narrow, and that it would take a very long time for any considerable body of cavalry to cross even if there was no opposition, and secondly, that the crossings were still under the enemy's fire.[96]

The senior commanders within the Cavalry Corps have been criticised for making much of their difficulties and seeing little of their opportunities.[97] It would seem that this was the case here. Greenly in particular seems to have allowed himself to be persuaded that a further advance across the canal was not possible. Left alone, Seely might have pushed on, but he was both the subordinate commander and a yeomanry officer faced with Greenly the regular. Seely himself described the lack of options left to him:

> It would, of course, have been madness to have sent more men over the little bridge we had made, even if it had been possible to get them across in the face of the increased rifle fire. They would have been lost in the darkness, and could have done no good.[98]

Moore has suggested that Major General MacAndrew, the commander of the 5th Cavalry Division, already displeased by the dismounting of the 7th Dragoon Guards in Marcoing, appears to have been in more aggressive mood, and may have continued to attack,[99] but he was away in Marcoing and command of the Canadians reverted to Greenly.

Kavanagh, as corps commander, must also bear some responsibility. The plan of attack called for the cavalry to be ready to move by $Z + 2\frac{1}{2}$, that is 8.50am. The 1st Cavalry Division, under the command of IV Corps, began its advance by this time, indeed half an hour ahead of time. However, it was not until nearly 3 hours later, at 11.40am, that the Cavalry Corps commander saw fit to order the advance of the 5th Cavalry Division. Meanwhile the 2nd Cavalry Division was ordered forward to Gouzeaucourt, and then apparently forgotten about until 1.20pm, when Greenly sent for further orders. The result of this was that infantry and tanks had been in Les Rues Vertes for around 2 hours before any substantial force of cavalry arrived, by which time the bridge had been broken and the German defence had thickened decidedly. In this climate of hesitation and delay it is easy to see why Greenly felt there was not enough daylight left to continue.

A final puzzling feature of the cavalry advance to Masnières is the question of Mon Plaisir bridge. This was highlighted by Wilfrid Miles in the Official History.[100] Approximately a mile (1.6km) east of the bridge in Masnières was a second crossing of the river and canal via a wooden bridge sheltered from fire by the river valley and screened by trees. This was intact and entirely suitable for cavalry. This bridge had been identified in a survey compiled by the Third Army intelligence branch, but the information was not circulated,[101] although it did appear explicitly in the operation orders of the 29th Division as it formed part of the fourth phase objectives of the 88th Brigade.[102] It was also depicted on both the 1:20,000 and 1:10,000 map sheets. Strangely, no reference to it appears in any of the operational orders for the Cavalry Corps, nor was it brought to the attention of Greenly when he met Seely, and Brigadier General Nelson of the 88th Brigade and the latter's brigade major, both of whom ought to have been familiar with the orders for the 88th Brigade. The only reference to the bridge in cavalry records is in the Canadian Cavalry Brigade war diary, where at around 4.00pm four guns of the machine-gun squadron were deployed 'to support the infantry [presumably of 88th Brigade] who were being pressed back at Mon Plaisir bridge'. In addition, B Battery RCHA came into action covering the crossing.[103] It is difficult to see how such a large oversight could have occurred. It remains possible that this crossing was rendered impassable by some circumstance known to the men present at the time but not recorded. If not, it must be added to the list of higher command failures of 20 November.

No further action was undertaken by the cavalry on 20 November. Cavalry Corps HQ contacted the 29th Division at 6.25pm to ask if any assistance from the 2nd or 5th Cavalry Divisions would be required overnight. As no support was requested, orders were issued for both divisions to withdraw to their forward concentration areas. Unfortunately communications with the 5th Division were very slow, and those with the 2nd Division had broken down almost entirely as their wireless had broken, and the head of the telephone cable from corps headquarters was lost in the dark. The cavalry tracks had also deteriorated in the continuing rain such as to be virtually impassable at night. As a result both divisions were counter-ordered at 9.15pm to stay were they were and carry on with the advance in the morning. Only the 4th Cavalry Brigade (of the 2nd Cavalry Division) at the rear of the column on the Villers Plouch–Marcoing route received the orders early enough to move, and they fell back to Villers Faucon.[104] For the remainder of the cavalry regiments strung out across the battlefield the situation was reminiscent of the April nights at Arras seven months before. Private Knight of the 2nd Dragoon Guards (with the 1st Cavalry Division) described the situation:

> It was raining. A dismal rain. Real November stuff that gradually wetted us through until eventually we could feel it trickling through our puttees. For hours we stood by our horses. Then at midnight we were told to off-saddle and peg down for the night. The prospect was by no means a cheerful one but we lay down behind the horses to get what little sleep we could.[105]

* * *

During the night of 20/21 November the embattled German defenders of Flesquières were advised that they could no longer be supported, and they withdrew. Thus by dawn on 21 November the luckless 51st Division was able to consolidate its second 'Brown Line' objectives.[106] Orders were issued overnight by IV Corps for the attack to be continued on the left towards Bourlon by the 62nd Division, and on the right towards Fontaine by the 51st Division. The 1st Cavalry Division was instructed to support the advance of IV Corps by detaching one regiment to support the 62nd Division, with the remainder continuing to try to advance west of the canal.[107] Mullen's lead brigade of the 1st Cavalry Division, the 2nd Cavalry Brigade, was already committed to the defence of Noyelles and the canal crossings, and indeed heavy German counter-attacks were to be made on these positions throughout the day.[108] He therefore called up the 1st Cavalry Brigade, which had spent the previous day in reserve around Trescault. One regiment, the 11th Hussars, was detached to support the 62nd Division while the remaining two regiments, the 2nd Dragoon Guards (Queen's Bays) and the 5th Dragoon Guards (now returned from their operations with the 2nd Cavalry Brigade the day before), were to support the 51st Division.[109]

Starting at about 6.00am the 51st Division advanced, occupying Flesquières and moving on to overtake positions along the Graincourt–Marcoing road with relatively little opposition. Next they faced a partially constructed defensive line running from north of the Bois des Neuf, across the front of Cantaing, and up to Bourlon Wood. An attack on this position was prepared for 10.00am, with the as-yet-unengaged 154th Brigade of the 51st Division leading. This attack was to be supported by artillery and by thirteen tanks of B Battalion, 2nd Tank Brigade. Unfortunately orders only reached the tanks at 9.00am, giving them little chance of reaching the start line in time. Seeing no tanks by 10.30, Brigadier General Buchanan commanding the 154th Brigade launched his Highlanders into the attack unsupported, with pipers leading. This assault rapidly foundered in the face of severe enemy machine-gun fire, and the brigade was pinned down short of Cantaing village.[110]

The 1st Cavalry Brigade, meanwhile, had been maintaining touch with the 51st Division via contact patrols.[111] Moving off from a position to the east of Havrincourt at 9.40am they reached the southern side of Premy Chapel ridge, west of Marcoing, at 10.25. From there elements of the advanced guard regiment, the 2nd Dragoon Guards (Bays) advanced north-east over the ridge towards the Bois des Neuf. At about 10.45 the infantry attack was observed, and the brigade RHA battery (I Battery) was brought into action to shell Cantaing in support of the infantry. Despite their support, the infantry attack was seen to be held up. At 11.15 the tanks finally arrived, and seven (some sources suggest thirteen[112]) tanks made their way over Premy Chapel ridge towards Cantaing, drawing heavy machine-gun fire as they advanced. By about noon the tanks were making good progress into the village, but were unsupported by any infantry. Anxious about the fate of his unsupported tanks in the village, the colonel of B Battalion sent a request for assistance to Brigadier General Makins commanding the 1st Cavalry Brigade. In response, all three squadrons of the Queens Bays moved north along the canal and galloped the village from the east. Private Knight of the Bays, recovering from his soaking overnight, described events:

> At last the orders came: Half-sections right, walk march! Form sections! Head, left wheel! Draw swords! Trot! Form Troop! Form column of half squadron! Gallop!
>
> The village lay about three-quarters of a mile away. We galloped fiercely to the outskirts, rapidly formed sections and got on to the road, numbers 1 and 2 troops cantering into the village first. Donelly the Irishman went raving mad, cutting and thrusting wildly at retreaing Germans. Indescribable scenes followed. The order came to dismount. Germans emerged from dugouts in all directions, some giving themselves up, others making a fight of it with a few bombs. No. 1 troop received a bomb in its midst. The bomb throwers were accounted for with rifle and revolver.[113]

By 1.40pm the village was reported clear of enemy. Realising the importance of the position, Makins rapidly reinforced the Bays with a squadron of 5th Dragoon Guards, and as signs of a counter-attack were observed around 2.00pm the defences of the village were further enhanced with six guns from the brigade machine-gun squadron. These troops continued to defend the village for the remainder of the day, being relieved by infantry of the 6th and 51st Divisions overnight.

Clearly the arrival of the tanks had retrieved the situation and made a success out of what could very easily have been a disaster. (Unfortunately the lack of progress of the 62nd Division towards Bourlon persuaded General Harper, commanding the 51st Division, to call a halt to the advance, and any advantage gained was thus thrown away.[114]) The Bays also seem to have got away with very light casualties, only one man being recorded killed, and three officers and thirty-four men wounded.[115]

The action can be viewed as evidence of the success of mounted cavalry working in cooperation with tanks, a fact that few commentators on the battle seem to have acknowledged. Smithers was scathing about the rôle of the cavalry:

> In addition to the Highlanders and Captain Raikes' tanks there was a cavalry brigade. What it was expected to achieve was unclear. An officer who watched attempts of cavalry and infantry to co-operate with the tanks in the open ground south of Bourlon Wood was much impressed with the difficulties of co-ordinating cavalry with tanks. When MG fire was met the horsemen had to go so far back to get cover that they lost touch and the tank was left alone on the objective for a long time before the cavalry could be communicated with and got forward again. This should hardly have come as a surprise; there was no place for animals in such a battle.[116]

Other writers simply ignore the presence of the cavalry, attributing the fall of the village to the 4th Gordon Highlanders, who were in the lead of the 154th Brigade attack.[117] Brigadier General Makins perhaps anticipated such counter-claims for the village, stating in the 1st Cavalry Brigade report:

> The village was soon over-run by the Bays. The 4th Gordons who had reached a trench to the S. of the village, then came into the village but retired again later. Lt Barnard [commanding the lead squadron of Bays] never saw any infantry in the village when he got there and the whole credit of taking Cantaing is entirely due to the Tanks supported by the Bays.[118]

One has to be somewhat sceptical of this claim as Makins could hardly be considered unbiased, but even if the Gordons were able to make a simultaneous advance on the west of the village, the cavalry was nonetheless able to contribute significantly to the battle, contrary to the widely perceived wisdom that cavalry could not work successfully with tanks.

The capture of Cantaing also marked the last mounted action in the offensive battle. The 2nd and 5th Cavalry Divisions had been held in readiness to advance via Marcoing and Masnières after a further infantry attack on the Masnières–Beaurevoir Line to the east of the canal, but this attack failed to make any progress against a greatly reinforced German line. On the evening of 21 November both divisions were withdrawn, and although the 1st Cavalry Division was initially retained in the battle area, and the 4th Cavalry Division moved forward to relieve the 5th, these two were also withdrawn on the 22nd.

Elements of the 1st and 2nd Cavalry Divisions were to play a significant part in the struggle for Bourlon Wood between 25 and 27 November, but this fighting was carried out entirely on foot, the divisions forming dismounted battalions from each of their brigades. The use of precious cavalry soldiers in this way reflects Charteris' prediction before the offensive began that ultimately the attack had been launched with too few troops. It also reflects the increasing desperation with which the Third Army command continued to press the attack, refusing to acknowledge that the offensive had essentially halted on 22 November.

* * *

Over the following days British attention continued to be focused on the stalemate battle for Bourlon Wood and the adjacent village. Meanwhile the Germans were making plans of their own. The reinforcements which had been rushed to the area meant that they were in a position not only to halt the British offensive, but also to contemplate a counter-attack of their own to reverse the British gains and restore the Hindenburg Line front. Preparations at the headquarters of Crown Prince Rupprecht's group of armies, in whose sector Cambrai lay, began on 24 November. This was followed by a conference with Ludendorff on the 27th, after which a formal order to the German *Second Army* was issued. The broad outline of the attack was as follows. A main thrust was to be launched at the internal south-eastern angle of the British salient by the Caudry and Busigny groups of German divisions, with the aim of striking across the base of the salient towards Metz en Couture. This would be accompanied by a thrust south by the Arras group of divisions to the west of Bourlon Wood. At worst this would cut off the British troops in the head of the salient around Fontaine, Marcoing and Masnières, and at best offered the possibility of rolling up the British line towards Arras from the south-east.[119]

The British Third Army commanders seem to have been taken largely by surprise by this attack when it fell on 30 November. Partly they were absorbed in the fighting for Bourlon, where a counter-attack was expected (and indeed delivered by the Arras group of German forces). Also they had been influenced by unduly optimistic intelligence assessments of the German inability to mount such an attack after the losses of the Cambrai battle thus far and in Flanders. In any event the lack of available forces meant that even had they been aware of the German plans there was little they could have done to oppose them. The British line around the salient continued to be held by the divisions of III and IV Corps which had participated in the original attack ten days before. To the south VII Corps, which was to bear the brunt of the German southern thrust, was spread out occupying a thinly held and poorly constructed line.[120]

The northern arm of the German attack made little progress, at great cost in German casualties. No cavalry were engaged. The southern attack, however, resulted in the involvement of three of the five British cavalry divisions in the subsequent fighting. Of particular significance was the attack by the German *34th* and *208th Divisions* of the Busigny group, which attacked at the extreme southern end of the German offensive front, between Vendhuille in the south and Banteux in the north. These troops were faced initially by the British VII Corps on a section of the line which had not formed part of the British attack front on 20 November, and which was relatively ill-prepared for the storm that was to descend upon it.

The German attack on 30 November began with a bombardment of gradually increasing intensity upon the northern half of the VII Corps' front, held by the 55th Division. This was followed at 7.00am by infiltration by small columns of German infantry (in a style which was to be used on a larger scale the following year), supported by low flying aircraft, gas and *minenwerfer* bombardment, and covered by smoke and the natural mist of early morning. This initial attack was enormously successful. Within hours Villers Guislain and Gouzeaucourt had been captured and a gap approximately 5 miles (8 km) north to south and 3 miles (4.5 km) deep had been torn in the British defences. Many guns had been captured and what opposition continued was mostly provided by scratch forces of rear-echelon troops.[121]

Largely by coincidence, part of the Cavalry Corps was in the area to the rear of VII Corps when the German blow struck. As a result, when Lieutenant General Snow of VII Corps appealed for reinforcements the cavalry were the natural choice for Third Army to commit to the battle to halt the German advance. The Cavalry Corps headquarters was at that time at Villers Carbonnel, south of Peronne, and approximately 16 miles (25 km) from the German break-in. All but one of the cavalry divisions were also some distance away from the fighting: the 4th and 5th Divisions were at Athies and Monchy-Lagache respectively, a few miles from the corps headquarters, while the 1st and 3rd Divisions were at Bray and Querrieu, further to the west. Only the 2nd Cavalry Division was in the immediate Cambrai area, at Fins, still recovering its dismounted battalions from their action in Bourlon Wood.[122]

Cavalry Corps HQ was telephoned by Third Army with news of the attack at 8.30am. At that point, by coincidence, the cavalry divisions had already begun to prepare a move into the VII Corps line to take over dismounted from the 24th Division, holding the southern half of the corps front. These orders were rapidly rescinded and the 5th Cavalry Division was ordered up to Villers Faucon, where the 55th Division had its headquarters. Shortly after this the 4th Cavalry Division was ordered to follow in support of the 5th, and with admirable despatch Kavanagh himself followed by motor car, taking the commanders of the 4th and 5th Cavalry Divisions, Kennedy and MacAndrew, with him and opening an advanced corps headquarters at Villers Faucon by 10.45am.[123] At about this time the 2nd Cavalry Division, nearest the northern end of the German break-in, was 'placed at the disposal' of III Corps command.[124] This was a sensible move as the German attack had struck the junction of the two corps, and while the 55th Division and VII Corps lay to the south of the incursion, III Corps troops mostly lay to the north. In allocating this division to the defending infantry corps Kavanagh also devolved responsibility for his artillery to them, as the RHA batteries of the 2nd Cavalry Division (operating under III Corps) and the 4th Cavalry Division were all handed over to the 55th Division.[125] This was an understandable move as the 55th Division had had its gun lines largely overrun, and was desperately short of artillery (although several of these gun positions were to be rapidly recaptured as the day progressed). The unfortunate consequence was that it denuded the cavalry themselves of what little integral artillery they possessed, and this was to be a significant factor in the fighting of the next few days.

The first cavalry into action on 30 November were from the 2nd Cavalry Division. As already stated, this division was at Fins awaiting the return of one of its dismounted battalions. At about 10.30am orders were received to reinforce the line at Gouzeaucourt, about 4 miles (6.5 km) to the east. The 5th Cavalry Brigade, formed of the 20th Hussars, 12th Lancers and 2nd Dragoons (Scots Greys), was allocated as advanced guard, and departed at around 11.00am, with the 20th Hussars (who had been in the process of arranging regimental baths for that morning) as vanguard. Approaching Gouzeaucourt, patrols reported the village in German hands, opposed on the ridge to the west by a thinly held line of assorted British stragglers and 470th Field Company, Royal Engineers. Fire from the village made forward progress impossible so the Hussars dismounted and reinforced the line.[126]

At about the same time the 1st Guards Brigade arrived on the left of the cavalry opposite Gouzeaucourt. The Guards Division had been initially allocated to VII Corps but this was changed as III Corps' need seemed greater; unfortunately this confusion of orders meant that only the 1st Brigade, operating alone, moved into the line. Notwithstanding their lack of support and numbers, the 1st Battalion, Irish Guards and the 2nd and 3rd Battalions, Coldstream Guards, carrying the 20th Hussars with them on their right flank, attacked into and through Gouzeaucourt at midday. Further progress was checked beyond the village but a new line was established which was held by the Guards and cavalry for the remainder of the day.[127]

While Gouzeaucourt was falling to the Guards and Hussars, the lead elements of the 5th Cavalry Division arrived at Villers Faucon. The leading Ambala Brigade reached there at 12.15pm,[128] having travelled some 11 miles (18 km) at a brisk trot in only just over an hour; most of the officers of the brigade had only the vaguest idea of where they were.[129] Orders from Kavanagh at the Cavalry Corps advanced HQ followed at 1.10pm:

> The Cav. Corps will advance in a northerly direction with a view to attacking the enemy's flank between Villers Guislain and Gouzeaucourt and seizing the Gonnelieu ridge. The 5th Cav. Div. will move at once with objective the enemy's flank between Villers Guislain and Gouzeaucourt. It will be supported by the 4th Cav. Div. In accordance with the situation as it develops.[130]

The 5th Cavalry Division moved off from Villers Faucon shortly after, with the 8th Hussars of the Ambala Brigade leading. These lead troops were broadly heading for Gauche Wood and Gouzeaucourt with the aim of linking up with the Guards and 2nd Cavalry Division to the north, but they still had very little idea of the position of their own and the enemy's troops, or indeed where they were themselves. On arrival at Vaucelette Farm at around 2.30pm they compared maps with the infantry holding the line along Revelon Ridge and a better picture of the situation was gained.[131] The 8th Hussars pushed on but soon drew fire from the direction of Gauche Wood and then became entangled in the trenches and wire of the British second line, which ran to the west of the wood. Abandoning their horses, they took up position in a sunken road to the west of the wood. The second regiment of the brigade, the 9th Hodson's Horse, attempted to move up on the left (north) of the Hussars in support but got no further than the sunken road, about 600 yards (550m) from the wood. A German counter-attack was, however, repulsed from the direction of the wood, and by 4.00pm, as it grew dark, contact had been made by Hodson's Horse with the 20th Hussars to the north, and a stable defensive line was established just west of the railway line from Gouzeaucourt in the north to Revelon Ridge in the south.[132]

A feature of the Hodson's Horse advance was that it was made mounted. This was effective where the ground was clear but where bottlenecks were created in crossing the abundant wire in the area German artillery was able to inflict significant casualties. Lieutenant Colonel Rowcroft, who rode with the regiment, recalled:

> The passage of the defile and advance by C Squadron had been so rapid that the enemy's artillery had not had time to get on to the

troops. However as D Squadron started to follow C through the gap in the wire, there was a different tale to tell, and the leading troop was literally blown to pieces.[133]

There is little direct evidence of Kavanagh's view of the battle on 30 November, but it is possible to infer from what few clues exist that he felt this was a decisive moment for the cavalry, and that Third Army had placed responsibility for stopping the Germans in his hands. His rapid advance by motor to his advanced headquarters is a symptom of this. His insistence upon mounted attacks was apparent the following day, as will be discussed later, but it seems likely that he adopted a similar tone on the 30th. The Cavalry Corps war diary records that at 3.15pm 'GOC [Kavanagh] rode up to GOC 5th Cav. Div. HQ [MacAndrew] ... Ambala and Secunderabad Brigades had just been directed *mounted* on Gauche Wood.'[134] (Author's emphasis) If indeed he did insist on mounted attacks on 30 November, it suggests he had misread the battle. Had the Germans been advancing in large bodies across open ground then a sharp mounted blow might have sent them reeling, but in fact their advance was by infiltration of small parties across ground which, although behind the British front line, was still part of the 'battle zone', and so heavily wired and cut by trenches. Also by midday the German advance had largely run out of steam and their forces were consolidating in entrenched positions. In short Kavanagh seems to have anticipated a return to 'open warfare' which had not actually occurred.

Fortunately the local commanders were not so deceived, and both the 8th Hussars and Hodson's Horse rapidly dismounted and fought on foot. Another lesson had also been learned. In his account of events contained in the corps war diary, Lieutenant Colonel Maunsell observed:

> As it was now clear that there was no hope of any further advance, the led horses were all sent back some three miles, well out of the way. The mistake of Monchy-le-Preux, where 700 horses were shelled to death in the streets of the village owing to no orders having been received to send them away, was not repeated.[135]

The remaining two brigades of the 5th Cavalry Division followed the Ambala Brigade between 3.00 and 4.00pm. The Secunderabad Brigade swung north to extend the line on the left of Hodson's Horse, but on approaching Gouzeau-court they made contact with the 5th Cavalry Brigade (2nd Cavalry Division), which was already filling that gap so the Secunderabad Brigade retired to a position in reserve to the west. An attack on Gonnelieu, one of the original corps objectives, was considered, and 'Patrols were sent towards Gonnelieu with a view to a mounted attack, but the place was found to be defended by wire and machine guns.'[136] Brigadier General Gregory, commanding the brigade, decided that this attack stood no chance of success and it was not attempted. (It is perhaps fortunate that at the northern end of the line he was not in good communication with Kavanagh.)

The Canadian Cavalry Brigade meanwhile moved up on the right (south) of the Ambala Brigade, taking up positions around Vaucelette Farm, and it was in these positions that the 5th Cavalry Division spent the night, the 18th Lancers (of the Ambala Brigade) relieving the 8th Hussars in the front line after dark.[137]

* * *

During the night 30 November/1 December orders were drawn up for a renewal of the British counter-attack at dawn the following day. Unlike the previous day, when few had been available, a significant number of tanks were found to support this attack, and a combined infantry, cavalry and tank assault was envisaged. Orders were issued by the Cavalry Corps headquarters at 6.40pm on the 30th:

> The 5th Cavalry Division, with the Lucknow Cavalry Brigade attached to it [from 4th Division], will attack Gauche Wood and Villers Guislain tomorrow 1st December, co-operating with 14 tanks, 8 of which will be directed on Gauche Wood and 6 on Villers Guislain. . . .
>
> 4th Cavalry Division less Lucknow Cavalry Brigade will be assembled west of Peiziere by 6.30am with the object of taking advantage of the advance of the tanks and seizing Villers Ridge.[138]

[Author's note: the villages of Peiziere and Epehy are conjoined and either name may appear on maps.]

A conference of the leading brigade commanders and a liaison officer from the tanks was held at 5th Cavalry Division headquarters at 1.15am where the details were worked out.[139] The 1st Guards Brigade, supported by twenty tanks, would attack Gauche Wood from the north. Simultaneously, on the right (south) of the Guards, the Ambala Brigade of the 5th Cavalry Division would attack the wood on foot from the west, supported by a further six tanks. The Secunderabad Brigade would take up a supporting position to the west of the Ambala Brigade, mounted. The Canadian Brigade would cover the southern shoulder of the attack. Meanwhile further south the Lucknow Brigade (of 4th Cavalry Division but under temporary command of the 5th) would attack towards Villers Guislain, supported by nine tanks, on the south-east side of the Peiziere–Villers road. In turn, on their right this attack would be supported by the remaining Mhow and Sialkot Brigades of the 4th Division, attacking north and east 'to take advantage of the advance of the tanks'.[140]

To mount such a coordinated attack over unfamiliar ground in the few remaining hours of darkness was a difficult undertaking, particularly for the tanks, as Colonel Maunsell observed:

> Conditions for tank co-operation in the contemplated attack on 1st December were extremely unfavourable. The machines were a long way from the points of assembly. It was dark, and there had been no time to reconnoitre lines of approach and find out the state of affairs in general. The uncertainty as to the locality of our own troops made things difficult enough for infantry and cavalry. It was infinitely worse for the tanks, especially as the terrain was absolutely new, and the machines are by nature extraordinarily blind.[141]

Nor was the artillery support for the attack remotely adequate. The two RHA batteries of the 5th Cavalry Division were to support the Gauche Wood attack, while the third RCHA battery was lent by the Canadians to support the Lucknow Brigade. 'Anyone with the slightest experience of France,' Maunsell remarked, 'would know that this was a mere fleabite.'[142]

In spite of these disadvantages, the northern part of the attack the following morning was a striking success. The 1st Guards Brigade waited about ten minutes for their supporting tanks, but on seeing no sign of them simply took Gauche Wood at a rush, supported only by the fire of their brigade machine-gun company. The 18th Lancers, the lead assaulting regiment of the Ambala Brigade, supported this attack and helped mop up the wood; indeed, as officer casualties in the Guards were so heavy, the officers of the 18th Lancers took temporary command of the forces in the wood.[143] The tanks allocated to support the Lancers arrived on time but rapidly lost direction and instead of heading east towards the wood, swung north across the face of the wood, and in passing shot up the trenches occupied by Hodson's Horse, inflicting several casualties.[144] Some eventually entered the wood from the north but only at about 8.30am, after the battle was substantially over.[145] Seely describes a curious incident during this battle which demonstrates another type of lack of communications, and one of the continuing difficulties Indian cavalrymen encountered in France:

> As I stood there I saw three Indian cavalrymen coming towards me with fixed bayonets, and in the centre an officer of the Coldstream Guards. I afterwards learnt that he had crawled out into the open under very heavy rifle fire to bring succour to one of my Strathcona's who had been shot through the thigh bone.... The three Indian cavalrymen mistook him for a German officer, and having arrested him, were bringing him back to our lines. By great good fortune

I knew one of the Indians, and induced them to stand aside and to release the officer.[146]

Further south events took a rather different turn. The Lucknow Brigade, with the 36th (Jacobs') Horse leading, were to attack towards Villers Guislain from a position south-east of Vaucelette Farm at 6.20am. At 5.45am, just over half an hour before they were due to set off, a message was received that the tanks allocated to the attack would not reach the rendezvous in time and would move off from a point a mile (1.6km) to the north-west, at Genin Well Copse.[147] This would place the tanks some distance away and on the other side of the ridge running along the Peiziere–Villers road. Brigadier General Gage, commanding the Lucknow Brigade, frantically sought to check his brigade's advance (Jacobs' Horse were contacted less than five minutes before they were to move off), and redeploy the force a mile to the west. This was achieved by 6.50am, but no tanks were contacted.[148]

Gage assumed that since the tanks were on his left their advance would converge with that of his brigade towards the objective (Villers Guislain); anxious that the tanks might have gone on ahead without support, and keen to make good his rôle as flank protection for the attack on Gauche Wood, he ordered the Jacobs' Horse into the attack. Gage was unaware not only that the tanks' start point had been altered but also that their axis of advance had also been changed to send all the tanks towards Gauche Wood, thus no tanks would enter his brigade area at all. As a result, Jacobs' Horse were left to advance with no tank support, little or no artillery support as the brigade RHA had been detached, and in increasing daylight. In the face of heavy German artillery and machine-gun fire the attack progressed no more than about 100 yards (100m) before becoming pinned down in the network of British second-line trenches ahead of them. This was a great relief to the scratch force of rear echelon troops holding those trenches but did not carry the brigade anywhere near Villers Guislain.[149]

Worse was to follow on the right of the Lucknow Brigade, and here the involvement of Kavanagh and Cavalry Corps headquarters in the conduct of affairs was starkly highlighted. On the right of the Lucknow Brigade, temporarily under 5th Cavalry Division command, lay the remainder of the 4th Cavalry Division, the Mhow Brigade leading with the Sialkot Brigade in support. Their orders had been to advance 'taking advantage of the advance of the tanks and seizing Villers Ridge'.[150] Wilfrid Miles also claims in the *Official History* that 'Mounted action was insisted upon by Lieut. General Kavanagh.'[151] The brigade was concentrated to the north of Peiziere by 6.30am, ready to go, and under artillery fire; however, seeing no tank attack developing and aware that the Lucknow Brigade had made no progress, Brigadier General Neil Haig, commanding the Mhow Brigade, made no move.

The Cavalry Corps war diary is somewhat coy about what happened next. No mention of the Mhow Brigade appears in the diary itself apart from a report of its advance at 8.45am. In the attached 'Report on Operations' events are described thus:

> The Corps Commander, who had sent a Staff Officer to the 4th Cavalry Division, to report on their progress, telephoned at about 7.45am to GOC 4th Cavalry Division, ordering him to commence the advance on the objective allotted to him in the Corps Order. He had not moved earlier in view of the fact that the advance of the tanks with Lucknow Brigade had not materialised.[152]

Also contained in the Corps war diary is the typescript 'The battle of Epehy', by Colonel Maunsell, excerpts of which have been quoted already, and which formed the basis of his later account of events published in the *Cavalry Journal.*[153] Associated with this are letters from both Neil Haig, commanding Mhow Brigade itself, and Major General Kennedy, commanding the 4th Cavalry Division. The letters are somewhat more revealing. Haig states:

> The attack on Villers Guislain was by direct order of the Corps Commander.... I went up to Alfred Kennedy's HQ and explained the enemy's situation to him, and asked him to come down to my HQ himself.... Kennedy quite agreed with me that an attack on this position was impracticable and said he would go and talk to the Corps Commander on the telephone at once and explain the situation.[154]

Kennedy's letter gives an account of this conversation:

Kavanagh: 'How is your attack getting on?'

Kennedy: 'My attack? Why, it has not started as the dismounted attack has not made any progress. The tanks failed to turn up and there is nothing doing.'

Kavanagh: 'Rot! You have to carry out your attack as ordered.'

Kennedy: 'But my orders were to take advantage of any success gained in the mounted [*sic*] attack and as I say there has not been any success.'

Kavanagh: 'You have to carry out your attack at once.'

Kennedy: 'If you order me to do so I will try it.'

(I may say the Corps Commander was evidently very annoyed, and from the first, spoke very rudely.)[155]

Haig continues:

> Kennedy returned later and informed me that he had explained the situation carefully, that the Corps Commander was very annoyed at the delay and ordered the attack to take place at once.
>
> While I was issuing my orders ... one of the Corps staff rode up and said to me 'then can I inform the Corps Commander that you have great hopes of success?' I told him that he could go back and tell the Corps Commander that I didn't think we had a 'Dog's bloody earthly.' He returned and told the Corps Commander that I was not optimistic.[156]

Higher commanders in the rear forcing their subordinates into pointlessly costly attacks is something of a First World War cliché, and was a rarer event than popularly believed, but on this occasion at least Kavanagh was doing precisely that. Kennedy and Haig were thus left with no option but to press ahead with an attack in which they had no confidence. Haig's report of subsequent events appears in the Mhow Brigade war diary,[157] and was reprinted verbatim in the *Cavalry Journal* after his death.[158] Much of what follows is drawn from that account. Kennedy passed a formal order to Mhow Brigade at 8.15am. 'You are to endeavour to push towards your objective supported by the artillery.' The form of words itself speaks volumes about his lack of expectation of success. The situation which was presented to Haig was as follows: the brigade lay at Peiziere and the adjoining village of Epehy. Approximately 5,000 yards (4,500m) to the north-east lay Villers Guislain, on the brigade objective, Villers Ridge. The terrain in between was largely open and unobstructed, sloping down to the canal to the east, but with higher ground forming the shape of a capital 'E'. The ridge carrying the road between the two villages formed the spine to the west, with a ridge to the south around Epehy, a central ridge, known on British maps as 'Lark Spur', and Villers Ridge to the north. Two re-entrants ran westwards from the canal. The southerly of these was 'Catelet Valley' and the northern 'Targelle Ravine'; two southward projections of this northern valley were known as 'Quail' and 'Pigeon' Ravines, although neither is more than a gentle depression in broadly rolling country. Cutting off the eastern ends of these features was the former British line, now occupied by the Germans and principally consisting of a series of fortified posts connected by communication trenches. To the west, about two-thirds of the way along the road to Villers, lay a 'Raperie' or 'Beet Factory' that had been occupied and fortified by the Germans.

Haig's plan was that the 2nd Lancers, supported by one squadron of the 6th (Inniskilling) Dragoons, should swing wide to the east, following a road along the northern face of Catelet Valley, before turning north via Pigeon Ravine on to Villers Ridge. Meanwhile the remaining three squadrons of the Inniskillings would pass along the east side of the main Villers road, dropping into Quail Ravine and the southward turn at the eastern end of Targelle Ravine, in order to gain some shelter from, and bypass, the beet factory. The 38th (Central India) Horse would remain in support, as would the Sialkot Brigade.

The 2nd Lancers moved off through Epehy at around 9.00am. The regiment had been on its way into the trenches when recalled on 30 November so the men were without swords or lances. These had to be handed out from wagons as the men rode off and many went into action without either.[159] Shelling was intense from the start. The regiment (followed by C Squadron Inniskillings and a brigade machine-gun section) deployed beyond the village into column of squadrons in line of troop columns, and set off at a gallop down Catelet Valley. They came under heavy machine-gun fire from in front and from the higher ground on both flanks, but rode on until they reached the rear of the former British positions, a trench known as Kildare Trench and the associated Kildare Post. The fresh German wire behind the post was jumped, or gaps found, and the Lancers captured the trench after some hand-to-hand fighting. Fortunately the trench ran along the line of a pre-existing sunken road, so it was possible to get some horses under cover, as the lancers were rapidly pinned down in this position. The remaining horses had to be sent back up the valley and suffered severely on the return trip. Haig summed up the resulting situation:

> A German position had been captured and was occupied by about 200 men 2nd Lancers, 36 men Inniskilling Dragoons, 4 machine guns 11th MG squadron and in addition there were 169 horses in the position, which greatly interfered with the movement of the garrison and the evacuation of the wounded.[160]

The Lancers gave a fine account of themselves, and Lance Dafadar Gobind Singh won a VC for his bravery in carrying messages back up the valley to brigade HQ.[161] The opportunity for a mounted attack was also a great boost to regimental morale, as is shown in a letter home from Jemadar Jiwan Singh:

> Thanks be to God, the attack was made with the utmost bravery and it achieved splendid results. The fury of our charge and the ardour of our war cries so alarmed the enemy that he left his trenches and fled. At first we were assailed by machine-gun fire like a rain storm from left and right, and afterwards from the front, but how could the cowardly Germans stand before the onslaught of the braves of the Khalsa![162]

Sadly all this effort contributed little to the objectives of the attack. The 2nd Lancers were to remain cut off in Kildare Trench for the rest of the day, fighting an at times desperate struggle with bombs and machine guns, and only withdrawing under cover of darkness.

The remainder of the Inniskilling Dragoons, meanwhile, were unaware that this would be the fate of the Lancers, and seeing them move off to the east at about 9.35am, took this as their cue to begin their own advance. In similar formation to the Lancers, squadron column of line of troop columns, extended, they set out from north of Peiziere, but unlike the Lancers who had the slight cover of a valley, the first part of the Inniskillings' route as far as the beet factory was completely exposed. Also, due to an oversight, and the absence of C Squadron, which normally led the column but was away supporting the Lancers, the attack was led by D Squadron, with the machine-gun section immediately behind it, instead of at the rear of the column. Intense fire was encountered almost immediately, but the Dragoons pushed on at a gallop. Despite their best efforts, however, the task was hopeless. D Squadron and the machine guns got as far as the beet factory itself before being surrounded and forced to surrender, while Lieutenant Colonel Paterson, leading the rear two squadrons, pulled up while 600 yards distant and withdrew to Peiziere. The Inniskillings lost 102 casualties and over 150 horses in a little under ten minutes. The machine-gun section, consisting of two officers, fifty-three other ranks and eighty-seven horses, was a total loss, all killed or captured. The widely quoted remarks of Colonel Maunsell concerning this attack bear repetition here: 'The point of attempting a mounted attack under the circumstances seems incomprehensible. In the case of the Inniskillings, not one single element that has conduced to the success in mounted attacks since, and including, the time of Napoleon was present.'[163] Sadly this fact was known to Haig and Kennedy before the operation was attempted; it seems that only Kavanagh, at Cavalry Corps headquarters, believed there was any chance of success.

Haig's final effort to press forward the attack came at 10.10am. Two squadrons of the Mhow Brigade reserve regiment, the Central India Horse, were sent to try to push down the north side of Catelet Valley and support the 2nd Lancers. Despite advancing on foot, these troops rapidly came under heavy machine-gun fire and could make no progress. One squadron in fact became pinned down on Lark Spur and was forced to remain there until darkness fell.

The result of the morning's operations was that while the 2nd Lancers occupied a position at the eastern end of Catelet Valley, and the Guards and the Ambala Brigade held Gauche Wood, a large westward salient lay between the two, still occupied by the enemy. In particular German machine guns were active on the railway embankment north of Vaucelette Farm, in the area known as Chapel Crossing,[164] and the beet factory was still strongly held. Nonetheless, it is highly questionable whether the Germans had either the will or the ability to push on south-westwards beyond the positions they had gained on 30 November. Their activities seem to have been limited to local counter-attacks against thrusts by the cavalry. Kavanagh, however, felt that a further effort to dislodge them was required. At about midday he rode forward to the

4th and 5th Cavalry Divisions' HQ just to the west of Peiziere, summoning Kennedy and MacAndrew to arrange further assaults during the afternoon.[165] Orders were issued for an attack by the Canadian Cavalry Brigade towards Chapel Crossing, linking up with the south end of Gauche Wood, while the Lucknow Brigade, now returned to 4th Division command, would attack towards the beet factory, supported by the Mhow Brigade on its right. Orders for an attack at 3.00pm were issued at 12.40. This order did not reach Haig at Mhow Brigade until 2.15pm, owing to the weight of shelling on Peiziere. His response was to point out the parlous state of his brigade after the disasters of the morning: '4th Cavalry Division were informed that the total available force in the hand of the G.O.C. Mhow Cav. Bde. consisted of two weak squadrons of Inniskilling Dragoons, one squadron of CIH and two machine guns.'[166] Nonetheless an attack plan was developed requiring the remaining squadron of the Central India Horse to push forward, assisted by the two squadrons of that regiment already trapped on Lark Spur. 'OC Inniskilling Dragoons was informed that in the case of success in this attack, the remains of his two squadrons would act mounted.'[167]

Once again the artillery support for an attack on foot against entrenched enemy with large numbers of machine guns was limited to little more than the intrinsic RHA and RCHA batteries of the two divisions. This was simply not enough to make any impression on the enemy. The Canadian attack was initially successful. Lord Strathcona's Horse, with support from a squadron of the Royal Canadian Dragoons, were able to evict the Germans from Chapel Crossing and link up with the southern end of Gauche Wood, but that was as far as they were able to go.[168] To the south of them the troopers of the Lucknow Brigade were presented with the same obstacles they had faced in the morning, but with no new resources with which to attempt them. Nor were they advised of the Canadian attack on their flank so no proper coordination was possible. Jacobs' Horse led the attack towards the beet factory, advancing in short rushes, but each attempt was met with rising casualties and the attack stalled after a few hundred yards.[169] At least 'as no attack appeared to develop on the left flank' the Mhow Brigade was spared the necessity of further effort, and the squadrons of the Central India Horse were not sent forward.[170]

The attack by the Canadians on Chapel Crossing marked the end of significant offensive operations on the Cavalry Corps front. Overnight the brigades in the line were relieved by the reserve brigades of the two divisions, the Secunderabad on the 5th Division front and the Sialkot on the 4th. The Germans were content to hold the ground gained and although fighting continued to the north, the German flank opposite the cavalry remained quiet. The Cavalry Corps was finally relieved by III and VI Corps on 6 December, and the corps forward headquarters at Villers Faucon was closed on that day.[171]

By that time the British salient, gained on 20 November, had largely been evacuated and returned to German hands.

* * *

Clearly the offensive at Cambrai failed to achieve the objectives desired of it by its planners, and much of the ground gained was rapidly lost as a consequence of the German counter-offensive of 30 November. A series of recriminations rapidly followed, culminating in both 'questions in the House' and several official enquiries.[172] These tended to focus on the reasons why the Germans made such good progress on 30 November, and dwelt little on the actions of the cavalry. Unofficially, however, the feeling was quick to develop that the cavalry had failed to live up to the opportunity presented to it by the tank and infantry attack. Home noted in his diary on 10 December: 'There is a lot of talk about the Cavalry just now; people seem to think that we should have got through on 20 November.'[173] This view that the cavalry failed has been picked up by most subsequent literature on the battle.[174]

Two major criticisms have been made of the cavalry. First, it has been argued that Kavanagh and the Cavalry Corps headquarters were too far in the rear to properly control the battle, and thus missed what fleeting opportunities for advance occurred. Combined with this is criticism of Kavanagh himself as a commander. This view was first promulgated by J.F.C. Fuller, and is adopted more or less verbatim by Tim Travers, quoting the former, 'Meanwhile, J.F.C. Fuller knew that Kavanagh was miles away from the battle and was "surely the worst Cavalry general in all history".'[175] The performance of Kavanagh will be examined in more detail later, suffice to say at this point that part of the problem was intrinsic in the command structure, not in the person of the commander. This criticism was also voiced by those involved in the battle itself. General Woollcombe is reported to have remarked to his ADC at IV Corps 'that the cavalry had cost us our chance'.[176] Smithers in his 1992 work once again quoted Colonel Baker-Carr of the Tank Corps: 'What a chance that day was missed! Never before and never again was such an opportunity offered.'[177] Interestingly, Smithers, while keen to quote Baker-Carr's castigation of the cavalry, signally neglects the remarks in mitigation of their performance which followed in the original work:

> Why, then, did the cavalry not avail itself of this golden opportunity? It is a difficult question to answer, though one fact which is known has an important bearing on the subject, namely that cavalry leaders were strictly prohibited from taking any action without the permission of superior authority. This in itself largely explains their astonishing inactivity.[178]

Mullens, the commander with responsibility for the advance of the 1st Cavalry Division on 20 November, stated his own case in 'Lessons to be drawn from the Operations of the 1st Cavalry Division in the battle which began on November 20th 1917',[179] written less than a month after the event. In this he pointed out that after the experience of previous battles, close touch was maintained directly with the attacking infantry divisions, and as a result 'Reports, both accurate and prompt, were constantly received of the progress of the attack.' In the light of this he argued:

> Opportunities for the employment of cavalry are of so fleeting a nature that the GOC leading Cavalry Division and the GOC leading Cavalry Brigade, who are the individuals on the spot, should be held responsible for taking advantage of any opportunities which occur. Time does not admit of sending the information back to the rear and for re-transmission to the front. . . .
>
> It is most urgently represented that the leading Cavalry Division should be given the plan and should be allowed to carry out the task allotted in the best way that offers.

He went on to catalogue the 'counter-orders' he had received in the course of the day. It is clear that there is a good deal of merit in his argument. The interference of Cavalry Corps HQ, and possibly of Kavanagh himself, as well as that of IV Corps HQ, significantly slowed the progress of the 1st Cavalry Division. Kavanagh also failed to push the 2nd and 5th Divisions forward with adequate vigour, abandoning the 2nd Division on the side of the road for several hours and forgetting about it.

General Woollcombe and IV Corps naturally took issue with almost every point made by Mullens, denying any responsibility for the command delays. Some of this controversy has been described earlier. The IV Corps report summarising the exchange of orders between themselves and the 1st Cavalry Division concludes: 'It is not seen how any of these orders [HP.14 et seq.] impeded the advance of 1st Cavalry Division, or in any way interfered with the execution of the original orders. The only object of the various orders was to hasten the action of the cavalry.'[180]

However, no matter what the 'object' of the orders may have been or the good intentions of IV Corps, it is difficult not to sympathise with Mullens. Woollcombe's argument that the messages contained only 'information' is a weak one, notwithstanding the fact that the said information was grossly inaccurate. The orders in the afternoon to move over Premy Chapel ridge were also a clear change from the original planned line of advance. That confusion and delay resulted is hardly surprising. The staff of Cavalry Corps advanced headquarters must also shoulder some of the responsibility. Their follow-up message regarding Flesquières can only be regarded as a direct order to the

1st Cavalry Division to advance by that route. Given the circuitous channels of communications and complex command structure, Mullens can hardly have been expected to ignore an order from Kavanagh on the grounds that since 6.15am he had been under IV Corps rather than Cavalry Corps command. Kavanagh made no reference to this in his comments on the performance of the division but it is tempting to suggest that this interference in the chain of command was at his behest. Either way the Cavalry Corps war diary would seem to imply that they were under the impression that they were passing on the intent, if not the actual wording, of IV Corps' wishes.[181]

It should also be borne in mind that the 1st Cavalry Division was extremely constrained in its freedom of movement. If the Hindenburg Support Line is taken into account, the German defensive systems extended through Flesquières and some distance to the east of (beyond) Ribecourt. Thus the division was not in a position simply to change direction and outflank defended positions in this part of the battlefield. Later on this would be possible, but not at this stage of the advance. The rôle of the cavalry was to move and fight flexibly beyond the lines of the enemy's fixed defences, but up to that point they were in the hands of the infantry and tanks who must first punch a hole through those defences for their advance. Whatever the protestations of Woollcombe and IV Corps, it was not the rôle of the cavalry to assist in the capture of Flesquières, which lay within the frontal part of the German defensive system and was thus part of the first phase of the attack. Cooperation with the cavalry was not planned until the later move on Bourlon and Fontaine. Harper's 51st Division conspicuously failed to capture Flesquières in the early stages of the battle and it was this which blocked the advance of the cavalry, and not *vice versa*. This was summed up by Cyril Falls when he observed: 'The Cavalry action on a grand scale had been a complete failure. Whatever chances of success it may have had were extinguished by the failure to take Flesquières.'[182]

The second criticism levelled at the cavalry is of lack of initiative at lower levels of command. Both Robert Woollcombe[183] and Stephen Badsey[184] have argued that years of inactivity had led to a cavalry force that was listless and timid, and incapable at all levels of decisive action. A curious further twist to these arguments is the view offered by Smithers that 'fortunately for themselves, the British cavalry did nothing',[185] his argument being that had the cavalry pushed forward, their self-evident uselessness and vulnerability to enemy machine guns would have led to senseless slaughter. Even Anglesey, who is normally reluctant to heap criticism on his chosen subjects, follows this line, observing that the inactivity of the cavalry divisions was 'fully justified'[186] and 'how lucky it was that there were not more "thrusters" in command'.[187]

Kavanagh, writing in February 1918, was generally supportive of his sub-ordinates, but took a similar line:

I am confident that Major General Mullens did everything in his power to carry out the instructions originally given him by IV Corps. The only criticism I have had to make on the action of the 1st Cavalry Division on the 20th November is that GOC 2nd Cavalry Brigade when he finally started to advance by the Bois des Neufs [*sic*] and carry out the original instructions given him, was slow in doing so, and did not appear to have pushed forward and supported his leading regiment with sufficient determination and resolution. His difficulties, however, were very great as his brigade was stretched out on a single narrow road with trenches and wire on either side for a long distance and their progress was of necessity slow.[188]

Others have also been critical of this, citing the presence of a company of tanks behind Premy Chapel ridge, tasked with cooperation with the cavalry but left unused.[189]

Simple reflection on the rôle of the 2nd Cavalry Brigade demonstrates that this view does no justice to the commanders at the 'sharp end'. Leaving their points of concentration shortly after midnight, the 4th Dragoon Guards were to be lead regiment all day as the narrowness of the advance route did not offer the option of relieving them with another regiment. Thus they were responsible for the advance to Trescault, for patrolling towards Flesquières in the morning, for the dismounted assault on Ribecourt at 2.00pm, for patrolling over Premy Chapel ridge prior to the abortive attempt at encirclement of Flesquières, and finally for attacking La Folie at the gallop at last light. By this time they had been marching and fighting for 16 hours, and so their conduct is perhaps more remarkable for its continued aggressiveness than for the lack of it.

It is also clear that Beale-Brown and Sewell had still not ruled out the capture of Cantaing at last light. The deployment of one squadron frontally on foot towards the village (B Squadron, 4th Dragoon Guards), while a second (A Squadron) attempted to gallop it via a flank is straight out of the pages of *Cavalry Training*. As Beale-Brown observed, 'It was now too late and too dark'[190] to wait for guns and to seek out the cooperation of tanks. Indeed, had he done so the same criticism of hesitation might have been levelled with greater justification. Instead his regiments continued to fight flexibly and aggressively, relying on their own internal resources. Further, as Sewell pointed out (quoted earlier), the presence of the enemy on the east bank of the canal, effectively in the rear of any attack towards Cantaing, made it a dangerous undertaking. Had the brigade not been held up for 3 hours earlier in the day by the events before Flesquières, the result may have been quite different. Add to this the exploits of the Fort Garry Horse across the St Quentin Canal and it is apparent that at regimental level at least there was no lack of 'cavalry spirit'.

Higher up the chain of command, however, the accusation of indecisiveness carries more weight. Of the cavalry divisional commanders, Mullens seems to have pushed on, but Greenly (in command of the 2nd Cavalry Division) was clearly reluctant to take any kind of chance in crossing the canal at Masnières on the evening of 20 November. The rôle of corps commanders, both of infantry and cavalry, has already been considered. The conclusions of the inquiry into the Cambrai battle, although principally concerned with the events of 30 November, were that while no blame could be attached to any commanders at corps level or above, there were failures lower down and that in particular 'junior officers, NCOs and men' had been at fault.[191] This is clearly untrue. It is arguable that in the cavalry at least the reverse was the case, and that while regimental and brigade commanders took the fight to the enemy as far as possible, they were let down by inertia and indecisiveness at each successive level of higher command.

* * *

Part of the command and control problem which plagued the cavalry throughout 1916 and 1917 was the number of tiers or levels of command through which its orders had to pass. One of these levels was that of the Cavalry Corps itself. This calls into question the function and usefulness of the corps as an institution. Given the conclusions above, that the failure to get the cavalry forward on 20 November was in large part due to the interference of the Cavalry Corps HQ, and the widespread criticism of its commander which follows on from this, an obvious wider question arises. Did the Cavalry Corps and its leader have any positive rôle to play? Would a series of independent cavalry divisions under GHQ control, as was briefly the case in 1916 (described in Chapter 2), have been a better option, with divisions serving directly under infantry corps command?

The answer to this lies in precisely what a 'corps' represents, and two interpretations of this are possible. First, 'corps' may be used in the sense implied in the term 'Regiments and Corps of the British Army', that is in an essentially 'cap-badge' rôle as a supra-regimental organisation of specialist troops of one kind or another. Obvious examples of this are the Royal Flying Corps (RFC), the Machine Gun Corps (MGC) formed in October 1915, and its offspring (formerly the Heavy Branch MGC) the Tank Corps. Besides an important moral rôle in supplying their members with a corporate identity, these formations were vital to their constituent units as they provided not only a centre for training and for the development of specialist equipment relevant to the corps' rôle, but also a voice in the ever more clamorous debate over manpower and resources. There is little doubt that the Cavalry Corps had an important function in this regard. The supply and training of the cavalry, particularly over the winter, was the responsibility of the corps, as has been discussed in earlier chapters. The moral value of the corps was also important, as emphasised by Home on the break-up of the British and Indian Cavalry Corps in March 1916: 'As regards the Cavalry the Corps formation has been done away with, ... I am heartbroken over their decision. We have all worked hard for this old Corps and hoped one day it would be used in open warfare.'[192] His contrasting joy at its reinstatement in September 1916 is evident: 'It is very nice to be amongst the old Cavalry once more. We are going to have all five Divisions and it will be a great day for us when we get going.'[193] This morale factor should not be underestimated; the cavalry suffered from a steady drain of its manpower to those young corps mentioned above, the tanks and the RFC, and anything that raised the profile and prestige of the cavalry was vital to its continuing success.

Thus the administrative value of the Cavalry Corps is not in doubt. What is much more questionable, however, is its operational function. This relates to the second definition of a 'corps' as a formation of a number of divisions, containing all arms and capable of limited independent action. This concept of a corps can be traced in large part to the armies of Napoleon a hundred years or more earlier. Its character and function in the BEF in the First World War have been thoroughly examined by Andy Simpson in both his unpublished 2001 thesis,[194] and his recent published paper in Gary Sheffield and Dan Todman's *Command and Control on the Western Front*.[195] While Simpson does not deal explicitly with the Cavalry Corps (indeed it is absent even from the list of corps excluded from his study[196]), his examination of the function of and definition of the rôle of other corps serves as a useful point of comparison with that of the cavalry.

Simpson points out that in 1914 the BEF had not fully resolved the question of corps function. While two corps were deployed to France this was largely because a force of six infantry divisions was considered too large to be controlled directly by the commander in chief.[197] The concept of self-contained all-arms forces was applied at divisional level, each infantry division having integral artillery, signal and engineer components as well as the necessary ambulance and supply train, and a squadron of divisional cavalry. During 1914 the cavalry was similarly organised at the divisional level, having the same integral assets, RHA batteries, mounted signal, engineer and medical units.[198] Thus both infantry and cavalry divisions could be considered as independent units, and indeed functioned as such. It has been noted in Chapter 2, however, that in the cavalry in particular many of these assets existed at brigade level, and that at the outbreak of war even the divisional structure, let alone that of the corps, had to be evolved *ad hoc*.

From late 1915, however, the relationship between the function of division and corps began to change, and from the Somme offensive of 1916 onwards a new system had developed. Simpson identifies four main functions of corps after this period.[199] The first of these relates to artillery. Prior to each organised offensive large numbers of additional guns would typically be assembled. These fell under the command of the corps artillery adviser, initially the Brigadier General Royal Artillery (BGRA), later redesignated the General Officer Commanding Royal Artillery (GOCRA). These officers controlled a force of artillery vastly larger than that assembled from within the divisions comprising the corps, and also took control of the artillery of those divisions, organising it to support the operations of the corps as a whole, supporting each division in turn as the operation required. In addition, one of the offensive lessons that was gradually appreciated by the commanders of the BEF in the course of the war was that it was unrealistic to expect troops to operate effectively beyond the protective umbrella provided by this artillery.

The three further corps' functions devolve from the presence of this artillery: administration, planning and reconnaissance. As the corps' larger guns were relatively immobile, corps tended to remain geographically quite static. The corps would remain in place while divisions rotated in and out of the area, and indeed different army headquarters might also come and go from above the corps. Meanwhile the corps took control of administration within its area: roads, railways, supply dumps, the supply of ammunition (particularly to the artillery) and so on were all controlled by corps. This increasing concentration of assets at corps rather than divisional level is reflected in the concentration of the individual cavalry squadrons previously allocated at divisional level into a 'corps cavalry regiment' in May 1916.[200] As a consequence of these factors, when an operation was being developed much of the detailed planning would take place at corps level. Decisions about objectives would be made in conference between corps and army, and the artillery fire-plan developed accordingly by the GOCRA. Individual divisions were responsible only for putting their troops in at the right time under the protection of this barrage. Finally, in support of its artillery, most corps had a dedicated RFC squadron available to direct artillery fire and conduct reconnaissance. Thus much of the information supplied to divisional and brigade commanders would have its origins at corps. This was the case not only before an attack began but, as Simpson emphasises, during the attack itself, where the 'big picture' was best understood at corps level, supplied by information from individual divisions and directly from contact aircraft. This picture was in turn fed back down the chain of command to the front-line troops.

If the presence of Kavanagh and the Cavalry Corps headquarters within the chain of command during an offensive, as they were at Cambrai, is to be judged, then Simpson's corps function criteria provide a very useful comparison. It rapidly becomes apparent that the Cavalry Corps HQ provided few if any of these functions. Above all, as the rôle of the infantry corps grew from the presence of its guns, so that of the Cavalry Corps declined in equal measure.

Equipped only with its integral divisional RHA brigades, the artillery strength of the Cavalry Corps was in relative terms insignificant. Thus it was not able to directly support its constituent divisions. Nor did it command the local administrative infrastructure, or possess special local knowledge to assist those formations. A squadron of RFC aircraft was directly attached to the Cavalry Corps, charged with providing information and communication,[201] but in the absence of guns to direct, one of the key functions of corps aircraft was lost. Also, in the event the weather on 20 November was such that little useful aerial reconnaissance was possible.[202]

Given these constraints, the placing of the 1st Cavalry Division under the operational control of IV Corps on 20 November seems not only the better choice of command arrangements but practically the *only* sensible option. Were the division to be controlled by the Cavalry Corps headquarters, that headquarters would have no practical support (in the form of artillery) to provide to the division, and as it would not be receiving information on the progress of the adjacent infantry divisions and its aircraft were struggling, no help in the form of information would be forthcoming either.

In short, the Cavalry Corps had no useful operational rôle on 20 November. Its presence in the chain of command served only to hinder the advance of the cavalry divisions. It is also arguable that had the 2nd and 5th Cavalry Divisions not waited on Kavanagh's word to advance but simply moved up according to the timetable behind the advance of III Corps (or been under their direct control), then the Canadian Cavalry Brigade might have reached the St Quentin Canal as much as 2 hours earlier. The consequences which might have flowed from that are a matter for speculation, but could have been significant. Before developing this idea too far, however, one of the other key rôles of the infantry corps must be considered, that is the provision of a heavy artillery umbrella for operations. It has been shown in a previous chapter that the advance of the cavalry at Arras was severely hindered by the fact that it outran its artillery support. In spite of efforts to provide flanking fire from heavy guns to the south, the artillery command was insufficiently flexible to achieve this. Had significant forces of cavalry been able to cross the St Quentin Canal on 20 November, they may well have been able to inflict significant damage on unorganised German rear echelon units, but it is likely that had they encountered significant organised resistance this lack of guns would have become a significant factor in their ability to make any further progress.

Serious questions also surround the rôle of the Cavalry Corps and Kavanagh on 30 November/1 December. There is no doubt that the arrival of the 20th Hussars and the Guards on 30 November helped to restore the line around the German break-in at Gouzeaucourt. Kavanagh's subsequent handling of the battle, however, was seriously flawed. Little or no information is available to determine what Kavanagh himself thought about the situation, and his attitudes have principally to be inferred from his actions and the orders he gave. It seems his primary error was to believe (wrongly as it turned out) that the Germans in this area were intent on a further advance, when in fact they were a flank guard content to consolidate their positions on their early gains. From this mis-apprehension flowed a series of further errors. The first of these was that the German forces would present themselves as blocks of troops advancing across open country, and that they would thus be vulnerable to mounted attack, when in fact they had never ventured far beyond the existing British rear trench lines and had wired themselves in.

The next mistake was to believe that the situation was grave enough to commit his corps to battle come-what-may regardless of the ultimate cost. This climate of panic was not exclusive to the Cavalry Corps headquarters and pervaded a number of parts of the British forces at that time. The BEF by this point in the war was accustomed to being strategically on the offensive; the Germans had organised virtually no operational level offensive battles since Verdun, restricting themselves to local counter-attacks. Thus any big German attack would be a severe shock. This was compounded by the fact that Allied intelligence had, as discussed earlier, seriously misjudged the reserves available to the Germans and their capacity for offensive action. The initial success of the German attack, which took a substantial bite several miles deep out of VII Corps' front, would have added to this sense of shock. This shock and surprise seems to have seriously affected Kavanagh's judgement.

The result of these factors was a strange development. The Cavalry Corps war diary refers several times to the 'Cavalry Corps line',[203] and indeed the corps was given responsibility for the area between III Corps in the north and VII Corps in the south, where the German attack was centred. The allocation of a sector of the front to the Cavalry Corps implies that the cavalry would be capable of holding such a line in a similar fashion to an infantry corps. While they were indeed able to create a defence, it has been demonstrated that the Cavalry Corps lacked a large proportion of the infrastructure and assets considered normal in an infantry corps, in particular in terms of artillery. Thus to expect them to function in the same way was demanding a lot. Rather than recognising the inherent weakness of his formation, and concentrating on a conservative, defensive strategy, Kavanagh seems to have decided that 1 December represented a historic opportunity for the Cavalry Corps to show its mettle and in some way 'save the day'. Thus he launched a series of increasingly desperate counter-attacks, each of which lacked all the basic ingredients for success: planning, intelligence, knowledge of ground, coordination with flanking units and above all guns. The price for this ambition (paid by the Mhow Brigade in particular) has already been described.

An interesting contrast with the activities of the Cavalry Corps commander at Cambrai is provided by the commander of the Tank Corps, Brigadier General

Elles. His 'corps' was essentially an administrative, cap-badge organisation, with no tactical command rôle. His rather theatrical gesture of leading the attack of H Battalion himself aboard the tank 'Hilda' flying a large and newly invented corps flag is widely quoted.[204] However, he had been heavily involved in the planning of the attack and logistical preparations, and the battalions of his corps were fully integrated into the command structure of the corps and divisions they were supporting. He was thus left with essentially nothing to do once the offensive had begun, except perhaps try to lead by example. It was also pointed out by Brigadier General Percy Hobart (himself a famous tank-man) that since all of the Tank Corps vehicles were in the first wave of the attack, Elles did not have to worry about being in a position to command any reserves later.[205] His acceptance of this is reflected in his own 'Tank Corps Special Order' issued before the battle: 'All that hard work and ingenuity can achieve has been done in the way of preparation. It remains for unit commanders and for tank crews to complete the work by judgement and pluck in the battle itself.'[206]

This relinquishing of operational control in the battle itself might have served as a useful model for the Cavalry Corps commander. It is not known to what extent Kavanagh would have been aware of Elles' approach, but even had he been, it is unlikely that he would have thought it relevant. The Tank Corps, while growing in stature, had yet to establish any form or separate identity comparable to that of the cavalry. Tanks were still simply adjuncts to the infantry battle like machine guns or trench mortars. The concept of armour as a separate 'arm' and the possibility of distinct armoured formations had not yet developed. Indeed, armoured cars had been integrated into cavalry formations in the same way as they had into infantry formations (as in 1918 tanks would be). Thus the rôles of tanks and cavalry would have appeared far less analogous to the contemporary eye than they do today.

* * *

Discussion of the rôle of the Tank Corps leads naturally on to the relationship between cavalry and tanks on the battlefield. The techno–centric and rather anti-cavalry stance of much of the writing on Cambrai has already been touched on earlier in this chapter. However, the operations at Cantaing on 21 November and (less successfully) on 1 December have shown that rather than cavalry and tanks being opposed, or mutually exclusive, forms of warfare, battlefield co-operation was both possible and planned-for from the outset. Such cooperation had been foreseen by the cavalry commanders, and special instructions for such operations were issued before the battle (see Appendix 4.1). Previous cavalry cooperation with armour, in the form of armoured cars, has been discussed in earlier chapters, and what is notable about these instructions is that they do not suggest that tanks are new to the cavalry, or that they require new tactics, rather that previous experience of cavalry–armour cooperation remains valid. Paragraph (d) of the notes is especially illuminating: '(d) Tanks should be used as pivots for the Cavalry. They are really moving Machine Guns heavily armed, and though they do not have the pace of Armoured Motors they should be used on the same principle.'[207]

Cavalry had been operating in conjunction with armoured cars since the Somme battles of 1916, and their successes in this regard during the German retreat to the Hindenburg Line in the spring of 1917 have already been examined in Chapter 3. Thus far from being new and wonderful, the cavalry attitude to tanks may be characterised as 'like armoured cars, but slower'.

It is useful to examine each of the ways in which horses and armour were expected to cooperate, and the degree of success in each case. The primary function of the tanks was to do the work previously carried out by preliminary bombardment – to provide routes of advance through the German wire. For the infantry this was simply a matter of advancing in the wake of each tank and stepping over the crushed-down wire entanglement. For the cavalry the job was rather more complex. As was the case in the opening phase of both the Somme and Arras offensives, the routes of 'cavalry tracks' were identified for the lines of advance of the cavalry divisions. Three such routes were identified. 'Cavalry track battalions' were then assembled, one each from the dismounted elements of each division,[208] and it was the job of these troops to clear the line of advance in each case. To assist with the wire clearance twelve specially adapted wire-clearing tanks were placed at the disposal of these parties, equipped with a large grapnel attached to the rear of the tank by a hawser.[209] The idea was that the grapnel would be dragged behind the tank to break or drag aside the wire entanglement. The Tank Corps was content with the effectiveness of this approach, reporting

> Wire pulled back to form gaps of at least 60 yards in every belt of wire to the final objective, just after midday on 20th November.
>
> Stretch of wire limited to 60 yards definitely but much more could be done per tank if necessary. After pulling the wire away the ground is absolutely clear of every scrap of wire or obstruction such as posts etcetera.[210]

However, this was not necessarily the case. Third Army Instructions, after allocating the tanks, had warned that: '6. Too great a reliance cannot be placed in the capabilities of the wire-pulling tanks. You must therefore be prepared to clear away any wire which still blocks your advance on any of the three routes.'[211]

This was good advice. Maunsell related in the *Cavalry Journal* how 'Certain tanks were detailed to assist our working parties clear the wire. The passages made by them did not enable the horses to get through. . . . Even after they had cleared a space, however, the denseness of the grass tangled up with odd bits of wire, iron stakes, etcetera, needed a lot of clearing.'[212] This view was expressed immediately after the battle in the 1st Cavalry Division report: 'It was noted that the tracks made through the belts of wire by the passage of the tanks were not practicable for Cavalry. Several such passages were personally explored and in no case was it possible to ride a horse through.'[213] Nor was wire the only obstacle. The commander of the 4th Cavalry Division Track Battalion reported that no fewer than twenty-six separate trench lines had to be either ramped or bridged on his line of advance, a job for which tanks provided no assistance.[214]

It should not therefore be assumed that the tanks somehow swept a clear corridor ahead of the cavalry along which all they had to do was ride forward. The assertions of Colonel Baker-Carr, commander of the 1st Tank Brigade, that 'On each section of the front, gaps in the wire, a quarter of a mile or more wide, had been made; the "going" was splendid, and from midday onwards, except in a few isolated spots, organised resistance had ceased to exist,'[215] should be regarded with extreme scepticism. Rather, as had been the case in previous offensives, the cavalry cut, dug and bridged its way forward under its own power, albeit assisted by the wire-pullers. It is a tribute to the skill of the cavalry track battalions that once again these tracks were ready on schedule.

Cooperation between cavalry and tanks in the exploitation phase of the 20 November battle was never properly tested, as that phase of the battle never really took place (as has been discussed at some length). The cavalry were, however, able to cooperate successfully with tanks on two occasions, admittedly on a small scale. The first was the support gained by the Northumberland Hussars at le Quennet Farm on 20 November, and the second was the attack on Cantaing by the Queens Bays the following day. Both of these small fights showed that tank firepower and cavalry mobility could be successfully combined, and both events have been overlooked by those such as Tim Travers who are keen to emphasise the contrast between the two arms.

Curiously, one of the problems highlighted by Wilfrid Miles in the Official History, and reiterated by Travers,[216] was the fact that where the tanks were successful, and pushed through the German organised defences into more open ground, they out-ran their infantry supports. The infantry, who by that time had been following on foot some 8,000 yards (7km), had become extremely tired. As Miles puts it, 'the Tank Corps had already come to the conclusion that some form of rapid transportation was needed by the infantry'.[217] A four-legged answer to this problem was perhaps not as far away as those fixated on technological solutions have suggested.

Travers also acknowledges that the tanks needed artillery as well as infantry support in order to be effective, but his thesis continues that the failure of this cooperation was a result of inflexibility on the part of the infantry and gunners who were not able to keep up with the new flexible warfare carried out by the tanks.[218] This argument misses an essential point about the tanks at Cambrai, which was precisely their lack of tactical flexibility. The initial tank attack was highly successful, but only because each tank had a pre-prepared objective and a thoroughly reconnoitred route to it. Once unleashed, the tanks were only able to crawl along their pre-ordained route. They were virtually blind and communication with them was almost impossible. The suggestion that commanders were able to summon up tanks to participate in spontaneous exploitation operations neglects these basic facts.

The experience of the Cavalry Corps in cooperating with tanks after the German counter-attack on 1 December is instructive in revealing the shortcomings of tanks in anything like a fluid battle. A variety of commentators, including the commander in chief, Haig, congratulated the Tank Corps on the strenuous efforts made to put tanks in the field on 30 November. Sixty-three tanks were deployed and Fuller called it 'one of the most remarkable tank achievements of the war'.[219] Yet given that the Tank Corps had started with 378 fighting tanks only ten days before,[220] to field only slightly more than 15 per cent of that number shows the massive difficulties faced by the tanks in responding to any kind of unforeseen circumstance. (The Cavalry Corps, by contrast, was able to respond to the same events with a much larger portion of its strength. The news of the German attack was received at 8.30am, the cavalry had an advance HQ set up at Villers Faucon by 10.30 and elements of three divisions in action by noon.)

Even once these tanks had been provided, their contribution to the battle was variable. Tanks were allocated to cooperate with the Guards in their recapture of Gouzeaucourt, but did not arrive until after the fighting was over. The following day tanks were again allocated to support the Guards on the attack on Gauche Wood. These failed to arrive, while those supporting the complementary attack on the wood by the 5th Cavalry Division lost direction and shot up Hodson's Horse before entering the wood after the fighting had ended. Lieutenant Colonel Maunsell commented in his report on these events: 'The actual presence of the tanks was more of a danger than an asset, for they attracted fire of every description and many casualties occurred to men standing in their neighbourhood. They were, in consequence, requested to withdraw.'[221] The war diary of the Ambala Brigade records a similar sentiment in its 'Lessons of 1st December': 'Keep away from tanks in the advance and send them away the minute the objective is reached – they draw fire.'[222] To the south the tanks allocated to lead the attack of the Lucknow and Mhow Brigades of the 4th Cavalry Division were not only unable to reach the arranged rendezvous, but when launched took the wrong line and took no part in the cavalry attack, with tragic consequences for the Mhow Brigade.

The conclusion suggested by these events is that cavalry–tank cooperation was certainly possible, but was very difficult to achieve *ad-hoc* except on a very small scale. It required a significant degree of planning, particularly on behalf of the tanks if they were to be able to participate at the right place and at the right time. Also, where this cooperation broke down, as often it did, the failure was by no means always attributable to the 'medieval' horsemen. Mechanised warfare was in its infancy and the tank-men still had a good deal to learn; meanwhile there was still plenty of room on the battlefield for the flexible mobility provided by the horse, as was to be demonstrated as the war moved into its final year.

Chapter 5

From Operation *Michael* to the 'Hundred Days', 1918

As regards the Cavalry – people at home ask, 'They had a great chance at Cambrai – is it any use keeping them? They will never have such a chance again.' That is the crux of the whole matter – on this they may do anything – make the Cavalry into latrine caretakers. I shall be glad to have a rest – that is that.

Brigadier General A. Home, BGGS Cavalry Corps,
22 December 1917[1]

John Terraine commented that in January 1918 'The British Army in France was now at one of its lowest ebbs of the War',[2] and as Home's remark above suggests, this malaise extended equally into the ranks of the cavalry. There was a feeling that Cambrai represented their best chance, and while supporters of the mounted arm were merely disappointed, those who opposed the presence of the cavalry in France took the opportunity to use them as a scapegoat for the failures of the offensive. Ironically, the cavalry was about to reach what was perhaps its peak of effectiveness in the whole war, as well as undergoing some of its severest tests yet.

Unfortunately this crisis of faith in mounted troops coincided with (or possibly contributed to) one of the fiercer periods of conflict in the on–going dispute between Haig, as commander in chief in France, and the prime minister Lloyd George and his war cabinet.[3] In summary this may be characterised as an argument between Lloyd George and his followers, who had lost faith in a decisive result in France, at least in the short term, and with it faith in Haig as commander in chief, and Haig himself, who felt that France was the only decisive theatre of the war. The result was a starvation of the BEF of manpower and resources, at a critical time when many observers including Haig felt that the collapse of Russia had placed Germany in an ideal position to mount a large attack in the west (a view that was to be vindicated from March 1918).

Within this broader context of manpower shortages, the cavalry was an easy target for reduction or even complete disbandment. The maintenance of five cavalry divisions in France had been challenged by the War Office as early as

May 1917, when Haig was asked to consider the dismounting of at least one division. He was also reprimanded by the War Office for the diversion of cavalry reinforcements:

> In this connection it is noticed that of the cavalry drafts lately dispatched as reinforcements for Infantry units in your command, 1,000 have apparently retransferred to cavalry. The Army Council desire to emphasize that drafts sent from this country for a particular arm should not be diverted to another arm without previous reference to, and sanction of, the War Office.[4]

Haig felt strongly, as he always had, that a powerful force of cavalry remained a vital part of his offensive – and indeed defensive – capability, and that to remove it was short-sighted folly. He set out his views at length in a letter to the War Office on 28 June 1917:

> I hold strongly that as the war develops a time will come possibly at no very distant date when the employment of cavalry in masses will not only [be] feasible but urgently necessary in order to turn a favorable situation to full account.
>
> I consider it of such importance that the cavalry required for this purpose should be constantly available, and fully trained, that I am unable to concur either in any reduction of the five Cavalry Divisions now in France, or in their constant readiness for action in masses being impaired by using any part of them as Divisional, Corps, or Army Cavalry even as a temporary measure.[5]

These remarks also demonstrate Haig's continuing attachment, discussed in respect of each of the earlier offensives covered by this study, to the idea of massed cavalry exploitation, which was never to be realised. However, his desire to retain the cavalry intact, albeit for the wrong reasons, is commendable.

The outcome of this contest was a partial victory for the War Office. Although the cavalry divisions initially remained unaffected, all but three of the corps cavalry regiments (mostly regiments of yeomanry distributed among the infantry corps) were dismounted in October 1917.[6] As will appear later, this short-sighted decision was to impact on the Cavalry Corps later in 1918. The Prime Minister, supported by Winston Churchill (who had taken over from Lloyd George as Minister of Munitions, and was seeking additional manpower for his tank-based ambitions), also returned to the subject in December 1917. A minute of the Cabinet Committee on Manpower spelled out their position:

> The Prime Minister stated that he gathered that the Chief of the Imperial General Staff [Wilson] was in substantial agreement with

the desirability of using the personnel of the Cavalry in other arms of the Service, notably in Tanks, in the Air Service and Artillery.

General Smuts pointed out that the American Army would require a large number of horses and the British Cavalry horses might be used for this purpose and a great saving of tonnage effected thereby.[7]

This time Haig, fighting to retain his own job, was unsuccessful in his defence of the cavalry. The result of this was a reduction in strength of the Cavalry Corps in France from five divisions to three, and an accompanying re-organisation of the remaining troops. This was completed in early March 1918 (see Appendix 5.1).[8] As part of this reorganisation, the Indian regiments from within the 4th and 5th Cavalry Divisions were dispatched to Palestine. The Canadian Brigade and four of the British regiments remaining from these divisions were retained in France (the exception being the 1st (Kings) Dragoon Guards, who had already been sent to India in October 1917). Within the three remaining cavalry divisions, all of the yeomanry regiments (with the exception of the Queen's Own Oxfordshire Hussars) and the three regiments of Household Cavalry were removed, the latter to be dismounted as machine-gunners. These spaces were then filled by the British regiments from the former Indian cavalry divisions. The result was that the 1st Cavalry Division remained almost un-changed (only the Bedfordshire Yeomanry being replaced by the 8th Hussars). The 2nd Cavalry Division was entirely unchanged, while the 3rd Cavalry Division lost three regiments of yeomanry and three of Household Cavalry, which were replaced by three British regiments from the Indian divisions, and the Canadian Cavalry Brigade, complete. The four regiments of yeomanry removed from the cavalry divisions were originally intended to be converted to cyclists. The regiments had petitioned to be motor machine-gunners instead and this was initially agreed, but in the end the units were broken up to provide reinforcements to the regiments remaining within the Cavalry Corps to make up losses suffered during the March fighting.[9]

The ostensible purpose of this move was to increase the cavalry force in Palestine, and at the same time to save shipping in the provision of supplies to the cavalry in France. In fact neither of these objectives was achieved. Badsey has demonstrated that the saving in shipping across the Channel was easily eclipsed by the shipping required for the movements between France and the East,[10] and the net gain to General Allenby in Palestine fell to only two regiments, as having received a reinforcement of eleven regiments from France and elsewhere, he was ordered to return nine yeomanry regiments for dismounted service in France as machine-gunners.[11] The outcome of this vast reshuffle was simply to reduce significantly the fighting power of the Cavalry Corps in France at the outset of what was to be its busiest year, without providing a major boost to numbers in other theatres or any significant logistical savings.

*   *   *

A substantial German attack was widely predicted in the spring of 1918. The collapse of Russia had freed large numbers of German troops to fight in the west, while the build-up of American forces in France meant that the window of opportunity for the Germans would not last long. Haig himself told the War Cabinet in January that 'the coming four months would be <u>the critical period of the war</u>'.[12] The likely point of attack was recognised equally clearly: the southern, thinly defended portion of the British line around St Quentin, with the aim of driving a wedge between the British and French armies south of that point. Such an attack would fall principally on the British Fifth Army under General Gough, and the southern portion of General Byng's Third Army.

There is not space to discuss this attack as a whole, but the British defensive strategy may be briefly summarised. While the BEF had spent the war to date largely on an offensive footing, the lessons of the increasingly sophisticated German systems of defence had been learnt equally well by the British by 1918. In particular the use of deep defensive positions and 'elasticity' in the face of attack had become the basis of the defence, drawing the enemy into a previously determined 'battle zone' behind the thinly defended front line, where counter-attacks would be launched.[13] Unfortunately, in the Fifth Army area much of the rearward parts of this defensive system existed only as lines on maps, or as 'spit-locked' trenches only a few inches deep. The forces defending them were also thinly spread. Not only had an additional sector of the front been taken over from the French, but the divisions expected to hold it were reduced, in common with all the British (but not Dominion) divisions in France, from twelve battalions to nine. This was a response to manpower shortages, but each division was still expected to defend the same extent of front, and to act in all ways as if it were still twelve battalions strong.[14]

All three cavalry divisions (of the recently much reduced corps) were placed in support of the Fifth Army front. They were spread out approximately 12 miles behind the front line, with the 1st Cavalry Division based at Flamicourt (just outside Peronne) supporting XIX Corps; the 2nd Cavalry Division at Quesmy in the south near Noyon, and the 3rd Cavalry Division in the centre at Athies, opposite St Quentin. The latter two divisions were tasked to support III Corps at the extreme south of the British line.[15] Unfortunately, the standing orders for these units in the event of an attack were based on a misapprehension. As has been seen earlier, for example at Cambrai, it was not uncommon for cavalry brigades to form dismounted units, usually of weak battalion strength, for service in the trenches. Fifth Army's plan anticipated a fight contained within the organised defence lines of the 'battle zone', or at worst the similar but less fortified 'rear zone'. Thus it was expected that the cavalry would contribute to this fighting on foot within these defensive systems. Major Preston, who fought in these battles as a machine-gun officer, and whose lengthy accounts of the events of 1918 in the *Cavalry Journal* form a significant source for this chapter, commented: 'For years our cavalry leaders had prepared and hoped for a 'Gap', but they had always visualised the gap made by us in the German line. The possibility of the enemy making such a gap in *our* line occurred to few, if any of them.'[16]

The German blow fell on the misty morning of 21 March. In many areas the British defences were rapidly overwhelmed. In particular, to the south of St Quentin, where the 2nd and 3rd Cavalry Divisions were in support of III Corps, the German advance completely penetrated the 'battle zone' and pushed on into unfortified rear areas. Between noon and 2.00pm on 21 March the 2nd Cavalry Division was dismounted and bussed forward to take up positions alongside the infantry on a defensive line along the Crozat Canal. The 3rd Cavalry Division followed in similar fashion on 22 March. The led horses were evacuated to Carlepont, 22km (14 miles) to the west near Noyon. The cavalrymen of these two divisions were to carry out a fighting retreat on foot of nearly 30km (20 miles) west and south past Noyon over the next five days before being reunited with their horses on 27 March.[17] In the north the 1st Cavalry Division was similarly dismounted on 21 March and fought for two days without its horses in support of XIX Corps.[18] The narrative of this period is one of constant small delaying actions followed by repeated retreats to new positions, and it will not be presented in detail here,[19] but some comment is required on the wisdom of using the cavalry in this way. The 3rd Cavalry Division produced an analysis of the March fighting, 'Points brought to notice during recent operations',[20] and Preston devoted a substantial section to 'Lessons Learnt from the Battle'.[21] Both agree that the tactical effectiveness of the cavalry during this period was seriously hampered, and they highlight a series of issues.

The first is that the cavalryman was simply not equipped to fight on foot for long periods. He was not issued a back-pack and equipment had to be extemporised, usually by creating a roll of greatcoat and groundsheet, worn *en-banderole* rather unsatisfactorily. His mobility was of course also substantially reduced. This latter point applied in particular to the supporting machine guns. When units were moved forward by bus many Vickers and Hotchkiss teams were forced to abandon their pack-horses and had to carry all their guns, equipment and ammunition on foot. Preston describes his own experience, where of the twelve guns in his squadron only four could be brought into action because his men simply could not carry enough ammunition, and he was reduced to driving to III Corps headquarters in a borrowed car to collect more belt boxes.[22] Only in the Canadian Cavalry Brigade was the commander of the machine-gun squadron 'wise enough' to insist on retaining his pack–horses when the unit was dismounted.[23] The situation was even worse in the 1st Cavalry Division, where the whole of the 2nd Machine Gun Squadron, which normally would have provided integral fire support to the 2nd Cavalry Brigade, had been detached and loaned to the infantry of the 66th Division.[24]

A similar situation applied to the artillery. Prior to the German attack all of the Cavalry Corps' integral RHA brigades were detached and incorporated into the relevant infantry corps' artillery defence structures. This would have been fine had the battle remained static but as soon as the Germans broke through the cavalry divisions were forced to operate without their normal mobile artillery support (an experience perhaps familiar to those cavalrymen involved in the December fighting at Cambrai the previous year). The 3rd Brigade RHA did not rejoin its parent 3rd Cavalry Division until 25 March, by which time it had fired away all its 13-pdr ammunition and as a result had to be sent to the rear in search of additional supplies.[25]

The cavalry were thus forced into action without the mobility (and incidentally shock capability) provided by their horses, and with inadequate machine-gun and artillery support. Given these various disadvantages, the dismounted cavalry acquitted themselves well in the days following the German breakthrough. Middlebrook is dismissive of their rôle in the early stages of the fighting, suggesting that their 'performance as infantry was of unproved and doubtful value'[26] and commenting that in the years prior to 1918 'the cavalry had been almost useless to the allied cause'.[27] Preston, however, as might be expected, takes a different view:

> The dismounted cavalry compared very favourably with the infantry. On no single occasion during these operations were cavalry driven back by a frontal attack: they only vacated a position when ordered to do so in consequence of withdrawals by people on their flanks.[28]

He attributes this success at least in part to the overall quality of the cavalry units compared with their infantry counterparts in 1918. While many infantry units had been virtually wiped out in earlier offensives and made up with drafts of ever-deteriorating quality, the cavalry 'still had a fair proportion of their pre-war officers and NCOs'.[29] In addition the cavalry had received substantial training in 'open' rather than trench warfare and were much more comfortable in the fluid fighting that characterised the early days of the battle. It is ironic that Haig had fought for the retention of the cavalry in anticipation of precisely this kind of fighting, albeit on the other side of the line, but at the same time the defensive scheme developed by GHQ and Fifth Army had deprived them of almost all of their tactical advantages, throwing them into battle as inappropriately equipped and ill-supported infantry.

The cost to the Cavalry Corps of this fighting was substantial. The corps as a whole suffered 4,142 casualties (including over 200 officers) between 21 March and 7 April. This equates to an average of approximately 125 casualties of all types (killed, wounded or missing) in each regiment, roughly 25–30 per cent of their fighting strength.[30] However, as discussed earlier, the fortunate coincidence of the dismounting of a number of yeomanry regiments immediately prior to the offensive meant that many of these experienced cavalry soldiers could be reincorporated into the corps *en-bloc* and the overall fighting quality of the reconstituted units was left undiminished.

* * *

Despite the pre-planned dismounting of the majority of the Cavalry Corps on 21–22 March, it rapidly became obvious that mounted troops were urgently required. Unfortunately, the led horses had been moved so far from their regiments that remounting formal units was not possible. Thus on 23 March orders were issued to the 2nd and 3rd Cavalry Divisions' headquarters to form scratch units out of those men available among the horse-holders and other rear echelon troops. Each regiment was ordered to find fifty men; this produced a mounted force of about 750, to which were added 600 infantry, mostly return-ing leave-men. As no integral machine guns were available, eight Lewis guns and their crews from 13 Balloon Company were added to the force. O Battery RHA was also found to provide artillery support. The whole was placed under the command of Major General Harman of the 3rd Cavalry Division, becoming 'Harman's Detachment'.[31]

The principal function of Harman's Detachment over the next few days was to provide mounted officers' reconnaissance patrols reporting to III Corps headquarters, a rôle which was vital in supplying information on the German, and indeed Allied, dispositions. However, the detachment was also involved in one mounted action which, while not of enormous strategic significance in the offensive as a whole, is of particular interest.

On 24 March III Corps, along with the dismounted portions of the 2nd and 3rd Cavalry Divisions and a number of attached French units, held a line running north-west to south-east from a point a few miles south-east of Ham, to the river Oise in the south. Strong German thrusts at the northern end of this line broke the link with XVIII Corps to the north and temporarily created a gap around the flank of the III Corps line. On the morning of the 24th, Harman's Detachment was behind this northern flank of III Corps at Berlancourt. At 8.30am the force was ordered forward to establish the situation on this potentially open flank and to reorganise and support the various infantry units in that area, in particular reforming a defensive line around the village of Villeselve.[32]

A detailed account of what followed is contained in the 3rd Cavalry Division war diary.[33] The mounted troops formed from the 7th and Canadian Cavalry Brigades moved to the east of Villeselve and made contact with the French units at the northern end of the III Corps line, forming a north-facing defensive flank. The remaining mounted men, those of the 6th Cavalry Brigade under Major Williams (10th Hussars), were ordered forward north-east through Villeselve to make contact with and throw back the advancing Germans 'using the sword only'. The force under Williams' command consisted of three fifty-man troops drawn from the three regiments of the brigade, the 10th Hussars (Lieutenant Ednam), the Royals (Lieutenant Cubitt) and the 3rd Dragoon Guards (Lieutenant Vincent).

This small force advanced north-eastwards along the road to Villeselve, turning northwards into a sunken lane leading to the hamlet of Collezy. At this point they came under machine-gun fire from the north and north-east and took temporary shelter behind a large farm to the south of Collezy. The Germans were found to be concentrated around two copses about 1,000 yards (900m) to the north-east, firing at least four machine guns. Williams immediately ordered a charge in 'infantry attack' formation; the 3rd Dragoon Guards formed the first wave, in loose line, followed by the 10th Hussars in similar formation, while the Royals formed the third line, in section columns as flank guards. The force crossed the intervening 1,000 yards at full gallop with swords drawn, over plough for the last 200 yards, cheering loudly as they closed with the enemy. As the 3rd Dragoon Guards' line swung east to attack the easternmost copse, the Germans facing them broke and ran into the trees, but the Dragoons dismounted and followed, shooting several as they fled. Twelve prisoners were captured. Meanwhile the 10th Hussars and the Royals rode at the western copse, where the greater part of the enemy lay. Between seventy and a hundred Germans were killed, mostly with the sword, and a further ninety-four were made prisoner. Three machine guns were captured or destroyed.

Albert Turp, a Farrier Sergeant with the Royals, was a participant in this charge, and later recalled:

> We had of course been taught that a cavalry charge should be carried out in line six inches from knee to knee, but it didn't work out like that in practice and we were soon a pretty ragged line of horsemen at full gallop. We took the Germans quite by surprise and they faced us as best they could, for there can't be anything more frightening to an infantryman than the sight of a line of cavalry charging at full gallop with drawn swords.
>
> I remembered my old training and the old sword exercise. As our line overrode the Germans I made a regulation point at a man on my offside and my sword went through his neck and out the other side.

The pace of my horse carried my sword clear and then I took a German on my nearside, and I remember the jar as my point took him in the collarbone and knocked him over. As we galloped on the enemy broke and ran ...[34]

In the event, although the supporting infantry were able to restore the line as a result of this charge, further withdrawals followed within a few hours and the ground was once again lost. However, this encounter is of interest as it shows the effect of shock action against troops in the open (as opposed to in trenches), particularly against men unprepared to meet a mounted opponent. The inability of machine guns alone to halt charging cavalry was also demonstrated, although the cost to the 6th Cavalry Brigade detachment was severe: out of roughly 150 men, seventy-three became casualties (six killed, the remainder wounded).[35] The potency of this fast-moving form of fighting was to be demonstrated again on a larger scale later in the year during the Amiens battle in August, as well as in October (described later in this chapter).

*   *   *

After several more days of retreat, all three cavalry divisions were reunited with their horses. The 1st Cavalry division was remounted on 24 March, and the 2nd and 3rd Cavalry Divisions on 26–27 March.[36] One other significant mounted engagement followed on 30 March at Moreuil Wood. By this time the German advance had penetrated to within 16km (10 miles) of Amiens. In the event this was to be the high-water mark of the offensive, but that of course was not apparent at the time, and the defence of the city was considered critical as its fall would sever rail communications between the BEF to the north and the French to the south. On 28 March General Gough was relieved of command of Fifth Army and his place taken by General Rawlinson (although the force continued to be known as 'Fifth Army'). Rawlinson was given the specific responsibility of defending Amiens with what remained of Gough's force, and all three cavalry divisions were to be concentrated near the city for this purpose.[37]

The events following were described in the *Cavalry Journal* by Major General Pitman,[38] who had taken over command of the 2nd Cavalry Division from Major General Greenly on 22 March.[39] The division had forced marched north towards Amiens over two days and arrived at Boves, 8km (5 miles) south-east of the city, on the night of 29 March. The division was four brigades strong, having the Canadian Cavalry Brigade attached from the 3rd Cavalry Division, the remainder of which was still some distance away to the south. The 1st Cavalry Division was meanwhile engaged in holding the line to the east of the city. In the early hours of 30 March information was received of a strong German thrust north-west towards Amiens along and to the south of the line of the Amiens–Roye road. If continued, this would carry the Germans on to high ground in the triangle formed by the junction of the rivers Avre (flowing south-east to north-west) and Luce (flowing east to west), virtually overlooking Amiens. The village of Moreuil lay in the valley of the Avre to the south, while the high ground between the rivers was occupied by the Bois de Moreuil, a triangular wood with one angle towards Amiens in the north-west and its base along the Moreuil to Demuin road on the south-east.

At 7.00am on the morning of 30 March orders were passed by telephone to the 2nd Cavalry Division from XIX Corps to advance as far as Moreuil and restore the line. Pitman travelled by car to brief his two nearest brigades in person. These were the 3rd Cavalry Brigade, which was ordered to move around to the north of Moreuil Wood, and the Canadian Cavalry Brigade, which he ordered to advance directly westwards across the Avre to the threatened point.[40] The Canadians arrived at Castel in the Avre valley opposite the wood at about 9.15am.[41] The brigade commander, Brigadier General 'Jack' Seely (encountered earlier at Cambrai), was up with the leading troops and he ordered his advanced guard regiment, the Royal Canadian Dragoons, to attack the wood. The leading squadron under Captain Nordheimer was to attack the nearest (north-western) corner of the wood while the two following squadrons were to circle around the wood to north and south and link up behind it. Captain Nordheimer's men were able to establish themselves in the north-western corner of the wood, but came under heavy rifle and machine-gun fire along the south-western side of the wood. Captain Nordheimer himself was fatally wounded. The second squadron under Captain Newcomen attempted to push along the south-western side of the wood towards the southern corner but only reached about half-way along the face of the wood before being forced into cover in the trees. The third squadron under Major Timmis galloped along the north face of the wood but came under such heavy fire from the wood and points further east that Timmis was forced to swing left and take shelter in some dead ground north of the wood.[42]

A few minutes later the second regiment of the brigade, Lord Strathcona's Horse, arrived at the north-western corner of the wood. One squadron (Captain Trotter) was dismounted and sent eastwards through the trees to clear the northern face of the wood. A second squadron under Lieutenant Flowerdew was sent to follow Timmis' Royal Canadian Dragoons, mounted, around the north-eastern corner of the wood. Thanks to the work of Trotter's men, Flowerdew was able to reach the north-eastern corner of the wood without difficulty. These men were followed by the third squadron of Lord Strathcona's Horse under Lieutenant Morgan, who dismounted at the eastern end of the north face of the wood. Morgan's dismounted squadron, along with Trotter's men from that regiment and the survivors of Nordheimer's Royal Canadian

Dragoons, were then organised into a line by the Strathcona's commander Lieutenant Colonel MacDonald, and began to sweep south through the wood.[43]

The events that followed have become the stuff of legend: Lieutenant Flowerdew was to be awarded a posthumous Victoria Cross, and the scene of his action painted by Alfred Munnings – an image that Anglesey chose for the dust-jacket of the relevant volume of his *History of the British Cavalry*. However, the sources differ on what actually took place, and whether indeed the event was a magnificent charge or a disorganised scuffle, with at least part of the mounted combat resulting from an attempt by Flowerdew's men to escape the attentions of their supposed victims.

The action began when Flowerdew mounted a bank at the north-eastern corner of the wood; confronted with a force of Germans, he then charged down the eastern face of the wood before ostensibly rallying, charging back through the enemy and finally retiring into the eastern face of the wood. Seely, the brigade commander (who was not present at the charge), gave an account in his own memoirs based on the VC citation of 'two lines of enemy each about sixty strong, with machine guns in the centre and flanks; one line being about two hundred yards behind the other'. Anglesey relies heavily on Seely's account and interprets these two lines to be a line of Germans forced out of the wood by the dismounted parties, and a second line of reinforcements approaching the wood. Seely's account is, however, highly coloured and is not necessarily to be considered reliable. His record of his conversation with Flowerdew is representative:

> I galloped up to Flowerdew, who commanded the leading squadron of Strathcona's; as we rode along together I told him that his was the most adventurous task of all, but that I was confident he would succeed. With his gentle smile he turned to me and said: 'I know, sir, I know, it is a splendid moment. I will try not to fail you.'[44]

It is hard not to be cynical about the *Boy's Own* quality of this narrative. Pitman more prosaically described the target of the attack as 'a party of about 300 of the enemy retiring from the wood'.[45] This corresponds with the description given in the Canadian Cavalry Brigade war diary.[46] The Strathcona's war diary on the other hand describes '2 lines of machine-guns, about 20 in all',[47] although this is likely to be an exaggeration. An altogether different perspective is provided by a German account of the action, translated and published in the *Cavalry Journal* in 1927:

> a small body of Strathcona's Dragoons, some sixty in number, succeeded in breaking right through the front line and pushing on in rear of the leading companies in the direction of Moreuil. Here they came upon a platoon of No. 2 Company [of *101st Grenadiers*] in

the act of being relieved, and by this platoon and by a machine-gun section of the 2nd Battalion the Canadians were received with a most murderous fire. Only a few of the dragoons succeeded in making their escape . . . A small scattered party of them came suddenly on the rear of No. 7 Company and endeavoured . . . to cut their way through. But very few, however, succeeded in doing so; not one of them allowed himself to be taken prisoner – each man had kept the last round in his pistol for himself![48]

The last sentence clearly shows that hyperbole was not limited to Seely's version of events. Unlike German cavalry, pistols in the Canadian cavalry were the preserve of officers, NCOs and specialists. What is not disputed is that Flowerdew's squadron suffered very heavily. Seely, quoting the VC citation, put their loss at 'about 70 per cent'.[49] The Strathcona's war diary gives losses for the action as a whole among all three squadrons at 157 out of the 350 present, 'including horseholders etc'[50] (or nearly 45 per cent). No doubt many of these were Flowerdew's men.

No information has been uncovered concerning German casualties. British accounts refer only to 'killing many with the sword'.[51] Nor is it clear what effect on the fight as a whole the charge produced. The Strathcona's war diary was in no doubt that 'their action had a great moral effect on those of the enemy who were still fighting in the wood. Hearing the clatter of hooves behind them and thinking themselves surrounded, their resistance to our dismounted troops slackened considerably.'[52]

However, it is not clear whether the troops attacked were already retreating out of the wood or were reinforcing it, or even, as the German account suggests, both. What is clear is that the struggle for the wood continued for at least another 6 hours. Not only were all the Canadians engaged but as the 3rd Cavalry Brigade arrived, its squadrons were also committed to the fight; the 4th Hussars joined the struggle on the south-western face of the wood at about 10.00am, supported by the 16th Lancers at about 12.15pm and finally the 5th Lancers at about 3.00pm, until 'The whole of the 3rd Cavalry Brigade was thus in action in the wood'.[53] Nor was the whole wood captured: although the cavalry were able to occupy the majority of the eastern face of the wood, the southern tip adjacent to Moreuil itself continued to hold out.

The Canadian Cavalry Brigade narrative admits:

The losses were severe, most regiments having lost from half to one third of their officers, and a similar proportion of their men, and it would have been impossible to have held the wood but for the prompt arrival of General Bell-Smythe's [3rd Cavalry] Brigade who reinforced our weak points and bore the brunt of the fierce fighting later in the day on the western face of the wood.[54]

Nevertheless, the cavalry were able to hold on until 2.30am on 31 March when the two brigades were relieved by infantry of the 8th Division.[55]

Thus the German advance towards Amiens had been halted on this part of the front, and congratulatory telegrams were sent from Rawlinson to the 2nd Cavalry Division headquarters.[56] While the action as a whole was successful, however, its individual parts are subject to a degree of criticism. Pitman offered a summary of his views on the performance of his own division. He comments favourably on the function of the division as a mobile reserve: when the German advance was identified, his mounted troops were able to respond quickly to plug the gap. He is critical, however, of Seely's tactics on arriving at the wood, commenting that 'The tactical handling of the Canadian Cavalry Brigade at Moreuil Wood on March 30 must not be taken as an example of how to make use of available troops.'[57]

Seely seems to have been overcome by a sense of the urgency of the occasion and committed troops to battle as and when they arrived. Thus the three Royal Canadian Dragoons squadrons were committed towards three separate objectives widely dispersed, and as Lord Strathcona's Horse arrived they too were broken up in a similar fashion. Also these troops were committed to battle without the support of artillery or machine guns, even though both were present with the brigade. All the evidence suggests that the German *101st Grenadiers* had been in possession of the wood for some time, and indeed they were about to undergo a relief when the Canadians arrived.[58] Thus it was not a race for the ground. A more considered and better prepared attack might well have achieved the same result at less cost. As it was, the fight was quickly left in the hands of junior squadron commanders and it succeeded owing to a combination of their aggression and skill combined with a degree of surprise on the part of the Germans. Any credit gained by the Canadians in this fighting did not save their already unpopular commander: Seely was relieved of his command of the Canadian Cavalry Brigade on 21 May 1918 and replaced by his able subordinate Lieutenant Colonel R.W. Paterson (formerly commanding officer of the Fort Garry Horse).

Flowerdew's charge itself does not appear to have been decisive. Indeed, it is possible to read in the German account of the charge not a squadron rallying to charge back through its foes, but a disorganised effort to cut an escape back along the route of the charge, followed by a flight into the cover of the trees. What it did provide, however, as was also the case at Villeselve, was a moral effect, not only on the Germans immediately present but on wider British public opinion. Moreuil Wood and Flowerdew's VC were extremely valuable as what in modern parlance would be termed 'good PR' in what were otherwise dark times for the BEF. The battle also occurred at the turning point of the campaign; no further advance towards Amiens was achieved by the Germans, although to what extent the small action at Moreuil Wood was a key to that is questionable.

What the Moreuil Wood fight does show, however, notwithstanding the usefulness or otherwise of Flowerdew's heroics, is that the cavalry remained a mobile and effective fighting force. No doubt Seely could have done a better job in command, but his brigade was still able to move at speed to the threatened point and successfully retake a piece of strategically important ground from the enemy, in the face of machine guns and artillery. Heavy losses were incurred, but it was not the one-sided massacre of popular imagination.

* * *

As the front stabilised, the Cavalry Corps remained in action up until 7 April when the last elements were relieved in the line and the divisions withdrew to rear areas. Their performance since 21 March was assessed very favourably at the time. Home commented on 25 March, 'The Cavalry barometer stands very high again, it was very low a month ago.'[59] This praise was repeated by General Gough in his own account of the battle in his memoir *Fifth Army*:

> The cavalry had played a great part in the battle. Their mobility, and their capacity to cross any country on horses and therefore to get rapidly from place to place, made them far more powerful then their mere numbers would suggest.... Their great value during these ten days should never be forgotten. Had the Germans been able to make use of cavalry of the same calibre during these events it is more than probable that the whole course of the battle would have been altered.[60]

Even the staunchest opponents of the cavalry in more modern writing have been forced to acknowledge the rôle of the cavalry in the March retreat and, as Gough highlighted, the importance of the lack of equivalent German cavalry in the attacking force.

The German lack of cavalry was recently (2006) considered by David Zabecki in his detailed study of the German March offensive. He concluded that two factors influenced this decision. First, that unlike the much vilified Haig, Ludendorff discounted cavalry from his calculations on the Western Front at an early stage; none of his doctrinal publications of this period even consider mounted troops.[61] Secondly, the German army suffered from a chronic shortage of transport, both motor and equine, and to bring even the infantry divisions involved in operation *Michael* up to establishment of transport, thirteen divisions in the East had to be stripped of their transport vehicles and horses, and rendered essentially immobile. Thus with every available horse pulling wagons for the infantry, and very poor stocks of fodder to feed even those horses, remounting a significant force of cavalrymen was never a realistic possibility.[62] Ludendorff himself described this situation in his memoirs:

> Trench warfare offered no scope for cavalry. The formation of regiments of dismounted cavalry ... was now continued.... Their horses were urgently required for the reorganization of the artillery and for our transport. The wastage in horses was extraordinarily high, and the import from neutral countries hardly worth consideration. The homeland and the occupied districts could not make good the shortage. There were many gaps.[63]

Thus the non-use of cavalry by the Germans in March 1918 was not a strategic miscalculation but a logistical necessity.

What is not widely appreciated about the British cavalry during the campaign is that, as was examined earlier, the cavalry divisions achieved much of their success precisely *without* the mobility so praised by Gough, as his defensive plan denied them their horses, machine guns and artillery for most of the first half of the battle. What he could not remove, however, was their training and experience, proving that mobile warfare rests at least as much in the mind of the soldier as in his means of transport. As has been demonstrated in earlier chapters, at regimental and troop level the cavalry continued to be a flexible and highly professional force. As Home put it in his diary of 16 April 1918: 'Thank Heaven we still have three Cavalry Divisions made of the old stuff and properly officered. We can stop a breakthrough anywhere.'[64] Hyperbole perhaps, but based on a strong grain of truth.

The effectiveness, particularly the moral effect, of small groups of mounted men against un-entrenched opponents was also demonstrated – even the scratch mounted forces available were able to overawe and defeat opponents armed with machine guns. Unfortunately, as Moreuil Wood was to demonstrate, question marks still hung over the capabilities of the higher commanders. It is arguable that this encounter was won by the aggression and determination of leaders at squadron and troop level, despite (rather than because of) the control exercised by their brigade commander.

As with the disappointments after Cambrai the previous year, recriminations and scapegoating were quick to follow the March–April fighting. Fortunately the spotlight had temporarily moved away from the cavalry. The chief casualty was General Gough, who was removed from command of Fifth Army on 28 March and replaced by General Rawlinson.[65] It is probable that, quite apart from the failure or otherwise of the defence in the March fighting, Gough was a victim of the on-going feud between the Prime Minister and Haig. Charteris recorded on 5 April:

He [the Prime Minister] is of course looking for a scapegoat for the disaster to the Fifth Army and has apparently decided to go for Gough. DH [Haig] is furious about this. It would certainly be most unfair if Gough were held responsible. He had a dozen divisions to hold a front of 42 miles and he was attacked by 50 divisions.[66]

Gough was a close friend of Haig, and as such a suitable surrogate for the commander in chief himself. Ironically, it would appear that Gough's loss was Kavanagh's gain. The Cavalry Corps commander had (perhaps deservedly) not come out well in the aftermath of Cambrai, and it seemed likely that it would be he who would be sacrificed. Kavanagh mentioned in a note to the commander of the 1st Cavalry Division, Major General Mullens, on 27 February 'it seems I am for home'.[67] However, this did not happen. The performance of his corps, in contrast to that of Fifth Army in general, transferred the pressure to Gough, who it seems had previously supported Kavanagh's dismissal. Home recorded in his diary of 25 March:

Heard on 22 [March] that the CC [Corps Commander: Kavanagh] was going to be sent home, so got Barrow to let me go out on the 26th to see what was the matter. I found that Goughie was the matter and had evidently reported badly on the CC – this was the result. Luckily the CC was in a strong position and the result is that Goughie has gone home and that Henry Rawlinson succeeds him.[68]

Given that both Gough and Kavanagh were close to Haig, and both, like their commander in chief, were cavalrymen, it seems unusual that they should apparently be in competition, but if nothing else it further contradicts the myth that there was some form of cavalry 'club' in the upper reaches of the BEF. For the present, however, the Cavalry Corps retained its commander and as an arm its star was at least briefly in the ascendant.

*   *   *

The German attack towards Amiens in March 1918 was followed by a series of other blows, falling all along the length of the Allied front. None, however, was to make gains as significant as those made against Fifth Army and gradually the German offensive resources were worn down. The last great attack was made on the Marne front on 15 July 1918, and while initially successful was rapidly contained, and French and American counter-attacks followed. The balance thus started to shift as the Allies looked to change to the offensive themselves.

On 24 July, while the Marne fighting was still in progress, General Foch as overall Allied commander called a conference with the three national commanders in chief, Haig, Pershing and Petain, to outline his offensive plans.[69] It was these plans which provided the basis for the Anglo–French offensive of

8 August. If the degree of success of that offensive is to be judged, and the rôle of the cavalry in it assessed, then the original objectives of the battle need to be considered in some detail. Foch spelled out three areas where attacks were required to relieve pressure on the Allied front, in particular on the railway system behind the front. Two of these areas, around Château Thierry and St Mihiel, lay in the Franco–American portion of the front, but the third lay opposite Amiens where the salient created in March threatened not only the Paris–Amiens railway, but also the junction point of the French and British armies. He further defined his ideas concerning this third area in a formal order issued on 28 July:

1. The object of the operations is to disengage Amiens and the Paris–Amiens railway, also to defeat and drive back the enemy established between the Somme and the Avre.
2. To do so the offensive, covered in the north by the Somme, will be pushed as far as possible in the direction of Roye[70] [about 40km (25 miles) south-east of Amiens].

Prior to this, beginning around 5 July, General Rawlinson, in command of what had now become the British Fourth Army, had been developing an offensive plan to relieve the pressure on Amiens,[71] so when presented with Foch's scheme this accorded well with his own plans. Rawlinson, as has been alluded to earlier, was more of a 'Bite and Hold' general, and his plans for relieving Amiens reflected this. He was also guided by the terrain. The attack front lay between the river Somme in the north, running broadly west to east, and the junction with the French First Army, running south–east along the Amiens–Roye road. The ground within this triangle was highly suitable for an attack: the terrain was rolling, and the going firm with minimal shell damage. The initial German defences were also relatively weak, having been extemporised after their March attack: 'their front line consisting of very rough trenches with no dugouts worthy of the name, and few communication trenches'.[72] However, the opportunities for an advance in this area were not limitless. At a distance of about 10km (6 miles) east of the existing front lay the 'Old' or 'Outer Amiens Defence Line'. This was a system constructed in 1916 which had originally faced east, and thus was mostly wired behind the trenches when attacked from the west, but it still represented a potentially defensible position. A few miles further east still lay the edge of the old Somme battlefield from 1916:

a wide stretch of country which had been fought over in the 1916 Somme battles and was completely covered with shell-holes and pieces of old wire, overgrown with thistles and rank grass. This shell-crater area – the near edge of which was a line running roughly north and south through Foucaucourt – was extremely difficult for infantry and well-nigh impossible for tanks and cavalry.[73]

Rawlinson thus developed a plan with strictly limited objectives, aiming at an advance to the 'Old Amiens Defence Line' and a consolidation there. This would still represent an advance of about 10km (6 miles) on a front about 16km (10 miles) wide, substantial progress by the standards of the Western Front.

The attack was initially scheduled for 10 August. It would be led by two corps: on the left the Australian Corps (of five divisions) between the Somme river in the north and the Amiens–Chaulnes railway line to the south; and on the right the Canadian Corps (of four Canadian and one British divisions) south of the railway and extending south as far as the boundary with the French along the Amiens–Roye road. To the north of the Somme III Corps would provide a flanking attack, and to the south of the Roye road the French XXXI Corps would advance in parallel with the Canadians. Supporting the infantry attack were over 500 tanks of various kinds, in particular seventy-two of the new Whippet light tanks (of which more later).[74]

All three divisions of the reduced Cavalry Corps were to be used in the offensive. In contrast to Rawlinson's approach to cavalry two years earlier, this time they were fully integrated into the attack. Two divisions were to move up as soon as the battle started, leapfrog through the infantry and push on to capture the more distant targets. The 3rd Cavalry Division was placed under the command of the Canadian Corps on the southern side of the advance, while one brigade (1st Cavalry Brigade) of the 1st Cavalry Division was placed under Australian Corps' control immediately north of the railway. Each cavalry brigade would be assisted by a company of sixteen Whippet tanks. The 2nd Cavalry Division and the remainder of the 1st Cavalry Division would remain in reserve under Cavalry Corps' control, but unlike in earlier battles no word from Corps HQ would be required to launch the leading brigades, which would advance automatically under local control. In the light of the command and control problems of previous offensives, discussed earlier, this devolution of command was critical to the success of the cavalry, and is one of the most significant aspects of this battle. The mission of the cavalry was stated explicitly in the 'General Staff Instructions' drawn up between 1 and 4 August: '(a) The first mission of the Cavalry Corps on 'Z' day will be to secure the line of the outer Amiens defences, and hold it until relieved by infantry of the Canadian Corps.'[75]

This plan had a great deal to recommend it. Rawlinson and his staff appear to have learned the lessons of Arras and Cambrai the year before. The new deeper defence systems used by both sides by this point in the war not only provided an environment with much more opportunity and freedom of movement for mounted troops, but also their very depth created a need for forces that could advance faster than men simply on foot, to tackle the deeper recesses of the defensive system itself. This reflects a change from the vision of cavalry performing a 'breakthrough' function after the local tactical battle was complete, to one of their integrated participation in the tactical battle itself. The devolution of command to infantry corps commanders had also been tried before, with varying degrees of success, but this time the cavalry were not simply to wait until their chosen commander launched them forward, but were to advance independently and carry on their mission without external prompting. The integration of cavalry and light tanks was also a progressive step, but the success or otherwise of this will be examined later.

Had the battle of Amiens, and the operational success of the cavalry in it, been judged by historians on the basis of the plans drawn up prior to 4 August, no doubt it would have been judged an unqualified success (except of course for those who, as with the Messines battle in 1917, might have criticised its *lack* of ambition). However, Haig and Foch met again on 3 August.[76] By this time Foch was so pleased with the progress of the counter-attacks on the Marne that he pressed for a widening of the objectives for the Amiens offensive. The battle had already been brought forward two days to 8 August in order to increase the pressure on German reserves, and perhaps he saw the opportunity for inflicting a significant defeat on the enemy. Haig responded by naming a series of deeper objectives, not only Roye and Chaulnes themselves, on the near edge of the destroyed zone but also Ham, 24km (15 miles) to the east of Roye, beyond the river Somme–Canal du Nord line.[77] This was embodied in an addition to the orders for the Cavalry Corps issued on 6 August:

> 6. With the above object in view, the Cavalry Corps, as soon as they have accomplished their first mission (*vide* Fourth Army no. 32 (G) para. 13 (a) [quoted above]), will push forward in the direction of the line Roye–Chaulnes with the least possible delay.[78]

It was characteristic of Haig to add 'wider horizons' to the limited plans of his subordinates, and it is arguable that in this case, as in many others, these ambitions were unrealistic. Here, however, it must be asked to what extent he really believed in these objectives and whether their inclusion was more of a political gesture to Foch than a military expectation. What is certain is that the failure of the offensive to reach further than Rawlinson's original target, the Old Amiens Defence Line, has provided ammunition to critics of both Haig and the cavalry ever since.

* * *

In preparation for the offensive the Cavalry Corps was brought up to positions to the west of Amiens, and then on the night of 7/8 August filed through the town to an assembly area in the V between the Amiens–St Quentin and

Amiens–Roye roads. This move was made in a single column over 28km (18 miles) long but, apart from a delay caused by a broken-down tank, passed without mishap.[79] The divisions were formed up by 2.30am, prior to Zero-hour for the infantry which was due at 4.20am. The battle began at 4.20 with, as at Cambrai, no preliminary bombardment but with creeping barrages ahead of the infantry and tanks. The infantry were rapidly on and through the German first lines, and as the day dawned to a thick mist 'the issue of the day was never in doubt'.[80]

The 3rd Cavalry Division was tasked to support the Canadian Corps on the right (southern) side of the attack. Their line of advance lay roughly south-east towards the 'Outer Defence Line' at le Quesnel. This would take the division across the only significant obstacle on the battlefield, the east–west flowing river Luce. Thus two contingencies were prepared for: a crossing by the bridges at Ignaucourt, or failing that a push further east around the head of the river valley. Almost as soon as the battle began patrols of the Fort Garry Horse (Canadian Cavalry Brigade) were on the move to establish the viability of these bridges. Lieutenant Colonel Ewing Paterson, who was temporarily in command of the 7th Cavalry Brigade, wrote an account of events for the *Cavalry Journal* in 1921. He observed one critical change in the usual arrangements:

> this decision [to advance] was left entirely to the GOC 3rd Cavalry Division without having to await orders from Infantry Corps or Division Headquarters, as had so often happened in previous engagements, the consequence having been that the fleeting opportunity had nearly always been lost.[81]

Thus unshackled from the dead hand of higher command, at 5.40am, only just over an hour after Zero, the division began its move along a prepared cavalry track up to the front line and across. Infantry fighting was continuing on either side of the cavalry line of march as they advanced.

At 9.15 the bridges were reported intact and the division began its first 'bound' as far as the river valley on the south side of the Luce at Ignaucourt.[82] The first troops across the river were Lord Strathcona's Horse at 9.20am, and this regiment then pushed on southwards to the boundary with the French on the Amiens–Roye road. Here they met up with 'Brutinel's Independent Force', a column of Canadian motor machine-guns, cyclists and truck-mounted mortars tasked with protecting the flank of the attack along the road, capturing fifty prisoners and a gun en route.[83] The two leading brigades of the division, Canadian on the right and 7th on the left, were formed up across the river with their accompanying Whippet tanks, supporting RHA and RCHA batteries, and machine-guns by 11.00am. Again without the necessity for further orders, the two brigades then pushed on to their next objectives.[84]

On the right (south) the Canadian Cavalry Brigade advanced towards Beaucourt village, and Beaucourt Wood to the east of it. While the initial advance was made rapidly on horseback, with few casualties due to the speed of movement, as the village and wood were reached the Canadians were forced into a dismounted fire-fight. Eight Whippets attempted to support this attack but they too were forced back by fire from a German field gun used in the anti-tank rôle. Beaucourt village was eventually captured after a fierce fight, but it was not until reinforcements of Canadian infantry arrived at about 4.30 in the afternoon that the wood to the east fell.[85]

On the left of the Canadians the 7th Cavalry Brigade advanced eastwards. They were faced with the village of Cayeux on their left front near the Luce valley, then the trees of Cayeux Wood stretching for over a mile (2km) south-wards along a crest of higher ground. To the right was a gap of about half a mile (1km) to the woods and village of Beaucourt. Ewing Paterson, in command of the brigade, described it as 'a most formidable looking position'.[86] The brigade advanced with the Inniskillings (6th Dragoons) on the right and the 7th Dragoon Guards on the left, with the 17th Lancers in reserve. The Inniskillings were brought to a halt in a copse some distance short of Beaucourt Wood, forcing the 7th Dragoon Guards to swing left (eastwards). The latter regiment was now faced with the length of Cayeux Wood, and 'without a moment's hesitation gave the order to charge, and with one loud yell ... were down the hill, across the open space, up the rise and into the copse, capturing the key to the position'.[87]

Due to their being echeloned by the change of face to the left, each squadron of the 7th Dragoon Guards made a separate assault into the edge of the southern part of the woods, but each was individually successful. Over one hundred prisoners were captured (although some subsequently escaped), as well as in excess of twenty machine-guns and a battery of field artillery.

Capitalising on this success, the 17th Lancers pushed through the wood on the left (north) of the 7th Dragoons, but on emerging from the wood towards Caix, the next village to the east, they came under heavy fire. Paterson himself had his horse shot from under him. In a textbook response, the 17th Lancers threw a squadron to the north, successfully outflanking the offending guns, and the advance continued, reaching the 'Amiens Outer Defence Line' and the divisional first objective by 2.30pm. A number of further prisoners were captured along the way, including several complete field hospitals and more artillery pieces.[88]

Ewing Paterson reviewed his brigade's actions and provided several observa-tions. Speed was of the essence: the German machine-gunners were unable to bring fire effectively on men charging towards them, and it was only in the last 60 yards that significant casualties were suffered; moreover 'once the men were on top of the enemy they put up no fight and appeared completely demoralised'.[89] He was warm in his praise for his supporting RHA battery and the initiative of its commander, but his supporting tanks had simply been left behind by the rapidity of the advance. He summed up the moral effect of large numbers of British cavalry appearing in what had been the German rear areas: 'A German officer when asked why he and his men had surrendered, said "Look, look," pointing around the country, "and wherever you look you see British cavalry".'[90]

After the capture of Beaucourt Wood to the south later in the afternoon by Canadian infantry, the last brigade of the 3rd Cavalry Division, the 6th, was pushed through between the two advanced brigades and took up a position along the Outer Defence Line south of the 7th Cavalry Brigade. The Canadian Cavalry Brigade had already been relieved by infantry during the afternoon and in due course the rather depleted 7th Cavalry Brigade was replaced by infantry at around 9.00pm, while the fresher 6th Cavalry Brigade held part of the line overnight.[91] As the two brigades of the 3rd Cavalry Division withdrew that night Paterson suggests they 'had good cause to be content'.[92] The division had advanced 11km (7 miles) and captured large numbers of prisoners and equipment. With the exception of the village of le Quesnel on the extreme right, all the divisional first objectives had been reached.

Advancing alongside the 3rd Cavalry Division to the north was the 1st Cavalry Division. The rôle of this division was divided: the 9th Cavalry Brigade, advancing south of the Amiens–Chaulnes railway line, was to move through the northernmost part of the Canadian Corps line, while the 1st Cavalry Brigade advanced to the north of the railway, under the immediate command of the Australian Corps. The 2nd Cavalry Brigade and the divisional headquarters would follow the 9th Brigade south of the railway. Not only was this line of advance not hindered by the river crossing required of the 3rd Cavalry Division, but also each brigade could rest its inner flank on the railway line, a useful aid to direction in the foggy morning.[93]

On the 9th Brigade front south of the railway the advance was led by the 15th Hussars on the left and the 19th Hussars on the right. Both had some initial difficulty crossing the debris of the old front lines, but by 11.00am the two regiments had passed through the advancing Canadian infantry at Guillaucourt, about 6km (4 miles) beyond the front line, and just short of the infantry's second ('Red Line') objective.[94] At 11.15am the Hussars were ordered forward on to their objectives in the Old Amiens Defence Line.[95] The historian of the 15th Hussars described the subsequent moves:

> There is little doubt that many felt that this moment was worth all the years of waiting. As the 15th swept past the position just captured by the Canadians, these latter leapt to their feet, and loudly cheered the regiment as it passed by. The distance to be covered was

about two thousand yards, and almost at once the 15th came under machine-gun fire, a few men and horses fell, but the momentum was gained, the forward rush continued, and in a remarkably short time all squadrons reached their objectives, dismounted and occupied the old trenches.[96]

Once again speed and aggression had proved effective in the face of machine-gun fire, and the brigade objectives were all achieved by around 1.00pm.

In due course the 2nd Cavalry Brigade (in reserve to this point) was sent forward to prolong the line to the right of the 9th Cavalry Brigade and link up with the left of the 3rd Cavalry Division to the south, thus by around 1.30pm the whole of the Outer Defence Line south of the railway, with the exception of the southernmost portion around le Quesnel, was in cavalry hands. During the afternoon the 2nd Cavalry Brigade pushed patrols out beyond the line to reconnoitre the villages further east, but these were met with heavy fire and it became apparent that the German defences were hardening and no further advance was possible.[97]

To the north of the railway the 1st Cavalry Brigade advanced with the 2nd Dragoon Guards (Queen's Bays) in the lead. At about 9.15am the Bays passed through the Australian infantry on their 'Red Line' objective just short of the village of Harbonnieres. Coming under fire as they came into sight of the village, two squadrons of the Bays galloped forward, gaining a position in a valley south of the village and near the railway line. In the process a number of Germans were killed or captured and several machine guns overrun. A further attempt was made to move north-east, circling around the rear of the village anti-clockwise, but this was beaten back by heavy fire from the line of a road leading out of the village to the south-west. An attempt was then made to clear this opposition using Whippet tanks, but this too was beaten back with the loss of two tanks knocked out and one broken down, as well as further losses among the cavalry. At this point the regiment consolidated its position to the south of the village, with a south-facing defensive flank along the railway, supported by machine-guns and by the brigade RHA battery on a ridge to the rear.[98]

At about 9.45 the 5th Dragoon Guards were ordered forward around the north side of Harbonnieres, their mission essentially to ignore resistance from the village and ride on to the Outer Defence Line. This was quickly accomplished (at a trot) despite taking fire from the north side of the village, and the 5th Dragoons pushed on across the trench line. At this point three trains were sighted in the distance, one of which was disabled by an aerial bomb before being famously captured by A Squadron, complete with its full complement of German soldiers allegedly returning from leave.[99] Two squadrons of the 5th Dragoon Guards continued to cause havoc beyond the Outer Defence Line until about 10.30am, overrunning a dressing station near Vauvillers and three batteries of artillery, although it was only possible to disable a few of the guns of the latter before abandoning them. Both squadrons then withdrew to the Defence Line.[100]

During this period it would appear that the remaining resistance in Harbonnieres itself had collapsed, prompted by the arrival of the 5th Australian Division infantry at about 10.30am, as the cavalry war diaries do not record any further fighting for the village, and by 12.15pm Brigadier General Sewell commanding the 1st Cavalry Brigade was able to report to the 1st Cavalry Division that his brigade was established on its objective along the Amiens Outer Defence Line.[101] Unfortunately heavy fire from the village of Vauvillers in particular made any advance beyond this objective impractical.

By early afternoon on 8 August the Cavalry Corps had achieved all its initial objectives. Their orders were now to wait on the consolidated Outer Defence Line until relieved by the infantry, before pushing on more deeply into the German rear areas. Vigorous patrolling was carried out beyond the Defence Line, but it became increasingly apparent that German reinforcements were arriving and the defence hardening. Thus no further advances were made that day. Rawlinson, however, remained optimistic and new objectives based on an advance of another 8km (5 miles) on 9 August were assigned.[102] Infantry attacks were launched on the following days, and the cavalry brought up in readiness each time to exploit any gains made. But although the front was advanced most of the distance initially proposed by Rawlinson, almost to Chaulnes, it was clear that, as so often had been the case in the past, the offensive had run out of steam. Rawlinson put an official end to operations on 11 August, ordering the Cavalry Corps back into reserve around Amiens.[103]

* * *

The operational success or otherwise of the cavalry forms the main subject of this book. Unfortunately, in the case of the Amiens battle the criteria by which this might be judged vary according to the standpoint and biases of the judges, and not all have been kind to the cavalry. The commander in chief, Haig, seems to have been well pleased with the performance of the cavalry on 8 August. He recorded in his diary on 13 August 1918:

> General Kavanagh explained to me the nature of the operations carried out by the cavalry. These were highly successful, and I feel sure that without the rapid advance of the cavalry the effect of the surprise attack of the 8th would have been much less and very probably the Amiens outer defence line would not have been gained either so soon or so cheaply.[104]

It would seem difficult to contradict this verdict. The Cavalry Corps had captured virtually all its primary objectives by lunchtime on the first day of the offensive. Their haul of prisoners was also impressive: Preston estimates this at about 3,000[105] out of an overall total for the British and Dominion forces of around 18,000.[106] Large numbers of machine guns were also overrun, as well as several batteries of artillery, several hospitals and at least one train (the 5th Dragoon Guards claimed twenty officers and 740 other ranks as prisoners from this one capture alone).[107] In terms of equipment capture, as well as personnel, it is also likely that the impact of the cavalry on the German defenders was under-represented in the statistics as in many cases prisoners were passed back to the infantry, or simply ignored as the cavalrymen rode on towards their objectives.[108] The moral effect of the cavalry on the defenders should not be underestimated either. The opinion of one German officer on large numbers of horsemen loose in his rear areas has already been quoted.

Various figures are available for casualties. Preston provided a figure (up to 12 August) of 1,054 human casualties in the Cavalry Corps,[109] although by his own admission the figures vary. Edmonds in the *Official History* offered a lower figure of 887 (with a horse loss of 1,800), out of a total loss of all arms in the offensive of 22,202.[110] The latter figure represents an average of something over one thousand casualties per participating infantry division (including those in reserve). The cavalry was not significantly involved in the fighting after the first day, but a thousand casualties over three divisions is not an excessive loss compared with that of the infantry. Within the Cavalry Corps the casualties were fairly evenly spread, although naturally those brigades most heavily involved in the fighting suffered most heavily; the Canadian Cavalry Brigade suffered most heavily, with 196 casualties, of whom twenty-five were killed.

Clearly, contrary to the widely held misconception both during the war and since, where the going was good machine guns alone were not an insuperable obstacle to mounted troops. Preston summarised the position:

> These three days' operations showed the great value of mounted troops in exploiting the success of a surprise infantry attack *so long as the ground was such as to permit rapid movement* [Preston's emphasis]. It was not so much the actual enemy machine-guns that held up the cavalrymen in the latter stages, as the fact that the broken ground prevented manoeuvres to avoid and outflank these machine-guns. And it cannot be too strongly emphasised that the infantry and tanks were equally unable to cope with these conditions.[111]

The verdict of subsequent historians has not been as kind to the cavalry. As elsewhere, the official historian Sir James Edmonds led the attack, claiming 'the attempts to use cavalry as a mounted arm in direct attack before every machine gun had been captured or silenced brought little profit in spite of the gallant efforts of the squadrons'.[112] Others were less subtle; McWilliams and Steel observed as recently as 2001, 'The glaring failure of the day was the performance of the cavalry.'[113] Schreiber, in his work on the Canadian Corps, claimed that 'the stubborn resistance of German machine-gunners', combined with artillery, meant that the cavalry were riding to 'certain death'[114] and elsewhere that the use of cavalry was 'a pathetic attempt to fulfil the atavistic hopes and beliefs of old cavalry officers, including Field Marshal Haig'.[115] Sadly such extravagant opinions occur with depressing regularity in the literature of the war. The views of Prior and Wilson, and John Terraine, as was the case with earlier battles, fall along similar lines.

It would appear that criticism of the rôle of the cavalry on 8 August has had as its focus two main points. The first point is that no 'breakthrough' occurred, and it is argued that the cavalry had no rôle in the battle unless a breakthrough was achieved. Secondly, the horsemen did not cooperate effectively with the tanks, thus not only failing to produce significant results in combination, but also hampering the tanks from achieving the success that might have been possible had they operated on their own. As McWilliams and Steel put it, 'The Whippet tanks were seriously handicapped by being attached to the cavalry.'[116]

The first of these criticisms can be linked to Haig's extension of the objectives. As so often in the past, he did not allow his vision to be constrained by a 'Bite and Hold' attack, and suggested the possibility of a deeper and more complete success. It is questionable to what extent Haig himself believed that this would occur, and to what extent it was a gesture towards Foch, who was eager for results that would support his attacks in the south. However, once the revised orders of 4 and 5 August had been issued, mentioning the Roye–Chaulnes Line and even Ham, away to the east, these objectives became the criteria by which the offensive as a whole, the success of the cavalry and even Haig himself have subsequently been judged. This is despite the fact that these revised orders made very little difference to the operation as carried out; the basis of the operation continued to be the limited attack up to the Amiens Outer Defence Line originally conceived by Rawlinson. Were the success of the operation to be judged on the basis of Rawlinson's original plan up to 4 August (to which hardly any changes were made in spite of Haig's promptings), it could only be judged a success.

Criticism of the cavalry can also be attributed to a failure to acknowledge the *tactical* rôle of mounted troops. This study has shown that as the battlefield deepened from the start of 1917 onwards, and the German defences became more flexible, the opportunities for mounted troops to contribute significantly to an all-arms battle at the tactical level grew steadily and 8 August 1918 represented a high point in this process. Not only was the rôle of the cavalry in capturing local tactical objectives early in the battle fully acknowledged in Rawlinson's plan, but their positioning well forward at the start of the battle, without the necessity for orders from corps commanders before advancing, allowed them to live up to their potential. Many commentators, however, remain wedded to the idea that the only rôle for cavalry was one of exploitation, and that their contribution to a tactical 'Bite and Hold' battle was minimal or superfluous. Prior and Wilson observed, 'The cavalry, for example, would only play a part if Haig's wildest dreams came true [i.e., a complete breakthrough]; Rawlinson's more modest purposes could be accomplished without them.'[117] This view neglects the important part played by the cavalry in attaining those 'modest purposes' not only more quickly but, as Haig commented (quoted above), more 'cheaply', as the Cavalry Corps casualty figures testify.

The second platform for criticism of the cavalry was the success or otherwise of cooperation with tanks (already discussed in some detail in Chapter 4 in relation to the Cambrai battle). Whippet tanks were attached to each brigade, but this, as at Cambrai, led to a good deal of scapegoating of the cavalry for the failures of the tanks. This criticism followed two strands. The first of these was that somehow the tanks could and should have been used on their own in some grand deep penetration operation. McWilliams and Steel summarised this argument:

> The tank officers had anticipated a powerful, concentrated thrust that would swing south and ravage the German rear areas ahead of the French First Army. Tied to the vulnerable cavalry, however, the Whippets were spread out over a wide front, which reduced their impact and eliminated the possibility of a concerted swing southward.[118]

Anglesey traces the origin of this piece of wild speculation to Fuller, while pointing out that it was Fuller himself who proposed the combination of Whippets with cavalry to Rawlinson in the first place.[119] The Whippet tank under discussion, in spite of its glamorous name, was only marginally quicker than its larger Mark V colleagues: 7mph (12kmh) on good going but only half that cross-country, and it was certainly no more reliable mechanically. Thus the idea of massed tank exploitation was no more viable in August 1918 than it had been in December 1917. In any case, as has been discussed earlier, the broken terrain beyond the Outer Defence Line would have been as much a bar to tank advance as it would to horses. Thus the suggestion that tanks could have achieved what cavalry did not remains a fiction in the minds of tank enthusiasts rather than a realistic possibility. Nonetheless the tank supporters were quick to make their point. Home was painfully aware of this within a few days of the battle, writing on 12 August:

> The Cavalry had a chance of doing a job and carried it out splendidly. In the papers a great deal of credit is given to the tanks, especially the Whippets, they being the latest toy. We shall have to get a tame correspondent and have the S. African business once more: nothing but advertisement.[120]

The second strand of criticism related to the success or otherwise of the direct cooperation between the horsemen and the tanks. The historian of the 6th Tank Battalion offered a comment on this in 1919, which has become the standard view among later historians:

> As a result of the Amiens battles, it was found that the present Whippet was not suitable to operate with mounted troops. One of two things invariably occurred; either the cavalry wanted to move forward at the gallop, in which case they out-distanced the Whippet, or the Whippets were able to move forward and the cavalry were prevented by machine-gun fire or barrage.[121]

The first part of this statement is undoubtedly accurate. After the early phases of the battle the tanks struggled to keep up with the cavalry. With the cavalry brigades advancing as rapidly as they did, this is hardly surprising. Lieutenant Colonel E. Paterson, commanding the 7th Cavalry Brigade, stated: 'The Whippet tanks, owing to the rapid advance from Bois-de-Morgemont and the difficulties of bad going and steep undulations, never appeared in the picture.'[122]

The second part of the argument, that the tanks were able to get forward where cavalry were not, is not supported by the evidence. In fact it was coming under fire that often prompted the cavalry to gallop in the first place, rapid movement being a proven tactic in the face of enemy machine guns. The war diary of Lord Strathcona's Horse bears this out:

> A heavy crossfire of MGs developing from Beaucourt, it was considered inadvisable to move more slowly under this fire, and Major Torrance was ordered to get on to the more covered position without reference to the tanks.... The distance between the Advance Squadron and the main body at this time had become considerable because in accordance with instructions the main body had not sent ahead of the Whippets.[123]

Thus the tanks were often left behind precisely because the cavalry were under fire. Equally unfortunately for the tanks, the contrast between the perceived vulnerability of cavalry to machine-gun fire and the relative invulnerability of tanks was not borne out by reality either. As has been shown, the cavalry were able to use their mobility to minimise casualties. Tanks on the other hand drew fire and were vulnerable to anti-tank fire from German artillery (fired both indirectly and in the specific anti-tank rôle over open sights), but lacked the protection of rapid mobility. They were thus no more able to confront well emplaced enemy troops by frontal attack than were the cavalry. The losses of three tanks in the unsuccessful attack to the south of Harbonnieres demonstrated this, and the two tanks brought up to support the failing Canadian

Cavalry Brigade attack against Beaucourt were equally unsuccessful.[124] In fact no occasions have been identified on 8 August where the cavalry advance was halted but the tanks were able to push on.

Only where there was good ground and room to manoeuvre were tanks alone, cavalry alone or the two in concert able to progress. Where this was possible, useful cooperation took place. Tanks cooperated with the 1st Cavalry Brigade in the clearance of Bayonvillers, and joined with the initially successful advance of the Bays along the north side of the railway 'obtaining very good practice on all kinds of targets'[125] before joining in the attacks around Harbonnieres. The two arms, mechanical and equine, were thus a good deal less mutually incompatible than may have been argued. Nonetheless the cavalry remained sceptical of the immediate potential of the Whippets, and worried about their impact on the mobility of horse-mounted troops. An after-action report prepared by the Cavalry Corps at the end of August observed:

> (a) the recent operations have proved that:
>
> > (i) these tanks cannot keep up with the advanced bodies of Cavalry fighting in open warfare, and that therefore if an attempt is made to use them, the action of the Cavalry is delayed and opportunities lost.[126]

Thus 'the task given to Whippet tanks should be a strictly limited one'.[127]

A significant amount of space has been given to this debate but, although the tanks may have been lauded in the press of the day, it is easy to over-emphasise any contemporary split between supporters of mechanical technology and those of horseflesh. Only with the benefit of hindsight, and the wholesale replacement of equine by petrol power in the later twentieth century, has it been possible to envisage a wholly mechanical, horseless army. Such a vision simply did not exist between 1914 and 1918, and those such as Travers,[128] who have castigated the commanders of the day for not embracing the technology more fully, essentially miss this point. It should also be remembered that significant numbers of tank officers were cavalrymen – the commander of the 6th Tank Battalion is listed in operational orders as 'Lieutenant Colonel C.M. Truman (12th Lancers)'.[129] Clearly his new job did not override his old regimental affiliation. Thus while problems of cooperation undoubtedly existed, these should not be viewed as a 'rivalry' between 'old' and 'new' arms, but more as a developing mobile arm (mechanical and equine) seeking to absorb a new piece of equipment.

One of the most telling facts which challenges the supposed anti-horse stance of the tank enthusiasts is the preferred mode of transport of tank officers. The nature of the tanks of the day meant that communication among the crew of a single tank was very difficult, and tank to tank communication essentially impossible. The result of this was that at Cambrai most tank officers in the rôle of section leader or above (excepting of course, famously, their brigadier) advanced on foot. This allowed them the flexibility to move around and liaise with their infantry counterparts.[130] When 'Whippet' tanks were introduced to cooperate with the cavalry, the faster pace of advance meant that these officers simply rode not tanks but horses. The history of the 6th Tank Battalion records: 'The difficulties of company commanders in keeping touch with the tanks on such a wide front were enormous, and they were compelled to be mounted. This fact largely accounted for our heavy casualties among senior officers.'[131]

Nor was this practice limited to operations in cooperation with cavalry. A posthumous Victoria Cross was awarded to Captain Richard West of the 6th Tank Battalion for his actions during two operations in August and September 1918. His citation records that he commanded from horseback, and had several horses shot under him, before becoming a casualty himself. On both occasions he was cooperating with infantry formations: 'He therefore rode forward on horseback to our front infantry line in order to keep in touch with the progress of the battle and to be in a position to launch his tanks at the right moment.'[132]

Clearly these men had no quibble with the use of horses on their newly 'mechanised' battlefield.

This discussion, however, has more to do with the historiography of the battle than with the operation itself. In summary, 8 August was a significant operational success, in which the Cavalry Corps (assisted by the tanks) played no small part. At last a plan had been evolved which placed the cavalry well forward in the right place at the right time, with realistic objectives, and removed the dead hand of corps level command. This allowed the local commanders to act with boldness and initiative within an ever-deepening battlefield, the outer reaches of which were at the limits of the tactical range of a conventional infantry and artillery attack. The battle also pointed the way to how the war would ultimately be won: not by a sweeping mobile victory but by well organised localised blows of overwhelming power, delivered with an ever-increasing frequency. Unfortunately, the usefulness of cavalry in the latter type of fighting, rather than the former, seems to have been widely overlooked.

* * *

Even as the last phases of the fighting around Amiens were in progress, a further diminution of the power of the cavalry was being contemplated. On 25 July Sir Henry Wilson in his capacity as Chief of the Imperial General Staff produced a lengthy document, entitled 'British Military Policy 1918–19'.[133] Among other things this document laid out the notorious 'Plan 1919', whereby the final offensive against the Germans would be delayed for a full year.

Haig was dismissive of much of its content, but Wilson's remarks concerning the cavalry were significant. He argued that one cavalry division should be dismounted entirely and used as tank or machine-gun troops. A second could be retained under GHQ command but this would no longer require the corps headquarters establishment, which could be reduced to a simple training inspectorate. The third remaining cavalry division would be broken up as corps cavalry, 'the need for which has been greatly felt during this year's campaign'.[134] This last remark is somewhat ironic as it was Wilson who was instrumental in the dismounting of almost all of the corps cavalry in October 1917. Wilson continued to push this policy at a conference of senior officers on 11 August, despite Kavanagh's protestations. Home, recording the meeting, commented: 'The CC [Kavanagh] tackled the latter [Wilson] on the question of doing away with the Cavalry Corps. HW said that he intended doing so. They will regret it.'[135]

The timing of these meetings was unfortunate. While the Amiens attack had been very successful, it was widely accepted that now the battlefront had reached the destroyed zone of the previous years' fighting, there would be little further opportunity for large-scale mounted action, at least until the British armies emerged on the far side of the Hindenburg Line and the German prepared defences. At the same time Wilson was right in that, as the armies advanced, the need for mounted troops in the corps and divisional cavalry rôle was acute. As the historian of the Oxfordshire Hussars put it, 'the moment the war became one of movement every unit in the Army, from corps down to platoon, began screaming for mounted troops to help them – their previous opinion of their uselessness having suddenly changed'.[136] Kavanagh and Haig were thus forced to accede to the demands for dispersal of some of the remaining cavalry among the advancing armies, while trying to retain a mounted striking force in the Cavalry Corps. Haig continued to look beyond the immediate fighting to a point when the wholesale German retreat would begin and mounted troops would be vital. He wrote in his diary on 1 September:

> I therefore wished the Cavalry Corps to be kept as strong as possible, and at the present time merely to detach the *minimum* number of squadrons necessary for Divisional and Corps requirements. By this procedure I hoped to have an efficient Cavalry Corps ready to act vigorously when the decisive moment comes, and reap the fruits of victory.[137]

Nonetheless on 4 September he directed Kavanagh to break up the 2nd Cavalry Division, sending a brigade to each of the First, Third and Fourth Armies. This provided twenty-seven squadrons; a further twelve squadrons remained in still-mounted corps cavalry regiments, notably those from the Dominions, including the King Edward's Horse, the Canadian Light Horse and the 13th Australian Light Horse. Thus thirty-nine squadrons were available for the fifty-nine divisions of the BEF. The duties of these small parties of mounted men, operating often in small troop or patrol-sized units, were unglamorous but constant, keeping the advancing infantry in touch with the enemy. There is not space in this study to provide the detail of all these small operations, and many have been thoroughly described in Preston's exhaustive account in the *Cavalry Journal*,[138] but his conclusions are instructive:

> There can, however, be no doubt that the decision to break up one cavalry division was the only wise one under the circumstances. Some people might think that *army* cavalry was a luxury, but in September 1918 *divisional* cavalry was clearly a necessity. Once the final British advance began, infantry divisional commanders and brigadiers needed mounted men almost every day.[139]

Little can be said against this: the squadrons had to go. If any blame is to be apportioned, it should fall on Henry Wilson, who in 1917 had dismounted the troops whom these men replaced. Unfortunately as a consequence it left the Cavalry Corps pitifully weak. Haig still clung to his view that a moment would come for the cavalry. He had already tried to bolster its strength with the addition of the 4th (Guards) Brigade infantry in buses, as well as additional motor machine-gun batteries 'with the object of exploiting the situation which I hope will arise after we get the Marquion–Canal du Nord line'.[140] Interestingly, the attachment of infantry in buses to the cavalry was not an innovation of 1918; indeed, it can be seen in Haig's plan for Loos in 1915, showing the continuity of thinking of the commander in chief, if not of the wider Cavalry Corps. Even with these additions, a force of six cavalry (and one infantry) brigades on the whole front of the BEF was never going to be decisive. Preston made the rather telling comparison with the forces under Allenby in Palestine, where the impact of mounted troops was undeniable:

> Sir Edmund Allenby had 4 cavalry divisions to 7 infantry divisions, as compared with Sir Douglas Haig's 3 cavalry divisions to 59 infantry divisions, and the strength of the hostile forces in each case is even more significant; the Turks had only 3,000 sabres and 32,000 rifles – equivalent to 1 cavalry and 4 infantry divisions – whereas on September 25th 1918 the Germans had no less than 71 divisions opposite the British.[141]

In the light of these figures the Cavalry Corps, however effective it might be on a local level, was becoming strategically somewhat irrelevant.

As the force shrank, Haig became ever more guarded about its use, commenting on 6 September 'I do not propose to employ the Cavalry Corps until I judge the situation favourable for obtaining decisive results.'[142] Meanwhile the corps would be withdrawn for training to prepare them for such a day. A large scale 'Scheme' was carried out by the Cavalry Corps on 17 September, based on the exploitation of a collapse of organised enemy defences. Haig rode out in person to observe this exercise and wrote a lengthy critique of its results to be circulated to regimental commanders and above.[143] The time taken out of the commander in chief's schedule for this kind of micro-management is questionable, but it clearly demonstrates his continuing aspirations for the corps. Home's view on the matter was more sanguine: 'I hate these Schemes. They are so much more difficult to arrange than actual fighting.' However, 'the Chief enjoyed his day with the Cavalry. It was luckily a fine warm day and that has a great deal to do with the tempers of the great.'[144]

*   *   *

When the dispersal of the 2nd Cavalry Division and Haig's conflicting ambitions for a unified cavalry force are considered, these must be placed in the context of the pattern of fighting which had developed by 1918. Haig clearly believed that the BEF was on the cusp of a significant change from the trench warfare familiar up to that point to a flowing, *mobile,* battle, pursuing a defeated and demoralised enemy. It has become a pattern among scholars to identify a period starting with Amiens on 8 August when this new warfare took place, and indeed the term 'The Hundred Days' has been borrowed from its original context describing the Waterloo campaign of 1815, to cover the three-and-a-half months between Amiens and the Armistice on 11 November. Edmonds suggests that this term was current as early as 1919, when Sir Archibald Montgomery-Massingberd published *The Story of the Fourth Army in the 'Battle of the Hundred Days', August 8th to November 11th 1918.*[145] However, the question must be asked to what extent the combat of this period was significantly different from that which had passed before, and if so what brought the change about?

It is true that from Amiens onwards the BEF was consistently successful and the battlefront was more 'mobile' than it had been for years, but while a series of victorious attacks moved the armies across France, the character of each of these attacks was not dissimilar to those which had gone before. The presence of the former battlefields of 1916 and 1917 and their influence has been discussed already, and it is possible to divide the 'Hundred Days' into two phases, the fighting up to and through the Hindenburg Line from August to the end of September, and a more mobile phase after that. Sheffield considered these 'first fifty days' and observed:

> In spite of the dramatic nature of the initial advance, the Battle of
> Amiens in many respects followed the pattern of previous battles.

Like the first day of Arras, initial success became more difficult to exploit as impetus ran down on subsequent days and resistance grew stronger.[146]

He further describes the BEF 'sequencing a series of shallow battles rather than persevering with futile attempts to fight deep battles of penetration'.[147] This presents a vision of fighting methods and conditions which are very similar to what had gone before, the difference being that the 'learning curve'[148] which the British forces had followed had refined their approach to battle to the degree that, in combination with an equivalent decline in German resources and fighting quality, local victories could be achieved. Looking specifically at the cavalry, a direct tactical lineage can be traced between what the Cavalry Corps achieved in August 1918, and what it strove towards at Arras and Cambrai (with the varying amounts of success discussed in earlier chapters). While it has been argued in this chapter that the cavalry played a valuable rôle in the battle of Amiens, this was not necessarily because the nature of the fighting had fundamentally changed (compared with Arras or Cambrai), but rather because the cavalry had developed their skills within the existing context.

This leaves the second 'fifty days' after the breaking of the Hindenburg Line, which many have seen as a period of true 'open warfare'. Again the change in the nature of the fighting seems to have been anticipated more than realised. Haig held his remaining cavalry divisions in readiness for their great exploitation manoeuvre, but in the event only committed them to action once, on 8–9 October, in a battle which was a significant success for the cavalry (discussed later) but not the crushing blow to a defeated enemy which he might have expected. Kavanagh was asked by Haig in 1919 to sum up his thoughts on this period. Kavanagh in reply described a situation: '(b) When after continued defeats the enemy's morale is so lowered that he is ripe for the action of masses of cavalry.' He went on: 'The situation described in (b) had been arrived at on the morning of the Armistice, and two cavalry divisions were on the march east of the Scheldt, when orders were received to stop them.'[149]

Apparently, in the eyes of the GOC Cavalry Corps, the moment which Haig had been waiting for did not arise until the last moments of the conflict, by which time (perhaps recognising that fact) the Germans had given in. Indeed, a week before the Armistice Haig offered the use of the Cavalry Corps to Generals Byng and Rawlinson (commanding Third and Fourth Armies respectively) and both declined the offer,[150] despite the fact that both had shown themselves amenable to the use of cavalry in the past.

Another development during 1918 which some scholars have viewed as a key indicator of the changing nature of the fighting is the 'all-arms mobile force', what Griffith called with some hyperbole the 'Cavalry brigade battle group'.[151]

Cavalry had been cooperating successfully with armoured cars, and indeed with their own integral brigade-level machine guns and artillery since 1916, and cooperated successfully with cyclists at Arras in 1917, but attention has focused on the creation in 1918 of *ad-hoc* all-arms forces including truck-borne infantry and mortars, as well as cyclists. Thus the character and performance of these forces requires examination.

The first instance of the formation of such a unit in 1918 was 'Brutinels Independent Force', assembled for the Amiens battle of 8 August.[152] This force did not include any cavalry, consisting entirely of motor machine-guns, cyclists and truck-mounted trench-mortars, nor was it particularly flexible, being essentially tied by its wheeled vehicles to the Amiens–Roye road which was its line of advance. Its 'independence' was also questionable, since the unit was not intended to penetrate deeply into the German position but rather to run up and down the road acting as a flank-guard to the Canadian Corps to the north. Its rôle was therefore a strictly limited one, of a specialist character, rather than a step towards genuine mobile warfare.

At the start of September the same commander was called upon to lead a similar force during the assault on the Drocourt–Quèant or 'D–Q' Line, part of the Hindenburg system of defences. The Canadian Corps, part of First Army, was to attack this defensive system on 2 September, with an axis of advance along the Arras–Cambrai road. In addition to the D–Q defences themselves, the possibility existed of achieving a bridgehead across the Canal du Nord, where the road crossed the canal some 6km (4 miles) beyond the German front lines. Using the road as a line of advance, a plan was developed for a force consisting of two motor machine gun brigades, an artillery battery, a cyclist battalion and trench-mortars in motor-lorries to push through the main infantry attack and drive on down the road to the canal at Marquion. This time the force would be accompanied by two regiments of cavalry: the 10th Hussars from 6th Cavalry Brigade and the Canadian Light Horse, acting as the Canadian corps cavalry, along with a section of 6th Machine Gun Squadron.[153]

The cavalry portion of the force included the officer commanding the 10th Hussars, Lieutenant Colonel Whitmore (encountered previously at Monchy in 1917), who provided a scathing critique of this operation in the *Cavalry Journal* in 1925.[154] Whitmore points out that as the column was likely to pass beyond the infantry, into the area bombarded by its supporting artillery, a corridor was left 1,000 yards (950m) wide astride the road which was excluded from the Allied creeping barrage. It was down this 'cylindrical funnel' that the force would advance. As he explained, his difficulties were manifold:

> If he [the force commander] deviates more than 500 yards on either side of his centre of advance he comes under the bombardment of the artillery, both heavy and light, of his own attacking corps. His

area of operations is certain to be bombarded by the enemy holding the crossings in front of him. He has no opportunity of disposing of his horses when a dismounted attack on the canal crossing becomes necessary. And the road by which he has advanced has by now become seriously obstructed by all conditions of traffic which necessarily follows in the wake of a successful attack.[155]

Fortunately for Whitmore and his men, the fighting on this attack front remained too heavy all day for the force to advance, and the Germans withdrew behind the canal overnight on 2/3 September, hence their services were not required. What would have become of them had this foolhardy scheme been attempted is not pleasant to contemplate.

Thus the assembly of a 'mobile force' by optimistic operational planners did not necessarily imply a realistic prospect of 'mobile warfare' actually taking place. Merely assembling the troops does not automatically predicate the appropriate conditions for their employment. It is arguable that Haig, as so often in the past, laid out a vision of a mobile war of pursuit, but that this never really came about. At the same time a series of battles were fought, conducted in a style which had much in common with the offensives of the preceding years. However, the increasing success and quickening tempo of what were in fact 'Bite and Hold' battles led to the impression, both among Haig's subordinate commanders and among later scholars, that a truly 'mobile' phase of the war had arrived. Much of the success of this process was due to the BEF's ability in 1918 to equip and supply repeated large-scale attacks on different parts of the front only days apart, instead of the months of logistical build-up which were required earlier in the war. However, even this successful attacking cycle could only be maintained at a certain level. It is arguable that had a German collapse such as Haig envisioned actually taken place, the Allied logistical effort, which was stretched almost to breaking point already by the existing speed of advance, would have been unable to cope with a faster movement.[156]

The presence of the Cavalry Corps on the battlefield at Amiens, and again in October, has also contributed to the impression of the 'new' character of the fighting. For many observers this is a clear indicator of a change in the nature of the war, given that in previous years their participation was presumed to be impossible. As has been shown, this latter impression is wrong, and mounted troops had a legitimate place in the fighting of 1916 and 1917. Thus no wholesale change in the character of the fighting was required for the Cavalry Corps to be successfully involved in 1918. Travers has criticised the high command of the BEF in 1918 for not embracing what he sees as a technological alternative to the 'semi-traditional forms of warfare'[157] carried on in 1918. He vastly overstates the potential of the available technology as an alternative, but his stress on continuity (or 'tradition') supports the idea of a continuum between the fighting of 1918 and what went before.

Much of this debate over the character of the war and the nature of offensive tactics has focused at a high level, particularly on the ambitions of Haig and his army commanders. At the same time, however, the war was being fought and won at a lower command level. The nature of the German defence allowed attacks to be carried out not only at corps and army level but also by individual divisions and even brigades. This type of attack, when carried out in 1916 or 1917, has rightly been criticised, but in 1918 it was a key part of keeping the pressure on the retreating German forces. It has been argued[158] that the 'mobile' character of the war is evident at this level, whether or not it is apparent in large-scale set-piece attacks.

For example in early October the 55th (West Lancashire) Division formed all-arms advanced guards in its infantry brigades 'so as to follow up rapidly should any considerable retirement of the enemy take place'.[159] Each infantry brigade in the division was allocated an 18-pdr battery and a machine-gun company as well as trench mortars on GS wagons, plus medical and engineer units. Cavalry was included in each force from the corps cavalry regiment, but this consisted only of a section – i.e., a corporal's patrol of eight men – hardly a battle-winning number of mounted troops. This force would be unleashed on the enemy when a suitable moment arrived by the issuing of a 'Scurry' telegram. However: 'As events turned out, the method of withdrawal of the enemy did not enable the Corps to issue any definite order for an advance at a particular time, and consequently the "Scurry" telegram was never issued from Divisional HQ.'[160] Thus even at this lower level of command, while the expectation of a mobile battle had trickled down from above, this did not necessarily translate into actual mobile fighting.

Nonetheless, a study both of Preston's account of 1918 in the *Cavalry Journal*[161] and of individual regimental histories[162] does show these small forces of cavalry in daily contact with the enemy, in a way which was not the case earlier in the war. There is no doubt that cavalry troops were able to fulfil in 1918 a rôle which had been a traditional part of their duties for several hundred years and had only fallen out of use since 1915: that of reconnaissance. It was in reconnaissance, as well as dispatch riding and prisoner control, that the regiments of cavalry dispersed as corps troops in August 1918 earned their keep. The German withdrawal meant that each time they broke contact with the advancing British troops their new positions had to be identified before an attack could be developed.

Good intelligence and communications are a vital part of military operations. Thus the rôle of the cavalry as reconnaissance troops was a vital one and should not be underestimated. It is not the same, however, as the use of mounted soldiers in the actual assault on those enemy positions or in the exploitation of any success. Once the latest German rearguards had been located, the assault upon them was typically an infantry and artillery affair. Indeed, even if the local commanders had wanted to include horsemen in their plans of attack the cavalry were simply not there in sufficient numbers. A regiment of cavalry per infantry corps equates to a squadron per division, and a troop (thirty or so men) per infantry brigade. Deduct those engaged on communications duties and prisoner escort, and each infantry brigade commander was left with little more than a handful of cavalrymen under the charge of a junior NCO.

This scarcity of 'mobile' resources was not limited to the cavalry. Griffith has successfully demonstrated that as the front of attack widened to incorporate the whole of the BEF in 1918, the number of tanks available to any one division was pitifully small and attacks were typically mounted without tank support.[163] Thus far from commanders spurning these mobile options, the 'semi-traditional' infantry/artillery battle which Travers criticises was forced upon the BEF by the unprecedented scale of the fighting.

* * *

The mounted soldiers distributed along the front as corps and divisional cavalry continued to be in action almost daily until the moment of the Armistice (and in some cases for a few hours after it), but only one opportunity arose for large-scale cavalry action. This was during the 'Second Battle of Le Cateau' between 8 and 10 October. By the beginning of October the BEF had penetrated the last of the significant German defences. The assault of 29 September had carried Fourth Army through the main Hindenburg defence line (memorably with the assault of the 46th Division across the St Quentin Canal at Riqueval), and continuing attacks up to 5 October overcame the supporting Hindenburg Support and Beaurevoir Lines.[164] Haig's 'Second Phase' of the campaign, that beyond the formal trench lines, was potentially about to begin.[165]

By 5 October Fourth Army occupied a line facing broadly north–east, about 10km (6 miles) beyond the line of the St Quentin Canal, and beyond the recently captured villages of Beaurevoir and Montbrehain. Their axis of advance followed a Roman road which branched off the St Quentin–Cambrai road at Riqueval then ran straight north–east, passing just to the north of Le Cateau 20km (12 miles) from the front line of 5 October, and ultimately on to Mauberge and Mons. On 5 October General Rawlinson issued orders for an attack by three corps (IX, II American and XIII) astride the road, with the objective of a line through the villages of Serain and Premont. The attack would be on a front of approximately 12km (8 miles) with infantry objectives around 6km (4 miles) into the German position.[166] The Cavalry Corps was tasked with exploitation beyond the infantry objective line, potentially as far as Le Cateau but specifically as far as the railway station and junction at Busigny, approximately 10km (6 miles) beyond the infantry start line. The cavalry attack would be made initially by the 1st Cavalry Division with the 3rd Cavalry Division in support. The order to advance would rest with the corps commander (a retrograde step in command and control compared with the automatic advance at Amiens), but unlike on previous occasions Kavanagh placed himself at the forward headquarters of the 1st Cavalry Division early in the battle so as to be well placed to judge the moment to move.[167]

Starting at 5.10am, the infantry assault was initially successful. Fighting for the objective villages of Premont and Serain was reported to the 1st Cavalry Division headquarters by 9.00am and in response to this the lead brigade (9th Cavalry Brigade) of the 1st Cavalry Division was sent up to try to get through between the two villages.[168] This advance was described by the historian of the 15th Hussars:

> ... the countryside presented an attractive appearance. The broad belt of destroyed and devastated areas had now been left behind, and stretched out to view lay the rolling highly cultivated countryside of agricultural France, untouched by war since 1914....
>
> Nevertheless this peaceful prospect was deceitful, for the German retreat was not by any means disorganised, and the rearguards were most skilfully placed.[169]

The lead regiment, the 19th Hussars, rapidly encountered heavy fire. Kavanagh characteristically ordered the division to push on in strength, but Major General Mullens, commanding the 1st Cavalry Division, made his own reconnaissance and determined that 'there were no signs of a disorganised retreat, and considerable resistance from both machine gun and artillery had been met with'.[170] He therefore pushed his two remaining brigades out to either flank to try to find a way around the two villages.

The period from 11.00am to around 2.00pm was filled by a series of increasingly desperate efforts by the three cavalry brigades to get forward, but without success. They made a number of relatively costly and ultimately unsuccessful mounted attacks on German machine-gun and artillery positions. To the south of the villages two troops of the 19th Hussars did succeed in capturing a battery of field guns at the point of the sword, but in so doing took so many casualties that, realising their weakness, their erstwhile prisoners turned on them with hand-grenades and the cavalrymen were driven off with further casualties.[171] One of the fatalities was Lieutenant Colonel Franks, who had led the regiment since 1915; all the officers who accompanied him in the attack also became casualties. The event was described by Squadron Sergeant Major Brunton of C Squadron:

> The charge was sounded, squadrons rapidly formed into line, and away we went hell for leather; it was a mad ride through shell fire.

We rode clean through the guns, killing many gunners by the sword.
Those that were spared bombed us as we passed through.[172]

Nor were casualties among the cavalry restricted to those charging artillery batteries. German aerial bombing was also a problem, particularly where the cavalry were forced to dismount, as led horses made a tempting target and could make no reply if attacked.[173]

By mid-afternoon Rawlinson decided that the infantry attack by XIII and II American Corps should be renewed, and the cavalry were withdrawn in readiness to support this attack; however, by 4.00pm it became apparent that this renewed assault would have to wait until the following day. Water supply was also becoming a significant problem, so the cavalry divisions were withdrawn west of Beaurevoir overnight. Even after this withdrawal the corps continued to be troubled by German aerial bombing, which caused several casualties.[174] Preston argued that this intensive bombing of the cavalry was a specific German tactic born of their fear of the potential of the corps, but he offers no evidence of this from the German side.[175]

It must be acknowledged that 8 October was not a particularly successful day for the cavalry. The German defences had not deteriorated to the degree seen on 8 August, allowing freedom of movement within and behind their lines, and their careful positioning of machine guns and artillery, combined with close air support, shows that they were by no means a spent force. Preston excuses this by arguing that the Cavalry Corps and divisional commanders were mindful of Haig's strictures on keeping the corps intact, and that they were thus less aggressive than they might have been. He describes the 1st Cavalry Division casualties (at around 200) as 'light' and further argues that 'the principle [was] accepted that, in the attack, reserves should be used to exploit a success rather than redeem a failure; and that if there was no success it was better to admit it and try again another day in another way'.[176] These two observations are hard to reconcile with the evidence of the war diaries; clearly the 19th Hussars sustained significant losses around Serain and Premont. Also, far from finding 'another way', Kavanagh responded to the news that they were held up by ordering Mullens 'to push on to Maretz in force'[177] (i.e., straight up the Roman road) with the remainder of the division, clearly precisely attempting to 'redeem a failure'. Fortunately Mullens chose a liberal interpretation of this order, throwing the 1st and 2nd Cavalry Brigades out to the flanks, albeit without making any greater progress.

The following day was more successful. Having ended the day on 8 October on a line through the villages of Premont and Serain, Fourth Army repeated the attack on 9 October. The infantry objectives this time were to be the villages of Maretz and then Honnechy and Maurois, representing an infantry advance of another 8km (5 miles) along the Le Cateau road. The attack on this part of the front was to be carried out by XIII Corps supported by the Cavalry Corps, which would once again seek to exploit towards and beyond Le Cateau.[178] As the 1st Cavalry Division had borne the brunt of the fighting the day before, the two cavalry divisions were exchanged and the 3rd Cavalry Division would lead the advance with the 7th Cavalry Brigade as advanced guard, keeping in close touch with the infantry.[179]

After a 5.20am start in thick mist the infantry once again made rapid progress. The headquarters of the 3rd Cavalry Division received word at 8.45am that the infantry had taken the village of Maretz (an advance of about 4km (2½ miles)) and that 'touch with retreating enemy had been temporarily lost'.[180] Clearly an opportunity had presented itself for the cavalry which had not arisen the day before. In response to this Major General Harman, commanding the 3rd Cavalry Division, ordered an advance. The leading 7th Cavalry Brigade had been broken up into patrols and spread along the front in contact with the infantry. It would take time to reform this brigade as a striking force so Harman ordered the two remaining brigades to leapfrog through the advanced guard brigade and the infantry and push on towards Le Cateau, the 6th Cavalry Brigade on the southern side of the main axial road and the Canadian Cavalry Brigade to the north.

First into action were the Canadians. The leading regiment, the Fort Garry Horse, reached the limit of the infantry advance to the north-east of Maretz at about 9.30am. The infantry had been held up by significant German machine-gun fire from the edge of the Bois de Gattigny, about one mile (1.6km) ahead. The machine guns accompanying the Fort Garry Horse and the four guns of A Battery RCHA were quickly brought into action against the edge of the wood, and at about 11.00am a mounted attack was launched, one troop of Fort Garry Horse attacking frontally while a further four troops swung left and entered the woods from the west. The frontal attack was extremely costly and 'most of the troop became casualties'. But the flanking attack succeeded in clearing the wood, and 'killing a great number of the enemy with the sword'.[181] Around 200 prisoners were captured, along with a 5.9-inch howitzer, an anti-tank rifle, a trench mortar and around forty machine-guns,[182] many of the latter abandoned in the face of the frontal charge.

While this attack was in progress Lord Strathcona's Horse had extended the left of the Fort Garry Horse in a wide flanking move around the northern end of the Bois de Gattigny, pushing on towards and to the south of the village of Bertry and capturing further prisoners; a party of thirty fleeing from the Fort Garry attack to the south, and a group of forty-five enemy who were success-fully charged by one squadron of Lord Strathcona's Horse in a line of rifle pits north of the wood.[183] By midday the Canadian Cavalry Brigade was within striking distance of (and taking machine-gun fire from) the villages of Maurois and Honnechy, astride the Le Cateau road, the original infantry objectives.

To the south of the main road the 6th Cavalry Brigade had joined the leading infantry on a line close to the railway south-west of (and short of) Honnechy, but heavy fire was encountered from the village and the infantry attack stalled at about 11.00am. The brigade commander, Ewing Paterson, made his own reconnaissance at about 11.30am, and was told that the infantry 'were so exhausted and the resistance so strong that it was not intended to advance further that day'.[184] At about 11.50am a conference was held of all the senior cavalry commanders. Kavanagh was present, along with General Harman, commanding the 3rd Cavalry Division, and Brigadiers E. Paterson (6th Cavalry Brigade) and R.W. Paterson (Canadian Cavalry Brigade).[185] It was decided that 'a vigorous attempt should be made to capture Honnechy and Reumont [the next village a further mile (1.6km) up the road] or the whole advance would peter out'.[186] The plan called for a frontal assault on Honnechy by the Royal Dragoons and 10th Hussars, while the 3rd Dragoon Guards circled the village to the south and the Fort Garry Horse attacked from the north. The flanks would be protected by the remainder of the Canadian Cavalry Brigade to the north and by the Inniskilling Dragoons to the south, borrowed from the 7th Cavalry Brigade for the purpose. The attack was timed for 2.00pm, at which time the infantry attack would also be renewed.

When the commander of the Canadian Cavalry Brigade returned to his headquarters he discovered that in fact the northern village, Maurois, had already fallen to an attack by two troops of the Fort Garry Horse.[187] Thus when the divisional attack began at 2.00pm the Royal Dragoons were able to pass to the north of Maurois (which masked them from Honnechy, still in German hands) and push on towards Reumont, recrossing the Roman road and taking up a position to the south-east of the village, while the Canadians encircled it from the north. The German garrison of Reumont withdrew, but a number were captured before they could escape, the Fort Garry Horse also 'killing a number of the enemy with the sword'[188] – no doubt those who did not surrender with sufficient alacrity.

Meanwhile to the south the 3rd Dragoon Guards moved around Honnechy to attack the village from the south-east. They were under heavy fire from their flank and rear (despite the efforts of the Inniskillings to provide flank protection) and had to close up to pass under the embanked railway line via a bridge over the Honnechy–Busigny road. They soon opened out again and approached the village at a gallop. The attack was a rapid success. Honnechy was occupied by 2.40pm,[189] and infantry of XIII Corps followed the Dragoons in and were able to complete the clearance of the village shortly after.

Thus by about 3.00pm the 3rd Cavalry Division occupied a line facing north-east from south of Reumont across the road and as far north as Troisvilles (captured earlier by Lord Strathcona's Horse). At about this time word was received via Fourth Army that German units retreating from the fighting opposite Third Army to the north were passing across the front of the cavalry on the Inchy–Le Cateau road. This traffic was brought under artillery fire by a battery of 4.5-inch howitzers attached to the Canadian Cavalry Brigade, as well as their own RCHA guns.[190] Meanwhile the 6th Cavalry Brigade was ordered to advance on Le Cateau and cut the roads leading out of the town. Unfortunately most of this brigade were dismounted and holding positions south of Reumont and the strength of the opposition ahead of them made any further advance impossible. The plan was therefore revised to send the Canadians forward north of the Roman road, supported by the 7th Cavalry Brigade.[191]

The Canadians advanced at about 5.00pm and in fading light Lord Strathcona's Horse established a line of posts cutting the road from Inchy along a front facing north-west from Troisvilles to above Neuvilly. On their right the Royal Canadian Dragoons, hardly engaged so far that day, pushed forward to the high ground overlooking the river Selle. The lack of progress of the 6th Cavalry Brigade south of the Roman road meant that the Fort Garry Horse had to form another defensive flank on the right along the line of the road overlooking Le Cateau. The Canadian Cavalry Brigade was thus strung out in an elongated rectangle with one regiment on each of three faces. These posts were to be held until daylight on 10 October, when the Canadian Cavalry Brigade was relieved and the 7th Cavalry Brigade took over the positions.[192]

The high ground overlooking the river Selle and the villages of Montay and Neuvilly marked the limit of the cavalry advance. Orders were issued for the 7th Cavalry Brigade to push on across the river on 10 October, but advancing patrols soon came under heavy fire and it was apparent that the Germans had consolidated their positions on the far bank. General Kavanagh recalled both cavalry divisions into reserve in the course of the day and they took no further significant part in the fighting.[193] In fact, such was the strength of the German position that it was to be a week before Fourth Army renewed its attack, by which time artillery had been brought forward and a new set-piece assault prepared.[194]

Clearly 9 October was a much more successful day from a cavalry point of view. The 3rd Cavalry Division had advanced about 14km (8 miles) from the infantry start line on a front of about 5km (3 miles) and over four hundred prisoners had been captured, along with more than a hundred machine guns, and various field pieces, trench mortars and other equipment. Furthermore the rapidity of their retreat had prevented the Germans from carrying out their routine destruction of the abandoned villages, a fact which, if not of great significance to the advancing Fourth Army, was certainly important to the inhabitants.[195] Nonetheless it was on this day's fighting that Sir James Edmonds gave his widely quoted verdict that 'the cavalry had done nothing that the infantry, with artillery support and cyclists, could not have done for itself at less cost'.[196]

This remark has gained such wide currency that it deserves detailed examination, and it can be challenged on a number of points. If the infantry advances of 8 and 9 October are measured, both show an advance of around 6km (4 miles). Although the cavalry was not able to progress on 8 October, it was able to get forward about 13km (8 miles) on the 9th. In each case the infantry attack was launched at around 5.00am and by about 9.00am had more or less run out of steam; references occur in the war diaries to the 'exhaustion' of the infantry. It is no coincidence that the range of an 18-lb field piece was around 6,500 yards – 6km (4 miles).[197] It is thus probably fair to say that a set-piece infantry attack had the potential to get forward only as far as the reach of its barrage, or about 7–8 km (5 miles) at most. A hiatus would then occur, at which point either the German defence was sufficiently dislocated to allow cavalry to push through, as on 9 October, and effectively 'double' the gains made, or alternatively the Germans continued to resist to the point that a renewed set-piece was required. Edmonds' assertion that infantry could have pushed on a further 8km (5 miles) without cavalry assistance is deeply questionable. Also, his qualification that the infantry could do so 'with artillery support' misses the essential point that beyond the range of the guns firing from behind the start line, that artillery support was very difficult to provide. The presence of the cavalry was thus arguably an important element which could 'add value' to an attack by increasing the gains made beyond what was possible with infantry alone.[198] That this was not possible every time does not detract from its usefulness on the occasions when it was.

Whether or not the infantry could have made similar gains 'at less cost' is also open to question. In addition to the approximately 200 casualties in the 1st Cavalry Division on 8 October, the 3rd Cavalry Division suffered a further 395 human casualties on 9 October.[199] This represents an average of 300 per division over both days, a figure remarkably similar to that suffered in the Amiens fighting of 8 August. No detailed infantry loss figures for these two days have been identified, but that the infantry would have done better in terms of casualties is unlikely.

It has also been argued that after the 'heavy defeat'[200] of 8 October the German army planned to re-establish a defence behind the river Selle and that on the 9th 'only weak rearguards faced the Allied forces'.[201] Many of the defenders withdrew overnight on 8/9 October to occupy the Hermann position beyond the river, and only 'defended localities' remained facing XIII Corps and the cavalry the next day.[202] There is no doubt that the cavalry found their advance on the 9th possible in a way that it had not been the day before. However, it is equally true that those rearguards were strong enough to require a significant set-piece infantry attack, and, as just discussed, the potential depth of that attack was limited; only by the use of cavalry was it possible to bring Fourth Army into a position to challenge the new defences along the Selle within 24 hours (albeit these were not formally attacked until some days later). Contact with and pressure on the enemy were thus maintained in a way which would not have been possible without mounted forces.

* * *

Preston concluded his study of 1918 thus:

> It may or may not be true to say that we should have defeated the Germans just the same in the autumn of 1918 even without our cavalry. But it is certainly true that, had it not been for that same cavalry, there would have been no autumn advance at all for the Germans would have defeated us in the spring.[203]

Preston was clear that the rôle played by the cavalry in defence in March was crucial, but that later on its importance was more arguable. The success or failure of the German March offensive was at times finely balanced, and probably hung on a range of factors, any one of which might be seen as critical. No doubt the part played by the cavalry was important. However, it was equally the case that the cavalry was quite poorly handled, both in terms of its dismounting at a vital point in the battle and also in the tactics applied by Seely at Moreuil Wood. Thus while the troops themselves deserve a great deal of credit, that owing to their leaders is rather less.

In August 1918 there seems to have been, at some levels within the BEF at least, a full appreciation of what cavalry could do and how to integrate them into the developing all-arms battle. Amiens on 8 August was a model example of how to integrate mounted forces into a set-piece attack and get the best out of them. Much of the credit for this falls ironically to Rawlinson, who in the past had not seemed keen to embrace the potential of cavalry. The design of the infantry attack on 8 August and the rôle allocated to the cavalry both show a clear continuity with the battles of 1917; lessons appear to have been learned and tactics developed which proved highly successful on the day. The 9 October fighting showed that this was not an isolated episode, but that a system had been developed whereby the limited progress achievable by a well-executed infantry attack could be significantly expanded upon by well-handled cavalry. In short, while an ultimate 'breakthrough' was never at issue, a 5-mile gain could be converted into a 10-mile gain by the well-timed intervention of mounted troops. Unfortunately, Haig's wider ambitions, and the ammunition this provided for his critics, have meant that this tactical achievement has largely been neglected.

After Amiens, however, the ever-widening extent of the offensive and the increasing tempo of attacks meant that the small number of horsemen available to the BEF was never going to be more than an occasional presence in what continued to be an infantry and artillery fight. The proportion of cavalrymen in the manpower of the BEF in France and Belgium on 11 November 1918 is recorded in official statistics as 0.56 per cent of the total force, or 0.77 per cent of the combatant strength (this latter figure compares with 58.19 per cent for the infantry, or more comparably 0.62 per cent for cyclists).[204] Haig's constant campaigning to retain any cavalrymen he could was laudable insofar as more mounted troops would no doubt have been useful, but it was ultimately based on a false premise. He continued, as he had since 1916, to believe in a day when the German defences would be broken to the extent that an independent force of cavalry could sweep through and create havoc in their rear areas. This day never came. Thus he was doing the right thing for the wrong reasons. There is little evidence that he ever truly recognised the tactical function of cavalry *within* the German defensive systems and in cooperation with other arms, preferring still to see them as an independent exploitation force.

The degree to which the fighting ever evolved into the 'mobile' or 'semi-mobile' warfare advocated by some historians is also questionable. Various all-arms columns were assembled, no doubt following the urgings of the commander in chief, but there is little evidence of actual combat by these forces. Certainly the value of both cavalry and armoured cars or motor machine-gunners grew as the year progressed, but this was essentially in the rôle of reconnaissance units. The set-piece fighting still remained the domain of the infantry and guns, with the occasional assistance of a few tanks, if for no other reason than that too few cavalry were available.

Chapter 6

Conclusions

At 11.00am the Armistice came into force and the fighting ended. Thank God!

Archibald Home, BGGS Cavalry Corps, Diary, 11 November 1918[1]

It is clear that between 1914 and 1918 the cavalry were effective in combat at a tactical level, in spite of the prevailing conditions of the battlefield (or as effective as their infantry counterparts, at any rate). The first factor in their favour was their mobility. The premise that the cavalry were incapable of moving around on the battlefields of the Western Front is simply false. Barbed wire and shell holes, while a challenge, were not insurmountable obstacles, and the character of the battlefield did not in and of itself prevent the cavalry from participating in the fighting. A good deal of effort had to be put into the preparation of cavalry tracks and in forward planning, but this was no more or less of a problem for the cavalry than it was for other arms. Indeed, the Tank Corps, supposedly the solution to the problem of trenches and barbed wire, arguably never reached a degree of mobility comparable to the cavalry. Thus the battlefield was not necessarily any more hostile an environment for a horseman than it was for any other soldier. The character of this battlefield also evolved as the war progressed, and far from becoming more hostile, actually created ever greater opportunities for cavalry action.

The battle of 14 July 1916 clearly demonstrated the ability of mounted troops to move around the battlefield. Nor is there any evidence in later operations that ground was a significant constraint. At Cambrai in 1917 it was not the ground but command and control issues which delayed the cavalry advance. Amiens and other battles in 1918 showed that when these command issues were at least partially resolved, the cavalry were able to move deep into the German positions and on to objectives beyond the immediate reach of the infantry.

The fighting at Monchy-le-Preux during the Arras battle also showed that the cavalry possessed a firepower capability disproportionate to their small numbers due to the presence of large numbers of machine guns, both the Vickers of the MGC(C) and the Hotchkiss guns integral to the regiments themselves. This firepower, combined with their mobility, made the cavalry a potent force on the battlefield. Their ability to move ahead of the advancing infantry and to take and defend ground was demonstrated on a number of occasions. The combination of mobility and firepower has a very modern ring to it, but it excludes the third, and at least equally important, tool at the disposal of a mounted soldier: shock action with cold steel. The ability of mounted troops to seize ground and to hold it with rifle firepower and automatic weapons is a concept found more acceptable by those critical of the cavalry arm. It would be quite possible to accept all that has been argued for so far, while still holding on to the idea that shock action – i.e., cavalrymen charging with sword or lance in hand – was nonetheless obsolete. For many writers the very idea of a soldier using cold steel from horseback stands as a metaphor for obsolescence, or, as Badsey put it, 'as a touchstone of all that is reactionary, foolish and futile'.[2] On some occasions mounted shock creeps into the narratives of these historians, but it is excused as somehow peculiar or exceptional. A.J.P. Taylor described the action of the 7th Dragoon Guards at High Wood as 'a sight unique on the Western Front'.[3] Similarly, while the earlier comments from Prior and Wilson concerning the cavalry at High Wood have already been examined, they revisited the subject in their 2005 work *The Somme*: 'Nevertheless they [the 7th Dragoon Guards] actually managed to spear sixteen Germans with their lances (certainly one of the strangest episodes in all the fighting on the Western Front and sixteen of the unluckiest victims).'[4]

The suggestion is that these events were so bizarre and unusual as to be of no account – a German soldier might equally live in fear of being struck by lightning. Traditionally also 'cavalry charges' have been viewed as a feature of the fighting of 1914 and of the latter days of 1918, and as such as indicators of the different character of the war during those periods. While this may have been the case in 1914, the evidence of 1916 and 1917 serves to undermine the supposed separate character of 1918. There was a strong continuity between the style of warfare before and into 1918, and the evidence of shock combat further supports this.

This book has described not one or two but a whole series of episodes of shock action. Table 6.1 lists those occasions discussed herein when a significant force of cavalry (at least a squadron) attacked enemy forces and inflicted casualties with close-quarter weapons (sword, lance or revolver). This excludes occasions when the Germans fled as the cavalry approached and no contact was made, but does include occasions where although contact was reached, the cavalry were ultimately unsuccessful, as the issue here is closing with cold steel, rather than holding ground.

Twenty separate fights are included. High Wood was far from unique, indeed the spread of these actions across almost all the major operations of the last three years of the war (with the exception of those around Ypres) shows that such combat was relatively commonplace and certainly was not suicidal, as some have attempted to suggest. This is not to suggest that shock was always

Table 6.1: Occasions of Arme Blanche Combat, 1916–1918

Location	Date	Offensive/Operation
High Wood	July 1916	Somme
Gueudecourt	September 1916	Somme
Guyencourt	March 1917	Advance to Hindenburg Line
Saulcourt	March 1917	Advance to Hindenburg Line
Villers Faucon	March 1917	Advance to Hindenburg Line
Monchy-le-Preux	April 1917	Arras
La Folie Château	November 1917	Cambrai
Cantaing	November 1917	Cambrai
Noyelles	November 1917	Cambrai
Manières–Crevecoeur Road	November 1917	Cambrai
Catelet Valley ('Kildare Trench')	December 1917	Cambrai
Collezy	March 1918	Operation 'Michael'
Moreuil Wood	March 1918	Operation 'Michael'
Cayeux Wood	August 1918	Amiens
Harbonnieres	August 1918	Amiens
Vauvillers	August 1918	Amiens
Premont	August 1918	Amiens
Gattigny Wood	October 1918	2nd Le Cateau
Honnechy	October 1918	2nd Le Cateau
Reumont	October 1918	2nd Le Cateau

the best choice; the attack of the Inniskillings at Epehy during the German counter-attack at Cambrai is an example of a costly and hopeless failure. However, as has been explained, this attack was forced on the local commanders from above, rather than being a tactic selected by the men on the spot. Their response to their orders on that day showed that regimental and brigade commanders at least, while happy to include the mounted charge in their portfolio of options, knew equally well when it was not appropriate.

The significant morale effect of sword-armed horsemen in rear areas should also not be underestimated. Several instances have been highlighted earlier where German forces were significantly demoralised by the prospect of being attacked at close quarters by horsemen, and fled or surrendered in consequence. The counter-balancing positive effect on Allied foot troops is also significant. Both at Arras and at Amiens cavalry were cheered on their way by the infantry, creating the wider impression that the battle must be going well somewhere if they were advancing. The importance of the absence of cavalry from the German order of battle in March 1918, given the fragile morale of the retreating Allied troops, has also been discussed, and this no doubt stems from a fear not that they might outflank or shoot at the retreating troops, but that they would literally 'ride them down' with swords. Thus the 'arme blanche' was by no means obsolete, and the sword, like the bayonet, was simply one of an arsenal of weapons that included the machine gun, the rifle and the artillery shell.

The effectiveness of the cavalry was also enhanced by the character of the soldiers within its ranks. To a much greater extent than was possible in the infantry, cavalry units were kept up to strength with experienced men (there were no 'New Army' cavalry regiments). Even in March 1918 the dissolution of the yeomanry units in the Cavalry Corps and their posting into the regular regiments meant that the proportion of 'old soldiers' in these units was very high. Training for Haig's vision of independent operations behind the front, albeit on the German side of the line, also meant that these men were much more comfortable on a fluid battlefield. This was relevant defensively in March 1918, as well as in attack. Cavalry soldiers were more used to extemporising defensive lines with their flanks unsupported than were their infantry colleagues. A criticism of the cavalry was that trench warfare had left them tactically stale and inflexible, but if anything in 1918 the reverse was true: it was their infantry counterparts who were most disconcerted by leaving the trenches.

Unfortunately, while disproportionate firepower, mobility and where appropriate its shock capability were critical to the effectiveness of cavalry, on various occasions, particularly in defence, the senior command managed to deny them each of these advantages. The lack of heavy artillery in the Cavalry Corps (as well as other corps assets typical in infantry corps) has already been discussed. Both at Cambrai in 1917 and in March 1918 this problem was exacerbated by the removal of RHA batteries from the cavalry brigades at crucial moments, thus denying them what little integral artillery firepower they had. Machine-gun units were sometimes also detached. In spite of this the cavalry were expected to make infantry-style counter-attacks without the support of any significant bombardment. These attacks, for example at Cambrai, were predictably costly and unsuccessful.

The premature dismounting of the cavalry in March 1918 (and the removal of the horses many miles to the rear) was also a mistake. Not only did this deny the corps its vital mobility, which would have been a great asset in the fluid fighting of that period, it also had a further impact on its firepower. The cavalry were not equipped to transport their machine guns, and more importantly supply them with ammunition, without their horses. Thus the removal of the horses not only slowed the cavalry down radically, it also left them with significantly less combat power. The dismounting of the cavalry also denied them their shock capability. The creation of *ad-hoc* mounted units in 1918 and the occasions when these were used in a shock rôle, such as at Collezy on 24 March, demonstrate that had there been more mounted troops available, this tactic might well have proved more widely useful.

*   *   *

The study of any aspect of the war between 1914 and 1918 rapidly reveals the evolving character of the war; each offensive and campaigning season was different from those which had preceded it. Scholars vary over the degree to which this evolution was a product of technological change, increasing expertise among the soldiers or their leaders, or even a blind 'natural selection' process. A key concept in the study of this process in the Allied armies is the idea of the 'Learning curve': the idea that the British army in particular learned gradually from its mistakes, and over time developed a highly effective and indeed war-winning range of fighting techniques.

It is hard to see much evidence of evolution in the cavalry arm below brigade level. In fact, the reverse appears to be true. As the war progressed the cavalry increasingly fell back on tactical methods that came straight from the pre-war pages of *Cavalry Training*. This should not, however, be regarded as a retrograde or unfortunate step. The cavalry tactics described in that book were the result of long and at times heated debate, and were in fact remarkably appropriate to the conditions of the war. The emphasis on the use of firepower to suppress objectives while highly mobile forces advanced by a flank to finally close with cold steel made good use of the varied capabilities of the cavalry. The continuity of manpower in the cavalry discussed above was also probably a factor. Whereas the infantry regiments of the pre-war BEF were almost entirely destroyed in the first years of the war, to be replaced by a 'New Army' requiring fresh training and with little tactical or doctrinal background to fall back on, the cavalry units were able to retain much of their pre-war 'tactical culture' through continuity of manpower.

In spite of this, the rôle of the cavalry did evolve as the war progressed. It was not so much that the cavalry changed, but that the nature of the war changed around it. In short, the battlefield became more 'cavalry-friendly' as the war itself evolved. The key to the widening rôle of cavalry was the development of the 'post-Somme' deep defensive system. In 1916, as British forces repeatedly hurled themselves at a very strong but very shallow German defensive line, there was little rôle for the cavalry as the 'breach' envisioned by Haig was never created. Subsequently, as the Germans moved to a far deeper but more porous defensive system, the importance of horsemen grew in proportion. A lower density of defences and strongpoints with gaps between, rather than solidly defended lines, offered ready-made 'gaps' for the cavalry to exploit, not by riding on to capture railheads deep in the rear, but rather by outflanking and attacking positions within the fighting zones themselves (the 'battle zone' and 'counter-attack zone' of the German system). The cavalry were also called upon to take advantage of the increasing fluidity of the battlefield to seize by *coups de main* objectives that would then be temporarily defended by automatic weapons before being handed on to supporting infantry.

Gueudecourt in 1916, Monchy in 1917 and Honnechy and Reumont in October 1918 were all examples of this practice.

The ever-increasing depth of German defensive systems from the battle of Arras onwards also created the problem that a 'Bite and Hold' attack, however ambitious, was limited in its potential by the battle range of its principal weapon: marching infantry. It had been demonstrated, and seems to have been understood by 1918, that the maximum assault depth that could be expected of infantry on foot was about 5,000 yards (4.5km). With defensive systems developing to depths of 10,000 yards (9km) or more, this would never be decisive. Despite experiments in the mechanical transportation of troops in tanks (which poisoned them with fumes and moved slower than the infantry could walk) or lorries (which were vulnerable to fire and had no realistic cross-country mobility), the horse remained the only practical means of projecting rifle and more particularly machine-gun strength into the furthest parts of the enemy defences.

A clear opportunity can therefore be identified on the evolving battlefield of the Western Front for the successful use of mounted troops. However, this is with the benefit of hindsight. The question arises whether this opportunity was ever fully identified at the time, and whether the cavalry was handled appropriately, at all levels of command, to take full advantage of it. Secondly, while the BEF was predominantly on an offensive footing strategically, several occasions arose where the cavalry was forced to fight *defensively*, in particular in March 1918. Here it is arguable that a misunderstanding and misapplication of deep-defence principles was to put the British Fifth Army at a distinct disadvantage.

* * *

It has been argued that below brigade level the cavalry was tactically effective and remained so throughout the war without much alteration to its methods. Clearly, however, its rôle in operations changed as the war progressed. This was a product not only of the changing character of the fighting, but also of the interaction between those changes, and the developing understanding by higher commanders of how cavalry could be included in operations.

Inevitably any analysis of this process begins with Douglas Haig, the commander in chief of the BEF during much of the war. The cavalry owed a substantial debt to Haig for its very survival on the Western Front. He was a powerful advocate for retention of mounted forces on several occasions, particularly after Cambrai and in early 1918. However, his keen support for the arm should not be confused with a clear understanding of its rôle. At a tactical level Haig had a very modern concept of how cavalry should function. He advocated combined-arms tactics, extensive use of machine-guns, and a fire-power and shock balance which was vindicated on several occasions during the war. The continuing applicability of the tenets of his 1912 *Cavalry Training* in the spring of 1917 or in 1918 has been described. Unfortunately, at an operational level it is arguable that Haig misunderstood the nature of the war from 1915 right up to November 1918, not only in the sphere of the cavalry but right across the board. His plans and objectives for the Somme battles of 1916 began with, and persisted with, the idea that the German defences were susceptible to a 'breakthrough': that the trench system was a finite, rigid structure which would fail catastrophically if put under enough pressure (analogous to a dam bursting). The rôle he envisioned for mounted troops was one of flowing through and exploiting this breach (real or metaphorical) in the enemy defences. His anticipation of this long-awaited event was apparent in his thinking concerning every subsequent offensive, and indeed he was still preparing for this change in the nature of the fighting when he arranged for the Cavalry Corps field exercises of September 1918.

Evidence of this unchanging outlook is contained in the Cavalry Corps war diary. Haig wrote to the Cavalry Corps commander, Kavanagh, and Lieutenant General Ivor Maxse (in his rôle as Inspector General of Training) on 6 September 1918 with his thoughts about the proposed cavalry field day, stating: 'I do not propose to employ the Cavalry corps until I judge the situation favourable for obtaining decisive results.'[5] Appended to this letter was a copy of the notes of a meeting held by Haig with army commanders two years earlier, on 18 March 1916, the content of which he presumably still considered relevant, viz: 'The action of mounted troops in the offensive battle under existing trench warfare conditions follows on the action of infantry and artillery, who must first effect a breach in the enemy's outer systems of defence.'[6]

In short he saw the cavalry rôle in September 1918 in identical terms to that of March 1916. It is arguable that this return to 'mobile warfare' anticipated by Haig never happened, even in 1918. What took place instead was a more subtle change in the character of the fighting *within* both sides' defensive systems, and it was this process that led to the development of an environment in which mounted troops had ever-increasing scope for action.

Among Haig's subordinates, the army commanders of the BEF, the degree of recognition of these changes was variable. Gough, for example, was quick to see the new potential for cavalry, but others, like Rawlinson, were slower, albeit the latter had a greater opportunity in the final phase of the war to embrace and make use of the new tactical realities. In the planning for 1 July 1916 there is little evidence of any appreciation of a rôle for the cavalry in the initial infantry and artillery battle. Haig was wedded to the idea of deep exploitation, and Rawlinson, commanding Fourth Army, was not a believer in a breakthrough and had no use for horsemen in his limited 'Bite and Hold' plan. Indeed, there was little reason for him to seek it: the German defences, and thus his planned 'bite', were both comparatively shallow. Nor as the fighting progressed did Rawlinson include the cavalry in his subsequent plans. His orders for September delayed their advance until after the artillery had moved up, showing clearly that he did not consider them an important part of the battle he was intending to fight.

At Arras in April 1917 General Allenby produced a slightly more progressive plan than that used on the Somme, in that it brought the cavalry divisions involved in the offensive closer to the attack front. Indeed, the cavalry divisions' 'final positions of readiness' were beyond the infantry start line – an innovative step. However, there was little expectation that the cavalry would be involved in the fight *within* the German defences. No move was expected of the cavalry until the infantry had reached their final 'Green Line' objectives. The order for the cavalry to move, even to their 'final positions of readiness', was not received by the corps until more than 9 hours after the battle had begun (2.40pm, after a 'Z' hour of 5.30am). This left little time or daylight for the cavalry to contribute to the battle. It is also arguable that the fighting around Monchy on 11 April, which brought the cavalry into action, was not intended as a combined-arms fight within the German deep defences (albeit that is what it became), but the result of Allenby's misapprehension that a genuine breakthrough had been achieved and that his forces were 'pursuing a defeated enemy'.

At Cambrai in the autumn of 1917 General Byng did not push the cavalry as far forward at the outset, having 'advanced concentration areas' around 8km (5 miles) behind the front lines at Fins. However, a set time was provided for their forward movement, 2½ hours after the infantry attack began at 6.20am. Indeed, the 1st Cavalry Division moved off ahead of schedule, only 2 hours after the battle had begun. Unfortunately after that, as has been described, ambiguities in the chain of command and Kavanagh's (no doubt well-meaning) interference effectively wrote the cavalry out of a significant rôle in the battle, and left them subject to unjustified vilification ever after.

Interestingly, it might be argued that the confusion developed precisely as a consequence of attempts by the two corps commanders concerned, Woollcombe and Kavanagh, to involve the cavalry in the fight *within* the German defences and divert them from their breakthrough/exploitation rôle. It has also been argued that the cavalry were able both to survive and to fight quite effectively within the confines of the German positions west of the St Quentin canal, as the activities of Brigadier General Beale-Browne's 2nd Cavalry Brigade demonstrated. However, these *ad-hoc* successes should not be taken as justification for the actions of those higher commanders. If the cavalry was intended to fight within the defended zone this should have been planned for from the start; there was no place for this kind of chopping and changing during a First World War offensive.

Only in 1918, and ironically in the hands of General Rawlinson, who appeared such a sceptic in 1916, did the Cavalry Corps finally operate in a pre-planned rôle within a combined-arms 'Bite and Hold' battle. Even then this was tempered by the broader ambitions of Haig, who continued to await the collapse of German resistance. Nor did Rawlinson apparently see cavalry as always a necessity in his attacking schemes; later, in the first week of November, when both he and his colleague at Third Army, General Byng, were offered use of the Cavalry Corps again, both declined.

Another key factor in the failure of the cavalry units to reach their full potential in these offensives was the nature of the communications available to their commanders. The presence of wireless sets within the cavalry at Cambrai, for example, has been commented upon. Contact aircraft were also available, but in spite of these advances the telephone or more often the dispatch rider or messenger were the principal means by which higher commanders could follow a battle. These lines of communication were simply too slow to allow commanders above divisional level to exercise real-time command over their troops. Time and again the cavalry were forced to wait until released by corps and army commanders before they could move forward. This all too often meant that they were late in setting off, and missed exactly the fleeting opportunities it was their job to exploit. Only at Amiens, where start times were pre-programmed and required no higher approval, were the cavalry able to move quickly into the battle.

These difficulties were exacerbated by the pyramidal structure of the lines of communication. Adjacent units in the front line were connected only by a chain which led back through numerous tiers of headquarters, via corps or even army command. The ability of cavalry commanders to cooperate effectively with their colleagues from other arms was severely hampered by this. The 14 July 1916 fighting is an example of this, where brigade and divisional commanders of infantry and cavalry were able to physically meet on the battlefield, but lacked the authority to spontaneously cooperate with each other without reference to higher commanders who were inevitably out of touch with events.

Only one army commander, General Gough, seems to have clearly grasped these problems and their impact on the potential of cavalry in trench fighting, and to have done so at an early stage; interestingly, he was also a cavalryman. In August 1916, as the Somme battles raged, GHQ distributed to army commanders a document submitted by Gough, in which he in turn credited the ideas of the commander of the 3rd Cavalry Division, Major General Vaughan. In it Haig's idea of a widespread collapse of resistance was rejected:

1. It is never safe to say that the enemy is demoralized as a whole. Demoralization, especially in trench warfare, only affects a portion of the hostile troops at a time and is only temporary. Our aim

must be to get the cavalry in contact with those troops that are
temporarily demoralized.[7]

Gough argued that a combination of detailed planning, good communications
and close cooperation between arms would be required to bring this about.
He advocated the allocation of a 'zone of action' to each cavalry division, and
giving the divisional commander freedom to act independently within that
area. He rejected the top-down command which was to blight subsequent
offensives,

> 5. The governing factor of the whole question is, with whom should
> the decision for the cavalry to intervene lie? If with the Army
> Commander or the Corps Commander, owing to the delays
> involved in getting the information back, and the orders out, it
> will probably be impossible for the cavalry to take advantage of
> any temporary demoralization.[8]

The paper ended with the rather rueful conclusion: 'Unless some such scheme
is adopted there is little probability of the cavalry intervening at the right time
and place.'[9] Unfortunately both at Arras and at Cambrai he was to be proved
right. Gough has widely been characterised as a cavalry-obsessed 'Thruster'
sharing Haig's unrealistic dream of a breakthrough. The 1916 paper suggests a
much more thoughtful approach to mounted warfare, at odds with that of
Haig. Evidence of this can be seen in the preparations for the Fifth Army attack
at Bullecourt in support of the Arras offensive in April 1917. Here Gough was
provided with one cavalry division to support his attack, ostensibly with the aim
of linking up with the two cavalry divisions allocated to Third Army. However,
at an army commanders' conference prior to the battle he objected that since
his operation was intended only to capture a portion of the Hindenburg Line
defences, the cavalry division would not be needed. In the event he retained it
at Haig's insistence.[10] (It saw no action.)

Hints of Gough's vision for the cavalry can be detected in his plan for the
Ypres battle in July 1917. Here was an offensive designed as a high-tempo
sequence of shallow 'Bite and Hold' attacks, supported at local level by forces
of cavalry integrated into the infantry attack. Unfortunately any analysis of
Gough's aspirations or tactical innovations for the Ypres battle becomes
clouded by the failure of the offensive as a whole. This was followed by his use
as a scapegoat for the failures of the defence in March 1918 (and here it has been
argued the cavalry *was* rather poorly handled at the higher command levels),
leading to his dismissal at the end of March 1918. It was thus left to Rawlinson
to see through the victories of 1918.

Within the Cavalry Corps itself, the effectiveness of the arm also suffered
due to the inadequacies of its commander, Kavanagh. The disastrous effects of

his desire to be involved in the chain of command during the Cambrai battle in 1917 have been discussed. During the same battle he can also be accused of misunderstanding the appropriateness or otherwise of shock action in defence. Kavanagh seems to have turned to mounted action not in response to its immediate tactical appropriateness (in terms of ground or opponents) but rather in proportion to his own concept of the criticalness of the moment. He was prepared on 30 November 1917 to attempt (as he saw it) to 'save the day' by launching a series of cavalry charges which the commanders on the ground knew to be suicidal. In the event only one was actually carried out, but it was a disaster for the Inniskillings who were obliged to attempt it. Similarly, at a lower level of command, Brigadier Seely's handling of the Canadian Cavalry Brigade at Moreuil Wood in 1918 is open to similar criticism. 'Desperate times require desperate measures' but it is equally true that cooler heads might have handled both of these crises less hastily and with less drama, and ultimately with fewer losses to the cavalry.

Overall, it is hard to see much skilful leadership or doctrinal originality in the higher ranks of the mounted arm. The corps was rather unimaginatively led. That it was able to perform so well came down to the individual skills and morale of its soldiers and junior leaders. Before too harsh a judgement is made of its senior commanders, however, it must be remembered that their rôle was not only to direct the operations of the corps but also to lead it morally and create the required *esprit de corps*. In this latter function Kavanagh emerges in a better light. Little evidence of the character of 'Black Jack' Kavanagh has been uncovered, but it seems that he was highly regarded both by Haig (who, as has been shown, treated him on a par with army commanders, rather than with his peers commanding infantry corps) and by his subordinates. On his appointment to lead the Cavalry Corps in September 1916, Home commented, 'I am glad Kavanagh is going to command as he is a real leader of men, and knows his job, has a mind of his own.'[11] His reputation as a fighting soldier had been made in command of the 7th Cavalry Brigade in the fierce fighting around Ypres in October 1914, and a judgement on him at that period was offered by one of his soldiers whose views featured earlier, Corporal of Horse Lloyd of the Life Guards:

> Our brigade seemed to get a call almost every time we were out, so we became known to the troops in the salient as 'Kavanagh's Fire Brigade' ... The shortage of casualties on those occasions was largely due to the masterly way in which we were handled by our Brigadier. He never spared us, but wherever the brigade went he took the lead, and there was no braver man in it than himself.[12]

One interpretation of this is that while Kavanagh was a brave and popular leader, capable of inspiring his men, his grasp of the niceties of higher command was lacking. This would accord with his tendency to respond to crises with aggression, either directly on the telephone to his subordinates, or indirectly in ordering mounted charges (both of which occurred on 1 December 1917), rather than by taking a more considered approach. Such a 'thruster' might be a success at brigade level, but commanding a corps was a different, more subtle, matter.

* * *

There remains also the question of the relationship between cavalry and tanks. Cavalry and tanks have been set out essentially in opposition by many historians of the First World War. Simply put, the argument runs that trench warfare had rendered the cavalry redundant, then the appearance of tanks broke the deadlock, but the reappearance of cavalry (and cavalry commanders) on the newly mobile battlefield then interfered with the potential of the new tanks to win the war. This is, of course, a gross oversimplification but it goes to the heart of the matter: a choice is offered between old-style horses or the new armour, and the two are mutually exclusive.

It has been shown that while there was a degree of inter–corps and inter–arm rivalry, this opposition between horse and engine simply did not exist during the war itself. Despite the growth in mechanical transport in the BEF the horse remained by far the dominant form of motive power on the Western Front (aside from railways), and no one would have seriously suggested that the horse might be removed from the military scene altogether. Thus armoured forces developed within a framework in which the presence of horses was taken for granted. Nor did armour appear on the battlefield suddenly or fully developed. Armoured cars (as opposed to tanks) had been in France since the opening shots of the war in 1914, and their cooperation with cavalry from 1916 onwards has been discussed. Thus the cavalry were able to assimilate the appearance of tanks on the battlefield much more smoothly and organically than has been widely acknowledged. This inter–relationship is exemplified by the fact that in 1918 ex–cavalrymen were riding in tanks and the commanders of tank battalions were on horseback.

Criticism of the cavalry has also stemmed from a misunderstanding of the capabilities of the tanks. The heavy tanks (Marks I to V) simply were not weapons of exploitation. Brigadier General Hobart commented of Cambrai: 'The Mk IV tank was not a suitable weapon for mobile warfare ... The task given to the Tank Corps by the Army was to get the infantry through the Hindenburg Line.'[13] The job of these vehicles was to crush the wire, to allow the infantry into the German defences, and to destroy machine-gun positions. It was not to drive on into the enemy rear areas, nor would they have been capable of doing so. Thus while there is little doubt that the cavalry failed in its task of exploitation at Cambrai, this was not a task that could or should have been performed by tanks.

Even with the arrival of the Whippet in 1918 the Tank Corps still did not have a weapon capable of deep exploitation, and indeed although it was classed as a 'light tank', the Whippet was only marginally faster than its heavy counterparts. Thus these vehicles could not have superseded the cavalry, as some have suggested. Thus in no sense did the appearance of tanks render the cavalry obsolete. Sometimes the two arms were able to cooperate directly together on the same part of the battlefield, on other occasions this was less successful; most often, however, they were in different places with different jobs to do. Cavalry and tanks should be seen as two complementary components of the wider BEF fighting machine, each doing their job within an increasingly coordinated and successful overall package which included infantry, guns, aircraft and all the other instruments of war.

The transition from the 'trench warfare' of 1916 to the supposedly 'mobile warfare' of 1918 was also a much more gradual and less marked process than has been previously suggested. The battlefield started to deepen with the changes in German defensive methods at the end of 1916, and this trend continued until the end of the fighting. Further, the moving battlefront of 1918 was created more by an increasing tempo of fighting, made possible by improved logistics, and by the frequent iteration of 'Bite and Hold' attacks, than by any great 'revolution' in how the war was fought. Tanks were an important part of this evolving picture, but they were not necessarily the catalysts for any dramatic change. Indeed, by the latter stages of 1918 the scale of the fighting and the width of the active front, exacerbated by the relative scarcity of tanks and the difficulty of moving them between attacking corps, meant that tanks became a luxury during that fighting rather than a necessity.[14] It is therefore possible to see the circumstances of the Tank Corps and the Cavalry Corps as analogous rather than opposed, both contributing to, and participating in, but neither dominating, an evolving infantry and artillery battle. Also by 1918 this battle was taking place on such a scale that neither corps was numerically in a position to make more than a marginal contribution.

✻   ✻   ✻

The final question that arises is that of 'success'. Was the Cavalry Corps able to achieve the objectives set out for it by those planning its rôle in the battles in which it participated? Given the tactical effectiveness at lower levels of command discussed earlier in this chapter, this question is focused more at the operational level (that is to say, in operations at the scale of corps and army). Was the cavalry able to play its larger part in each offensive as a whole and fulfil its commander's objectives?

The short answer to this is that it was not; the cavalry was mostly unsuccessful at an operational level. However, this failure was not inevitable and intrinsic to the cavalry as an arm, but was the result of a combination of factors which do not relate to the troops themselves but to their commanders. This can be seen in each individual offensive. In 1916 the rôle of the cavalry as defined by Haig and Rawlinson was the exploitation of a breakthrough of the German positions. That this breakthrough was not achieved was not the responsibility of the cavalry, despite the odium which has fallen on them as a result. Similarly at Arras in 1917 the cavalry could not reach the deep objectives defined for them by Third Army. Again, however, it is arguable that these objectives were unrealistic and reflected General Allenby's misreading of the battle as it developed. The offensive at Cambrai in 1917 was stunningly successful in its early stages, and there is no doubt that the cavalry failed to take full advantage of this situation. However, this was the result of command and control failures outside the control of the cavalry divisions themselves, rather than their own ineffectiveness. Only at Amiens in 1918 were the cavalry completely successful in obtaining the goals initially set out for them in the offensive. Unfortunately, even here Haig inserted into the plan deeper objectives which were completely unrealistic, and these have remained to cast a shadow over the achievements of the corps on that day. Thus operational success always eluded the cavalry, but this had more to do with exaggerated expectations than failures within the corps.

There is a further reason why the contribution of the cavalry to the outcome of the war was not decisive. They were present in the BEF in such small numbers that they could only play a small part in comparison to their colleagues in other arms, and as the war developed in 1917 and 1918 to allow greater potential for the cavalry to contribute, their numbers in proportion to the size of the BEF as a whole dwindled almost into insignificance. The question of whether 'more cavalry, better led' would have been helpful on the Western Front is ultimately like many counterfactual arguments, somewhat sterile, but it is reasonable to argue that the cavalry units that were present, when offered the chance to get into battle, acquitted themselves well and proved that at brigade and regimental level the cavalry was an effective fighting arm.

*   *   *

As bells rang to mark the Armistice at 11.00am on 11 November 1918 many members of the BEF laid aside their rifles and finally let themselves contemplate a return to home and civilian life. In the cavalry things were somewhat different, for two reasons. First, many of these men were still regular soldiers; they had served before the war and would continue to do so after. Some units were immediately involved in following up the retreating German army, and occupying bridgeheads across the Rhine. Secondly, unlike a rifle, a horse remains as demanding a beast in peacetime as it is in war. Armistice day, therefore, was in many units nearly 'business as usual'. The historian of the 15th Hussars records:

> At 11am orders were received that hostilities had ceased, the trumpeters of the Regiment sounded the Regimental call, and then Cease Fire; the men gave a loud cheer. The call to Stables was sounded, and all then proceeded prosaically to groom and look after the horses.[15]

Corporal of Horse Lloyd missed the celebrations at the front as he was still in hospital recovering from a serious wound inflicted by a German aerial bomb dropped on his tent during the German offensive of March 1918. He was not alone; casualties among other ranks of the cavalry in the BEF amounted to 19,051, of whom 4,421 had died. It is interesting to compare the statistics for different fighting arms of the British army over all theatres of war. In all, 23 per cent of the cavalry were killed (or died of wounds) and 66 per cent were wounded at least once, compared with figures for the infantry of 20 per cent and 64 per cent respectively. The proportion of officer casualties to other ranks was also significantly higher in the cavalry than in any other arm.[16] If nothing else, this gives the lie to the argument that the cavalry failed to 'do their bit' on the Western Front. However, the last word should perhaps go to Lloyd:

> During the best years of my life I had given to it [the cavalry] the best that was in me, and received precious little in return. I would gladly go through it all again for the sake of the good times spent in company of the great fellows of all ranks who were my comrades.[17]

Appendix 1

A British Cavalry Regiment in Typical Attack Formation

'Squadron column in line of troop columns'

Note: only basic fighting elements have been shown; medical and signal units might also be present, as well as attached MGC(C) troops. Column intervals between squadrons have also been shortened: these might be up to 200 yards. An Indian-based regiment would have four squadrons each of three troop columns. (Drawn from *Cavalry Training, 1912*, ch. 4.)

```
                                        ENEMY
B Squadron
T                        T         Sqn HQ      T                    T
IIII   <Deployment Distance>  IIII              IIII                 IIII
IIII                     IIII                   IIII                 IIII

IIII                     IIII                   IIII                 IIII
IIII                     IIII                   IIII                 IIII

IIII                     IIII                   IIII                 IIII
IIII                     IIII                   IIII                 IIII

IIII                     IIII                   IIII                 IIII
IIIIH                    IIIIH                  IIIIH                IIIIH
                                       Regt HQ
C Squadron
T                        T         Sqn HQ      T                    T
IIII                     IIII                   IIII                 IIII
IIII                     IIII                   IIII                 IIII

IIII                     IIII                   IIII                 IIII
IIII                     IIII                   IIII                 IIII

IIII                     IIII                   IIII                 IIII
IIII                     IIII                   IIII                 IIII

IIII                     IIII                   IIII                 IIII
IIIIH                    IIIIH                  IIIIH                IIIIH

A Squadron
T                        T         Sqn HQ      T                    T
IIII                     IIII                   IIII                 IIII
IIII                     IIII                   IIII                 IIII

IIII                     IIII                   IIII                 IIII
IIII                     IIII                   IIII                 IIII

IIII                     IIII                   IIII                 IIII
IIII                     IIII                   IIII                 IIII

IIII                     IIII                   IIII                 IIII
IIIIH                    IIIIH                  IIIIH                IIIIH
```

Key

T — Troop leader (subaltern)

IIII — 8-man section in two ranks
IIII — (commanded by corporal)

IIII — Hotchkiss-gun section
IIIIH

The Deployment Distance had to be of sufficient width to allow the troop to form into a two-rank line of Sections; a minimum of 40 yards, often much more.

Appendix 2

A Note on the Recent Cavalry Fighting up to 7 April 1917, issued by the General Staff, April 1917

The following deductions are drawn from the experience of the cavalry recently acting on the front of the advance over open country:-

(a) Very careful reconnaissance of the ground, as well as the enemy's position, before attacking is essential. Reconnaissance by aeroplane is not sufficient. Patrols must be used freely, usually mounted by day and dismounted by night.

(b) When the locality to be attacked lies in a depression, it is often advisable to allot objectives on rising ground beyond. This gives a better chance of cutting off a retreating enemy and prevents losses, especially to led horses, from hostile bombardment directed on the locality after its capture.

(c) Short, sharp bombardments immediately prior to attack (registration having been carried out unostentatiously beforehand) gave good results. Very careful observation is required to enable a lift to be made at the right moment. Cavalry will seldom, if ever, have enough guns to set up a regular barrage, but with careful arrangements for observation, and a rapid and bold advance of the artillery if the attack succeeds, it should be possible to give some cover to the advance, to shell the retiring enemy, to search for likely hostile observation parties, and to engage a counter-attack.

(d) Advances were made successfully over exposed ground moving at a gallop, extended.

(e) Combination of rapid turning movements with frontal attacks and covering fire (to hold the enemy's attention) gave good results. Armoured cars proved very useful in frontal attacks and seemed to attract most of the hostile fire.

(f) When attacking, a sudden opening of hostile machine-gun or rifle fire from a flank may be dealt with by detaching a troop or squadron to gallop at the gun or riflemen while the main body continues its advance.

(g) Rapidity of execution is essential. Any hesitation after a decision has once been formed is fatal. Manoeuvring for ground and cover from view during an advance, if delay is entailed, will seldom give results sufficient to compensate for the loss of time involved.

(h) It is advisable, in attacking localities, to tell off pursuing detachments beforehand. They must follow the attack closely. A limit should usually be laid down beyond which pursuit is not to go. Within this limit pursuing detachments must act with extreme boldness.

GENERAL HEADQUARTERS, 10 April 1917
(PRO Ref; WO33/816)

Appendix 3

Human Casualties, 3rd Cavalry Division, 9–11 April 1917

Unit		11 April						Total 9–11 April					
		Officers			Other Ranks			Officers			Other Ranks		
		Killed	Wounded	Missing	Killed	Wounded	Missing	Killed	Wounded	Missing	Killed	Wounded	Missing
3rd Cavalry Division													
6th Brigade	Brigade HQ	1				1		1				3	3
	3rd D.G.		3		19	68	2		2	2	18	75	
	1st R.D.				2	22	1		1	1	2	28	
	Nth. Som. Yeo.		4		4	12			3		5	17	
	6th MG Sqn		2		1	5			2		3	4	
	C Battery RHA				3	14					3	16	
	Brigade Total	1	9		29	122	3	1	8	3	31	143	3
7th Brigade	Brigade HQ												
	1st Life Guards												
	2nd Life Guards												
	Leics Yeo.												
	7th MG Sqn												
	K Battery RHA					6						1	
	Brigade Total					6						1	
8th Brigade	Brigade HQ	1			2			1				2	
	RHG (Blues)	1	3		25	17	4	1	3		25	17	4
	10th Hussars	*2*	*7*		*18*	*150*	*5*	*2*	*7*		*18*	*150*	*5*
	Essex Yeo.	*1*	*12*		*8*	*94*	*10*	*1*	*12*		*8*	*94*	*10*
	8th MG Sqn		3			28	2		3			28	2
	G Battery RHA				3	14					3	14	
	Brigade Total	5	26		56	303	21	5	27		54	305	19
	Divisional Total	6	35		86	431	24	6	35		85	448	24

Notes: **Bold** figures are taken from tables in Preston (1931).

Italicised figures are from Whitmore (1920), where casualties are listed by name.

Other figures are extracted from divisional and brigade war diaries.

Discrepancies between Preston's overall totals and those for 11 April only reflect minor losses on the first two days of the offensive.

Appendix 4

Equine Casualties, Cavalry Corps, 1–14 April 1917

	Killed	Died	Destroyed	Total	Non Fatal Losses	Overall Total
1st Cav. Division	**31**	**55**	**55**	141	–	200 (est.)
2nd Cav. Division	**273**	**154**	**37**	464	308	772
3rd Cav. Division	**563**	**18**	**24**	603	382	985
Totals				1,208		1,957

Notes:

Bold figures are from Cavalry Corps DDVS war diary.
Other figures are from unit diaries.

Appendix 5

Notes on the Use of Tanks with Cavalry*

1. The sphere of activity and the radius of the tank is limited and the pace of advance is slow. These are the main disadvantages.
2. On the other hand, the tank can break through wire, move into villages held by Machine Guns and sit on strongpoints held.
3. Its use to Cavalry advancing is very great, but in legislating for Cavalry action supported by tanks the following points must be borne in mind.

   (a) Tanks work in sections of 3 tanks.
   (b) They must be given definite objectives, and successive waves of tanks must be used, instead of giving tanks successive objectives.
   (c) Cavalry must not wait for tanks, but must push on. On the other hand, if held up, the arrival of tanks will be of the utmost use.
   (d) Tanks should be used as pivots for the Cavalry. They are really moving Machine Guns heavily armed, and though they have not the pace of Armoured Motors they should be used on the same principle.
   (e) Therefore Cavalry use their mobility to get round the flanks of every village or position held by the enemy, whilst tanks move straight on it.

4. Attention is drawn to the Training Note on Tanks which has been issued to all concerned.

Cavalry Corps, 10 November 1917

* 'Cavalry Corps Instructions for Operations GY, Appendix C', Cavalry Corps GX 272/39, 10 November 1917, contained in Cavalry Corps War Diary, November 1917, Appendix VII, WO95/574.

Appendix 6

Reorganisation of the Cavalry Corps, March 1918

Orders of battle from Becke, A.F. (ed.), 1935, *Order of Battle of Divisions. Part 1: The Regular British Divisions* (HMSO London)

Cavalry Corps, November 1917				Cavalry Corps March 1918		
1st Cavalry Division						
1 Cav. Bde	2nd DG (Bays)	5th DG	11th Hus	*	*	*
2 Cav. Bde	4th DG	9th Lcrs	18th Hus	*	*	*
9 Cav. Bde	15th Hus	19th Hus	Beds Yeo.**	*	*	8th Hus
2nd Cavalry Division						
3 Cav. Bde	4th Hus	5th Lcrs	16th Lcrs	*	*	*
4 Cav. Bde	6th DG (Carab)	3rd Hus	Q Own Ox. Hus	*	*	*
5 Cav. Bde	2nd D (Greys)	12th Lcrs	20th Hus	*	*	*
3rd Cavalry Division						
6 Cav. Bde	3rd DG	R.Dgns	N. Som. Yeo.**	*	*	10th Hus
7 Cav. Bde	1st L. Gds	2nd L. Gds	Leics Yeo.**	7th DG	6th D (Innis)	17 Lcrs
8 Cav. Bde	R. Hse Gds	10th Hus	Essex Yeo.** (Can. Cav. Bde)	R. Can Dgns	L. Strath. Hse	Ft Garry Hse
4th Cavalry Division				Div. broken up		
Sialkot Cav. Bde	17th Lcrs	6th Cav.	19th Lcrs			
Ambala Cav. Bde	8th Hus	9th Hse	30th Lcrs			
Lucknow Cav. Bde	1st (Kings) DG	29th Lcrs	36th Hse			
5th Cavalry Division				Div. broken up		
Mhow Cav. Bde	6th D (Innis)	2nd Lcrs	38th Hse			
Secunderabad Cav. Bde	7th DG	20th Hse	34th Hse			
Canadian Cav. Bde	R. Can Dgns	L. Strath. Hse	Ft Garry Hse			

Notes:

* Unchanged

** Units broken up to reinforce Cavalry Divisions, April 1918

Indian Regiments shown shaded

Appendix 7

Additional Notes on the Plates

Plate 1. A fully equipped cavalryman of 1917–1918.
This image shows a fully equipped cavalryman of an unknown regiment photographed sometime after late 1916. A second photograph of the same man (not reproduced here) depicts him in side view. His sleeve badges show he is a lance corporal, with a crossed rifles badge indicating he is the best shot in the squadron. He has at least five years' service, indicated by two long service and good conduct chevrons, and one wound stripe.

His horse wears an equine gas mask on its nose-band, an item of kit that was seldom carried as it was rarely required. (The man himself carries a box respirator (issued in late 1916) on his back, but it is not visible in this photograph.) Note also the grooming brush attached to the picketing pegs, and a large white feed sack.

In many ways this man typifies the ideal of the great war cavalryman; he is a pre-war regular and a crack shot, and carries all he needs to live and fight independently on the battlefield.

(*Taylor Library*)

Plates 2 and 3. June 1916, Royal Canadian Horse Artillery assembling a trench bridge.
These are two of a series of photographs of the Canadian Cavalry Brigade, probably taken by the Canadian official photographer H.E. Knobel, during their preparations for the Somme offensive. Here gunners assemble a portable bridge. The original captions indicate that the whole construction process took one-and-a-half minutes.

The operations are being supervised by two officers (left) and a senior NCO (back, right). All of the men are wearing a cavalry-pattern water bottle and haversack, the latter secured by an '03 Pattern leather waist-belt.

The field gun in the second image is the standard 13-pounder QF (quick-firing) piece which equipped both RHA and RCHA units accompanying the cavalry divisions. This is the same type used on ceremonial occasions by the King's Troop, Royal Horse Artillery today. Later in the war many of these units up-gunned to the heavier 18-pounder version, as used by field artillery units.

(*Dept. of National Defence/Library and Archives Canada/PA-a000115 and a000132(1)*)

Plate 4. The Fort Garry Horse demonstrate a temporary trench bridge, June 1916.
Another photograph in the same series as Plates 2 and 3, here an officer of the Fort Garry Horse demonstrates the effectiveness of a recently erected folding 'Fort Garry' trench bridge. It could be crossed by horses in single file and could be positioned in under a minute. It would, however, require an obedient horse to ride over such a narrow structure; other photos in the series show men leading their horses over on foot.

(*Dept. of National Defence/Library and Archives Canada/PA-a000123(1)*)

Plate 5. A Canadian cavalry tool-pack horse, June 1916.
A cavalry tool-pack horse of the Canadian Cavalry Brigade. This horse is carrying ten standard British army GS shovels, as well as several RE pickaxes, a bundle of sand-bags and various

smaller tools. Although apparently unglamorous, these animals were critical to the battlefield effectiveness of cavalry units, allowing them to dig-in on objectives once captured. Tool-pack animals were key to the fighting at Monchy in 1917, as well as in the defensive fighting at Cambrai.

(Dept. of National Defence/Library and Archives Canada/PA-a000139(1))

Plate 6. Horse lines of the Fort Garry Horse, June 1916.
Another image from the June 1916 series showing horse lines of the Fort Garry Horse in a training camp in the rear. Saddles and rifle buckets can be seen lined up in front of the animals, and on the far right of the image are piled arms. The men are busy grooming, an activity which if time allowed took up several hours every day. The horses appear to be in good condition and have had their manes 'hogged' (shaved short) for active service. This is a somewhat idealised image as it shows a unit in good weather, well away from the combat area. Later in the war such tidy arrangements would have been less common, especially as the German air threat increased in 1917 and 1918.

(Dept. of National Defence/Library and Archives Canada/PA-a000052(2))

Plate 7. Makeshift horse lines behind the front line, winter 1916/17.
In contrast to the orderly lines of the previous summer, this image shows horse lines near the front over the harsh winter of 1916/17. The animals have been rugged-up, and their coats and manes allowed to grow against the cold. This is probably a temporary stopping place as where possible cavalry units tried to build temporary shelters for the horses or found billets in barns and other buildings.

(Taylor Library)

Plate 8. A complete cavalry regiment (the Fort Garry Horse) paraded by squadrons, June 1916.
A further picture from the June 1916 series depicting the Fort Garry Horse. Here the size and structure of a typical cavalry regiment is clearly demonstrated. The three squadrons are arranged side by side, with the four troops making up each squadron standing in two-rank lines one behind the other.

However, on operations it is unlikely that a regiment would ever deploy this densely; typically there would be gaps of up to 100 yards between squadrons and troops.

Note also that this represents only the fighting strength: not present are the limbers and wagons of the regiment's logistic tail, which would have added to the length of the column when the regiment was on the move.

(Dept. of National Defence/Library and Archives Canada/PA-a000027(1))

Plate 9. The 20th Deccan Horse in Carnoy valley prior to going into action at High Wood, July 1916.
This very famous photograph was taken on 14 July 1916 by the British official photographer Ernest Brooks. The men appear to be in jovial mood, waving their recently acquired steel helmets. The pennons on their lances have removed and replaced by a leather washer, intended to prevent the lance from penetrating too far through the enemy and getting stuck.

The horses are heavily laden with kit, including water buckets, an additional bandolier of ammunition around the neck, and fly fringes on their bridles. Visible also are rifle buckets, attached to the near (left) side of the saddle – a common practice in lancer units as it avoided the rifle butt interfering with use of the lance. Non-lance-armed troops normally carried the rifle on the off side.

(Taylor Library)

Plate 10. Members of the 9th Hodson's Horse pause to consult a map, near Vraignes, April 1917.
This is another Ernest Brooks photograph, showing the 9th Hodson's Horse (Ambala Brigade, 1st Indian Division) in the course of the follow-up of the German retreat to the Hindenburg Line. Vraignes lies within a few kilometres of Peronne on the river Somme.

The central figure is a Dafadar, the Indian NCO equivalent to a sergeant, while the man with the map is probably a Jemadar, or junior 'Viceroy's Commissioned Officer', roughly equivalent to a lieutenant. He carries a gas mask slung on his back.

All the men seem quite lightly equipped, with only the officer apparently carrying a sword. What is also noticeable is the quite small stature of the horse nearest the camera, which is barely more than a pony; however, smaller, lighter horses were often found to be just as hardy as larger traditional cavalry mounts, and often better suited to campaigning.

(Taylor Library)

Plate 11. Members of the 29th Lancers (Deccan Horse) near Pys, March 1917.
This photograph was taken by official photographer J.W. Brooke (not to be confused with Ernest Brooks) and shows the 29th Lancers (Lucknow Brigade, 1st Indian Division) following up the German retreat in the area of Bapaume. These men are in full marching order with forage sacks, swords, picketing gear, additional bandoliers and a variety of other baggage all visible.

The extent of the shelling of the battlefield by the end of the 1916 Somme campaign is apparent in the desolation of the landscape through which the column is passing.

(Taylor Library)

Plate 12. British cavalry crossing muddy ground near Mory in the spring of 1917.
Mory lies to the north of Bapaume. Here British Lancers, in full marching order with greatcoats against the cold, follow a muddy track across the desolate Somme battlefield in the winter of 1916/17. Notable again, as with the Indian lancers in earlier images, are the leather washers instead of pennons on their lances, and the rifles and mess tins attached to the near side of the saddle.

(Taylor Library)

Plate 13. British cavalry waiting to advance alongside the Arras–Cambrai road, April 1917.
One of Ernest Brooks' most famous photographs shows members of an unknown British cavalry unit awaiting the order to advance during the Arras battle in April 1917. The miserable conditions prevailing at the start of that battle are clear from the state of the ground and the faces of the men. This image is frequently reproduced as an exemplar of the lack of activity of British cavalry in the battle, or in the war at large, despite the significant role played by mounted troops in the first few days of the Arras offensive.

(Taylor Library)

Plate 14. British cavalry advancing along a cavalry track, 1917.
An official photograph of unknown date but probably taken in the course of 1917. The temporary bridge is typical of the type of construction used to cross trenches or other obstacles on 'cavalry tracks'. When the original photo is examined in detail, the two figures on the left appear to have been rather crudely re-touched, but nonetheless the unofficial headgear of the figure on the extreme left is of interest. Note also the large hay-net on the off side of the saddle of the fourth man from the left.

(Taylor Library)

Plate 15. Scots Greys mount up beside a road, May 1918.
A series of official photographs were taken in May 1918 at Brimeux, near Montreuil, of the 2nd Dragoons (Scots Greys). It is likely that this image is one of that sequence.

Early in the war attempts were made to dye the coats of the grey horses of this regiment to make them less conspicuous, but this was quickly abandoned. It would appear that the order to mount up has just been given as the men are caught in the act of stowing their rifles and adjusting their equipment. Several horses have broken rank while being mounted, and one or two men appear to be still on the ground.

A French clergyman on a bicycle also appears in the background, riding through the middle of the parade.

(Taylor Library)

Notes

Chapter 1

1. Marquis of Anglesey, 1997, *A History of the British Cavalry*, vol. VIII, 'The Western Front, 1915–1918; Epilogue 1919–1939' (Leo Cooper, London), p. xix.
2. Badsey, S., 1996, 'Cavalry and the Development of the Breakthrough Doctrine', in Griffith, P. (ed.), *British Fighting Methods in the Great War* (Frank Cass, London), pp. 138–74.
3. Badsey, S., 2008, *Doctrine and Reform in the British Cavalry 1880–1918* (Ashgate, Aldershot).
4. Badsey, S., 1981, *Fire and the Sword: The British Cavalry and the Arme Blanche Controversy 1871–1921* (Unpub Cambridge University Thesis).
5. Ibid., p. 359.
6. Holmes, R., 1996, 'The Last Hurrah: Cavalry on the Western Front, August–September 1914', in Cecil, H. and Liddle, P. (eds), *Facing Armageddon – The First World War Experienced* (Leo Cooper, London), p. 285.
7. Holmes, R., 2004, *Tommy, The British Soldier on the Western Front 1914–1918* (HarperCollins, London), pp. 435–50; Corrigan, G., 2003, *Mud, Blood and Poppycock, Britain and the First World War* (Cassell, London), pp. 139–60.
8. For example: Terraine, J., 1980, 'Cavalry Generals and the "G" in Gap', in *The Smoke and the Fire, Myths and Anti-myths of War 1861–1945* (Sidgwick & Jackson, London); Griffith, P., 1994, *Battle Tactics on the Western Front, The British Army's Art of Attack 1916–18* (Yale University Press, London); Prior, R. and Wilson, T., 1992, *Command on the Western Front, The Military Career of Sir Henry Rawlinson 1914–1918* (Blackwell, Oxford); Travers, T., 1987, *The Killing Ground: The British Army, the Western Front and the Emergence of Modern Warfare 1900–1918* (Allen & Unwin, London); Sheffield, G., 2001, *Forgotten Victory, the First World War: Myths and Realities* (Headline, London).
9. Badsey, 1981, p. 6.
10. Travers, 1987, 1990, p. 5.
11. Terraine, 1980, p. 162.
12. Badsey, 1996, p. 140.
13. Ibid.
14. See Terraine, 1980, p. 148, or Harris, J., 1996, 'The Rise of Armour', in Griffith (ed.), 1996, pp. 113–37.
15. Anglesey, 1997, pp. xx–xxii.
16. Terraine, 1980, pp. 161–9.
17. Neillands, R., 1998, *The Great War Generals on the Western Front 1914–18* (Robinson, London).
18. Anglesey, 1997, pp. xx–xxi.
19. Brown, I.M., 1998, *British Logistics on the Western Front 1914–1919* (Praeger, Connecticut).
20. Terraine, J., 1963, *Douglas Haig, The Educated Soldier* (Cassell, London, 2000), p. 21.
21. Edmonds J.E. (ed.), 1945, *History of the Great War Based on Official Documents, Military Operations France and Belgium 1918*. Vol. V: '26th September–11th November, The Advance to Victory' (HMSO, London), p. 196.
22. Terraine, J., 1978, *To Win a War – 1918 The Year of Victory* (Cassell, London, 2000), p. 190.
23. Terraine, J., 1982, *White Heat: The New Warfare 1914–18* (Sidgwick & Jackson, London), p. 317.
24. Terraine, 1982, p. 147.
25. Terraine, 1963, p. 380.
26. Terraine, 1982, p. 317.
27. Prior and Wilson, 1992, p. 201.

28. Miles, W. (ed.), 1938, *History of the Great War Based on Official Documents, Military Operations France and Belgium 1916*. Vol. II, '2nd July 1916 to the End of the Battles of the Somme' (Macmillan, London), pp. 85–7.
29. Sheffield, 2001, p. 144.
30. Ibid., p. 106.
31. *Cavalry Training 1912* (HMSO, London), p. 305.
32. OH, 1918, vol. V, p. 235.
33. Terraine, 1978, p. 192.
34. Terraine, 1982, p. 317.
35. Anglesey, 1997, p. 257.
36. Badsey, 1981, p. 316.
37. Anglesey, 1997, pp. 286–9.
38. Ibid, p. xx.
39. Brown, 1998, p. 66.
40. Anglesey, 1997, p. 289.
41. Badsey, 1981, p. 31.
42. Badsey, 1981.
43. Badsey, 1996.
44. For example: Johnson, H., 1994, *Breakthrough! Tactics, Technology and the Search for Victory on the Western Front in World War I* (Praesidio, Novato Ca.).
45. Phillips, G., 2002, 'The obsolescence of the Arme Blanche and Technological Determinism in British Military History', *War in History*, vol. 9(1), pp. 39–59.
46. Terraine, 1978, p. 111.
47. Prior and Wilson, 1992, p. 307.
48. Ibid., p. 323.
49. Phillips, 2002, p. 56.
50. Griffith, 1996, p. 16.
51. Badsey, 1981, p. 336.
52. As defined in Brown, 1998, p. 5.
53. Terraine, J., 1964, *General Jack's Diary – War on the Western Front 1914–1918* (Cassell, London, 2000), p. 229.
54. Terraine, 1982, p. 286.
55. Terraine, 1980, p. 164.
56. Terraine, 1982, p. 290.
57. Badsey, 1981.
58. Griffith, 1994, pp. 159–63.
59. Badsey, 1996.
60. Sheffield, 2001, p. 144.
61. Griffith, 1994, p. 161.
62. Sheffield, 2001, p. 144.
63. Harris, 1996, p. 113.
64. Travers, 1987, p. 97.
65. Anglesey, 1997, p. 42.
66. Griffith, 1994.
67. Ibid.
68. Morris, D., 1965, *The Washing of the Spears, The Rise and fall of the Great Zulu Nation* (Sphere, London, 1990).
69. War Office, *1914 Field Service Pocket Book* (HMSO, London, repr. David & Charles, Newton Abbot, 1971), p. 250.
70. Horne, A., 1996, *How Far from Austerlitz? Napoleon, 1805–1815* (Macmillan, London), p. 310.
71. Badsey, 2008, pp. 47–50.
72. All organisational details are extracted from: Becke, A.F. (ed.), 1935, *Order of Battle of Divisions; Part 1: The Regular British Divisions* (HMSO, London); or Becke, A.F. (ed.), 1945, *Order of Battle, Part 4: The Army Council, GHQs, Armies and Corps* (HMSO, London).
73. Anglesey, 1997, p. 63.
74. Ibid., pp. 204–5.
75. This debate is thoroughly examined in Badsey, 2008.
76. Tylden, G., 1965, *Horses and Saddlery* (J.A. Allen & Co., London), p. 154.
77. Badsey, 2008, p. 91.
78. Bridges, T., 1938, *Alarms and Excursions, Reminiscences of a Soldier* (Longmans, London), pp. 80–1.
79. War Office, *1914 Field Service Pocket Book*, p. 191.
80. See *Cavalry Training 1912* (HMSO, London), ch. IV.
81. Badsey, S., pers. comm.
82. A full account of these events is contained in Anglesey, 1996.
83. Heathcote, T.A., 1999, *The British Field Marshals, 1736–1997. A Biographical Dictionary* (Leo Cooper, London), pp. 21 and 66.
84. Anglesey, 1996, p. 222.
85. Badsey, 1981, p. 306.
86. For example: Holmes, R., 1995, *Riding the Retreat, Mons to the Marne Revisited* (Jonathan Cape, London); Anglesey, 1996.
87. Anglesey, 1996, p. 112.
88. Edmonds, J.E. (ed.), 1925, *History of the Great War Based on Official Documents, Military Operations France and Belgium 1914*. Vol. I, 'Mons, the retreat to the Seine, the Marne and the Aisne, August–

October 1914' (Macmillan, London), p. 50.
89. Bridges, 1938, p. 76.
90. Anglesey, 1996, p. 114.
91. Bridges, 1938, p. 78.
92. Ibid.
93. Anglesey, 1996, p. 141.
94. Terraine, J., 1960, *Mons, The Retreat to Victory* (Pan Books, London, 1972), p. 97.
95. 1st Cavalry Division War Diary, August 1914, Appendix 1, WO95/1096.
96. Ibid.
97. Terraine, 1960, p. 99.
98. Holmes, 1995, p. 139.
99. Letter of C.H. Leveson to Major Becke, 7 July 1918, 18th Hussars War Diary, August 1914, WO95/1113.
100. Holmes, 1995, p. 140.
101. Letter of C.H. Leveson.
102. 'Statement about the non-existence of wire during the charge of 9th Lancers, 24th August 1914', in 1st Cavalry Division War Diary, August 1914, WO95/1096.
103. Quoted in Anglesey, 1996, p. 122.
104. Letter of C.H. Leveson.
105. Anglesey, 1996, p. 124.
106. 1st Cavalry Division War Diary, August 1914, Appendix 1, WO95/1096.
107. Holmes, 1995, p. 140.
108. Anglesey, 1996, p. 124.
109. Holmes, 1995, p. 138.
110. Howard-Vyse R.G.H., 1921, 'The Fifth Cavalry Brigade at Cerizy, August 28th 1914', *Cavalry Journal*, vol. XI, p. 112.
111. 5th Cavalry Brigade War Diary, 28 August 1914, WO95/1138.
112. Stewart, P.F., 1950, *The History of the XII Royal Lancers (Princess of Wales's)* (Oxford University Press, London), p. 251.
113. Anon., typescript 'Moy 28th August, 1914', in 12th Lancers War Diary, August 1914, WO95/1140.
114. Howard-Vyse, 1921, p. 113.
115. Stewart, 1950, p. 251.
116. Anon., 'Moy 28th August, 1914'.
117. 20th Hussars War Diary, 28 August 1914, WO95/1140.
118. Anon., 'Moy 28th August, 1914'.
119. Howard-Vyse, 1921, p. 115.

120. Anglesey, 1996, p. 141nn.
121. Gough, H. (Gen. Sir), 1931, *The Fifth Army* (Hodder & Stoughton, London), p. 31.
122. Howard-Vyse, 1921, p. 117.
123. Ibid.
124. Wavell, A., 1946, *Allenby, Soldier and Statesman* (Harrap, London), p. 114.
125. Stewart, 1950, p. 255.
126. Anglesey, 1996, p. 205.
127. Omissi, D., 1999, *Indian Voices of the Great War – Soldiers' Letters 1914–18* (Macmillan, London), p. 1.
128. Sandhu, G., 1991, *I Serve – Saga of the Eighteenth Cavalry* (Lancer, New Delhi), p. 34.
129. Anglesey, 1996, p. 223.
130. Omissi, 1999, p. 364.
131. Ibid., p. 2.
132. Sandhu, 1991, p. 49.
133. Anglesey, 1996, p. 219.
134. Sandhu, 1991, p. 51.
135. Anglesey, 1997, p. 38.
136. Ibid., pp. 19–22.
137. Lloyd, R.A., 1938, *Trooper in the Tins*, reprinted as *Troop Horse and Trench, The Experiences of a British Lifeguardsman of the Household Cavalry Fighting on the Western Front during the First World War 1914–1918* (Leonaur, London, 2006), p. 100.
138. The background to Loos is summarised in Corrigan, G., 2006, *Loos 1915, The Unwanted Battle* (Spellmount, Stroud), pp. 1–19.
139. First Army Operation Order No. 95, 19 September 1915, WO95/158.
140. OH, 1915, vol. II, p. 156.
141. First Army Orders GS 164/8 (a), 11 September 1915, WO95/158.
142. GHQ Orders GS 164 (a), 12 September 1915, WO95/158.
143. 3rd Cavalry Division War Diary, 19 September 1915, WO95/1141.
144. First Army Operation Order No. 95, 19 September 1915, para. 5, WO95/158.
145. GHQ OAM 887, 21 September 1915, para. 3, in Cavalry Corps War Diary, September 1915, WO95/573.
146. Haig, Diary, 22 September 1915, p. 120, WO265/5.

147. Preston, T., 1937, 'The Third Cavalry Division at Loos', *Cavalry Journal,* vol. XXVII, p. 18.
148. Ibid., pp. 22–8.
149. Anglesey, 1997, p. 20.

Chapter 2
1. Anglesey, 1997, p. 42.
2. GHQ OA 512, 3 March 1916, WO95/574.
3. Badsey, 2008, p. 394.
4. GHQ GS 1428, 9 March 1916, WO95/574.
5. Badsey, 1996, p. 154.
6. Haig, diary, 9 April 1916, WO256/9.
7. Anglesey, 1997, p. 40.
8. *Cavalry Training 1912* (HMSO), pp. 268–71.
9. Gough, 1931, p. 132.
10. Secunderabad Cavalry Brigade HQ War Diary, 8 February 1916, WO95/1187.
11. 2nd Indian Cavalry Division War Diary, 18 June 1916, WO95/1180.
12. 9th LAC Battery War Diary, WO95/1182.
13. 34th Poona Horse War Diary, 9 May 1916, WO95/1187.
14. Secunderabad Cavalry Brigade HQ War Diary, 28 May 1916, WO95/1187.
15. Sandhu, G., 1981, *The Indian Cavalry* (Vision Books, New Delhi), p. 304.
16. 2nd Indian Cavalry Division War Diary, 3 June 1916, WO95/1180.
17. Anglesey, 1997, p. 38.
18. 2nd Indian Cavalry Division War Diary, 18 June 1916, WO95/1180.
19. Seely, J., 1930, *Adventure* (Heinemann, London), p. 221.
20. Anglesey, 1997, p. 48nn.
21. Canadian Cavalry Brigade War Diary, 27 May 1916, WO95/1083.
22. Ibid., 3 June 1916.
23. 'Secunderabad Cavalry Brigade Order No. 30', included as an appendix in Secunderabad Cavalry Brigade War Diary, 1 July 1916, WO95/1187.
24. '2nd Indian Cavalry Division Operation Order No. 3', 28 June 1916, para. 2, included as an appendix in 2nd Indian Cavalry Division War Diary, WO95/1180.
25. Lloyd, 1938, p. 226.
26. Keegan, J., 1976, *The Face of Battle* (Viking, New York), p. 242.
27. Neillands, R., 2001, *Attrition. The Great War on the Western Front 1916* (Robinson, London), p. 241.
28. Prior and Wilson, 1992, p. 35.
29. Liddell Hart, B.H., 1930, *The Real War* (Faber & Faber, London), p. 306.
30. Middlebrook, M., 1971, *The First Day on the Somme, 1 July 1916* (Allen Lane, London), p. 272.
31. Badsey, 1981, p. 306.
32. Edmonds, J.E. (ed.), 1932, *History of the Great War Based on Official Documents, Military Operations France and Belgium 1916*, vol. I, 'Sir Douglas Haig's command to the 1st July: The Battle of the Somme' (Macmillan, London), p. 249.
33. 'Plan for Offensive by the Fourth Army GX 3/1', 3 April 1916, Fourth Army file, WO158/233.
34. Haig, Diary, 5 April 1916, p. 66, WO256/9.
35. 'Plan for Offensive by the Fourth Army GX 3/1'.
36. 'GHQ letter OAD 710' of 12 April 1916, para. 3, Fourth Army file, WO158/233.
37. Cavalry Corps War Diary, 3 March 1916, WO95/574.
38. 'GHQ letter OAD 710', para. 6.
39. 'Amended plan submitted by Fourth Army to GHQ, 19 April 1916', para. 26, Fourth Army file, WO158/233.
40. Ibid.
41. GHQ letter OAD 876 to Sir H. Rawlinson, 16 May 1916, Fourth Army file, WO158/233.
42. Ibid., para. 4.
43. OH, 1916, vol. I, p. 311.
44. Ibid., p. 312.
45. 'GHQ letter OAD 12', 16 June 1916, para. 2(b)i, Fourth Army file, WO158/234.
46. 'Note of Commander-in-Chief's Instructions in amplification of OAD 12 issued 16 June 1916', OAD 17, 21 June 1916, para. 2, Fourth Army file, WO158/234.
47. Ibid., para. 5.
48. OH, 1916, vol. I, p. 267.
49. Badsey, 1996, p. 154.
50. Ibid., p. 155.
51. Gough, 1931, p. 136.

52. 'GHQ letter OAD 12', 16 June 1916, para. 1, Fourth Army file, WO158/234.
53. Prior & Wilson, 1992, p. 155.
54. 'Fourth Army Memorandum, 32/3/7G', 28 June 1916, Fourth Army file, WO158/234.
55. Ibid., para. 2.
56. OH, 1916, vol. I, pp. 251–2.
57. '2nd Indian Cavalry Division Operation Order No. 3', 28 June 1916, included as an appendix in the 2nd Indian Cavalry Division War Diary, WO95/1180.
58. 'Fourth Army Memorandum, 32/3/7G', 28 June 1916, Fourth Army file, WO158/234.
59. '2nd Indian Cavalry Division Operation Order No. 3', 28 June 1916, para. 2, included as an appendix in the 2nd Indian Cavalry Division War Diary, WO95/1180.
60. Horne, 1996, p. 224.
61. Sheffield, G., 2003, *The Somme* (Cassell, London, 2004), p. 22.
62. GHQ letter OAD 710, 12 April 1916, para. 6, Fourth Army file, WO158/233.
63. OH, 1916, vol. I, p. 267.
64. Secunderabad Cavalry Brigade HQ War Diary, 1 July 1916, WO95/1187.
65. Middlebrook, 1971, p. 226.
66. Ibid., p. 288.
67. Norman, T., 1984, *The Hell they called High Wood – The Somme 1916* (Patrick Stephens, Wellingborough), p. 45.
68. Lloyd, 1938, p. 229.
69. 2nd Indian Cavalry Division War Diary, 2–7 July 1916, WO95/1180.
70. OH, 1916, vol. I, p. 84.
71. Anglesey, 1997, p. 49.
72. Prior and Wilson, 1992, p. 193.
73. Terraine, 1963, p. 210.
74. 'Fourth Army Operation Order No. 4', 8 July 1916, Fourth Army file, WO158/234.
75. Quoted in Anglesey, 1997, p. 45.
76. OH, 1916, vol. I, p. 63.
77. Haig, diary, 13 July 1916, p. 19, WO256/11.
78. Liddell Hart, 1930, p. 322.
79. 'Fourth Army Operation Order No. 4', 8 July 1916, Fourth Army file, WO158/234.
80. Ibid.
81. Ibid., para. 4.
82. 'Instructions for the Action of Cavalry of Fourth Army on "Z" Day', 12 July 1916, para. 5, Fourth Army file, WO158/234.
83. Fourth Army Memorandum, 13 July 1916, para. 2.
84. Ibid., para. 4.
85. Prior and Wilson, 1992, p. 193.
86. 'Instructions to Br.-General C.L. Gregory, commanding Advanced Guard, 2nd Indian Cavalry Division', 14 July 1916, para. 3, WO95/1180.
87. XIII Corps Operation Order No. 25, 13 July 1916, para. 8, in XIII Corps War Diary, July 1916, WO95/895.
88. 'Order No. GS301/4', included as an appendix to the 2nd Indian Cavalry Division War Diary, 12 July 1916, WO95/1180.
89. Secunderabad Cavalry Brigade War Diary, July 1916, WO95/1187.
90. '3rd Division Operation Order No. 84', 13 July 1916, para. 26, in 3rd Division War Diary, July 1916, WO95/1377.
91. '2nd Indian Cavalry Division Operation Order No. 7', 13 July 1916, included as an appendix to the 2nd Indian Cavalry Division War Diary, WO95/1180.
92. Anglesey, 1997, p 43.
93. 'Secunderabad Cavalry Brigade Order No. 32', included as an appendix to the Secunderabad Cavalry Brigade War Diary, 14 July 1916, WO95/1187.
94. 2nd Indian Cavalry Division War Diary, 14 July 1916, WO95/1180.
95. Ibid.
96. 'Secunderabad Cavalry Brigade Narrative of Events, 14 July 1916', included as an appendix to the Secunderabad Cavalry Brigade War Diary, 14 July 1916, WO95/1187.
97. 20th Deccan Horse War Diary, 14 July 1916, WO95/1187.
98. 7th Dragoon Guards War Diary, 14 July 1916, WO95/1187.
99. 'Secunderabad Cavalry Brigade Narrative of Events, 14 July 1916'.
100. OH, 1916, vol. II, pp. 82–3.
101. 2nd Indian Cavalry Division War Diary, 14 July 1916, WO95/1180.
102. 9th LAC Battery War Diary, 14 July 1916, WO95/1182.

103. N Battery RHA War Diary, 14 July 1916, WO95/1188.

104. 2nd Indian Cavalry Division War Diary, 14 July 1916, WO95/1180.

105. Letter of 18 July 1916, quoted in Omissi, 1999, p. 209.

106. 7th Dragoon Guards War Diary, 14 July 1916, WO95/1187.

107. 2nd Indian Cavalry Division War Diary, 14 July 1916, WO95/1180.

108. OH, 1916, vol. II, p. 83.

109. Ibid., p. 84.

110. 'Secunderabad Cavalry Brigade Narrative of Events, 14 July 1916'.

111. Norman, 1984, p. 89.

112. 'Secunderabad Cavalry Brigade Narrative of Events, 14 July 1916'.

113. OH, 1916, vol. II, p. 85.

114. Ibid., p. 86.

115. Secunderabad Cavalry Brigade Signal Squadron War Diary, 14 July 1916, WO95/1188.

116. 'Secunderabad Cavalry Brigade Narrative of Events, 14 July 1916'.

117. Ibid.

118. Ibid.

119. N Battery RHA War Diary, 14 July 1916, WO95/1188.

120. 'Secunderabad Cavalry Brigade Narrative of Events, 14 July 1916'.

121. Ibid.

122. Army Message Form 'OC XX Deccan Horse, from SCB 119', attached to 20th Deccan Horse War Diary, 14 July 1916, WO95/1187.

123. Tennant, E., 1939, *The Royal Deccan Horse in the Great War* (Gale & Polden, Aldershot), p. 48.

124. Ibid., p. 49.

125. 'Secunderabad Cavalry Brigade Narrative of Events, 14 July 1916'.

126. Secunderabad Cavalry Brigade Signal Squadron War Diary, 14 July 1916, WO95/1188.

127. 'Secunderabad Cavalry Brigade Narrative of Events, 14 July 1916'.

128. 2nd Indian Cavalry Division War Diary, 14 July 1916, WO95/1180.

129. OH, 1916, vol. II, p. 85.

130. Ibid., p. 84.

131. Anglesey, 1997, p. 49.

132. Liddle, P., 1992, *The 1916 Battle of the Somme – A Reappraisal* (Wordsworth, London, 2001), p. 74.

133. Hart, P., 2005, *The Somme* (Cassell, London), p. 274.

134. Liddle, 1992, p. 74.

135. Canadian Cavalry Brigade War Diary, 15 July 1916, WO95/1083.

136. 'Secunderabad Cavalry Brigade – Casualties, 14 August [sic] 1916', included as an appendix to the Secunderabad Cavalry Brigade War Diary, 14 July 1916, WO95/1187.

137. N Battery RHA War Diary, 14 July 1916, WO95/1188.

138. Prior and Wilson, 1992, p. 201.

139. Macdonald, L., 1983, *Somme* (Michael Joseph, London), pp. 137–8.

140. For example in Anglesey, 1997, p. 53.

141. *1914 Field Service Pocket Book* (HMSO), p. 189.

142. Taylor, A.J.P., 1963, *The First World War, An Illustrated History* (Penguin, London, 1966), p. 140.

143. Seton, G., 1931, *Footslogger, An Autobiography* (Hutchinson, London), p. 164.

144. Letter of 2 August 1916, quoted in Omissi, 1999, p. 215.

145. Quoted in Liddle, 1992, p. 76.

146. Hudson, H., 1937, *History of the 19th King George's Own Lancers 1858–1921*, p. 160.

147. Badsey, 1996, p. 144.

148. 'Secunderabad Cavalry Brigade Order No. 32', included as an appendix to Secunderabad Cavalry Brigade War Diary, 14 July 1916, WO95/1187.

149. Secunderabad Cavalry Brigade Signal Squadron War Diary, 14 July 1916, WO95/1188.

150. 'Instructions for the Action of Cavalry of Fourth Army on "Z" Day', 12 July 1916, para. 2, Fourth Army file, WO158/234.

151. Jones, H.A., 1928, *Official History of the War. The War in the Air – being the story of the part played in the Great War by the Royal Air Force*, vol. II (Clarendon Press, Oxford), p. 228.

152. GHQ letter OAD 116, 19 August 1916, Fourth Army file, WO158/235.

153. GHQ letter OAD 131, 31 August 1916, para. 3, Fourth Army file, WO158/235.

154. Ibid., para. 5.
155. Fourth Army Instructions No. 299/17 (G), 11 September 1916, Fourth Army file, WO158/236.
156. Fourth Army Instructions No. 299/20 (G), 11 September 1916, para. 6, Fourth Army file, WO158/236.
157. 'Battle of Flers–Courcelette, Fourth Army Instruction in the event of a general advance', 13 September 1916. Quoted in OH, 1916, vol. II, appendix 22. Original not available in NA.
158. Ibid., para. 5.
159. Ibid., para. 9.
160. Home, A., *Diary*, pub. Briscoe, D. (ed.), 1985, *Diary of a World War I Cavalry Officer* (Costello, Tunbridge Wells), p. 119.
161. Ibid., p. 120 (15 September 1916).
162. Cavalry Corps GX 4/1 'Action of Cavalry Corps', 10 September 1916, included in Cavalry Corps War Diary Appendix V, WO95/574.
163. Memorandum attached to 'Cavalry Corps Operation Order No. 1', 13 September 1916, included in 1st Indian Cavalry Division War Diary, September 1916, WO95/1167.
164. Fourth Army Instructions No. 299/18(G), 11 September 1916, Fourth Army file, WO158/236.
165. 'Cavalry Corps Operation Order No. 1', 13 September 1916, included in 1st Indian Cavalry Division War Diary, September 1916, WO95/1167.
166. Cavalry Corps War Diary, 15 September 1916, WO95/574.
167. OH, 1916, vol. II, p. 343.
168. Cavalry Corps War Diary, 16 September 1916, WO95/574.
169. Cavalry Corps War Diary, 21 September 1916, WO95/574.
170. 'Cavalry Corps GC 126', included in Cavalry Corps War Diary, 18 September 1916, WO95/574.
171. 'Cavalry Corps Operation Order No. 5', included in Cavalry Corps War Diary, September 1916, WO95/574.
172. 'Cavalry Corps Operation Order No. 1, Appendix A', included in Cavalry Corps War Diary, September 1916, WO95/574.
173. 'GX 4/36 appended to Cavalry Corps Operation Order No. 5', included in Cavalry Corps War Diary, September 1916, WO95/574.
174. OH, 1916, vol. II, p. 370.
175. 'GX 4/36'.
176. 1st Indian Cavalry Division War Diary, 25 September 1916, WO95/1167.
177. OH, 1916, vol. II, p. 377.
178. 1st Indian Cavalry Division War Diary, 25 September 1916, WO95/1167.
179. Cavalry Corps War Diary, 25 September 1916, WO95/574.
180. 1st Indian Cavalry Division War Diary, 25 September 1916, WO 95/1167.
181. OH, 1916, vol. II, p. 382.
182. Ibid., p. 385.
183. Cavalry Corps War Diary, September 1916, Appendix XV, WO95/574.
184. Letter of 4 October 1916, quoted in Omissi, 1999, p. 242.
185. Sandhu, 1981, p. 304.
186. Hudson, 1937, p. 163.
187. Ibid., p. 160.
188. GHQ letter OAD 116, 19 August 1916, para. 1, Fourth Army file, WO158/235.
189. Terraine, 1963, p. 84.
190. Badsey, 1996, p. 142.
191. Lloyd, 1938, p. 227.

Chapter 3

1. Letter, Byng to Chetwoode, 30 May 1917, quoted in Badsey, 1981, p. 317.
2. Terraine, 1963. (Cassell, London), p. 289.
3. Fuller, J, 1920 'The Influence of Tanks on Cavalry Tactics', in *Cavalry Journal*, vol. X, p. 127.
4. Holmes, 1996, p. 285.
5. Terraine, 1963, p. 277.
6. Anglesey, 1997, p. 66.
7. Home, *Diary* (29 October 1916), in Briscoe, 1985, p. 124.
8. Cavalry Corps War Diary, November 1916, Appendix G1, WO95/574.
9. Falls, C. (ed.), 1940, *History of the Great War Based on Official Documents, Military Operations France and Belgium 1917*, vol. I, 'The German retreat to the Hindenburg Line and the Battles of Arras' (Macmillan, London), p. 64.
10. Home, *Diary* (10 October 1916), in Briscoe, 1985, p. 124.

11. Ibid., p. 126 (13 November 1916).
12. Cavalry Corps GX 41 'Winter Training', included in Cavalry Corps War Diary, September 1916, Appendix H, WO95/574.
13. Ibid., p. 1.
14. Darling, J.C., 1922, *20th Hussars in the Great War* (Privately Published, Lyndhurst, Hants), p. 73.
15. Ibid, p. 74.
16. Cavalry Corps GX 41 'Winter Training', p. 4, para. 3.
17. Ibid., p. 5, para. 9.
18. Home, *Diary* (18 January 1917), in Briscoe, 1985, p. 123.
19. 'Cavalry Corps OB 1835, 24/11/16', Cavalry Corps War Diary, November 1916, Appendix L, WO95/574.
20. Cavalry Corps AA&QMG Branch War Diary, 6 February 1917, WO95/574. See also Preston, T., 1920, 'The Machine Gun Corps (Cavalry), in France 1916–1918', part I, in *Cavalry Journal*, vol. X, pp. 262–731.
21. OH, 1917, vol. 1, p. 16.
22. Badsey, 1981, p. 318.
23. Cavalry Corps GX 42/1, Cavalry Corps War Diary, October 1916, WO95/574.
24. Cavalry Corps GX 96/30/1, Cavalry Corps War Diary, March 1917, Appendix C, WO95/574.
25. Preston, 1920, Part III, p. 488.
26. Cavalry Corps War Diary, March 1917, WO95/574.
27. Cavalry Corps DDVS War Diary, 4 October 1916, WO95/581.
28. Ibid., 15 October 1916.
29. Ibid., 27 November 1916.
30. 1st Cavalry Division ADVS War Diary, November 1916, WO95/1102.
31. Cavalry Corps DDVS War Diary, 13 April 1917, WO95/581.
32. Lloyd, 1938, p. 254.
33. Van Emden, R. (ed.), 1996, *Tickled to death to go. Memoirs of a cavalryman in the First World War* (Spellmount, Staplehurst), p. 126.
34. Darling, 1922, p. 75.
35. Cavalry Corps DDVS War Diary, 6 January 1917, WO95/581.
36. 3rd Cavalry Division ADVS War Diary, January 1917, WO95/1145.
37. OH, 1917, vol. 1, p. 162.
38. Preston, T., 1931, 'The Cavalry at Arras 1917', *Cavalry Journal*, vol. XXI, p. 521.
39. Wynne, G.C., 1940, *If Germany Attacks, The Battle in Depth in the West* (Faber, London), pp. 133–64.
40. Seely, 1930, p. 255.
41. OH, 1917, vol. I, pp. 93–4.
42. Ibid.
43. Terraine, 1963, p. 276.
44. GHQ letter OAD 337, 16 March 1917, Third Army file, WO158/223.
45. 'Cavalry Corps Operation Order No. 1', 19 March 1917, in Cavalry Corps War Diary, March 1917, Appendix A, WO95/574.
46. 5th Cavalry Division Operations Order No. 23, 19 March 1917, in 5th Cavalry Division War Diary, March 1917, Appendix 98, WO95/1152.
47. OH, 1917, vol. I, pp. 138–49.
48. 'Narrative of the Operations of the 5th Cavalry Division between March 24th and March 27th', contained in 5th Cavalry Division War Diary, March 1917, Appendix 102, WO95/1152.
49. Seely, 1930, p. 256.
50. Fort Garry Horse War Diary, 24 March 1917, WO95/1084.
51. 'Narrative of the Operations of the 5th Cavalry Division between March 24th and March 27th'.
52. 5th Cavalry Division War Diary, 25 March 1917, WO95/1152.
53. 'Narrative of the Operations of the 5th Cavalry Division between March 24th and March 27th', op. cit.
54. Seely, 1930, p. 257.
55. OH, 1917, vol. I, p. 135nn.
56. Ambala Cavalry Brigade War Diary, 26 March 1917, WO95/1164.
57. 18th Lancers War Diary, 26 March 12917, WO95/1164.
58. Ambala Cavalry Brigade War Diary, 26 March 1917, WO95/1164.
59. 'Narrative of the Operations of the 5th Cavalry Division between March 24th and March 27th'.
60. Canadian Cavalry Brigade War Diary, 27 March 1917, WO95/1083.
61. Ibid.
62. Ibid.

63. Anglesey, 1997, p. 73.
64. 8th Hussars War Diary, 27 March 1917, WO95/1164.
65. Ambala Cavalry Brigade War Diary, 27 March 1917, WO95/1164.
66. 9th LAC Battery War Diary, 27 March 1917, WO95/1163.
67. Home, *Diary* (29 March 1916), in Briscoe, 1985, p. 137.
68. 8th Hussars War Diary, 29 March 1917, WO95/1164.
69. 1/1st Royal Wiltshire Yeomanry War Diary, 30 March 1917, WO95/930.
70. Winter, D., 1978, *Death's Men, Soldiers of the Great War* (Penguin, London), p. 81.
71. Fort Garry Horse War Diary, 26 March 1917, WO95/1084.
72. Canadian Cavalry Brigade War Diary, 26 March 1917, WO95/1083.
73. *Cavalry Training 1912* (HMSO, London), p. 270.
74. General Staff, 1917, SS143: *Instructions for the Training of Platoons for Offensive Action 1917.*
75. Anglesey, 1997, p. 73.
76. Discussed in detail in Wynne, 1940, p. 150ff.
77. Home, *Diary* (31 October 1916), in Briscoe, 1985, p. 125.
78. OH, 1917, vol. 1, p. 544.
79. Terraine, 1963, p. 250.
80. OH, 1917, vol. 1, Chapters I and II.
81. GHQ Letter OAD 258, 2 January 1917, Third Army file, WO158/223.
82. Ibid., para. 1.
83. Ibid., para. 5.
84. Anglesey, 1997, pp. 74–5, 205.
85. Heathcote, 1999, p. 21.
86. Wavell, 1946, p. 134.
87. Heathcote, 1999, p. 23.
88. Wavell, 1946, p. 141.
89. James, L., 1993, *Imperial Warrior, The Life and Times of Field Marshal Viscount Allenby 1861–1936* (Weidenfeld & Nicholson, London), p. 83.
90. Terraine, 1963, p. 54.
91. Charteris, J., 1931, *At GHQ* (Cassell, London), p. 210.
92. Ibid.
93. James, 1993, p. 91.
94. Ibid., p. 74.
95. Wavell, 1946, p. 158.
96. Third Army Appreciation No. GS 1/15, 7 February 1917, Third Army file, WO158/223.
97. Ibid., para. 3.
98. Wavell, 1946, p. 140.
99. Johnson, J.H., 1995, *Stalemate! The Great Trench Warfare Battles of 1915–17* (A&AP, London), p. 99.
100. James, 1993, p. 95.
101. Terraine, 1963, pp. 280ff.
102. 'Instructions issued to the Cavalry Corps for offensive operations to be carried out by the Third Army', 5 April 1917, WO95/574.
103. 'Instructions to the Cavalry Corps, Third Army, No. GS 21/11', 3 April 1917, contained in Third Army War Diary, April 1917, WO95/361.
104. For example, the 37th Division Instructions No. 6, Administrative Arrangements (Q), 2 April 1917, paras II and XII, reproduced in OH, 1917, vol. 1, Appendix 35. Original not available in NA.
105. Cavalry Corps A&QMG War Diary, April 1917, Appendix A, WO95/577.
106. 'Cavalry Corps Operation Order No. 3', 8 April 1917, contained in Cavalry Corps War Diary, April 1917, Appendix VI, WO95/574.
107. Cavalry Corps War Diary, 5 April 1917, WO95/574.
108. Ibid., 7 April 1917.
109. Ibid., 8 April 1917.
110. OH, 1917, vol. 1, p. 201.
111. Ibid., p. 231.
112. Ibid., p. 225.
113. 'Cavalry Corps Operation Order No. 3', 8 April 1917, contained in Cavalry Corps War Diary, April 1917, Appendix VI, WO95/574.
114. Cavalry Corps War Diary, 9 April 1917, WO95/574.
115. Ibid.
116. Preston, 1931, p. 525.
117. Cavalry Corps War Diary, 9 April 1917, WO95/574.
118. Ibid.
119. Preston, 1931, p. 526.
120. OH, 1917, vol. 1, p. 237.
121. Cavalry Corps War Diary, 9 April 1917, WO95/574.

122. Ibid.
123. 1st Cavalry Division War Diary, 9 April 1917, WO95/1097.
124. Preston, 1931, p. 526.
125. OH, 1917, vol. 1, p. 237.
126. Carton de Wiart, A., 1950, *Happy Odyssey* (Jonathan Cape, London), p. 82.
127. Northamptonshire Yeomanry, VI Corps Cavalry, War Diary, 9 April 1917, WO95/792.
128. VI Cyclist Battalion War Diary, April 1917, Appendix 1 'Report on the action of 6th Cyclist Bttn during operations from 9th to 12th April 1917', WO95/792.
129. OH, 1917, vol. 1, p. 244.
130. Cavalry Corps War Diary, 9 April 1917, WO95/574.
131. Ibid.
132. OH, 1917, vol. 1, p. 244.
133. Ibid., p. 247.
134. Ibid., p. 249.
135. 1st Cavalry Division War Diary, 10 April 1917, WO95/1097.
136. 'Cavalry Corps Operation Order No. 4', 10 April 1917, contained in Cavalry Corps War Diary, April 1917, Appendix XVI, WO95/574.
137. 1st Cavalry Division War Diary, 10 April 1917, WO95/1097.
138. 'Operations of 1st Cavalry Brigade, April 10th and 11th' contained in 1st Cavalry Brigade War Diary, April 1917, Appendix A, WO95/1108.
139. Ibid.
140. 1st Cavalry Division War Diary, 10 April 1917, WO95/1097.
141. 5th Cavalry Brigade War Diary, 9 April 1917, WO95/1138.
142. Preston, 1931, p. 526.
143. 4th Cavalry Brigade War Diary, 9 April 1917, WO95/1135.
144. Ibid., 10 April 1917.
145. 'Cavalry Corps Operation Order No. 4'.
146. 3rd Cavalry Division War Diary, 10 April 1917, WO95/1141.
147. Ibid. 148. Ibid.
149. Cavalry Corps War Diary, 10 April 1917, WO95/574.
150. 8th Cavalry Brigade War Diary, 10 April 1917, WO95/1156.
151. Preston, 1931, p. 527.
152. Nicholls, J., 1990, *Cheerful Sacrifice, The Battle of Arras 1917* (Leo Cooper, London), p. 138.
153. 3rd Cavalry Division War Diary, 10 April 1917, WO95/1141.
154. 7th LAC Battery War Diary, 10 April 1917, WO95/1146.
155. Cavalry Corps War Diary, 10 April 1917, WO95/574.
156. 3rd Cavalry Division War Diary, 10 April 1917, WO95/1141.
157. Ibid.
158. Cavalry Corps War Diary, 10 April 1917, WO95/574.
159. OH, 1917, vol. 1, p. 251.
160. Lloyd, 1938, p. 256.
161. Preston, 1931, p. 528.
162. Ibid.
163. OH, 1917, vol. 1, p. 252.
164. 5th Cavalry Brigade War Diary, 10 April 1917, WO95/1138.
165. OH, 1917, vol. 1, p. 259.
166. 'Cavalry Corps Operation Order No. 5', 10 April 1917, contained in Cavalry Corps War Diary, April 1917, Appendix XXI, WO95/574.
167. Ibid., para. 4.
168. OH, 1917, vol. 1, p. 259.
169. Cavalry Corps War Diary, 11 April 1917, WO95/574.
170. OH, 1917, vol. 1, p. 263.
171. Ibid., p. 275.
172. 3rd Cavalry Division War Diary, 11 April 1917, WO95/1141.
173. Ibid.
174. Preston, 1931, p. 530.
175. 3rd Cavalry Division War Diary, 11 April 1917, WO95/1141.
176. '3rd Cavalry Division at Monchy 11th April 1917', contained in Cavalry Corps War Diary, April 1917, Appendix XXXV, WO95/574.
177. D.W. Cuddeford, quoted in Johnson, 1995, p. 108.
178. Letter from Capt. R. Gordon-Canning quoted in 'Notes: The Cavalry at Arras 1917', in *Cavalry Journal*, vol. XXII, 1932, p. 292.
179. 'Operations 8th Cavalry Brigade 9–12th April 1917', contained in 8th Cavalry Brigade War Diary, April 1917, WO95/1156.

180. Essex Yeomanry War Diary, 11 April 1917, WO95/1156.
181. Clarence Garnett interview, quoted in Nicholls, 1990, pp. 144–5.
182. '3rd Cavalry Division at Monchy 11th April 1917', para. 10, contained in Cavalry Corps War Diary, April 1917, Appendix XXXV, WO95/574.
183. Essex Yeomanry War Diary, 11 April 1917, WO95/1156.184. 8th Machine Gun Squadron War Diary, 11 April 1917, WO95/1156.
185. Essex Yeomanry War Diary, 11 April 1917, WO95/1156.
186. Ibid.
187. Preston, 1931, p. 530.
188. '3rd Cavalry Division at Monchy 11th April 1917', para. 7, contained in Cavalry Corps War Diary, April 1917, Appendix XXXV, WO95/574.
189. 3rd Cavalry Division War Diary, 11 April 1917, WO95/1141.
190. OH, 1917, vol. 1, p. 265.
191. '3rd Cavalry Division at Monchy 11th April 1917', para. 12, contained in Cavalry Corps War Diary, April 1917, Appendix XXXV, WO95/574.
192. OH, 1917, vol. 1, p. 266.
193. Whitmore, F., 1920, *The 10th PWO Royal Hussars and the Essex Yeomanry during the European War 1914–1918* (Benham & Co., Colchester), p. 106.
194. Preston, 1931, p. 533.
195. Preston, 1920, p. 495.
196. 3rd Cavalry Division War Diary, 11 April 1917, WO95/1141.
197. Preston, 1931, p. 533.
198. North Somerset Yeomanry War Diary, 11 April 1917, WO95/1153.
199. Preston, 1920, p. 495.
200. 3rd Cavalry Division War Diary, 11 April 1917, WO95/1141.
201. OH, 1917, vol. 1, p. 268.
202. Essex Yeomanry War Diary, 11 April 1917, WO95/1156.
203. OH, 1917, vol. 1, p. 273.
204. James, 1993, pp. 105ff.
205. Letter from Kavanagh to Allenby, 13 April 1917, contained in Cavalry Corps War Diary, April 1917, WO95/574.
206. Whitmore, 1920, p. 98.
207. Preston, 1931, p. 537.
208. Thomas, A., 1968, *A Life Apart* (Gollancz, London), p. 97.
209. For example, Anglesey, 1997, p. 91; Nichols, 1990, p. 147; Fox, C., 2000, *Battleground Europe: Monchy-le-Preux* (Leo Cooper, London), p. 42.
210. Brander, M., 1969, *The 10th Royal Hussars (Prince of Wales's Own)* (Leo Cooper, London), p. 97.
211. See for example Nichols, 1990, Fig. 19.
212. Fox, 2000, pp. 28–9.
213. Letter from Kavanagh to Allenby, 13 April 1917, contained in Cavalry Corps War Diary, April 1917, WO95/574.
214. Essex Yeomanry War Diary, 11 April 1917, WO 95/1156.
215. Quoted in Griffith, 1994, p. 79.
216. Third Army appreciation no. GS 1/15, 7 February 1917, Third Army file, WO158/223.
217. Whitmore, 1920, p. 100.
218. Ibid., p. 103.
219. 6th Cavalry Brigade War Diary, 11 April 1917, WO95/1152.
220. Letter from Kavanagh to Allenby, 13 April 1917, contained in Cavalry Corps War Diary, April 1917, WO95/574.
221. Telegram quoted in OH, 1917, vol. I, p. 259.
222. Letter of 10 April 1917, quoted in Gardner, B., 1965, *Allenby* (Cassell, London), p. 106.
223. OH, 1917, vol. I, p. 242.
224. Wynne, 1940, pp. 165ff.
225. Ibid., Sketch 13.
226. Spears, E.L., 1939, *Prelude to Victory* (Jonathan Cape, London), p. 432.
227. Ibid., p. 423.
228. 5th Cavalry Brigade War Diary, 11 April 1917, WO95/1138.
229. 2nd Cavalry Division ADVS War Diary, 11 April 1917, WO95/1122.
230. Quoted in Nicholls, 1990, p. 132.
231. 3rd Cavalry Division ADVS War Diary, April 1917, WO95/1145.
232. 2nd Cavalry Division ADVS War Diary, April 1917, WO95/1122.
233. 3rd Cavalry Division ADVS War Diary, April 1917, WO95/1145.
234. 5th Cavalry Brigade War Diary, 11 April 1917, WO95/1138.

235. 4th Cavalry Brigade War Diary, April 1917, WO95/1135.
236. 111th Brigade War Diary, 11 April 1917, WO95/2531.
237. Fox, 2000, p. 29.
238. Letter from R. Gordon-Canning, quoted in 'Notes: The Cavalry at Arras 1917', in *Cavalry Journal*, vol. XXII, 1932, p. 293.
239. OH, 1917, vol. I, p. 237.
240. Ibid.
241. Northamptonshire Yeomanry War Diary, 10 April 1917, WO95/792.

Chapter 4
1. Private papers of Major Hammond, letter to his wife of December 1917, Bovington Tank Museum Archive.
2. Woollcombe, R., 1967, *The First Tank Battle, Cambrai 1917* (Arthur Barker, London).
3. Cooper, B., 1967, *The Ironclads of Cambrai* (Pan Books, London).
4. Smithers, A.J., 1992, *Cambrai: the First Great Tank Battle, 1917* (Leo Cooper, London).
5. By Lieutenant Commander J. Wedgewood, MP for Newcastle-under-Lyme. Quoted in Moore, W., 1988, *A Wood Called Bourlon. The cover-up after Cambrai 1917* (Leo Cooper, London), p. 174.
6. Pitman, T.T., 1923, 'The part played by the British Cavalry in the surprise attack on Cambrai 1917', *Cavalry Journal*, vol. XIII, p. 235.
7. Miles, W. (ed.), 1948, *History of the Great War Based on Official Documents, Military Operations France and Belgium 1917* Vol III, 'The Battle of Cambrai' (HMSO, London).
8. Ibid., p. iv.
9. Woollcombe, 1967, pp. 126–39.
10. Smithers, 1992, p. 122.
11. Marquis of Anglesey, 1997.
12. Ibid., p. 100.
13. Terraine, 1963, p. 249.
14. Ibid., p. 297.
15. Ibid., p. 370.
16. Miles, 1948, pp. 4–5.
17. Cooper, 1967, p. 37.
18. Ibid., p. 54.
19. OH, 1917, vol. III, p. 6.
20. Ibid., p. 8.
21. Moore, 1988, p. 41.
22. Terraine, 1963, p. 379.
23. OH, 1917, vol. III, p. 9.
24. Charteris, 1931, pp. 267–8.
25. GHQ letter OAD 690, 3 November 1917, contained in Third Army War Diary, November 1917, WO95/367.
26. OH, 1917, vol. III, p. 18.
27. Third Army Plan, Operation 'GY', 13 November 1917, GS 56/68, para. 1., contained in Third Army War Diary, November 1917, WO95/367.
28. OH, 1917, vol. III, p. 19.
29. Ibid., p. 28.
30. 'Cavalry Corps Instructions for Operation GY', Cavalry Corps GX 272/39, 10 November 1917, contained in Cavalry Corps War Diary, November 1917, Appendix VII, WO95/574.
31. Pitman, 1923, p. 241.
32. Seely, 1930, p. 273.
33. 'Cavalry Corps Instructions for Operations GY', 10 November 1917, Appendix B, para. 6.
34. For details see OH, 1917, vol. III, pp. 50–64, or Woollcombe, 1967, pp. 68–81.
35. 'Narrative of Operations of 1st Cavalry Division, 20th to 27th November 1917', included in the 1st Cavalry Division War Diary, November 1917, Appendix 14, WO95/1097, p. 1.
36. 'Cavalry Corps report on operations commencing 20th Nov. 1917', contained in Cavalry Corps War Diary, November 1917, Appendix XXXII, WO95/574, p. 2.
37. 'Narrative of Operations of 1st Cavalry Division, 20th to 27th November 1917', p. 1.
38. Cavalry Corps War Diary, 20 November 1917, WO95/574.
39. Ibid.
40. For example Woollcombe, 1967, pp. 101–25.
41. IV Corps narrative of operations quoted in Woollcombe, 1967, p. 129.
42. Message form included in 'Lessons to be drawn from the Operations of the 1st Cavalry Division in the battle which began on November 20th 1917', report by Major General Mullens, 9 December 1917, WO158/429.

43. 'Note by IV Corps', in file with 'Lessons to be drawn from the Operations of the 1st Cavalry Division in the battle which began on November 20th 1917'.
44. Letter by Major General Mullens accompanying papers passed to Sir James Edmonds, 17 September 1945, WO95/1097.
45. Message form contained in the 1st Cavalry Division War Diary, 20 November 1917, WO95/1097.
46. 'Narrative of Operations of 2nd Cavalry Brigade on November 20th-21st 1917', contained in the 2nd Cavalry Brigade War Diary, November 1917, Appendix 16, WO95/1097.
47. Cavalry Corps War Diary, 20 November 1917, WO95/574.
48. 'Narrative of Operations of 1st Cavalry Division, 20th to 27th November, 1917', p. 1.
49. Ibid., p. 2.
50. 'Lessons to be drawn from the Operations of the 1st Cavalry Division in the battle which began on November 20th 1917', para. 4.
51. Ibid., 'Note by IV Corps', para. 4 (c).
52. Woollcombe, 1967, p. 133.
53. 'Lessons to be drawn from the Operations of the 1st Cavalry Division in the battle which began on November 20th 1917', message form attached to 'Note by IV Corps'.
54. Cavalry Corps War Diary, 20 November 1917, WO95/574.
55. 'Narrative of Operations of 2nd Cavalry Brigade on November 20th-21st 1917', p. 1.
56. 'Report on action of 4th Dragoon Guards, 20 November 1917', contained in 2nd Cavalry Brigade War Diary, November 1917, Appendix 16, WO95/1097.
57. Ibid.
58. Ibid., p. 2.
59. 2nd Cavalry Division Operations Order no. 34, 18 November 1917, contained in 2nd Cavalry Division War Diary, November 1917, WO95/1118.
60. 2nd Cavalry Division War Diary, 20 November 1917, WO95/1118.
61. OH, 1917, vol. III, pp. 62–4.
62. 1/1 Northumberland Hussars, III Corps Cavalry, War Diary, 20 November 1917, WO95/700.
63. Ibid.
64. Cavalry Corps War Diary, 20 November 1917, WO95/574.
65. Ibid.
66. OH, 1917, vol. III, p. 67.
67. Cavalry Corps War Diary, 20 November 1917, WO95/574.
68. 'Cavalry Corps report on operations commencing 20th Nov. 1917', contained in Cavalry Corps War Diary, November 1917, Appendix XXXII, WO95/574, p. 2.
69. Ibid., p. 3.
70. '5th Cavalry Division Summary of Operations, November 20th to 22nd', contained in the 5th Cavalry Division War Diary, November 1917, WO95/1162.
71. Secunderabad Cavalry Brigade War Diary, 20 November 1917, WO95/1162.
72. OH, 1917, vol. III, p. 74.
73. Lane's report forms Appendix B in '5th Cavalry Division Summary of Operations, November 20th to 22nd', op. cit.
74. '5th Cavalry Division Summary of Operations, November 20th to 22nd'.
75. For example Cooper, 1967, p. 112; Woollcombe, 1967, p. 84.
76. Cooper, 1967, p. 112.
77. Moore, 1988, p. 74.
78. Anon, quoted in Cooper, 1967, p. 113.
79. OH, 1917, vol. III, p. 68.
80. Fort Garry Horse War Diary, 20 November 1917, WO95/1084.
81. Private papers of Major Hammond, letter to his wife of December 1917, Bovington Tank Museum Archive.
82. Smithers, 1992, p. 116.
83. Contained in Fort Garry Horse War Diary, 20 November 1917, WO95/1084.
84. '2nd Cavalry Division – Narrative of Events from 20th November to 6th December 1917', contained in 2nd Cavalry Division War Diary, November 1917, WO95/1118.
85. Ibid.
86. Ibid.
87. Fort Garry Horse War Diary, 20 November 1917, WO95/1084.

88. Strachan, H., 1927, 'A squadron on its own', in *Cavalry Journal*, vol. XVII, pp. 240–51.

89. Cowen, W., 1928, 'Correspondence', in *Cavalry Journal*, vol. XVIII, pp. 470–7.

90. Figures from Strachan, 1927, p. 250.

91. Ibid., p. 241.

92. Ibid.

93. Ibid., p. 245.

94. Ibid., p. 251.

95. Cowen, 1928, p. 473.

96. 'Cavalry Corps report on operations commencing 20th Nov. 1917', p. 5.

97. For example Cooper, 1967, p. 119.

98. Seely, 1930, p. 275.

99. Moore, 1988, p. 76.

100. OH, 1917, vol. III, p. 70.

101. Ibid., p. 31.

102. 29th Division Order no. 167, 18 November 1917, contained in 29th Division War Diary, November 1917, WO95/2283.

103. Canadian Cavalry Brigade War Diary, 20 November 1917, WO95/1083.

104. 'Cavalry Corps report on operations commencing 20th Nov. 1917', p. 5.

105. Reminiscences of Private C. Knight, 2nd Dragoon Guards, quoted in Purdom, C.B. (ed.), 1930, *Everyman at War*, reprinted as *True World War I Stories. Sixty personal narratives of the war* (Robinson, London, 1999), pp. 159–66.

106. OH, 1917, vol. III, p. 108nn.

107. Cavalry Corps War Diary, 21 November 1917, WO95/574.

108. 'Narrative of operations of 1st Cavalry Division, 20th to 27th November, 1917', p. 2.

109. 'Action of 1st Cavalry Brigade, 20th–22nd November, 1917', included in 1st Cavalry Division War Diary, November 1917, Appendix 15, WO95/1097, p. 1.

110. OH, 1917, vol. III, p. 109.

111. What follows is drawn almost entirely from 'Action of 1st Cavalry Brigade, 20th–22nd November, 1917'.

112. OH, 1917, vol. III, p. 110.

113. Reminiscences of Private C. Knight, 2nd Dragoon Guards, quoted in Purdom, 1930, p. 162.

114. Ibid., p. 111.

115. 2nd Dragoon Guards War Diary, November 1917, WO95/1109.

116. Smithers, 1992, pp. 125–6.

117. For example De Pree, H., 1928, 'The Battle of Cambrai', *Journal of the Royal Artillery*, vol. LV, p. 224.

118. 'Action of 1st Cavalry Brigade, 20th–22nd November, 1917', p. 2.

119. OH, 1917, vol. III, pp. 174–5.

120. Ibid., p. 168.

121. Ibid., pp. 176–84.

122. 'Cavalry Corps Report on Operations between November 30th and December 6th 1917', contained in Cavalry Corps War Diary, December 1917, Appendix XVI–B, WO95/574.

123. Maunsell, E.B., 1926, 'The 4th and 5th Cavalry Divisions at the Battle of Epehy, November 30th to December 1st 1917', in *Cavalry Journal*, vol. XVI, p. 230.

124. Cavalry Corps War Diary, 30 November 1917, WO95/574.

125. Ibid.

126. Darling, 1922, p. 90.

127. OH, 1917, vol. III, pp. 189–90.

128. Ambala Cavalry Brigade War Diary, December 1917, Appendix A, WO95/1164.

129. Maunsell, 1926, p. 231.

130. Cavalry Corps War Diary, 30 November 1917, WO95/574.

131. Ambala Cavalry Brigade War Diary, December 1917, Appendix A, WO95/1164.

132. Ibid.

133. Rowcroft, C.H., 1923, 'The 9th Hodson's Horse at Cambrai 1917', *Cavalry Journal*, vol. XIII, p. 48.

134. Cavalry Corps War Diary, 30 November 1917, WO95/574.

135. Maunsell, Lieutenant Colonel, 'The Battle of Epehy', typescript contained in Cavalry Corps War Diary, December 1917, WO95/574.

136. 'Cavalry Corps Report on Operations between November 30th and December 6th 1917'.

137. Ambala Cavalry Brigade War Diary, December 1917, Appendix A, WO95/1164.

138. Cavalry Corps Order G 20, contained in Cavalry Corps War Diary, December 1917, Appendix X, WO95/574.

139. 'Cavalry Corps Report on Operations between November 30th and December 6th 1917'.
140. Maunsell, 1926, p. 237.
141. Ibid., p. 236.
142. Ibid., p. 243.
143. OH, 1917, vol. III, p. 239.
144. Rowcroft, 1923, p. 49.
145. Ambala Cavalry Brigade War Diary, December 1917, Appendix A, WO95/1164.
146. Seely, 1930, p. 285.
147. Message received by Cavalry Corps HQ at 5.15am, Cavalry Corps War Diary, December 1917, WO95/574, and received by Lucknow Brigade at 5.45am, Maunsell, 1926, p. 241.
148. Ibid., p. 241.
149. Ibid., p. 243.
150. Cavalry Corps Order G 20, contained in Cavalry Corps War Diary, December 1917, Appendix X, WO95/574.
151. OH, 1917, vol. III, p. 232.
152. 'Cavalry Corps Report on Operations between November 30th and December 6th 1917', p. 4.
153. Maunsell, 1926.
154. Letter of Brigadier General Haig to Colonel Maunsell, in Cavalry Corps War Diary, December 1917, WO95/574.
155. Letter of Major General Kennedy to Colonel Maunsell, in Cavalry Corps War Diary, December 1917, WO95/574.
156. Letter of Brigadier General Haig.
157. 'Operations carried out by the Mhow Cavalry Brigade on December 1st 1917', contained in Mhow Cavalry Brigade War Diary, December 1917, WO95/1160.
158. Anon, 1928, 'Operations carried out by the Mhow Cavalry Brigade on December 1st 1917', in *Cavalry Journal*, vol. XVIII, pp. 44–58.
159. Anon, 1928, 'The 2nd Lancers at Epehy', *Cavalry Journal*, vol. XVIII, pp. 566–8.
160. 'Operations carried out by the Mhow Cavalry Brigade on December 1st 1917', p. 4.
161. Anon, 1928, 'The 2nd Lancers at Epehy'.
162. Letter of 10 December 1917, quoted in Omissi, 1999, p. 339.
163. Maunsell, Typescript, para. 33, WO95/574.
164. Canadian Cavalry Brigade War Diary, 1 December 1917, WO95/1083.
165. Maunsell, 1926, p. 358.
166. 'Operations carried out by the Mhow Cavalry Brigade on December 1st 1917', contained in Mhow Cavalry Brigade War Diary, December 1917, WO95/1160, p. 7.
167. Ibid.
168. Canadian Cavalry Brigade War Diary, 1 December 1917, WO95/1083.
169. Maunsell, 1926, p. 360.
170. 'Operations carried out by the Mhow Cavalry Brigade on December 1st 1917', p. 7.
171. 'Cavalry Corps Report on Operations between November 30th and December 6th 1917', p. 7.
172. Summarised in Anglesey, 1997, p. 141nn.
173. Home, *Diary* (10 December 1917), in Briscoe, 1985, p. 159.
174. For example Woollcombe 1967, ch. 9 'The Failure of the Cavalry'.
175. Travers, 1992, p. 24.
176. Woollcombe, 1967, p. 136.
177. Quoted in Smithers, 1992, p. 122.
178. Baker-Carr, C.D., 1930, *From Chauffeur to Brigadier* (Ernest Benn, London), pp. 271–2.
179. 'Lessons to be drawn from the Operations of the 1st Cavalry Division in the battle which began on November 20th 1917', report by Major General Mullens, 9 December 1917, WO158/429.
180. 'Note by IV Corps', para. 4 (c).
181. Cavalry Corps War Diary, 20 November 1917, WO95/574.
182. Falls, C., 1922, *The History of the 36th (Ulster) Division* (Somme Assn. Facsimile edn, 1991, Belfast), p. 156.
183. Woollcombe, 1967, p. 136.
184. Badsey, 1981, p. 322.
185. Smithers, 1992, p. 118.
186. Anglesey, 1997, p. 158.
187. Ibid., p. 157.
188. Kavanagh C.M., manuscript note to General Mullens, 27 Feburary 1918, contained in 1st Cavalry Division War Diary, WO95/1097.
189. For example OH, 1917, vol. III, p. 282.
190. 'Narrative of Operations of 2nd Cavalry Brigade on November 20th–21st 1917', p. 1.

191. OH, 1917, vol. III p. 297.

192. Home, *Diary*, in Briscoe, 1985, p. 101.

193. Ibid., p. 120.

194. Simpson, A., 2001, 'The Operational Role of British Corps Command on the Western Front 1914–1918' (Unpub. UCL PhD thesis).

195. Simpson, A., 2004, 'British Corps Command on the Western Front, 1914–1918', in Sheffield, G. and Todman, D. (eds), *Command and Control on the Western Front, The British Army's Experience 1914–1918* (Spellmount, Staplehurst), pp. 97–118.

196. Simpson, 2001, p. 17.

197. Simpson, 2004, pp. 97–8.

198. *1914 Field Service Pocket Book* (HMSO), pp. 4–6.

199. Simpson, 2001, pp. 212–13.

200. Anglesey, 1997, p. 38.

201. 'Cavalry Corps Instructions for Operations GY', 10 November 1917, para. 8.

202. Pitman, 1923, p. 242.

203. Cavalry Corps War Diary, December 1917.

204. OH, 1917, vol. III, p. 54.

205. Hobart, P., 1935, 'Cambrai Battlefield Tour' (Unpub. typescript in Bovington Tank Museum Archive).

206. Tank Corps Special Order no. 6, 19 November 1917, contained in Tank Corps War Diary, November 1917, WO95/92.

207. 'Cavalry Corps Instructions for Operations GY, Appendix C', Cavalry Corps, GX 272/39, 10 November 1917, contained in Cavalry Corps War Diary, November 1917, Appendix VII, WO95/574.

208. Anglesey, 1997, pp. 113ff.

209. 'Third Army Instructions to Cavalry Corps', 13 November 1917, para. 5, contained in Third Army War Diary, November 1917, WO95/367.

210 'Report on Wire-Pulling Operations 20 November 1917', Bovington Tank Museum Archive.

211. 'Third Army Instructions to Cavalry Corps', 13 November 1917, para. 6, contained in Third Army War Diary, November 1917, WO95/367.

212. Maunsell, 1926, p. 135.

213. 'Lessons to be drawn from the Operations of the 1st Cavalry Division in the battle which began on November 20th 1917', report by Major General Mullens, 9 December 1917, WO158/429, para. 6.

214. Anglesey, 1997, pp. 113ff.

215. Baker-Carr, 1930, p. 271.

216. Travers, 1992, p. 23.

217. OH, 1917, vol. III, p. 289.

218. Travers, 1992, p. 23.

219. Quoted in Cooper, 1967, p. 173.

220. OH, 1917, vol. III, p. 28.

221. Maunsell, Typescript, WO95/574, para. 12.

222. Ambala Brigade War Diary, 1 December 1917, WO95/1164.

Chapter 5

1. Home, *Diary* (25 December 1917), in Briscoe, 1985, p. 160.

2. Terraine, 1963, p. 390.

3. Ibid., pp. 384–408; Edmonds, J.E. (ed.), 1935, *History of the Great War Based on Official Documents, Military Operations France and Belgium 1918* Vol. I, 'The German March offensive and its preliminaries' (Macmillan, London), chapters 1–4.

4. War Office letter to D. Haig, 12 May 1917, WO106/403.

5. Letter from Haig to War Office, 28 June 1917, WO106/403.

6. Messenger, C., 2005, *Call to Arms, The British Army 1914–18* (Weidenfeld & Nicholson, London), p. 195.

7. War Cabinet 293, Minute 17, December 1917, WO106/403.

8. Preston, T., 1932, 'The Cavalry in France March–April 1918', in *Cavalry Journal*, XXII, pp. 170–83, 326–41, 483–96; vol. XXIII, pp. 11–29, 161–78, 335–52, 500–16; vol. XXII, p. 171.

9. Ibid., vol. XXIII, p. 501.

10. Badsey, 1981, p. 333 and Appendix 2.

11. Anglesey, Marquis of, 1994, *A History of the British Cavalry*, vol. V, 'Egypt, Palestine and Syria 1914 to 1919' (Leo Cooper, London), p. 220.

12. Haig, Diary, 7 January 1918, p. 8, WO256/27.

13. This system is more fully described in Middlebrook, M., 1978, *The Kaiser's*

Battle, *21* March 1918, the first day of
the German Spring Offensive (Allen
Lane, London), pp. 74–82.

14. The impact of this is discussed in
Bryson, R., 1999, 'The Once and Future
Army', in Bond, B. (ed.), *'Look to your
Front'. Studies in the First World War by
the British Commission for Military History*
(Spellmount, Staplehurst), pp. 33–4.
15. Preston, 1932, vol. XXII, p. 173.
16. Ibid., vol. XXII, p. 174.
17. Ibid., vol. XXII, p. 178.
18. Ibid., vol. XXIII, p. 13.
19. Preston, 1932, provides an exhaustive
account of these actions.
20. 'Points brought to notice during recent
operations', 3rd Cavalry Division War
Diary, April 1918, WO95/1142.
21. Preston 1932, vol. XXIII, pp 502–16.
22. Ibid., vol. XXII, p. 488.
23. Ibid., vol. XXII, p. 180.
24. Ibid., vol. XXIII, p. 12.
25. Ibid., vol. XXII, p. 487.
26. Middlebrook, 1978, p. 105.
27. Ibid., p. 98.
28. Preston, 1932, vol. XXIII, p. 506.
29. Ibid.
30. Ibid., p. 500.
31. 'Narrative of operations carried out by
3rd Cavalry Division March 21st to
April 5th 1918', in 3rd Cavalry Division
War Diary, April 1918, WO95/1141.
32. Ibid., p. 3.
33. 'Action of 3rd Cavalry Division at
Villeselve', in 3rd Cavalry Division War
Diary, April 1918, Appendix III, WO95/
1141.
34. Albert Turp, quoted in Cusack, J. and
Herbert, I., 1972, *Scarlet Fever, A lifetime
with horses* (Cassell, London), p. 74.
35. Figures from 6th Cavalry Brigade War
Diary, March 1918, WO95/1152.
36. Preston, 1932, vol. XXII, p. 172.
37. Ibid., vol. XXIII, p. 177.
38. Pitman, 1923–24.
39. Preston, 1932, vol. XXII, p. 182.
40. Pitman, 1923–4, p. 362.
41. Anglesey, 1997, p. 203.
42. 'Narrative of Operations Canadian
Cavalry Brigade', in Canadian Cavalry
Brigade War Diary, April 1918, WO95/
1142.

43. Lord Strathcona's Horse War Diary,
30 March 1918, WO95/1085.
44. Seely, 1930, pp. 302–3.
45. Pitman, 1923–4, p. 364.
46. 'Narrative of Operations Canadian
Cavalry Brigade', in Canadian Cavalry
Brigade War Diary, April 1918, WO95/
1142.
47. Lord Strathcona's Horse War Diary,
30 March 1918, WO95/1085.
48. Von Falkenstein R., 1927, 'The attack
by Strathcona's Dragoons on the 2nd
Battalion, 101st Grenadiers on 30th
March 1918' (reprinted from *Militar-
Wochenblatt*, 11 February 1927), in translation with commentary as 'The two
sides of the wood', in *Cavalry Journal*,
vol. XVII, pp. 606–14, p. 608.
49. Seely, 1930, p. 303.
50. Lord Strathcona's Horse War Diary,
30 March 1918, WO95/1085.
51. Pitman, 1923–4, p. 364.
52. Lord Strathcona's Horse War Diary,
30 March 1918, WO95/1085.
53 'Operations 30th-31st March-1st April',
in 3rd Cavalry Brigade War Diary, April
1918, WO 95/1133.
54. 'Narrative of Operations Canadian
Cavalry Brigade', in Canadian Cavalry
Brigade War Diary, April 1918, WO95/
1142, p. 3.
55. Ibid.
56. Pitman, 1923–4, p. 62.
57. Ibid., p. 64.
58. Von Falkenstein, 1927, p. 606.
59. Home, *Diary* (25 March 1918), in Briscoe,
1985, p. 162.
60. Gough, 1931, p. 323.
61. Zabecki, D.T., 2006, *The German 1918
Offensives. A Case Study in the Operational Level of War* (Routledge, London),
p. 46.
62. Ibid., p. 88.
63. Ludendorff (no date), *My War Memories
1914–1918*, vol. I (Hutchinson, London),
p. 385.
64. Home, *Diary* (16 April 1918), in Briscoe,
1985, p. 168.
65. Preston, 1932, vol. XXIII, p. 177.
66. Charteris, 1931, p. 298.
67. Kavanagh, manuscript note to General
Mullens, 27 Feburary 1918, contained in

1st Cavalry Division War Diary, February 1918, WO95/1097.

68. Home, *Diary* (25 March 1918), in Briscoe, 1985, p. 162.

69. Edmonds, J.E. (ed.), 1947, *History of the Great War Based on Official Documents, Military Operations France and Belgium 1918*, vol. IV, '8th August-26th September, the Franco British Offensive' (HMSO, London), p. 1.

70. Ibid., pp. 2–3.

71. Ibid., p. 3.

72. Preston, T., 1934–6, 'The Cavalry in France August-November 1918', in *Cavalry Journal*, vol. XXIV, pp. 167–82, 338–58, 496–514; vol. XXV, pp. 7–27, 165–86, 332–51, 489–508; vol. XXVI, pp. 1–23, 170–83, 326–41, 483–96; vol. XXIV, p. 169.

73. Ibid., vol. XXIV, p. 170.

74. OH, 1918, vol. IV, pp. 16–24.

75. 'Fourth Army General Staff Instructions no. 32 (G), 31 July 1918', Fourth Army War Diary, August–September 1918, WO95/437.

76. OH, 1918, vol. IV, p. 28.

77. 'GHQ Operation Order of 5th August 1918, OAD 900/14', para. 2, Fourth Army War Diary, August–September 1918, WO95/437.

78. 'Fourth Army Operations Orders of 6 August 1918', Fourth Army War Diary, August–September 1918, WO95/437.

79. Home, *Diary* (8 August 1918), in Briscoe, 1985, p. 179.

80. Preston, 1934–6, vol. XXIV, p. 174.

81. Paterson, E., 1921, 'The Door Ajar', in *Cavalry Journal*, vol. XI, pp. 395–404, p. 397. Lieutenant Colonel Ewing Paterson is not to be confused with Brigadier General R.W. Paterson, commanding the Canadian Cavalry Brigade in the same division. Ewing Paterson also went on (as a brigadier general) to command the 6th Cavalry Brigade in October.

82. 'Canadian Cavalry Brigade Narrative of Operations – August 8th to August 11th 1918', in Canadian Cavalry Brigade War Diary, August 1918, WO95/1083.

83. 'Narrative and Diary of Operations of 3rd Cavalry Division from August 6th to August 11th 1918', contained in 3rd

Cavalry Division War Diary, August 1918, WO95/1142.

84. Preston, 1934–6, vol. XXIV, p. 174.

85. Ibid., p. 176.

86. Paterson, 1921, p. 402.

87. Ibid.

88. 'Narrative and Diary of Operations of 3rd Cavalry Division from August 6th to August 11th 1918', contained in 3rd Cavalry Division War Diary, August 1918, WO95/1142.

89. Paterson, 1921, p. 404.

90. Ibid.

91. 'Narrative and Diary of Operations of 3rd Cavalry Division from August 6th to August 11th 1918', contained in 3rd Cavalry Division War Diary, August 1918, WO95/1142.

92. Paterson, 1921, p. 404.

93. Preston, 1934–6, vol. XXIV, p. 338.

94. Ibid., p. 339.

95. 'Narrative of Operations, 1st Cavalry Division, 8th to 11th August 1918', contained in 1st Cavalry Division War Diary, August 1918, WO95/1097.

96. Carnock, Lord, 1932, *The History of the 15th The King's Hussars 1914–1922* (Naval & Military Press, Uckfield, reprint, no date), p. 186.

97. Preston, 1934–6, vol. XXIV, p. 345.

98. 'Narrative of Operations, 1st Cavalry Division, 8th to 11th August 1918', contained in 1st Cavalry Division War Diary, August 1918, pp. 2–3, WO95/1097.

99. Preston, 1934–6, vol. XXIV, p. 342.

100. 'Narrative of Operations, 1st Cavalry Division, 8th to 11th August 1918', contained in 1st Cavalry Division War Diary, August 1918, p. 2, WO95/1097.

101. Preston, 1934–6, vol. XXIV, p. 345.

102. Ibid., p. 348.

103. 'Fourth Army Operation Order no. 20/5G, 11 August 1918', para. 6, in Fourth Army War Diary, August 1918, WO95/437.

104. Haig, Diary, 13 August 1918, p. 30, WO256/34.

105. Preston, 1934–6, vol. XXIV, p. 356.

106. OH, 1918, vol. IV, p. 154.

107. Preston, 1934–6, vol. XXIV, p. 344.

108. Harris J.P., with Barr, N., 1998, *Amiens to the Armistice, The BEF in the Hundred*

Days' Campaign, 8th August to 11th November 1918* (Brassey's, London), p. 98.

109. Preston, 1934–6, vol. XXIV, p. 358.
110. OH, 1918, vol. IV, p. 160.
111. Preston, 1934–6, vol. XXIV, p. 357.
112. OH, 1918, vol. IV, p. 156.
113. McWilliams, J. and Steel, R., 2001, *Amiens: Dawn of Victory* (Dundurn Press, Toronto), p. 196.
114. Schreiber, S.B., 1997, *Shock Army of the British Empire, The Canadian Corps in the Last 100 Days of the Great War* (Praeger, Connecticut), p. 49.
115. Ibid., p. 57.
116. McWilliams and Steel, 2001, p. 196.
117. Prior and Wilson, 1992, p. 309.
118. McWilliams and Steel, 2001, p. 196.
119. Anglesey, 1997, p. 235.
120. Home, *Diary* (12 August 1918), in Briscoe, 1985, p. 180.
121. Anon, 1919, *The War History of the 6th Tank Battalion* (Private printing, reprinted by Naval & Military Press, undated), pp. 132–3.
122. Paterson, 1921, p. 404.
123. Lord Strathcona's Horse War Diary, 8 August 1918, WO95/1085.
124. 'Canadian Cavalry Brigade Narrative of Operations – August 8th to August 11th 1918', in Canadian Cavalry Brigade War Diary, August 1918, WO95/1083.
125. Report of Major Rycroft, B Company, 6th Tank Battalion, quoted in Fletcher, D., 1994, *Tanks and Trenches. First-hand accounts of tank warfare in the First World War* (Alan Sutton, Stroud), p. 142.
126. 'Notes on recent operations No. 6', Cavalry Corps GX 444/11, 24 August 1918, para. 8, Cavalry Corps War Diary, August 1918, WO95/575.
127. Ibid.
128. Travers, T., 1992, *How the War was Won. Command and Technology in the British Army on the Western Front 1917–1918* (Routledge, London), p. 175.
129. 'Instructions for the Amiens battle', Cavalry Corps GX 438/9, Cavalry Corps War Diary, August 1918, WO95/575.
130. Hobart, 1935, p. 40.
131. Anon, 1919, p. 132.

132. Maurice, F., 1919, *The Tank Corps Book of Honour* (Spottiswoode, Ballantyne & Co. London), p. 73.
133. OH, 1918, vol. IV, p. 12 and Appendix V.
134. 'British Military Policy 1918–19', CIGS, 25 July 1918, para. 56 (D), reproduced in OH, 1918, vol. IV, Appendix V, p. 545.
135. Home, *Diary* (11 August 1918), in Briscoe, 1985, p. 180.
136. Keith-Falconer, A., undated, *The Oxfordshire Hussars in the Great War (1914–1918)* (John Murray, London; Naval & Military Press Facsimile), p. 309.
137. Haig, Diary, 1 September 1918, p. 2, WO256/36.
138. Preston, 1934–6.
139. Ibid., vol. XXV, p. 10.
140. Haig, Diary, 25 August 1918, p. 61, WO256/35.
141. Preston, 1934–6, vol. XXVI, p. 19.
142. Haig, 'Memorandum to Cavalry Corps, 6 September 1918', contained in Cavalry Corps War Diary, September 1918, WO95/575.
143. 'Scheme of 17th September, Narrative of Operations' and notes by C. in C., in Cavalry Corps War Diary, September 1918, WO95/575.
144. Home, *Diary* (18 September 1918), in Briscoe, 1985, p. 183.
145. Edmonds, 1945, p. viii.
146. Sheffield, 2001, p. 202.
147. Ibid., p. 207.
148. See for example, Simpkins, P., 1996, 'The war experience of a typical Kitchener division: the 18th Division, 1914–1918', in Cecil, H. and Liddle, P. (eds), *Facing Armageddon – The First World War Experienced* (Leo Cooper, London), pp. 297–315.
149. Kavanagh to Haig, 14 February 1919, 'Cavalry in Modern War', contained in Cavalry Corps War Diary, WO95/575, pp. 1 and 4.
150. Haig, Diary, 5 November 1918, quoted in Sheffield, G. and Bourne, J., 2005, *Douglas Haig War Diaries and Letters 1914–1918* (Weidenfeld & Nicholson, London), p. 485.
151. Griffith, 1994, p. 161.
152. Preston, 1934–6, vol. XXIV, p. 176.

153. Ibid., p. 509.

154. Whitmore, F.H.D.C., 'Drocourt–Queant Line 2 September 1918', in *Cavalry Journal*, vol. XV, pp. 171–6.

155. Ibid., p. 174.

156. This is discussed in more detail in Harris, 1998, pp. 289–90.

157. Travers, 1992, p. 175.

158. Sheffield, G., pers. comm.

159. Coop, J.O., undated, *The Story of the 55th (West Lancashire) Division* (Daily Post Printers, Liverpool, Naval & Military Press Facsimile), p. 136.

160. Ibid., pp. 137–8.

161. Preston, 1934–6.

162. Keith-Falconer, undated, ch. X.

163. Griffith, 1994, pp. 166–8.

164. See Harris, 1998, pp. 218–36 for a summary of these operations.

165. Preston, 1934–6, vol. XXIV, p. 496.

166. Ibid., vol. XXV, p. 18.

167. 'Cavalry Corps Narrative of Operations 8th to 10th October 1918', in Cavalry Corps War Diary, October 1918, p. 1, WO95/575.

168. Ibid., p. 2.

169. Carnock, 1932, p. 198.

170. 'Cavalry Corps Narrative of Operations 8th to 10th October 1918', in Cavalry Corps War Diary, October 1918, p. 2, WO95/575.

171. Carnock, 1932, p. 200.

172. Quoted in Mallinson, A., 1993, *Light Dragoons, the Origins of a New Regiment* (Leo Cooper, London), p. 206.

173. Carnock, 1932, p. 200.

174. 'Cavalry Corps Narrative of Operations 8th to 10th October 1918', in Cavalry Corps War Diary, October 1918, p. 3, WO95/575.

175. Preston, 1934–6, vol. XXV, p. 26.

176. Ibid.

177. 'Cavalry Corps Narrative of Operations 8th to 10th October 1918', in Cavalry Corps War Diary, October 1918, p. 3, WO95/575.

178. Preston, 1934–6, vol. XXV, p. 165.

179. 'Cavalry Corps Narrative of Operations 8th to 10th October 1918', in Cavalry Corps War Diary, October 1918, p. 4, WO95/575.

180. '3rd Cavalry Division Narrative of Operations Oct. 8th -11th 1918', in 3rd Cavalry Division War Diary, October 1918, p. 2, WO95/1142.

181. 'Narrative of Operations Fort Garry Horse, 9-10-18', in Fort Garry Horse War Diary, October 1918, WO95/1084.

182. 'Canadian Cavalry Brigade, Narrative of Operations for period 8th-9th-10th October 1918', in Canadian Cavalry Brigade War Diary, October 1918, WO95/1083.

183. 'Narrative of Operations Lord Strathcona's Horse (RC), 9/10/18', in Lord Strathcona's Horse War Diary, October 1918, WO95/1085.

184. Preston, 1934–6, vol. XXV, p. 167.

185. 'Cavalry Corps Narrative of Operations 8th to 10th October 1918', in Cavalry Corps War Diary, October 1918, p. 4, WO95/575.

186. Preston, 1934–6, vol. XXV, p. 167.

187. 'Canadian Cavalry Brigade, Narrative of Operations for period 8th-9th-10th October 1918', in Canadian Cavalry Brigade War Diary, October 1918, WO95/1083.

188. Ibid., p. 3.

189. '3rd Cavalry Division Narrative of Operations Oct. 8th-11th 1918', in 3rd Cavalry Division War Diary, October 1918, p. 4, WO95/1142.

190. 'Canadian Cavalry Brigade, Narrative of Operations for period 8th-9th-10th October 1918', in Canadian Cavalry Brigade War Diary, October 1918, WO95/1083.

191. '3rd Cavalry Division Narrative of Operations Oct. 8th -11th 1918', in 3rd Cavalry Division War Diary, October 1918, p. 4, WO95/1142.

192. 'Canadian Cavalry Brigade, Narrative of Operations for period 8th-9th-10th October 1918', in Canadian Cavalry Brigade War Diary, October 1918, p. 4, WO95/1083.

193. 'Cavalry Corps Narrative of Operations 8th to 10th October 1918', in Cavalry Corps War Diary, October 1918, p. 5, WO95/575.

194. Preston, 1934–6, vol. XXV, p. 181.

195. 'Canadian Cavalry Brigade, Narrative of Operations for period 8th-9th-10th October 1918', in Canadian Cavalry Brigade War Diary, October 1918, p. 5, WO95/1083.
196. OH, 1918, vol. V, p. 235.
197. Harris, 1998, p. 46.
198. A concept outlined in Badsey, 1996, p. 163.
199. 'Cavalry Corps Narrative of Operations 8th to 10th October 1918', in Cavalry Corps War Diary, October 1918, p. 6, WO95/575.
200. Harris, 1998, p. 240.
201. Ibid.
202. OH, 1918, vol. V, p. 212.
203. Preston, 1934–6, vol. XXVI, p. 19.
204. War Office, undated, *Statistics of the Military Effort of the British Empire during the Great War* (HMSO, Naval & Military Press reprint, Heathfield).

Chapter 6

1. Home, *Diary*, in Briscoe, 1985, p. 190.
2. Badsey, 1981, p. 359.
3. Taylor, 1963, p. 140.
4. Prior, R. and Wilson, T., 2005, *The Somme* (Yale University Press, London), p. 134.

5. 'Training of Cavalry Corps in order to be able to exploit success after next great battle', letter from D. Haig to C. Kavanagh and I. Maxse, 6 September 1918, in Cavalry Corps War Diary, September 1918, WO95/575.
6. 'Extract from Notes of the Conference of Army Commanders held by the General, Commanding-in-Chief, at First Army Headquarters, AIRE at 11a.m. on the 18th March 1916', in Cavalry Corps War Diary, September 1918, WO95/575.
7. GHQ OAD 121, 24 August 1916, contained in Cavalry Corps War Diary, WO95/575.
8. Ibid., p. 2.
9. Ibid.
10. Falls, 1940, p. 181.
11. Home, *Diary* (1 September 1916), in Briscoe, 1985, p. 119.
12. Lloyd, 1938, p. 100.
13. Hobart, 1935, p. 29.
14. See Harris, with Barr, 1998, p. 297.
15. Carnock, 1932, p. 206.
16. Anglesey, 1997, p. 282.
17. Lloyd, 1938, p. 315.

Bibliography and Sources

Primary Sources

The principal source of primary material for this study was that contained in the unit war diaries and other documents held at the National Archives, Kew. These items are referenced by their NA box number, mostly originating in the WO95/ series.

War Cabinet papers WO106/403
D. Haig, Diary WO256/5, 9, 11, 27, 34, 36
First Army General Staff WO95/158
Third Army General Staff WO158/223; WO95/361, 367
Fourth Army General Staff WO158/233, 234, 235, 236; WO95/437
Fifth Army General Staff WO158/249
Cavalry Corps WO95/573, 574, 575, 581
XIII Corps WO95/895
1st Cavalry Division WO95/1096, 1097, 1102, 1108, 1109, 1113
2nd Cavalry Division WO95/1118, 1122, 1133, 1135, 1138, 1140
3rd Cavalry Division WO95/1085, 1141, 1142, 1145, 1146, 1152, 1153, 1156
1st Indian (4th Cavalry) Division WO95/1160, 1164, 1167
2nd Indian (5th cavalry) Division WO95/1083, 1084, 1163, 1152, 1180, 1182, 1187, 1188
Corps Cavalry Regiments WO 95/700, 737, 792, 930
Infantry units WO 95/1377, 1667, 2283, 2531

Additional material was also obtained from the archives of the Tank Museum, Bovington:
Hammond, P. (Major) Private papers
Hobart, P., 1935, 'Cambrai Battlefield Tour' (Unpub. typescript)
'Report on Wire-Pulling Operations. 20 November 1917' (Unpub. typescript)

Official Histories

The following volumes of the Official History of the War were consulted, these are referenced throughout as 'OH, Year, vol. no.'
Edmonds, J.E. (ed.), 1925, *History of the Great War Based on Official Documents, Military Operations France and Belgium 1914* Vol. I: 'Mons, the retreat to the Seine, the Marne and the Aisne, August–October 1914' (Macmillan, London)
Edmonds, J.E. (ed.), 1932, *History of the Great War Based on Official Documents, Military Operations France and Belgium 1916* Vol. I: 'Sir Douglas Haig's command to the 1st July: The Battle of the Somme' (Macmillan, London)
Edmonds, J.E. (ed.), 1935, *History of the Great War Based on Official Documents, Military Operations France and Belgium 1918* Vol. I: 'The German March offensive and its preliminaries' (Macmillan, London)

Edmonds, J.E. (ed.), 1936, *History of the Great War Based on Official Documents, Military Operations France and Belgium 1915* Vol. II: 'Battles of Aubers Ridge, Festubert and Loos' (Macmillan, London)

Edmonds, J.E. (ed.), 1937, *History of the Great War Based on Official Documents, Military Operations France and Belgium 1916* Vol. II: 'March–April: continuation of the German Offensive' (Macmillan, London)

Edmonds J.E. (ed.), 1945, *History of the Great War Based on Official Documents, Military Operations France and Belgium 1918* Vol. V: '26th September–11th November, The advance to Victory' (HMSO, London)

Edmonds J.E. (ed.), 1947, *History of the Great War Based on Official Documents, Military Operations France and Belgium 1918* Vol. IV: '8th August–26th September, the Franco-British Offensive' (HMSO, London)

Edmonds, J.E. (ed.), 1948, *History of the Great War Based on Official Documents, Military Operations France and Belgium 1917* Vol. II: '7th June to 10th November Messines and Third Ypres (Passchendaele)' (HMSO, London)

Falls, C. (ed.), 1940, *History of the Great War Based on Official Documents, Military Operations France and Belgium 1917* Vol. I: 'The German retreat to the Hindenburg Line and the Battles of Arras' (Macmillan, London)

Miles, W. (ed.), 1938, *History of the Great War Based on Official Documents, Military Operations France and Belgium 1916* Vol. II: '2nd July 1916 to the End of the Battles of the Somme' (Macmillan, London)

Miles, W. (ed.), 1948, *History of the Great War Based on Official Documents, Military Operations France and Belgium 1917* Vol. III: 'The Battle of Cambrai' (HMSO, London)

Other Official Publications

Becke, A.F. (ed.), 1935, *Order of Battle of Divisions Part 1: The Regular British Divisions* (HMSO, London)

Becke, A.F. (ed.), 1945, *Order of Battle Part 4: The Army Council, GHQs, Armies and Corps* (HMSO, London)

1914, *Field Service Pocket Book* (HMSO)

1912, *Cavalry Training* (HMSO)

Jones, H.A., 1928, *Official History of the War; The War in the Air – Being the story of the part played in the Great War by the Royal Air Force* Vol. II (Clarendon Press, Oxford)

War Office (undated), *Statistics of the Military Effort of the British Empire during the Great War* (HMSO, Naval & Military Press reprint, Heathfield)

Cavalry Journal

The *Cavalry Journal* resumed printing in 1919 and continued until the outbreak of the Second World War. During those years a substantial body of material concerning operations on the Western Front was published, much of it eye-witness accounts by participants. Thus many of these articles may be considered published *primary* sources.

Anon, 1928, 'Operations carried out by the Mhow Cavalry Brigade on December 1st 1917', vol. XVIII, pp. 44–58

Anon, 1928, 'The 2nd Lancers at Epehy', vol. XVIII, pp. 566–8

Cowen, W. (Captain), 1928, 'Correspondence', vol. XVIII, pp. 470–7

Fuller, J., 1920, 'The Influence of Tanks on Cavalry Tactics', vol. X, p. 127

Howard-Vyse, R.G.H., 1921, 'The Fifth Cavalry Brigade at Cerizy August 28th 1914', vol. XI

Maunsell, E.B. (Colonel), 1926, 'The 4th and 5th Cavalry Divisions at the Battle of Epehy, November 30th to December 1st 1917', vol. XVI, pp. 129–244, 351–63

Paterson E., 1921, 'The Door Ajar', vol. XI, pp. 395–404

Pitman, T.T. (Major General), 1923, 'The part played by the British Cavalry in the surprise attack on Cambrai 1917', vol. XIII, pp. 235–59

Pitman, T.T. (Major General), 1923–24, 'The operations of the Second Cavalry Division (with the Canadian Cavalry Brigade attached) in the defence of Amiens, March 30-April 1, 1918', vol. XIII, pp. 360–71 and vol. XIV, pp. 48–64

Preston, T., 1920–23, 'The Machine Gun Corps (Cavalry) in France 1916–1918', vol. X–XIII

Preston, T., 1931, 'The Cavalry at Arras 1917', vol. XXI, pp. 521–42

Preston, T., 1932, 'The Cavalry in France March–April 1918', vol. XXII, pp. 170–83, 326–41, 483–96; vol. XXIII, pp. 11–29, 161–78, 335–52, 500–16

Preston, T., 1934–6, 'The Cavalry in France August–November 1918', vol. XXIV, pp. 167–82, 338–58, 496–514; vol. XXV, pp. 7–27, 165–86, 332–51, 489–508; vol. XXVI, pp. 1–23

Preston, T., 1937, 'The Third Cavalry Division at Loos', vol. XXVII, pp. 17–30

Rowcroft, C.H., 1923, 'The 9th Hodson's Horse at Cambrai 1917', vol. XIII, pp. 47–50

Strachan, H. (Major), 1927, 'A squadron on its own', vol. XVII, pp. 240–51

Von Falkenstein, R., 1927, 'The attack by Strathcona's Dragoons on the 2nd Battalion, 101st Grenadiers on 30th March 1918' (reprinted from *Militar-Wochenblatt*, 11 February 1927), in translation with commentary as 'The two sides of the wood', vol. XVII, pp. 606–14

Whitmore, F.H.D.C. (Lieutenant Colonel), 'Drocourt–Quèant Line 2 September 1918', vol. XV, pp. 171–6

Unpublished University Theses

Badsey, S., 1981, 'Fire and the Sword: The British Cavalry and the Arme Blanche Controversy 1871–1921' (Unpub. Cambridge University PhD Thesis)

Simpson, A., 2001, 'The Operational Role of British Corps Command on the Western Front 1914–1918' (Unpub. University College London PhD Thesis)

Other Published Works

Anglesey, Marquis of, 1994, *A History of the British Cavalry*, vol. V, 'Egypt, Palestine and Syria 1914 to 1919' (Leo Cooper, London)

Anglesey, Marquis of, 1996, *A History of the British Cavalry 1816–1919*, vol. VII, The Curragh Incident and the Western Front 1914 (Leo Cooper, London)

Anglesey, Marquis of, 1997, *A History of the British Cavalry*, vol. VIII, 'The Western Front 1915–1918; Epilogue 1919–1939' (Leo Cooper, London)

Anon, 1919, *The War History of the 6th Tank Battalion* (Private printing, reprinted by Naval & Military Press, Uckfield)

Badsey, S., 1996, 'Cavalry and the Development of the Breakthrough Doctrine', in Griffith, P. (ed.), *British Fighting Methods in the Great War* (Frank Cass, London)

Badsey, S., 2008, *Doctrine and Reform in the British Cavalry 1880–1918* (Birmingham University)

Baker-Carr, C.D., 1930, *From Chauffeur to Brigadier* (Ernest Benn, London)

Brander, M., 1969, *The 10th Royal Hussars (Prince of Wales's Own)* (Leo Cooper, London)

Bridges, T. (Lieutenant General), 1938, *Alarms and Excursions, Reminiscences of a Soldier* (Longmans, London), pp. 80–1

Brown, I.M., 1998, *British Logistics on the Western Front 1914–1919* (Praeger, Connecticut)

Bryson, R., 1999, 'The Once and Future Army', in Bond, B. (ed.), *'Look to your Front'. Studies in the First World War by the British Commission for Military History* (Spellmount, Staplehurst)

Carnock, Lord, 1932, *The History of the 15th The King's Hussars 1914–1922* (Naval & Military Press, Uckfield)

Carton de Wiart, A., 1950, *Happy Odyssey* (Jonathan Cape, London),

Charteris, J. (Brigadier General), 1931. *At GHQ* (Cassell, London)

Coop, J.O., undated, *The Story of the 55th (West Lancashire) Division* (Daily Post Printers, Liverpool, Naval & Military Press Facsimile)

Cooper, B., 1967, *The Ironclads of Cambrai* (Pan Books, London)

Corrigan, G., 2003, *Mud, Blood and Poppycock. Britain and the First World War* (Cassell, London)

Corrigan, G., 2006, *Loos 1915, The Unwanted Battle* (Spellmount, Stroud)

Cusack, J. and Herbert, I., 1972, *Scarlet Fever. A lifetime with horses* (Cassell, London)

Darling, J.C. (Major), 1922, *The 20th Hussars in the Great War* (Private Pub., Lyndhurst, Hants)

De Pree, H. (Major General), 1928, 'The Battle of Cambrai', in *Journal of the Royal Artillery*, vol. LV

Falls, C., 1922, *The History of the 36th (Ulster) Division* (Somme Assn. Facsimile, Belfast, 1991)

Fletcher, D., 1994, *Tanks and Trenches. First hand accounts of tank warfare in the First World War* (Alan Sutton, Stroud)

Fox, C., 2000, *Battleground Europe, Monchy-le-Preux* (Leo Cooper, London)

Gardner, B., 1965, *Allenby* (Cassell, London)

Gough, H. (General Sir), 1931, *The Fifth Army* (Hodder & Stoughton, London)

Griffith, P., 1994, *Battle Tactics on the Western Front, The British Army's Art of Attack 1916–18* (Yale University Press, London)

Harris, J., 1996, 'The Rise of Armour', in Griffith (ed.), *British Fighting Methods in the Great War* (Frank Cass, London)

Harris J.P., with Barr, N., 1998, *Amiens to the Armistice. The BEF in the Hundred Days' Campaign, 8th August to 11th November 1918* (Brassey's, London)

Hart, P., 2005, *The Somme* (Cassell, London)

Heathcote, T.A., 1999, *British Field Marshals, 1736–1997, a Biographical Dictionary* (Leo Cooper, London)

Holmes, R., 1995, *Riding the Retreat, Mons to the Marne Revisited* (Jonathan Cape, London)

Holmes, R., 1996, 'The Last Hurrah: Cavalry on the Western Front, August–September 1914', in Cecil, H. and Liddle, P. (eds), *Facing Armageddon – The First World War Experienced* (Leo Cooper, London), pp. 278–94

Holmes, R., 2004, *Tommy, The British Soldier on the Western Front 1914–1918* (HarperCollins, London)

Home, A. (Brigadier General Sir), *Diary*, pub. Briscoe, D. (ed.), *Diary of a World War I Cavalry Officer* (Costello, Tunbridge Wells, 1985)

Horne, A., 1996, *How far from Austerlitz? Napoleon 1805–1815* (Macmillan, London, 1997)

Hudson, H. (General Sir), 1937, *History of the 19th King George's Own Lancers 1858–1921* (Gale & Polden, Aldershot)

James, L., 1993, *Imperial Warrior, The Life and Times of Field Marshal Viscount Allenby 1861–1936* (Weidenfeld & Nicholson, London)

Johnson, J.H., 1994, *Breakthrough! Tactics, Technology and the Search for Victory on the Western Front in World War I* (Praesidio, Novato Ca.)

Johnson J.H., 1995, *Stalemate! The Great Trench Warfare Battles of 1915–17* (A. & A.P., London)

Keegan, J., 1976, *The Face of Battle* (Viking, New York)

Keith-Falconer, A., undated, *The Oxfordshire Hussars in the Great War (1914–1918)* (John Murray, London, Naval & Military Press Facsimile)

Liddell Hart, B.H., 1930, *The Real War* (Faber & Faber, London)

Liddle, P., 1992, *The 1916 Battle of the Somme – A Reappraisal* (Wordsworth, London, 2001)

Lloyd, R.A., 1938, *Trooper in the Tins,* reprinted as *Troop Horse and Trench, The Experiences of a British Lifeguardsman of the Household Cavalry Fighting on the Western Front during the First World War 1914–1918* (Leonaur, London, 2006)

Ludendorff, undated, *My War Memories 1914–1918,* vol. I (Hutchinson, London)

Macdonald, L., 1983, *Somme* (Michael Joseph, London)

Mallinson, A., 1993, *Light Dragoons, the Origins of a New Regiment* (Leo Cooper, London)

Maurice, F., 1919, *The Tank Corps Book of Honour* (Spottiswoode, Ballantyne & Co., London)

McWilliams, J. and Steel, R., 2001, *Amiens Dawn of Victory* (Dundurn Press, Toronto)

Messenger, C., 2005, *Call to Arms, The British Army 1914–18* (Weidenfeld & Nicholson, London)

Middlebrook, M., 1971, *The First Day on the Somme, 1 July 1916* (Allen Lane, London)

Middlebrook, M., 1978, *The Kaiser's Battle, 21 March 1918, the first day of the German Spring Offensive* (Allen Lane, London)

Moore, W., 1988, *A Wood Called Bourlon, The cover-up after Cambrai 1917* (Leo Cooper, London)

Morris, D., 1965, *The Washing of the Spears, The Rise and Fall of the Great Zulu Nation* (Sphere, London, 1990)

Neillands, R., 1998, *The Great War Generals on the Western Front 1914–18* (Robinson, London)

Neillands, R., 2001, *Attrition, The Great War on the Western Front 1916* (Robinson, London)

Nicholls, J., 1990, *Cheerful Sacrifice, The Battle of Arras 1917* (Leo Cooper, London)

Norman, T., 1984, *The Hell they called High Wood – The Somme 1916* (Patrick Stephens, Wellingborough)

Omissi, D., 1999, *Indian Voices of the Great War – Soldiers' Letters 1914–18* (Macmillan, London)

Phillips, G., 2002, 'The obsolescence of the *Arme Blanche* and Technological Determinism in British Military History', in *War in History,* vol. 9(1), pp. 39–59

Prior, R. and Wilson, T., 1992, *Command on the Western Front, The Military Career of Sir Henry Rawlinson 1914–1918* (Blackwell, Oxford)

Prior, R. and Wilson, T., 2005 *The Somme* (Yale University Press, London)

Purdom, C.B. (ed.), 1930, *Everyman at War,* reprinted as *True World War I stories, Sixty personal narratives of the war* (Robinson, London, 1999)

Sandhu, G., 1981, *The Indian Cavalry* (Vision Books, New Delhi)

Sandhu, G., 1991, *I Serve – Saga of the Eighteenth Cavalry* (Lancer, New Delhi)

Schreiber, S.B., 1997, *Shock Army of the British Empire, The Canadian Corps in the Last 100 Days of the Great War* (Praeger, Connecticut)

Seely, J., 1930, *Adventure* (Heinemann, London)

Seton, G., 1931, *Footslogger, An Autobiography* (Hutchinson, London)

Sheffield, G., 2001, *Forgotten Victory, the First World War: Myths and Realities* (Headline, London)

Sheffield, G., 2003, *The Somme* (Cassell, London)

Sheffield, G. and Bourne, J., 2005, *Douglas Haig War Diaries and Letters 1914–1918* (Weidenfeld & Nicholson, London)

Simpkins, P., 1996, 'The war experience of a typical Kitchener division: the 18th Division, 1914–1918', in Cecil, H. and Liddle, P. (eds), *Facing Armageddon – The First World War Experienced* (Leo Cooper, London), pp. 297–315

Simpson, A., 2004, 'British Corps Command on the Western Front, 1914–1918', in Sheffield, G. and Todman, D. (eds), *Command and Control on the Western Front, The British Army's Experience 1914–1918* (Spellmount, Staplehurst), pp. 97–118

Smithers, A.J., 1992, *Cambrai: the First Great Tank Battle 1917* (Leo Cooper, London)

Spears, E.L. (Brigadier General), 1939, *Prelude to Victory* (Jonathan Cape, London)

Stewart, P.F., 1950, *The History of the XII Royal Lancers (Princess of Wales's)* (Oxford University Press, London)

Taylor, A.J.P., 1963, *The First World War, An Illustrated History* (Penguin, London, 1966)

Tennant, E., 1939, *The Royal Deccan Horse in the Great War* (Gale & Polden, Aldershot)

Terraine, J., 1960, *Mons, The Retreat to Victory* (Pan Books edition, London, 1972)

Terraine, J., 1963, *Douglas Haig, The Educated Soldier* (Cassell, London, 2000)

Terraine, J., 1964, *General Jack's Diary – War on the Western Front 1914–1918* (Cassell, London, 2000)

Terraine, J., 1978, *To Win a War – 1918 The Year of Victory* (Cassell, London, 2000)

Terraine, J., 1980, *The Smoke and the Fire, Myths and Anti-myths of War 1861–1945* (Sidgwick & Jackson, London)

Terraine, J., 1982, *White Heat: The New Warfare 1914–18* (Sidgwick & Jackson, London)

Thomas, A., 1968, *A Life Apart* (Gollancz, London)

Travers, T., 1987, 1990, *The Killing Ground: The British Army, the Western Front and the Emergence of Modern Warfare 1900–1918* (Allen & Unwin, London)

Travers, T., 1992, *How the War was Won, Command and Technology in the British Army on the Western Front, 1917–1918* (Routledge, London)

Tylden, G., 1965, *Horses and Saddlery* (J.A. Allen & Co., London)

Vandiver, F., 1997, 'Field Marshal Sir Douglas Haig and Passchendaele', in Liddle, P. (ed.), *Passchendaele in Perspective: The Third Battle of Ypres* (Leo Cooper, London)

Van Emden, R. ed.), 1996, *Tickled to death to go, Memoirs of a cavalryman in the First World War* (Spellmount, Staplehurst)

Wavell, A., 1946, *Allenby Soldier and Statesman* (Harrap, London)

Whitmore, F. (Lieutenant Colonel), 1920, *The 10th P.W.O. Royal Hussars and the Essex Yeomanry during the European War 1914–1918* (Benham & Co., Colchester)

Winter, D., 1978, *Death's Men, Soldiers of the Great War* (Penguin, London)

Woollcombe, R., 1967, *The First Tank Battle, Cambrai 1917* (Arthur Barker, London)

Wolff, L., 1958, *In Flanders Fields* (Longman's, London, 1960)

Wynne, G.C. (Captain), 1940, *If Germany Attacks, The Battle in Depth in the West* (Faber, London)

Zabecki, D.T., 2006, *The German 1918 Offensives, A Case Study in the Operational Level of War* (Routledge, London)

Index

Bullecourt 104, 107, 117, 240
Busigny 158, 222, 226
Buxton, Major (Essex Yeo.) 115
Byng, General Julian (Third Army) 4, 22, 86, 135, 136, 137, 143, 188, 218, 238, 239

Cabinet, War 186, 188
Caix 205
Cambrai 94, 108, 111, 114, 115, 116, 117, 137, 145, 146, 152, 158, 159, 219, 222
Cambrai, battle of (1917) 5, 9, 13, 15, 37, 87, 130, 133–184, 185, 194, 199, 200, 202, 204, 211, 214, 218, 231, 233, 234, 236, 238, 239, 240, 241, 242, 243, 244
Campbell, Captain (Ft Garry Hse) 151, 152
Campbell, Lieutenant Colonel (9L) 25, 26, 27, 28
Canadian Army,
    Canadian Light Horse 215, 219
    Fort Garry Horse 43, 60, 68, 96, 98, 99, 100, 150, 151, 174, 197, 204, 225, 226, 227
    Lord Strathcona's Horse 96, 97, 98, 99, 101, 164, 170, 194, 195, 196, 197, 204, 212, 225, 226, 227
    RCHA 100, 154, 164, 204, 225, 227
    Royal Canadian Dragoons 96, 98, 170, 194, 197, 227
Canal de l'Escault (Canal de St Quentin) 137, 138, 139, 140, 145, 174, 178, 222, 238
Canal du Nord 137, 203, 216, 219
Canche, River 110
Cantaing 140, 141, 143, 144, 145, 155, 156, 157, 158, 174, 180, 182, 233
Caporetto, battle of (1917) 136
Carlepont 189
Carnoy 58, 61, 77, 78
Carton de Wiart, Brigadier General (12th Bde) 111
Carvin 36
Casteau, action at (1914) 23–4
Castel 194
Catelet Valley 167, 168, 169, 233
Caton-Woodville, Richard 31
Caudry 158
Cavalry Training 1914 6, 14, 40, 88, 101, 174, 235, 237
Cavalry Journal 16, 31, 92, 131, 134, 151, 152, 166, 167, 181, 189, 193, 195, 204, 216, 219, 221
Cavan, Lord, Lieutenant General (XIV Corps) 79, 84

Cayeux 205, 233
Central Powers 17
Cerizy (Moy), action at (1914) 24, 25, 28–32
Chance, Lieutenant Roger (4DG) 26
Chapel Crossing 169, 170
'Chapel Hill' 112
Charteris, Brigadier General John 105, 136, 158, 199
Chateau Thierry 201
Chaulnes 202, 203, 206, 208, 210
Chetwoode, General Sir Phillip 17, 28, 30, 31
Chipilly 57
Churchill, Winston (Minister of Munitions) 186
Cliff, Major (3DG) 121
Collezy 192, 233, 234
Combles 79
Commons, House of 133
Conchy 110
Congreve, Lieutenant General Sir Walter VC (XIII Corps) 45, 55, 57, 62, 63, 72
Corrigan, Gordon 2
Courcelette 51, 78, 83
Cowen, Captain (Ft Garry Hse) 152, 153
Crask, Lance Corporal (8th Suffolk) 70
Crevecoeur 152
Crinchon, River 111, 117
Critchley, Major (LSH) 97
Croisilles 104
Croix 109
Crozat Canal 189
Cubitt, Lieutenant (1DG) 192
Cuddeford, Captain (HLI) 118
'Curragh Incident' (1914) 22
Curzon, Lord 34

Dardanelles 105
Darley, Captain (4DG) 144
Darling, Major (20H) 88, 89, 91, 129
Dawkins, Lieutenant (7DG) 148
De Lisle, Lieutenant General Sir Henry 24, 25, 27, 28, 32
Delville Wood 55, 64, 65, 66, 77
Demuin 194
Deputy Director Veterinary Services (DDVS) 129
Dernancourt 77, 78, 79, 80, 83
Desert Storm, Operation 12
Doulens 110
'Drocourt–Quéant Line' 117, 124, 219
Duisans 122